The Literature of Modern Arabia

The Literature of Modern Arabia

An Anthology

Edited by
Salma Khadra Jayyusi

Published by Kegan Paul International
London and New York
in association with
King Saud University, Riyadh

First published in 1988 by Kegan Paul International Ltd
11 New Fetter Lane, London EC4P 4EE

Distributed by
Associated Book Publishers (UK) Ltd
11 New Fetter Lane, London EC4P 4EE

Routledge, Chapman & Hall Inc.
29 West 35th Street
New York, NY 10001, USA

Produced by Worts-Power Associates

Set in Garamond
by Paragon Photoset, Aylesbury
and printed in Great Britain
by Short Run Press Ltd., Exeter

ISBN 07103-0261-4 (c)
07103-0263-0 (p)

Foreword

This large and authoritative volume offers, for the first time, a representative selection of the works of ninety-five of Arabia's best creative authors. It presents poetry, drama and short stories from Saudi Arabia, Yemen and the rest of the Gulf states. Sponsored by King Saud University in Riyadh, which was represented by a distinguished editorial board, it was edited by Salma Khadra Jayyusi, one of the Arab world's most prominent scholars of modern Arabic literature, and was prepared as part of the programme of PROTA, the Project of Translation from Arabic literature, which Jayyusi directs. Several well-known English-speaking poets and writers have cooperated with bilingual translators on producing high quality translations. The volume reflects the panorama of life in the Peninsula, the outlook, aspirations and contradictions which govern people's behaviour in times of great change, and is likely to modify many of the stereotyped attitudes and expectations of English-speaking readers.

Contents

8

9

11

FICTION

12

13

Acknowledgements

On behalf of the Editorial Board of King Saud University and the Editorial Board of PROTA (Project of Translation from Arabic) I would like to thank the esteemed President of King Saud University, Dr Mansour al-Turki and the university's Academic Council for making it possible for us, through a generous grant and much moral support, to prepare this volume. Under the guidance of such an illustrious scholar as Dr al-Turki, King Saud University has demonstrated, through this and other cultural enterprises, its pioneering spirit and its willingness to take on projects that aim at breaking new ground in the various fields of study covering the Arabian Peninsula and indeed often the whole of Arabic culture. This is well demonstrated in the present volume.

For my part, I would like to thank wholeheartedly the members of King Saud University Editorial Board: Dr Shukry Ayyad, who was Visiting Professor at the university, Dr Ahmad al-Dhobaib, Vice President for Graduate Studies and Scientific Research, Dr Mansour al-Hazimi, Chairman of the Arabic Department, and Dr Izzat A. Khattab, Chairman of the English Department, for giving me all the help needed for the completion of this task. I want to thank them especially for their trust and constant faith and encouragement, their hospitality, patience and open-heartedness. Indeed they, and Saudi Arabia which I visited four times during the course of this work, became home to me, an anchorage, a return to roots. With intelligent humour and a genuine love of literature, they brought a spirit of collegial harmony which has been for me an unforgettable experience.

We started this volume without having a comprehensive foundation to work from and build on, a situation which would normally have required many years of research to resolve. We were, however, able to finish this volume within the relatively short period of two years because of the assistance we obtained from scholars in Gulf and Yemeni studies, and from PROTA readers. Even in the best situations, where knowledge of

15

the field has already been attained or is readily available, the selection period is usually the most time-consuming part of any serious anthology. For his advice and help in providing books and a wide range of selections to choose from, my thanks are due to Dr Abd al-Aziz al-Maqalih, President of the University of Sanaa who, with the help of Abd al-Wadoud Sayf and Abd al-Bari Tahir, provided me with many selections from Yemeni poetry and fiction. I would also like to thank Dr Abdallah al-Muhanna, Professor of Arabic at the University of Kuwait, for providing selections from Kuwaiti poetry, and Dr Ahmad Kamal Zaki, Visiting Professor at King Saud University, for suggesting selections from Saudi literature. Last but not least, my heartfelt thanks go to Dr Ibrahim A. Ghulum, Professor of Arabic at the University of Bahrain, for sending us very useful material, much of which we used, from the short story and drama of Bahrain, Kuwait and the Emirates, together with his own knowledgeable comments on the selections and the authors chosen.

PROTA's readers, Dr Sharif Elmusa and Dr Lena Jayyusi, merit special thanks. It was because of their great help and their diligent and inspired work selecting from the many books we acquired that the picture of the Peninsula's literature was completed. Their commentaries and critical accounts of the literature they read, presented cogently and clearly, reflected not only their passion for literature, but also a high professional quality. Without their help, this volume would have been considerably delayed.

My thanks also go to Dr Issa Boullata, Professor of Arabic Literature at McGill University, and to Dr Adnan Haydar, Professor of Arabic at the University of Massachusetts in Amherst, both members of PROTA's Editorial Board, for helping us with the readings and selections as well. As usual, Dr Boullata undertook, with typical skill, some of the most difficult translation tasks in the poetry included and I thank him for this very much.

The great support this project and all other PROTA projects had from Dr Salih Jawad Altoma, Chairman of the Department of Near Eastern Languages and Cultures at Indiana University and member of PROTA's Administrative Board, has been instrumental in forwarding the cause of the project, and I thank him heartily, as I thank the other members of the Administrative Board, Dr Roger Allen, Dr Trevor Le Gassick and Dr Ernest McCarus for the enthusiastic support they have lent to this and other PROTA projects.

To Dr Michael Marmura, Professor of Islamic Philosophy at the University of Toronto, are due my thanks for his invaluable advice on points of translation of the quotations from the writings of Ibn Hazm and al-Jahiz in Mansour al-Hazimi's short story, 'The Nightingale's Triptych'.

To Dr Charles Doria, who lectures at Mason Gross School for the Arts at Rutgers University in New York, are due my thanks for his many inspiring suggestions on format and style and for his constant moral support.

Sulaiman al-Shaikh has been a sincere and enthusiastic friend of PROTA from the very inception of the project, and I thank him for his consistent help over the years, particularly for his great kindness in sending me literary material from Kuwaiti literature for this anthology.

And I also thank the Yemeni poet, Abd al-Rahman Fakhri for the invaluable information he gave me on Yemeni authors and on Yemen's recent history.

The erudition and passion for literature demonstrated by the distinguished translators who worked with me on this volume have been a source of inspiration and delight and I thank them very much. Working with them gave me new insights into the subtleties of language and confirmed my belief in the universality of literature and the essential harmony of creative minds everywhere.

The authors represented in this anthology, who readily answered our letters, sent us their books and gave us their quick and often enthusiastic permission to translate from their works, deserve our warmest thanks. Their happy co-operation has given us an added purpose and determination to continue this difficult task of bridging the cultural gap between the contemporary Arab world and the English-speaking world. It is only through the kind of confidence and co-operation that this anthology (and indeed the other anthologies of modern Arabic literature already finished by PROTA) had, that work on modern Arabic literature and culture can be facilitated and introduced in other languages as part of world culture.

I should also like to thank Muhammad al-Jeeli Ismail who was secretary to Dr Khattab at the University of King Saud, for his competent and much appreciated assistance. Similarly, I should like to acknowledge warmly the meticulous help of Erna Hoffmann and Gretchen Arnolds in preparing the final copy of this volume.

Salma Khadra Jayyusi

17

Preface

Seldom does a work that requires so much responsibility as this work did yield so much joy and aesthetic pleasure while working on it as this anthology has provided. Choosing representative selections from the rich and relatively little-known corpus of Arabic literature in the Arabian Peninsula was an arduous task. Original material has not always been readily available, and I had to make several trips to the Peninsula to secure the necessary source materials for this book. Moreover, no single work on the literature of the whole area exists. Even individual genres such as poetry, for example, are not covered comprehensively. Books of criticism, literary history and even anthologies are usually devoted to the poetry of this country, or to the short story or drama of that, or of a specific group of countries (such as the Gulf states, for example). The most flagrant omissions occur in books that treat modern Arabic literature in general. These general studies make little or no mention of the varied and flourishing literature which the Peninsula has produced in modern times. It was clear from the outset that, for some reason, the literature of Arabia, once the fountainhead of literary creativity in classical times, has veered away in modern times from the mainstream of Arabic literature, and for the most part critics and literary historians of Arabic literature in general have left it untreated. Therefore, it soon became clear that in working on a comprehensive anthology of the literature of the whole area, we were breaking new ground. In order to cover the area fairly and comprehensively, we had to depend on our own research and on advice from specialists in various fields of Gulf and Yemeni studies before we were able to form an overall picture of the relevant literatures. As we proceeded to read through this literature, we discovered, bit by bit, the originality and vigour of much of the literary output in the Peninsula; and consequently, the omissions began to look more serious and embarrassing. We discovered that all over the Peninsula there were poets and writers of fiction and drama who were creating a modernist literature, much of it of the high artistic standard achieved in the modernist literature of the rest of the Arab world. Our readings demonstrated as well the truth of what I have always maintained: that despite the fact that the Arab world at present constitutes many different states, its literature has always constituted, in many aspects, a unified corpus, enriched by local variations.

The present anthology offers representative examples of literature from Saudi Arabia and other Gulf states: Kuwait, Bahrain, Oman and the Emirates, as well as from North and South Yemen. It spans works created since the First World War, but the main emphasis has been on the contemporary period. This is because, first, this period reflects the highest artistic development and maturity of both poetry and fiction, and second, because this is the period that reveals the fundamental and deep changes that have occurred in the Gulf countries (including, of course, Saudi Arabia,) because of the oil boom, as well as in Yemen (both North and South) as an outcome of the two revolutions which have transformed many avenues of life in that country. As a result of these Peninsula-wide transformations, many of them radical and irreversible, the whole area is characterized by a teeming vitality and great expectations, but also by many deep contradictions and frustrations, as Dr Shukry Ayyad so well elucidates in the introduction to this anthology. The reader of this volume will discover all these attitudes reflected in the literature of this large region.

There are many people in the world who are interested in the Arabian Peninsula either because of its deep Islamic roots and rich cultural heritage or because of its immense wealth and strategic position. Whether for religious yearnings or for other interests, for many the area constitutes a focal point. One would expect many of these people to be eager to know more about its culture, its intellectual activity and the way its creativity has confronted the many problems and transformations created by sudden shifts in circumstance. Muslim idealists, who have always viewed the Arabian Peninsula as the corner-stone of Islamic values and morality, will find in this anthology, written by some of Arabia's best creative talents, a reassurance that great ideals are still the quest of its writers. On the other hand, others looking for opportunities in this dynamically developing area, will find in this anthology the other face of Arabia, a sensitive and compassionate face, vibrant with sympathy for life's conflicting experiences, a countenance sometimes pensive and nostalgic, sometimes humorous and confident, but one that is always earnest and sincere. This anthology will complete everyone's picture of the area and deepen their understanding of its people, as well as of the spirit that

19

directs the way they look at, and interact with, the world. I believe that the best way people on the outside can truly and fully discover Arabia's hidden conscience, its motivating impulse, its generosity, its pride, idealism and supreme dignity, is through reading its literature. It is then, through such an acquired familiarity with the experiences, the sentiments, the ideals and visions of Arabia's authors, that rigid stereotypes will be fractured and replaced with valid realities. As we read this literature, we became exhilarated by the fact that these writers, whether they came from a struggling country like Yemen, or were the heirs of Arabia's new affluence, are all writers with a message that is deeply ennobling and humanizing in its import, and as challenging as that of any writer in the vast Arab world.

Moreover, in this anthology scholars of Arabic culture and literature will find a great deal of information which has not been available before. This is the beginning, I hope, of an enduring process of acquaintanceship with a robust literary output that promises to be continuous and enriching. Without the knowledge of the literature of modern Arabia, the knowledge of Arabic literature as a whole would be, I believe, deficient and its picture incomplete.

However, before proceeding further, I must clarify a major difference concerning the literature of the Peninsula. Not all this literature shares a common background, for the contemporary Yemeni experience differs widely from that of the rest of the Peninsula. And even among the Gulf states themselves, the position of Saudi Arabia as the centre of the Muslim world differs from that of the rest of the Gulf states.

Before the sixties, South Yemen constituted a number of small British protectorates which, with Aden, which was a British colony then, formed a Federal Union. North Yemen, with its capital, Sanaa, was governed by the Imams, the country's hereditary rulers who governed with an iron fist. In 1962, the Yemeni revolution erupted in the North against Imam Ahmad ibn Yahya and his royalist forces. A protracted civil war resulted which, in 1969, ended with the defeat of the last of the Imams, Imam Badr ibn Ahmad, and the subsequent formation of a republic. The South revolted against the British in 1963 and gained its independence in 1967, forming a republic which eventually, in October 1978, created a socialist state. However, since 1974 the Yemenis have maintained an integrated union of writers which meets periodically either in Sanaa or Aden. Due to these political and social transformations, the Yemenis had to face all the numerous problems that accompany newly achieved freedom, besides those that result from a poverty-stricken, underdeveloped rural society. The reader of this anthology will see all the resultant problems

20

and contradictions in Yemeni society delineated with great sensitivity and urgency in contemporary Yemeni literature.

However, the greatest sudden change in the Peninsula took place in the oil-rich countries of Saudi Arabia and the other Gulf states. The Gulf countries often had the task of facing a complete change in life: change in occupations, in life-styles, in human relations, in the very topography of these countries, as new cities and towns mushroomed in the once arid desert. Many values were bound to change and the horizons of Arabia widened greatly, bringing in new ideas and a different vision of the world. However, it was Saudi Arabia which had the most arduous task of all. The country of Makkah and the holy Kaaba, as well as of Madinah with the Prophet's shrine, it is the home of the oldest Islamic traditions to which millions of Muslims aspire, traditions that must be kept alive, that can give coherence to the vast Muslim world. This entails a great responsibility. The dynamics of change, therefore, had to meet this responsibility, a historical responsibility fourteen centuries old. And it is a matter of the greatest interest to watch how so much effort was made during the past few decades to keep the balance between the onslaught of modernity and technology and the attachment to roots. Poetry and fiction sensed this and mirrored it, delineating a picture of confrontation and strife, and even sometimes of alienation.

It is this relationship between the literatures of Arabia and their respective societies which is one of the two major features that become immediately clear in this anthology. The other, which can only be realized through a comparative study of this anthology alongside other anthologies of general Arabic literature,[1] is the relationship between the literature of Arabia and mainstream Arabic literature, a relationship

---

1. See such anthologies of general Arabic literature as, *An Anthology of Modern Arabic Poetry*, ed. by Mounah Khouri and Hamid Algar, University of California Press, 1974; *Modern Arab Poets*, ed. by Issa Boullata, Heinemann, London, 1976; *Women of the Fertile Crescent*, ed. by Kamal Boullata, Three Continents Press, Washington, 1978; *Modern Poetry of the Arab World*, ed. by Abdallah al-Udhari, Penguin Books, 1986; and *An Anthology of Modern Arabic Poetry*, ed. Salma Khadra Jayyusi, Columbia University Press, New York, 1987. And see *Modern Arabic Short Stories*, ed. by Denys Johnson-Davies, Oxford University Press, 1967; *Arabic Writing Today: the Short Story*, ed. by Mahmoud Manzalaoui, American Research Center, Cairo, 1968; *Arabic Short Stories*, ed. by Denys Johnson-Davies, Quartet Books, London, 1983; and *Anthology of Arabic Fiction and Drama*, ed. by Salma Khadra Jayyusi, Columbia University Press, forthcoming.

which governs also artistic trends and techniques. I shall explain these two points below.

The difference in background between Yemeni and Gulf literatures has naturally produced differences in emphasis, visions and attitudes. Yemeni literature, for example, is deeply involved in the country's political life. It harbours a profound hatred for the pre-1962 past, which is usually depicted as a time of great stress and immeasurable suffering. The Gulf literature, on the other hand, looks back nostalgically at the pre-oil past, the past of seafaring and pearl diving, full of toil and hardship, it is true, of endeavours hardly ever requited and hopes hardly ever achieved, yet settled and well-rooted in place and time, and full of contentment and innocence, governed by a spirit of harmony and human brotherhood. As I have mentioned above, the changes which took place in the various societies of the Arabian Peninsula have produced a state of deracination which Dr Ayyad discusses cogently in his introduction. What I would like to emphasize here is that this literature is a literature of the human spirit at its best, endearing and liberating, with a deep and enduring love and a supreme commitment. As seen in its literature, 'the Arabian Peninsula is no desert that only flows with oil and riches; it is green with ordinary people, doing battle for everyday life; and green with unfamiliar foliage, and familiar faces and concerns. It is also a place that harbours ordeals, poverty and suffering ... and the young writers, men and women, write about it all, with detail, warmth and authenticity, and without fear.'[2]

On the other hand, Arab readers of this anthology will recognize in it part of their own experience, part of their instinctive knowledge of the world. One hopes that anthologies like this are capable of extending the plane of mutual recognition and reciprocal commitment among Arab writers and readers alike. They will find that the literature of Arabia is as committed 'to the struggle of Arab society in this critical period of change and transformation as any literature in the rest of the Arab world, reflecting the general social and psychological scene, and speaking of Arab achievement and failure, joy and sorrow, hopes and fears'.[3] Thus we see the Saudi and Yemeni poets lamenting the destruction of Beirut,

2. From a final assessment of the selections by Lena Jayyusi, written first in English and published in Arabic translation in *Al-Qabas* newspaper, Kuwait, 7 July 1985.
3. From a final assessment of the selections by Sharif Elmusa written in English and published in Arabic translation in *Al-Qabas*, *ibid*.

and expressing anger and frustration at political failure in Palestine, and joy over the undying nerve of resistance to all forms of aggression on the dignity and freedom of the individual and the nation.

Moreover, scholars of Arabic are bound to find that the artistic history of the various genres of literature in this region is an integral part of the artistic history of modern Arabic literature in general. Poetry, for example, has developed in the same way, with the same revolution in both form and content that has engaged Arab poets everywhere in the Arab world; the same quarrel between 'traditional' and 'modern' took place, and the same active experimentation. However, the contemporary poets of Arabia should not be seen as epigones, although the movement of modernism in the poetry of Arabia has come about in the wake of the modernist movement in the main centres of poetic activity in Beirut and Baghdad. The poets of Arabia have been selective in their choices of what to adopt, and have in many cases shown an authenticity and an originality quite their own. The verses of the Kuwaiti poet, Sulaiman al-Fulayyih are applicable to many:

> When will we strive, my friend, to be
> not as others imagine us
> but as we wish ourselves
>   to be?

The selections in this anthology were finalized in cooperation with my esteemed colleagues, Dr Shukry Ayyad, Dr Ahmad al-Dhobaib, Dr Mansour al-Hazimi and Dr Izzat Khattab, who formed the Editorial Board of King Saud University for this anthology. We met together several times in Riyadh, first to agree on the general subject areas to be included, then to agree on the final Arabic selections. Finally, when the English version of this anthology was completed in the United States and Britain with the cooperation of PROTA's distinguished team of translators, I went to Riyadh to finalize the anthology with the King Saud University Editorial Board.

We felt that the most direct way of presenting the selections in the anthology was to group them by genres, and, as far as the authors' names were concerned, to arrange these alphabetically. We felt that it would complicate matters enormously to arrange the selections by country, or to separate the authors by generations. This was the same situation I faced when arranging the final format of my *Anthology of Modern Arabic Poetry* (Columbia University Press, New York, 1987), for there are occasional authors of older generations who write a more modernist literature than the much younger authors, and any such strict arrangements by age would be confusing. We chose to represent drama by a single play mainly for reasons of space, particularly since Saqr al-Rushud's, *The Mud*,[4] which we translated, is a strong and absorbing piece of work, and very representative of the thematic preoccupation and artistic achievements of drama in the area. We also chose to give excerpts from one novel only, Hamza Bogary's *Saqifat al-Safa*,[5] for the same reasons, particularly because we introduced such well-known novelists as the Kuwaiti Ismail Fahd Ismail, and the Yemeni Zaid Mutee' Dammaj and Muhammad Abd al-Wali in their capacity as short story writers.

The method of translation into English employed follows PROTA's principles, as is the case with all PROTA books: first I give the selections to competent bilingual translators who enjoy a great sensitivity to literature, then to English-speaking poets and writers (according to the genre of the selection) who creatively modify the translated version, rephrasing it according to their own method of writing, without being influenced by the Arabic text or the Arab literary idiom. Translating between two non-related languages such as Arabic and English can be a very hazardous task, and it is very difficult for any direct translation to be completely free of the often magnetic effect of Arabic as a source language, particularly in the case of poetry translation. The two lots of translators are therefore indispensable to each other and both have an onerous task indeed. Although this double task has its difficulties, it also has its rewards. I hope that our efforts to produce a version as worthy of the original selections as possible is successful in conveying both the aesthetic and the semantic intentions of the authors.

The names of the translators are arranged according to the system by which the translation process has been conducted. Usually, the name of the first translator appears first, then the name of the English-speaking poet or writer, thus denoting the two stages of the work. This arrangement does not reflect any value judgement. Sometimes, however, the poet has found the version of the first translator complete and has left it as it is. All poems carrying the name of only the first translator belong to this category.

I have written the authors' names in this anthology in the easiest way for the English-speaking reader to pronounce. However, I have added a sheet

---

4. See Ali al-Ra'i, *Theatre in the Arab World*, Alam al-Ma'rifa, Kuwait, 1980, in which he assesses the drama in the Arabian Gulf, pp. 394–449; and see pp. 404–10 and 420–24 for his evaluation of al-Rushud's dramatic works.
5. *Saqifat al-Safa* is being translated into English by PROTA.

at the back of the book, which has a transliterated list of the authors' names according to the rules of transliteration set by the *New Encyclopaedia of Islam*.

A glossary of Arabic words presented in the anthology in English transliteration is to be found at the end of the volume.

Salma Khadra Jayyusi

Introduction

'The cradle of the Arabs' is how an Egyptian author described the Arabian Peninsula some forty years ago. At that time, the huge mineral wealth of this ancient territory was barely tapped and its immense surface barely scratched for relics of its long-forgotten history, but the Kaaba in Makkah was the holiest shrine of the Islamic faith, the site where pilgrimage rituals were performed once every year, where the 'smaller pilgrimage' was carried on daily without interruption, and towards which every Muslim directed his or her face in prayer at least five times a day.

Especially after the advent of Islam in the seventh century AD, Arab tribes had emigrated from the peninsula all over what is known as 'the Arab world', where they mingled with local stocks to such an extent that it became almost impossible, in a country like Egypt, to distinguish groups or even individuals of Arab descent from those of mixed origins. It is now an established fact that 'Arabism' refers primarily to a community of language and culture.

However, recent changes in the socio-economic sphere have introduced equal changes in historical outlook. All around the fringes of the desert, bleak hills, solitary islands, and vast expanses of gravel and sand are disclosing not only huge reservoirs of oil and gas, but also valuable testimonials of history. At Faw (midway between Makkah and Yemen, overlooking the north-west fringe of the Empty Quarter), at al-Taj (150 km north-west of Dhahran), at Failakah (a small island facing the coast of Kuwait), at al-ᶜAin (near Abu Dhabi), and at various ports of Oman, relics from ancient civilizations span more than three thousand years from the heyday of ancient Egyptian and Mesopotamian civilizations to the Hellenistic era. Showing marked influences from them all, together with some affinities with Indian cultures, they bear witness to the long-forgotten fact that the Arabian Peninsula was never cut off from the main civilizations of the ancient world. On the contrary, owing to its unique position bridging the three continents that made up the whole of the known world until modern times, as well as the important role it played in world trade, the region was precisely at the crossroads of these civilizations. Thus the whole of Arabian history demands revision, and this process holds significant implications for the present and the future.

The view which is just beginning to dawn upon researchers in Arab history and civilization is that the role assumed, willy-nilly, by the inhabitants of the Arabian Peninsula throughout the long periods which preceded the modern revolution in the means of communication, entailed the 'trading' of cultural values no less than material goods, between East and West, North and South. Naturally, Arab scholars will be more inclined to describe this phenomenon as 'mediation', 'homogenization', or even 'rejuvenation' rather than as a mere go-between. The earliest record of such a rule goes back to the Sumerian civilization, which historians consider either Semitic, Indo-European or both. We are on surer ground when we move on to Islam. That a unified Arab culture existed before Islam seems beyond doubt, although very little is known about such a culture. A long period of decadence reigned for about three centuries before Islam, when Byzantine influence receded from the western parts, especially north-west and south-west, and Persian hegemony was spread virtually over all the inhabited parts of Arabia. Although the Arabs in Yemen and the Hijaz were engaged in a bitter conflict with the Abyssinian kingdom, which was a Byzantine satellite, this does not seem to have had a lasting effect on the Arabs' general feeling of goodwill toward people and even governments of the Byzantine world. Owing to the persecution suffered by Muslims in Makkah during the first thirteen years of Muhammad's mission, the Prophet ordered a number of his followers to emigrate from Makkah to Abyssinia, where they remained, unmolested, for several years, in spite of the machinations of Makkan unbelievers. Regarded as a political gesture, we may infer that even the burgeoning city-state of Makkah maintained good relations with Persia, which had its satrap in Najran, not far to the south. Muhammad was also particularly friendly with the governor of Egypt. The Muslims considered the Byzantine emperor and the Persian king tyrants, but the Qur'an predicted a near victory for the Byzantines (*al-Rum*) after their temporary defeat by the Persians in AD 619, a hint that revealed where Muslim sympathies lay.

Although Arabia was penetrated by Persian culture, which was felt even in Makkah, Islam placed itself squarely in the heart of the Near Eastern traditions that had infiltrated into Christianized Europe. Islam was presented as a renovation of the religion of Abraham, and considered history mainly as the earthly struggle of eternal truth revealed through

27

God's messengers. Biblical stories provide recurrent motifs in the *suras* of the Qur'an, and even a later Christian story, that of the cave dwellers, is given a prominent place in 'The *Sura* of the Cave'. In contrast to the harshness of its attacks on Makkan unbelievers, the Qur'anic arguments with the differing sects of Christianity are rather lenient. In modern terms, it can be safely stated that Islam presented the different factions of 'People of the Book' (Christians and Jews) with a simpler ideology, which they were presumably able to accept as a universal religion.

Later chapters in the history of Islamic civilization conform well with the beginning. The Muslims easily absorbed Greek philosophy and science, which they transmitted back to Europe through Spain and Sicily, in the meantime winning the peoples of the Persian Empire and penetrating deeply into Asia. As a cultural project, Islam stretches beyond both religious conversion and political hegemony; its role in the sphere of cultural history is comparable only to that of the Greek civilization.

At this point a more basic comparison comes to mind. In spite of the huge geographical differences between 'the cradle of the Arabs' and that of the Greeks, there are also some striking similarities. Both consisted of small populated centres spread over the Aegean archipelago and the coasts of Asia Minor and Italy on the one hand, and scattered over a huge expanse of desert on the other. Both populations combined a feeling of nationhood together with local or tribal loyalties and a keen sense of individual freedom. Both were widely reputed as travellers (Arabs have their Ulysses in the famous Sinbad). Perhaps the Greeks were more fortunate: their task was easier. They salvaged what had remained of the moribund Egyptian and Babylonian civilizations and adapted them to the more nature-loving tribes of the Eastern Mediterranean; it was a little more difficult to adapt the teachings of Christ to the wilder tribes of Northern Europe. In the case of the Arabs it was far more difficult to bring the civilizations of the Far East and those of the Near East and the Eastern Mediterranean together. Arabs definitely opted for the latter, although they did not neglect the former. In the fourth century of the Islamic era (the eleventh century AD), a Muslim philosopher and mathematician, Abu al-Raihan al-Bairuni, made a long and extensive journey in the Indian Peninsula, learned Sanskrit, and described in detail the customs and beliefs of the Indians. Although he is remarkably objective in his statements, he does not hide his feeling of amazement towards the extremely populous and heterogeneous Indian pantheon. Ethnological and linguistic theories may posit a common origin for both European – including Greek – and Indian peoples, but if one is to generalize about civilizations, it is certainly safer to link the Arab innate belief in a supernatural order of things with the Greek logical explanation of natural phenomena, as against the Hindu conception of material chaos, out of which man has no hope of real escape but in complete withdrawal.

All this might seem far-fetched to a Western scholar; none the less, what is open to question is only the perspective or the proportions given to certain facts; the facts themselves are there to be judged and verified. Beyond any conclusions drawn, it is sufficient for the purposes of this introduction to state that the assumptions laid out here are present, consciously or subconsciously, integrally or partially, in the minds of most *modern* Arabs. Part of their dilemma, on the national as well as on the individual level, stems from the difficulty they experience in trying to bring these assumptions forward to the 'here and now' of their modern existence. Thus a unique situation obtains: over and above spatial extremes, temporal ones have to be brought together, some way or other.

Ironically, Islam helped to move trade routes from its cradle to the north and west, and Arabia itself, having few natural resources to support a stable society, relapsed into tribalism. It was only when Western imperialism started on its old project of swallowing up the whole of the Muslim Middle East that Arabs, including those of the Arabian Peninsula, became self-critical. Abd al-Aziz ibn Saᶜud, the founder of the present Saudi kingdom, distinguished himself among all Arab leaders by drawing completely on indigenous resources for the immense task of building a vigorous, new Arab Muslim society. Oil discoveries, coming later, have only helped to facilitate the progress which is now being realized at a spectacular pace. At the present stage of Arab awakening, identity is the keyword. While the cultural gap between Arab and Western societies, in spite of all the efforts made, does not seem to diminish, techtonic changes are restructuring the whole of the Arab world.

Impatience breeds anxiety, and the pulls of past history and future aspirations are sometimes too difficult to bear. Poets, for whom tradition is an essential part of existence, suffer most. Falling off between the two time opposites, a Yemeni poet laments:

> Still more far off, the morrow
>   on which we waste our yearning;
> Nor can we summon back
>   Yesterday – for it is unreturning.
>
> (Abdallah al-Baraduni, 'Between Two Voids')

The uncertainty of the poets' existence in time is paralleled by their feeling of estrangement and frustration in their own country and among

29

their own people. Whether young or old, Arab poets are mostly angry. In the same poem, al-Baraduni denounces corrupt and ignorant rulers in very clear terms:

> Successive rulers came;
> Pockets grew rife with gold;
> Who bought us knew not why,
> Nor he who sold us knew what he has sold.

The Kuwaiti poet Fahd al-Askar is scarcely less outspoken against the whole mighty lot, although he often couches his attacks in a tone of self-pity, as in 'Complaint':

> O my country, how
> Can a nightingale like me survive between
> A hissing snake and a croaking frog?
> How can I live among those
> Who hate me because I care for the poor?

The theme of alienation, running through the whole of the modern poetry of Arabia, takes different guises in each of the three trends represented in this collection (corresponding roughly to three generations of Arabian poets). Older poets are inclined to grandiose proclamations and melodramatic representations, with a big 'I' standing like a tent-pole. Similes and metaphors are often extended to approach the dimensions of symbol or allegory: moth (A. Qandeel), mirage, deserted valley (A. M. Al Khalifa). The omnipresent 'I' transforms itself, in Awwad's 'Figs and Sycamore', into a camera eye, painfully alive to the contradictions of social life. It yields to the private pleasures of philosophical meditation in Faqi's 'Myth of Immortality', but it is anguished meditation, coming from the 'depths' rather than the 'heights'.

It is curious, however, that there is hardly a poem that does not mention, be it in one line or two, the poet's solitary state. Even in a poem filled with pathos, like Qandeel's 'Death in Life', which laments the loss of the poet's young daughter, he must say:

> I dwelled apart in a world of phantasy,
> And made myself an alien from humanity.

A painful feeling of insignificance infuses bitterness in al-Hadrani's love poem, 'Fountain':

30

> You are not guilty; if the grass has withered and wilted
> and the streams are all dried up.
> You, who are you, my soul's companion, and
> who am I? We are no more than smoke
> blown about by the savage winds.

Although it could be misleading to dub this trend 'classical', we distinguish a more 'romantic' group among poets of the next generation (notably al-Qurashi and al-Gosaibi). With them the theme of estrangement takes a nostalgic turn: regret for the loss of original innocence, escape to realms of beauty, light, love. The poet's escape to these enchanted realms is frustrated by the actual touch of them. In Paris ('The Altar of Love') al-Qurashi is deeply disappointed:

> In Paris I felt the alienation
> Of a bereaved soul.
> And I sensed the death of all my dreams. . . .
> Is your gift to my thirsty soul a hungry mouthful
> a mirage, an abyss?
> You, who are a myth and a song
> That has inspired the deprivation of my country
> Whom poets have embellished with images of love.
> Your evil enchantment has blasted the flower of my years.

We can profitably compare this poem of al-Qurashi with al-Hadrani's 'Streets of Rome', where the feeling of estrangement stems from the national, rather than the individual character.

Al-Gosaibi creates an enchanted world of light, colour, music and exotic scents ('Song in a Tropical Night'), but he feels only 'an ecstasy of pain', sees 'a wedding . . . full of sorrow' and has nothing but gloomy thoughts to offer to his 'dark pearl', whose coming makes the air 'tremulous with dew, with fragrance, with light, with passion and colour', for:

> How can I be merry
> and compose verses
> that twinkle with the light of dawn?
> My poems are better unsaid!
> So say that it is the moon!

This last line, repeated through the poem like a refrain, suggests that the poet is making excuses, not for his lack of spirit but rather for his untimely effusiveness. While a more classical poet could say simply,

'When I suffer, it's for those who drift, . . . as if drowned' (al-Wugayyan, 'Tattered Sails'), al-Gosaibi effects an unexpected shift from the inside to the outside:

> As for me, do not ask about me
> My country is a rainless land
> I sail towards a dangerous goal . . .
> Say then, it is the moon!

For al-Gosaibi, love spells anxiety. He is either taking refuge in it, or falling back from it, or both. Two poems of his, 'Your Loving' and 'Love and Black Harbours', illustrate these changing moods, connected only by a dominating feeling of estrangement. In the first poem he seems to revel in the celestial bliss of love:

> . . . In the night of your love
> I play with stars, or touch the crescent or plenilune.

But, unable to forget the outer world, he continues:

> So also, like night, it abolishes
> Those false shapes which the hand of day had fashioned,
> Peacefully striding onwards to things that are sad and strange.

In the second poem the spectres of 'black harbours, representing all the inequities and uglinesses of social life, stand between the poet and his beloved'. The epilogue clinches the impossible situation:

> In vain I open my soul
> to your love:
> I have come back without a soul!

The latest trend in the modern poetry of Arabia may be described as modernist, although it retains some of the characteristics of the 'romantic' poetry of the sixties. There is the same effusiveness, especially in the longer poems. The intellectualized language is often penetrated by candid self-exposure. Mere incongruity is often sought in order to achieve stylistic effects. These foibles can easily be explained by the fact that most of these poets have not yet reached full maturity – an important consideration in a language with such a long tradition as Arabic. It is noteworthy, in spite of all this, that quite a few 'modernist' poems achieve real beauty. This is particularly true of the shorter ones, where the taut, sinewy form helps the poets to rid themselves of both classical bombast and romantic effusion. The effect sought after is one of urgency, immediacy: the young poets are not only angry, they can be also provocative, even insulting, as Abd al-Kareem al-Razihi is in his poem 'The Need for a Second Heaven and an Additional Hell':

> O sky vaulted with the glass
> of myth and bones of ancient legends
> sprouting out your stars
> those welts spread beautifully
> over your blue skin, reborn
> each evening from the germ of original sin,
> they climb all over your face
> like a graceful herd of
> glorious smallpox
>
> There is something dirty inside me
> I want to get rid of
> and toss into your basket
> woven of the sufferings of saints
> and fronds of mystical love.

Free verse, hashed sentences and symbolic imagery constitute the vehicle of most modernist poems. Although they still grate on most Arab ears, this reaction is itself part of the intended shock.

The language of modernist poetry makes it easier for the younger poets – among whom we can count a good number of women – to fuse in one gesture the themes of desire, anguish, expectation and even rebellion. The 'beloved' in Ismail al-Warith's 'Prayer to the Beloved' is clearly Yemen, or his own image of it. In 'Drinking from Her Eyes' by Muhammad Jabr al-Harbi the images of the everlasting female, the motherland and the haunting experience of the poem itself blend in one mood of estrangement, unending search and insatiable yearning. Qasim Haddad's short poem 'Dominion' is not just an experiment in graphic poetry; it expresses the extreme situation of being submerged in a host of contending emotions, more or less the same situation that he tried to encompass in his longer poem, 'The Sea has its Transformations,' with its striking image of a sea 'narrow, narrow like the pupil of an eye . . . We don't have enough of it to make a shirt for a child'. One gets the feeling that the obvious difference in 'space' between the two poems points to the theme of 'space' itself, dominating all human activity.

Yemeni poetry calls for special notice here. Although the new generation has produced its experiments too, the difference among the three trends mentioned above is not, perhaps, as clearly felt as it is in other parts of Arabia. All modern Yemeni literature is involved literature, and poetry is no exception. This common denominator has facilitated exchange among various trends: Abd al-Aziz al-Maqalih is essentially modernist, both in the complex structure of his poems and the novelty of his imagery; but in the stateliness of his syntax he is, probably, the most classical of all modernists; in his emotional exuberance he is perhaps the most romantic. This amalgam is only natural in an atmosphere of continuous social and political turmoil, which – although much less noticed by the outside world than that of the Palestinian or Lebanese scene – has never stopped since the end of the Second World War.

The development of fiction in modern Arabic literature, in general, shows notable differences from that of poetry. Whereas the poetic revival began with the imitation of models from the classical period, and only later became more or less directly influenced by English and French poetry, modern Arabic fiction came into being as imitations of free translations from English and French. Only lately have some leading Arab novelists (for example, the Egyptian, Naguib Mahfouz) begun using a narrative language that combines the style and technique of the traditional story-teller with those of modern fiction. The fact that the writing of fiction, like all other modern developments in Arabia, is a recent but quickly growing phenomenon helped to make such a blend come naturally to the Arabian writer.

The remarkable variety of style and atmosphere owe much to the natural setting of our stories, but we can also sense the effect of different cultural backgrounds, grafted on to indigenous habits of story-telling. 'Auntie Kadarjan' by Ahmad al-Siba‘i, one of the first exponents of the modern literary movement in Saudi Arabia, shows what a sensitive Arab writer can do with a congenial theme, although he leaves his reader with the impression that what we have here is a piece of autobiographical reminiscence rather than a short story after the Western tradition. 'The Nightingale's Triptych' by M. al-Hazimi presents an outstanding example for comparison in more than one respect. The author belongs to the middle generation, who were brought up in the same cultural setting described by Siba‘i, but became exposed to various influences through their studies and extensive travels in other parts of the Middle East and in Europe and the United States. 'The Nightingale's Triptych' combines, in a very peculiar manner, the natural sensitivity and polite irony noticed in Siba‘i with an at once amused, alienated and self-critical mood. The technique is seemingly free, but its audacity shows an interest in the experimental forms of the modern short story.

In mirroring the various cultural cross-currents, fiction is much more effective than poetry. Abd al-Rahman Fakhri may mention Tagore in a poem, but you feel how actually near you are to Tagore and the whole South Asian atmosphere when you read Salih Saeed Ba-Amer's story 'Dancing by the Light of the Moon'. We get something of the atmosphere of *The Arabian Nights* in Khalil al-Fuzay's 'The Storm' and Abd al-Hameed Ahmad's 'The Palm Tree Said to the Sea'. Mayfa Abd al-Rahman's 'What came between Aneesa and Me' captures the modern reader by its freshness and originality, while the fallen, solitary old teacher in Abdallah al-Salmi's 'Summer and Ashes' and the downtrodden wayfarer in Muhammad Hasan al-Harbi's 'An Ordinary Death' will remind him of some of Dostoevsky's characters. 'The *Hazeen* was Singing' by M. Abd al-Malik and 'Waiting' by M. S. Sayf are almost poetic in conception and texture, although they retain the traditional respect for plot. Siba'i Uthman's 'Silence and the Walls' verges on the surrealistic, while a modernist technique based on the newspaper report and depending almost exclusively on narration is used to much effect in the humorous story 'Why Fattoum al-Ward Hit her Neighbour' by M. al-Murr.

Other short stories keep to the structure of the 'classical' European short story, whose masters, de Maupassant and Chekhov have been known both to Arab writers and readers for a long time; but each one of these new writers has his own preferences and creates his own atmosphere. M. Alwan paints impressionistic sketches of the Asiri village, while H. A. Husain accompanies the stranger in a modern Saudi city, prying into his inner feelings as he studies his movements in the minutest details. Sulaiman al-Shatti is fond of playing the cares and complexities of ultra-modern ways of life against the lingering, wistful attachments to bygone days, which continue to disturb his characters' souls. Ismail Fahd Ismail is more concerned with the dilemma of the alienated intellectual (especially in his short novels, which could not be presented here), but he is also sensitive to the plight of weaker individuals who are either unduly afraid or insufficiently aware of the hostility of their surroundings.

With wide differences in mode, atmosphere and technique, the theme of deracination pervades the bulk of fiction produced in the Arabian Peninsula. 'Deracination', meaning both change and separation, corresponds well to the alienation which appears as a keynote in poetry. Although deracination is essentially a social phenomenon, it has emotional implications which give a certain poignance, akin to poetry, to most of the short stories included in this anthology, even such 'well-made' works as Layla al-Uthman's 'Pulling up Roots' and A. al-Qadi's 'The Final Ring'. As a symbol of change or progress the 'bridge' becomes the centre of action and supplies the title of two short stories in this collection. The 'elevator' plays a similar role in another. In typical symbolic fashion, both images express ambivalent attitudes, while a metaphor 'The Lake of Nothingness', as the title of still another short story, epitomises a downright indictment of the personal vices brought about by sudden capitalist developments. On the other hand, sudden affluence coupled with spiritual emptiness offers splendid material for comedy, as in Abd al-Hameed Ahmad's 'Khlalah SEL'. Romantic themes can never be absent in a society undergoing significant changes in ideals and outlook, but they are seldom treated with enough artistic restraint as they are in Ibrahim al-Nasir's 'Disappointment'. Conversely, the 'involved' character of Yemeni fiction is perhaps responsible for the realistic tone of such stories as 'Abu Rubbiya' and 'The Succession'. However, the variety of style and tone is remarkable between, say, the grim humour of 'The End of Old Amm Misfir', the sarcastic note of 'Brother, Pay Up and Get Out!' and the elaborate technique of 'The Butterflies'.

While 'change' may be an adequate description of the main theme in the short novella included in this anthology – 'The Journey', by the Yemeni Zaid Mutee͑ Dammaj – 'The Mud', a play by the Kuwaiti Saqr al-Rushud is perhaps better explained as a drama on the theme of deracination.

The device of gathering a motley group of social types on some means of transportation – a caravan, a carriage, a bus or an aeroplane – is common enough; but its success depends on how it is put to use. In 'The Journey' we meet specimens representing practically all types of middle-class Yemenis, but with enough leisure and acumen on the part of the narrator to distinguish them also as characters, before they disappear again among similar individuals in the crowded capital. The appearance of the emancipated young working woman brings the action into focus, and helps to display wide differences in attitudes.

'The Mud' is a modern tragedy. All the main characters – Tariq, Mariam, Fahd and Wafa' – are motivated only by selfish desires, which lead the most wicked of them to the point of crime. (The writer cleverly keeps its actual perpetration in doubt.) The only mainstay of their luxurious house (built of cement) is the mud man, Marzouq, the freed slave.

Three episodes have been selected from Hamza Bogary's novel, *Saqifat al-Safa*. Those who are fond of 'oriental' travelogues will find in this genuine account of facts and events much that would appeal to their exotic flair; but there is much more besides. In fact, the charm of these detailed accounts resides precisely in the fact that they are not related for their own sake. As in any autobiographical novel, much episodic material comes in, but this is so closely interwoven with the fabric of the novel, which consists in the growing consciousness of a sensitive creature, that the rich setting emphasizes the peculiar significance of the narrator's experience. Auntie Asma, Ustadh Umar, the water-carriers' society of freed slaves in old Makkah, etch themselves deeply in the memory; but they also serve, in the course of the novel, to mark the hero's painful progress towards a saner and more positive attitude to life.

To the English reader who is embarking on this book as a part of a serious study of the Middle East, or just as an adventure in reading to satisfy his or her 'ethnological' curiosity, a word might be said on the part of all who have worked on it. Before we got these texts together, none of us, I believe, had thought that they would constitute such a meaningful whole. That it does, was the discovery which we made to our own satisfaction. We also feared that, put in the English idiom, and in spite of all the care that would be given to the task of translation, much of it would be strange and would sustain a cultural gap difficult to transcend by the English-speaking reader, but we are more reassured now. And we do not intend this as a value judgement, to anticipate your own. After all, both the responsibility and the pleasure of value judgements, dear reader, are completely yours.

Shukry Ayyad

Poetry

Khadija al-Amri

Two Sprigs of Basil

Song, song, a few tears and a little rain
The hand of evening rises over the last rider
tossing his cloak into space.
The trace disappears.

Why do their caravans rest along the voice's horizon?
Why does the heart trust in such tents?

This is where awareness begins.
The ear has its own habitat but resists,
peeling off words to retain only echo
which would fashion a furious dagger
to plunge into distant depths.

Song, song, a few tears, a half-measure of madness
'Either you are or we are not'
Do I resemble the dream?
Perhaps you resemble it.
But your dreams end
and my dreaming is excessive, a daring guest
that crashes into life's voyage
without finding satisfaction – who can it be?

Song, song, a few tears and some conversation
bearing the fragrance of musk

When he spoke to me, my heart was cradling
the pulse of the north, transporting it into the south

When I awoke to his voice
my time became timeless, a distance dissolving . . .
An image of mountains set sail in my blood
and an olive tree forgotten by civilization
when it grew tall and lofty –
motherhood, a hope that may yet be attained
by sleeping over an ember in the south
When I spoke to him two sprigs of sweet basil
flowered at the crossroads of the heart –
holding a clutch of wormwood
I crossed over night's body
without a horse

At night, dissolving all distances
'Either you are or I am not'
I fashioned in his presence a mode for my belonging
kissed in him the forehead of the country that denied me
stones and eyes
I recorded birth on his two shores
dropped one year, another,
twenty

Shall I now ascend?
Nothing separates me from the elegy of years
but my desire for extinction – yet
why is extinction fearful
like children's happiness before innocence
is violated on a summer's night?

Tears arrive, tears, tears
leaving space
for the completion of madness
. . . I am certain now that betrayals come from
behind, civilizations are a sword,
all languages die,
and only the good-hearted
remain true to nature.

Translated by Lena Jayyusi and Naomi Shihab Nye

Fahd al-Askar   **KUWAIT**

Complaint

O my country, how
Can a nightingale like me survive between
A hissing snake and a croaking frog?
How can I live among those
Who hate me because I care for the poor?
Because I am frank of heart, and proud?
I would not have been in trouble
If I were one whose feelings are dead.
O my country, I have some claim on you
You rejected it, and yet you honoured
The claims of thugs and loafers.
If I had flattered you or cheated you,
You would not have cast me off
This was my punishment, my country:
Because I would not kow-tow before your stupid billy-goats
I was mewed up at home like a falcon
I was thirsty and you filled my cup
But I have drunk nothing but bitterness
I buried my dreams in the morning of my youth
Ever since I have regretted them
Would that youth had never dawned!
The baboon sports freely
On my country's land, and the jackal revels.
Irony! – The rights of those
Who work evil are protected
But those of the righteous are trampled upon.
And the convicted felon becomes a plaintive
Is it just, O Lord, that I should grieve

And be forced to complain of my wounds
Even to the knife itself?

Translated by Issa Boullata and John Heath-Stubbs

Abd al-Kareem al-Auda   **SAUDI ARABIA**

The Prologue

Through the Eastern streets
we hurried toward the
Caliph's benches,
hurried toward the Eastern hotel
on the outskirts of the city
to sit under the great awning
drinking our sad coffee
speaking of passion and affairs

We drank from the waters
of youthful desire
Life was abundant
and we were damp as birds
learning the word-tricks
touching their edges
their shorelike letters
that were our secret face
The Eastern hotel was gay
though sadness also dwelled there
It was set apart
surrounded by distances
and minarets
Was this the right time
for the prologue?
The silence in your eyes
was a preface for anguish
If not for sadness
we wouldn't have been together

unfolding the desert's hard heart
in love with the palms in Dareen

Our mornings were love
and circling questions
but we migrated through the night
to an exiled room
We blessed those who came
like trees, like rivers
desert scorpions
with no water or provisions, with nothing
to stir the ash of their desolation
except the roads whose endless
silence we had to break

Then we would hurry back
to the Eastern hotel
to remember how death
could also die
how hunger could starve
Terror was our song
for the road,
a song exploding
the passion of words

This is the time for prologues
and the silent pool in your eyes
is a spring for my thirsty poetry
You say the horizon is wide
that our street which they demolished
will never forget its childhood
You say
the horizon is a house
a school

You are my first poem
the children will write
in their notebooks
You are my first poem
in which I will write as I wish
about my homeland

about your eyes
those ponds where I swim
I will become the question
of a wanderer
homeless across the face
of the earth
The wilderness burns
with his desire
And you shall be the poem
of all times
when you see my questions
running to you, asking
of the seeds of love
and curses
Be then the most
merciful curse
or come out flashing
like the spark of exile.

Translated by Sargon Boulus and Naomi Shihab Nye

Muhammad Hasan Awwad   **SAUDI ARABIA**

Figs and Sycamore

Tired with work
I left my office one day
to stroll alone
and quietly at twilight
Here is the market
of the poor
shacks and stalls
where a huge crowd
mills around
A blind man
and a boy who leads
his skinny bare-backed donkey
among children playing
in grim joy
the sarcastic passersby
hawkers of firewood
the sneaky craftsman
the crook
the dangerous thief
Bedouins with their camels
downing their supper by hand
and here in the tiny shops
where Yemenites are lords
the Indian servant
goes around yelling:
Who has seen the bloody ram
and mother sheep with her twins?
There is a Javanese roaming

with a pair of eggs
he hopes to exchange for dinner
and black women half-naked sit
on their haunches
bubbly with delightful talk
selling their wares
beef jerky
sesame seeds
perfumes
one of them with peeled
almonds piled up high
A lame beggar in bitter silence
begs for alms
A woman passes by
selling sycamore fruit
The best of Syria and
Egypt, she yells. Taste of
honey. Fit to be eaten
by a prince!
Behind her in the corner
the corpse of a goat stinks
two weeks dead
in a strange accident
a Yemenite woman beggar
trying to steal it,
had to climb up a rickety house
making stones shower down
in an avalanche that buried it
Its broken body lies now
where flies and dogs have a feast
and probably wolves
would not hesitate
if they could trust
the milling crowd.
In the road a dog
is taking a leak
a chicken never tires
of pecking for grain
but there's only dung
and her efforts are wasted
A soldier comes along

to blow his whistle:
the mayor will be going this way
accompanied by the head
of the chamber of commerce
and the doctor from the south
and his brother
the newspaper editor
and the literary man
they want to spend some time
at the oasis of the grand sheik
And if you happen to ask
those sitting in the dirt
in a cloud of flies
about the grand sheik
they'd reply: He's the lord
who owns the palaces
and those great orchards
teeming with birds
where he entertains
the other lords
in the fresh open air
with figs and olives
and iced juices and grapes
on big, elegant carpets.

I went back to slave
at the mill
with the knowledge that figs
have their own eaters
who are different from those
who eat sycamore fruit.

Translated by Sargon Boulus

Time's Spindle

Morning into noon prolonged
and noon, in turn
            delivers us
to twilight come
as a florid sunset. Earth goes dim
for a time and then
the night lets down
            its shades,
                  we sleep

Day's messengers, back again,
herald the dawn
Blend into a river.
                  The sun, rising –
And so it turns,
The spindle of time.

This sun that turns
As you turn, do you know it?
Night, do you know where you are going?
Why do days line up
To circle through our lives?
Earth at evening,
Earth in the morning,
Tides that ebb and flow –

Plants in their turn
            glow and shimmer,
Then they wilt,
                  the wind
Carries them away, and man:
From the cradle he's rocked in
To the brink of his grave.

Translated by Sargon Boulus and Christopher Middleton

Abd al-Ilah al-Babtain   SAUDI ARABIA

The Road's Bend

She gathers her steps from the roads of this city
Wishing to depart, she asks me,
'Where do these roads lead, you with the aching feet?'
Her suddenness stunned me
spread in my blood like day
I stopped . . .
lit a cigarette for recollection
    of her face, her mysterious questions
(when did her blossoming face first inhabit me?
From which path did we walk out once together, towards the
    sadness of palm trees,
till I lost her on the road?)

I woke to her questioning voice,
purling words of fatigue,
'Where do these roads carry me? Answer!
Your reverie precedes light
but your silence lies fractured in my hand
Your sky contains no rain, no stars,
your land is not swept by wind,
and here is your silence, broken in my hand . . .'
Who, I wonder, will answer the heart's tremor
if silence takes root in the road,
and ripens over clumsy lips which mumble
of nights when pleasure grows flaccid,
of days skilled in eluding the debtors –
Tremble when morning surprises you,
when night takes you for a wistful excursion –

Who, I wonder, will answer if silence should break in the hands,
    if the road ravages the feet
if those who depart fasten their suitcases between the beloved's
    sorrow
and illusory joy

She turned, she cried,
silence drew me into its tunnel and I cried as well
Here I am, possessed by her face,
her face, my fate
Her sadness has become bread that persists in embossing my table,
a song that occupies the heart during the lull of desire's weeping
I trembled . . . I trembled . . .
but my silence still lay broken in her hands
– I will give you some answer,
bestow on you the absent filly
These roads will lead to the date palm that hangs suspended
    over our pain
She cried and turned,
threw something to the ground,
and walked hurriedly towards the bend.

Translated by Lena Jayyusi and Naomi Shihab Nye

I Search Sorrow . . . Happiness Conceals You

(TO MANY HEARTS THAT HOSTED MY PAIN ONE EVENING)

You come like a treacherous stab
No time speaks of you . . . no eyes desire you

So where did you come from?
And why did you relish betrayal on that rainy night?

Now you have a resting place between my silence and myself
so rise up and dance
There's a fountain full of sorrow sprinkled in the space
between my teardrops and my eyes
so rise up and drink
Our mornings are confronted by the stare of the impossible
Our nights have been abandoned by birds and light and wishes
I have waited for you since I awoke
since I began this solitary weeping
I learned how to hide my wound from a star in the sky,
from a stone in the road

You were between me and the time that arrived
bearing your ill omen
embracing the heart's flood that flowed from you
so where am I when I bar a door and leave a window open,
when I keep a vigil on land, and the sea overtakes me,
when I sleep through the day, and night awakens me to stand guard
over two solitary embers in my fireplace.

You lay between me and the time that came creeping,
stealing into these nights full of warmth
and wakefulness, of laughter sprinting across my father's
    forehead
as he returned each night to the sleeping brows of his children . . .
he would kiss them, concealing within them the aches of
    his departed day
only to awaken to a new morning, new cares that would steal
a few more minutes from his span of life.

And between me and the flirtatious wishes which drank
from my pain, so I lit up my night to transport them
to the morning that would not come . . . so steal them, then,
kill them . . . Now they have the colour of ash, the taste
of black, the smell of teardrops.

I have waited for you since I awoke –
How come you arrive like a hidden tremor?

No time speaks of you . . . no breast desires you,
so where did you come from?
Why do you enjoy passing across a road that glows
with wholesomeness?
Now you have a jug of misery and ill fortune, so
   sit yourself down upon these hearts . . .
drink what you will . . .
our nights have been abandoned by birds and light and wishes,
All that remains is a prayer upon the lips.

Translated by Lena Jayyusi and Naomi Shihab Nye

End of Death

I find no kinship with anything;
The world is alien, the times estranged –
As if I came in an age too soon or too late.
Or perhaps in an interim.

The seasons have lost their appointed hours,
The eyes of the sun and stars their keenness;
Those who swim with the tide have come,
Sowing their words upon the waters.

Oh time with no identity,
When the murderer's trade is one with the physician's;
Distinctions of contraries are blotted out,
And truth's arrow forgets to hit the target.

Its own fragrance is the death of the flower;
Even the innocent dew is suspect.
The juice of the grape has lost its fervour;
Sheer terror is the sole delight.

But what now can strike terror in us?
There is nothing at all that can put us in fear;
Murder is a lust and an opiate,
Only security is held in contempt.

Killing plays the part of its own assassin:
Today it comes in a novel guise –

A mark that displays the grace of beauty.
Who now will Azad[1] give her poison to?

No one is left – she must drain her own cup.

Earth's slumber holds the shoots of burgeoning
The end of death is the beginning of awakening
Here the dead become the seeds of new life –
Rain then, clouds, on whatever spot you will!

Translated by John Heath-Stubbs with the help of the Editor

The Kindness of the Enemy

This man, who is my enemy,
has threatened death or robbery.
Should he rob me, he will find
I own nothing – I won't mind.
Let him kill me – very well!
He'll free me from the prison-cell
which is called Life. So, in the end
My foe will prove a generous friend.

Translated by Sargon Boulus and John Heath-Stubbs

1. Azad was the Persian wife of the general, al-Aswad al-Ansi; she poisoned him at the demand of a Persian general in Yemen.

Between Two Voids

Dwindle and drain away
    All things that we have got
That which we hoped for seems
More unattainable and more remote.

Still more far off, the morrow
    on which we waste our yearning;
Nor can we summon back
Yesterday – for it is unreturning.

Between the day that's done
    and that which now draws near
We plant the wind, with which
We strive to build our castles in the air.

What we built falls to ruin
    What we would build must fail
We drive towards no port –
Before we found the wind we lost the sail.

Successive rulers came;
    Pockets grew rife with gold;
Who bought us knew not why,
Nor he who sold us knew what he has sold.

Giver or taker, both
    Crumble – and we abide
In poverty and hunger,
And yet we still retain our sneering pride.

Translated by Sargon Boulus and John Heath-Stubbs

Between the Knife and the Killer

Into his inner self he is exiled
By desolation howling all around,
But there his alienation casts him forth
Into a sea, still seeking for its bound.

The pass in front of him leads back to him;
More than the traveller is the road confused;
One half of him asks of the other. Comes
an answer, more than he who asked, bemused.

When, in the final hour, he seeks for death
He thrusts his breast upon the assassin's knife,
And sinking there within his murderer's grasp
Consumes away the remnants of his life.

His mouth is smaller than his anguished screams,
And greater than himself his burden seems.

Translated by Sargon Boulus and John Heath-Stubbs

Answers to One Question

Why is it that time past is yet to be?
It is because what's called futurity
Has passed away, a long, long time ago
It is because our faces are backwards set
Seeking for lost identity – even so
Because the singer greatly loved and yet
What thing it was he loved, he did not know.

Translated by Sargon Boulus and John Heath-Stubbs

Treachery of Words

You are a fool, as much as I,
Glibly accepting each untruth:
Meanness termed thrift, and innocence
The gullibility of youth.

Naked aggression we describe
As courage of the beast untamed;
and man's brutality to man
Is, for heroic worth, acclaimed!

Translated by Sargon Boulus and John Heath-Stubbs

Longing

He is athirst. The goblets
With thirst are all afire,
Though they are filled up to the brim,
Like mirrors that a lovely face desires.

Like moments of delight
That float before the eyes
Of one who's strength is ebbing out
Inch upon painful inch, until he dies.

He thirsts – not for the goblet;
The vine thirsts too, and so
Though he is eager to arrive,
The nearer that he draws, he treads more slow.

Here his quest ends, where ends
to be beginning prove;
Full of desire, he runs towards it,
Seeking no cure, to melt away in love.

He longs to be the hunter,
But as the prey, must flee;
In all his chaffering he finds
The only merchandise that's sold is He.

Translated by Sargon Boulus and John Heath-Stubbs

Ali al-Dumaini   **SAUDI ARABIA**

They Ask You

The loaves hide in your shirt
The pavements are proud of you
Those standing at prayer wonder
    about the right direction of Mecca

Enquire of your wounds for a way of escape
Enquire of the trembling moment
when you laughed secretly because
    you were accused about the birds
    and accused of a flux of language.
In your eyes
    are hidden the ceramic hour
    and the loaves
A street takes refuge in you from the blaze of the sun
The wind seeks shelter in your arms
(and here you are, like a mountain
                    like a rainbow forest
Everyone argues about you with the dew
                    and with the morning).

My Master,
My Master hiding your face with your own shirt-tail
Do you feel ashamed to be smaller than these wounds?
or will you secretly laugh when your reality
    encloses you
    between the dampness of the ceiling
    and the eternal loneliness at night
    Under the coins of those who own the earth

and amuse themselves selling you
    the howling of the winds.

When men weary me
or when my affairs weary others
I search my breast . . . I seek to find
if any bird of hope remains there yet
or my own small country?
Have the birds left their innocence there
or the Bedouins pitched their tents still?
Here I am:
     I have let down a pole into the sea
and have taken off my country clothes
and here is my foot getting near the water
    without becoming wet
I can sense in the sand the laughter of the dew
    the extension of space
    and the depth of the waters
I lower myself . . . I raise my voice
    and offer my death
    to the winds of friendly hands.
I shake off all people
wash my face in the leaf of a palm tree
Longing is knocking at every door
'Save God's Mecca with the rain of the trees
and with the trees of the rain
Lend this spirit its dagger
Here I stand at the sea side
stripped of my country clothes
Lend me the dew and the crescents
I ask You, God, for a country and a place of repose
and for an open path.'
The roads have darkened, the mists have turned
    into grey clouds
and you, my heart, are hung ensnared
    at the sides of the wall
Those who enter from the gate can touch you
You tempt the birds of the earth to roost around you
and build from the grasses of these sands
    a kingdom
    a gate that allows passersby to enter

but those within cannot get out.

The winds tempt others with you, but you
    they do not tempt
They make a guide of you
    before you are ever guided
They make you the resting place of pilgrims
You knight who whistle in the midst of the wilderness
    all things hear you
        and you do not hear them
    The names write you
        but you do not write them
And your heart, turning white in the morning
    and pale at night
    dripping with oil and water
You dance at the gate of silence
(blue . . . blue is that which shines in the dark
    but cannot be lit)
You watch those who enter, and those who go out
    the fugitive, the thief and the victim
    while you burn, and are aflame
Fortunate is he who embraces the branches of passion
who divulges the secret without faltering
and never comes near you at the gate.
You who have forgotten those whom you loved
The difference between you two is:
that the one remains on the road searching
and the other does not search, yet he finds the way
tapping on the trunks of palm trees
making rhythmical tunes on his staff at the gate
waking up a heart that is hanging without a shroud
a heart that's not been lost
but that's not found its way
or its abode.

Translated by May Jayyusi and John Heath-Stubbs

Muhammad al-Dumaini   SAUDI ARABIA

Cedar and Olives[1]

Embers raining in my heart . . .
Why do I cherish you?
And why do I cherish empty vanities?
How shall I wipe out falsehood,
The false veneer of an ancient death now blooming –
a country whose silence cries out loudly,
tears that fuelled nothing,
a fire consuming the neighbourhood,
a day that stretched out into a century,
a secret no longer a secret,
a sky that lends no shade,
and grass ignorant of sunshine?
Sidon is a hunted prey;
no trace is left for Beirut.
If Palestine began this woe,
why not say what happened in Beirut
    was doomed from the beginning?

Beirut's disaster is also ours.
The responsibility is ours too,
    for we came to think of Beirut
        only as Bank Street
and the broker at the gate of the airport
offering the bird to the tourist,
and the crowded corridor.
Tourist Hotel in Beirut is not pleased with us.

1. Cedar and olives are symbols for Lebanon and Palestine.

Whether the Palestinian stayed home
or fled to us, we share his woe.
He will not accept that I
am merciful with the enemy,
that I carry the vision, but stifle it with wine
and bend my head to suppress what is well known
though on the news I see my defeats
and carry, vicariously, my Arab banners.

We travelled far away
before we realized the secret of water
and saw the pictures of the slain
floating in our wells.
We saw how fighters in the trenches sing
with one voice,
how the hole around the olive tree stretched
to redden the cedars
(and, to think, once the cedars were green!).

On the news screen
hovered moss inhabited by sleep
and the official envoy reading
how the invasion[2] happened so quickly.
Summer in the hotel stopped, immobilized.
Alone we welcomed the flower in the coffin.

Now we are the tower of blown-up doors
imprisoned in death
letting eloquent language work instead of us.
Tourist Hotel, who remembers it?
Tourist Hotel, who knows it
lost under clouds of tears and ravaged bodies?

And so we do not witness to the obvious.
Pens are barren roses in our fingers.
They will not fade
until fire is kindled in us
in this long long war.

2. This is a reference to the Israeli invasion of Lebanon in June 1982 which
devastated the country, already greatly weakened by the long civil war.

If the Palestinian heart leaves or stays
Beirut will still love war,
Beirut transforms the earth into a bird
    and calls the water blood.
This is Beirut, and this is its long war
first and second,
third and fourth,
Beirut needs the dead to live,
the wounded to live,
    and the living
        to live.

Translated by May Jayyusi and Naomi Shihab Nye

Abd al-Rahman Fakhri   **YEMEN**

Identity Card

As it happens
my mind is silver
my heart of ivory and stone,
my tongue weighed down
with the Arabic language
For I am an Arab
and belong to this century
of balloons
and the Third World War
The language of the Hindus is also mine
when Tagore sings
I resemble a fiery peacock
in a fit of rage
or my neighbour's daughter
when she falls in love
and casts off her chains.
Flow on, O words
for everyone to read
and let me emerge
from the ink-pot
as if for the first time
I will not stretch my hand
out to you
you may have
to thrust me down the pit
towards the fountain of alphabet
O monsters, my friends!

Translated by Sargon Boulus and John Heath-Stubbs

A Favourite Habit

Have you ever tasted
the taste of bitterness?
while your conscience prepares for sleep?
In a while your spirit
will turn out the lamps
In a while you will stretch out
   dimensionless
and peel off yourself
the lessons you have learned,
your bills, and your hopes.
For the sake of rest
forget us, your friends
take absence upon yourself
You will pay
   today's price –
You will sleep
but only to wake
and wake, only to sleep
to grapple with our curses
upon yourself again.

Translated by Sargon Boulus and John Heath-Stubbs

From 'The Myth of Immortality'

1
How can a whisper so displease?
Conspiracy, confusion of
Wish-phantoms vanishing, darkest night. I wanted
Warmth of embers, I clutch ashes.

2
Time sweetly whispering: I can hear
A mystery which I alone encompass;
I wish I did not. Count your blessings,
You who know you do not know.

3
He was the essence of his age, and so serene,
Such clemency was his, everyone said.
His heart was broken, he was dead:
But for their neglect, need it have been?

4
No place to call my own, I travelled
Much between the desert and the sea.
I did not mix.
                    The higher up I went
The more the pit rose up to capture me.

5
Butterfly, beauty, not a piece of paper
Tossed aside, but freshness, winged, a flow –

I caught you, felt you flutter in my fingers,
Then, like all else, for love I let you go.

6
Here in my house, it seems,
I sweep with a thousand eyes
The four horizons. All too near
The sights, the chants, the cries —

Stricken by them with fear,
What if I gaze more far afield?
Would I see the other world
Still here, unknown, revealed?

7
Dying let me hear the tune I love:
Play the *rabab* for a while, by my bed.
It will be a moment only as I go,
My kinfolk, home, vanishing also;
Soon the layers of the dark
Fold back, to show
Those lights of mine I'm thinking of.

8
Change: you and I, we both have changed,
I said — idea, even spirit, and
Being, so much clay to the potter's hand.
From place to place around the self time ranged.

Pressing away, briefly, crevices of shade
Where self took shelter, for a time between.
Nothing was left but what it chose to mean:
From what it meant it chose the man it made.

9
Overwhelmed with pain I'd wake up
screaming, what if I were free of pain?
Is it really so strange
that I alone in the world
can find respite only in pain?
Or am I the only soul who knows

71

how rich suffering can be?
I see myself as a link
between a world that yearns
and a world that rejects.

10
I aspired to the summit
but went hurtling one day
down the endless pit.
Alone I dug in the solitary depths,
for a companion is
that rarest thing.
But the treasures uncovered
were tangible, true:
Had I taken the upward path
I'd only have lost my way
to find a slight glitter of gold.

11
Leaving nothing but dregs
to whomever came after me,
I distilled my pleasures.
Savouring sweet breezes and poison
draughts, worriedly, peacefully,
I went past any bound.
Honey turned hemlock
in my mouth, and ghosts wandered
my interior.
My early joys
take me, now, to task
and are my ruin.

12
He shuns the evening
once he owns the day
and woe to those
around him.
Whenever he's infatuated
with light, he leaves it
and seeks the dark.
Straining toward the highest

peak, he tumbles willingly
down to the pits.
And while mocking the hunters' traps,
he approaches the trap, with his own feet, there.

13
Oh soul! I hope it is not an illusion!
Will I lie in my grave
after a life of empty toil
yearning for immortality? Would a corpse
ever yearn? Would a corpse fear its future?
Immortality! My soul detects no bliss
in its setting sun.

14
Oh phantoms that light my way
at night like heavenly stars,
tending me on my lonesome road,
lightening my heavy journey!
You spirits of my friends! Do not
be stingy now with your secrets!
My anxious soul keeps reaching toward the unknown
but perceives nothing but dust!

15
I wished I were a budding rose
ripe with fragrance . . .
for what is earth without bowers
and fountains to please the eye?
Many suffer thirst in the wilderness
and after labouring greatly their fate catches up.
This earth has Edens, and it has deserts,
but in it we are its paradise and its hell.

16
His sensitivity keeps him
vigilant, his heart forever tremulous,
he has no escape.
A mere whisper intensifies his suffering,
a simple nod wounds him like a blade.
How he wished, like anyone, to have a heart

abounding with bliss,
but this was not to be. Forever he has
anguish in love, anguish in hate!
He can find his peace neither in things
near, nor in things far.

17
I am that man who lived enraptured
in the past. I returned to my senses now
and forgot your love, moving toward
distance and detachment.
Do not ask how this has happened,
how the farce became a serious matter.
Only ask your heart: How could it ever imagine
a free man could become a slave?

stanzas 1–8 translated by Sargon Boulus and Christopher Middleton;
stanzas 9–12 translated by Sargon Boulus and Naomi Shihab Nye;
stanzas 13–17 translated by Salma K. Jayyusi and Naomi Shihab Nye

Muhammad al-Fayiz   **KUWAIT**

Zero

I wonder at sand
That grows flowers.
I wonder at rocks
That emit fragrance.
I wonder at the brine
Which becomes potable
After it is cleansed
Of its salt.
I wonder at her who
For a long time
Tarried obediently
In the corners of her home,
But now publicizes her longing,
Releases her passion,
And sheds her protected status
To the winds –
While you still abide
At the same old place
Resembling a zero.

Translated by Issa Boullata and Naomi Shihab Nye

A Sailor's Memoirs[1]

(EXCERPTS FROM THE FIRST MEMOIR)

O land of fires
And dusty winds:
The sea is more compassionate
Than your shores
And the mast a better shelter
Than a pine forest.
O sea:
Your salt is more delicious
Than grapes of the city.
Take my sail, wind,
Steer my ship.
I will restore Sinbad's[2] tale
To the world.
And who is Sinbad?
There is a great difference
Between frenzied imagination
and the real giant
Freely crossing the seas
With sails and cables,
His will ascending above the clouds,

1. The 'Memoirs' of al-Fayiz were written in the 1960s to express nostalgia for the pearl-diving, sea-faring days of the Kuwaitis before oil, as the first example here shows, and wistfulness about the more sedentary life following the oil boom, as is exemplified by the second 'Memoir'.
2. Sinbad is the legendary sea-faring, treasure-seeking hero of *The Arabian Nights* and other folktales. He has often been used as an archetypal symbol of quest and adventure in contemporary Arabic poetry.

His blue-veined hand
Almost touching the stars.

My oil lamp gasps
Like my sleepless eyes
That watch the horizon
Looking for shores.
A storm blows it out
And the ship-singer sings:
'Candle light
From the gleam of her eyes
Melt my ribs with passion!'

As long as I live
The seas will be my abode.
When I die, a fathom of land.
Salt of the seas,
You will soon be honey,
This day will shine
Like her eyes.
Pull down the sails, companions,
Let the ship come to shore.
Singing the sea-song on board,
We return sadly to the city
From the summer journey,
But we will sail again
In winter rains.
Au revoir!

Translated by Issa Boullata and Naomi Shihab Nye

A Sailor's Memoirs

(EXCERPTS FROM THE TWENTIETH MEMOIR)

I don't believe in a sun
That illuminates caves
While my home remains steeped
In total darkness.
I don't believe in a land
Where thorns and cares
Are my share of its yield
While the harvest belongs to others.
Peace be to the Gulf breeze
Though others claim its pearls.
Peace to the sand of the shores,
Bed of dying dawn.
Peace to past memories that loom
Like a covey of pigeons crossing the sky.
Peace to returning ships
and their singers in moonlight.
Peace to the sails in the Gulf,
Roaming the seas, loving risk.
Peace to him who goes out pearl-diving,
And to him who returns from a voyage.
Peace be to women beating tambourines
And their triumphant vows that make dreams
Come true.
Peace be to a gathering in the dark
Lit up by songs and vibrant strings.
Peace to him who winds cables,
To our neighbourhoods in winter,
Their paths awash with rain.
Peace be to the neighbourhood water-carrier,
His jingling bells in the passageways.

Peace to the well in the morning,
Its sputtering bucket as it descends.
Peace to the brazier in winter
Around which are spun the evening tales.
Peace be to the rampart and its turrets,
The stones and boards of its gates.
Peace be to our quiet dwellings,
As still as the dead in their tombs.
They almost push away the huge buildings
To tell their own past stories.
I almost smell lost generations in them,
lying underneath us without veils.
They peep at me through the wall cracks
And complain of insomnia.
Peace! Peace! For I am gone
Like gathered clouds that pour down
To be drunk by hard rocks,
To fill skin-bags and streams.

Translated by Issa Boullata and Naomi Shihab Nye

Abdallah al-Faysal   **SAUDI ARABIA**

Doubts

Doubting you, I doubt my very soul
For you are part of me, we form one whole.

They say you've broken faith – can that be true,
When all that I desire is only you?

Your youthful, confident footsteps lead me on,
Now unreturning youth is almost gone.

Self-doubter, I am now betrayed, it seems
By that which had sustained my youthful dreams.

It is as if those dreams once more arise,
While youth departs, before my sleepless eyes.

What's told about you I mistrust and fear,
Yet, to what all men say, I lend an ear.

Shadows of doubt crowd round me and enslave,
Whilst through the nights in vain for sleep I crave:

As if night's caravan each evening came
And bruited to the world, my love, your name.

Yet what my ears have heard I'll not believe
And nothing to suspect in you perceive

Not credit all those rumours, though my heart
Through its own simple faith, feels bitter smart.

Do not depart from me – such pain and ache
I have endured, suspicious for your sake.

My soul still suffers in tormenting fires,
Because of all its dreams, doubts and desires.

Answer me then – since they report of you
That you have played me false. Are these things true?

Translated by Al-Sayyid Ishaq al-Khalifa Sharif and John Heath-Stubbs

Love's Wounds

Ask not of love's wounds – the heart has laid them in the tomb I say;
Ask not of love's tears when love has departed far away.

For the stricken heart remains neither joy nor ecstasy;
Only sleep will render it forgetful of its poverty.

All my unrequited dreams, all my withered senses weep;
Tired of roaming through the night, now I only ask for sleep.

What tormented once my breast – every fierce consuming flame
Has been quenched and stifled now, till mere ashes it became.

All the melodies of love, that once in my heart would ring,
beat against the barren rocks, with an empty echoing.

Do not ask why all our dreams Time has squandered recklessly
They're a story which is past, and revived it cannot be.

Do not ask why we are now emptied of desire and cold,
Or where songs of passion are, that we sweetly sang of old.

Hope is dead now, and I view, with the same indifference,
All the happiness of meeting and the pain of severance.

Now no more we fear the envious, once the very bane of life
Cutting short our sweetest pleasures with a sharp and cruel knife.

We have let the curtain fall on our loving, and it's plain,
Once the curtain has been drawn, there's no going back again.

Now the amorous moon that once shone upon us from the height,
Distant and more distant grows, parting from us through the night.

Now the garden of our love is made desolate and bare,
And instead of fragrant blossoms, we find thorns and briars there.

Do not ask me why – accept it – we are severed and must learn
That the past, when it is vanished, never, never can return.

Translated by Al-Sayyid Ishaq al-Khalifa Sharif and John Heath-Stubbs

Reproach

When, yesterday, among the crowd you turned
    Your head aside, eyes full of doubts the while,
Half in acquiescence and half chiding
    Hovered upon your lips an anxious smile.

Then I perceived that all my youthful years,
   All my past life was mirrored in your eyes;
And I had squandered it on trivial things
   And vanities, then did I realize

How I had duped myself, become indeed
   A slave to falsehood, and cut off from truth;
Alienated, even among my friends
   In the bright dewy freshness of our youth.

I knew not my own form in vigorous prime,
   And 'Who are you?' I asked in my confusion.
Turning to others then, they seemed to be
   Nothing but fleeting mirage and illusion.

Now my own heart I heard, and it rebuked me
   With its pulsating beat, and from my eyes,
Like waters welling from a limpid fountain,
   Under my eyelids the moist tears arise.

Then I returned and sought my private chamber
   But in that place your ghost was present too
How can I flee, when from you and towards you
   Is all my will, my passion all for you.

Translated by Al-Sayyid Ishaq al-Khalifa Sharif and John Heath-Stubbs

Sulaiman al-Fulayyih   **KUWAIT**

Being

Till when will we continue
    to engage in this madness?
When will we strive, my friend, to be
not as others imagine us
but as we wish ourselves
    to be?

Translated by Lena Jayyusi and Naomi Shihab Nye

Women

The women in this country are statues
They have been chiselled out of rock
Their hearts are piled high with emptiness
Their faces are stone and have no features

The women in this country have eyes of glass
They turn the other way and do not see a thing
The women in this country have lips of lead
Not knowing how to smile they only move them
When they're agitated

If they so much as glimpse the moon
The women in this country frown

Follies they have, kinships and friendships
But not the slightest trace
Is left on them by these

Translated by Lena Jayyusi and Christopher Middleton

A Pony for the Tribe

When will the promised
    pony come, people
        ask and ask and more
And more people are
    haggling over it, more and
        more people aspire
To manage it, more and more
    the chatter and the rumours
        multiply. When, when
Will the pony come,
    the promised pony?
        they ask, the bridle makers,

More and more of them
     fashion its bridle, the scribes
        are all bent on figuring
Its pedigree. It's really
     a farce. When will it come,
        when, the pony? More,
Plenty of people hope
     it won't come at all.
        The problem, they argue, is
Its imminence. When,
     when will the pony
        come? Others wonder –
Those who weave abortive plans
     about it, more and
        more of them, those who
Busily are rigging
     the gallows for whoever
        might be riding it.
The farce goes on, the
     questions multiply, the plots
        and the confusion –
When will the pony
     come? I'll tell you. Simply look
        at the sky, the clouds
Piling up, their folds
     dark, loaded with lightning, when
        the lightning flashes,
Then the pony will come,
     as lightning in lightning,
        thunder and earthquake.

Translated by Lena Jayyusi and Christopher Middleton

Clouds

What pain
  When the heart darkens gloomily
  Thick clouds
come crowding my mind, densely
densely,
gradually.
What sadness when thunder shakes
  the mountains of anguish in my heart
violently
violently it comes.
It destroys me,
this lightning
that gleams in the desert of my
  soul
but illuminates nothing!

Translated by Lena Jayyusi and Naomi Shihab Nye

Ghazi al-Gosaibi   **SAUDI ARABIA**

Love and Black Harbours

Before the word trembles like a frightened bird
pause and observe what weird,
what unknown things I have come back with
Vanish, and take your foolish fancies
with you.

I stand alone in this place
Dawn on the horizon
is a tired yet eager horse
Shyly the city
receives the kiss of morning
A sad perfume
clings to the handkerchief you left.

How cruelly breaks the dawn
when I return downcast
without my love
without the sunlight of your eyes
the enchantment of our meeting.

Do you know why
the shadow of a wall
springs up between us
whenever our longing
brings us together?
Why when we soar with the dream
a cloud of dust
brings us back to earth?

Why when poetry touches our souls
prose takes over with its words,
like dead coal?
Why? – Because the heart
has lost its innocence,
It was pure as a fountain
but now no more
Bold as an idea conceived in night.
It has come back
worn out by its journey
among black harbours
in troubled seas.

FIRST HARBOUR

I was an innocent
I was fond of playing
running alone
over the grass;
building a sand-castle
and toppling it over
the heads of my friends
Then I stood in this harbour
and saw a wolf-pack
with men's faces
whose greetings were with their claws
when they laughed
their fangs were full of menace
and in their fury
they devoured children.
It was there I learned how to fear!

SECOND HARBOUR

I was an innocent
My mother said Don't lie!

My father said
You will be safe if you remain true
I loved truthfulness
true of eye true of heart true
of word
Then I stood by this harbour
and heard men call
the ugliest
the most beautiful,
the most generous
a skinflint,
the mule potent,
the thief a man of honour:
It was there that I learned how to lie!

THIRD HARBOUR

I was an innocent
I owned nothing but illusions
and the stars on the horizon
and poetry notebooks
where my dreams nested.
Then I stood by this harbour
people asked
Do you own a house
as you own verse and its tinkling rhymes?
Do you have any land
besides the verdant lands of poetry?
There I was infected
with money fever.

I was an innocent
and a raw youth
who saw no difference
between one man and another
All were Adam's
children and Eve's
Then I stood by this harbour

and saw the lowly and the great
the beggar and the tycoon
One sits at ease
while the rest must stand,
one walks, and other men walk with him
one is welcomed by flunkeys
while the rest are left standing
on the doorstep
There I learned to love
the blaze of fame.

EPILOGUE

My sweet! The night
of hypocrisy, self-seeking and lies
has come between us now
In vain I open my soul
to your love:
I have come back without a soul!

Translated by Sargon Boulus and John Heath-Stubbs

Little Thoughts

If once we say 'No!'
we are purged of our
hypocrisy
and die in innocence, like children.

Spurred by a cause
even cowards fight.

To write a poem is like
a tune that leaps out
of a moment of life.

In a world of mirrors
the search for truth
is unending.

If I could forget my ego
for one moment
then I would find myself.

We lie
on the luminous side
of our dreams
when we die.

When you are a master
but do not feel exalted
When you are a slave
but do not feel debased
That is what it is like
to be a lover.

Translated by Sargon Boulus and John Heath-Stubbs

Song in a Tropical Night

Say that it is the moon
or the sea that is always burning
with waves and with desire
or the sand where gems
glisten and glow
where coconuts have a fragrance
rare in other fruit
Say that it is the trees then!
There is music in the forest
drums in an ecstasy of pain
a wedding which is full of sorrow
Say that it is the lute strings.

O my dark pearl!
most lovely at the journey's end
At your coming the air was tremulous with dew
with fragrance, with light, with passion and colour
I came,
tedium in my eyes
tedium even to my fingertips
my soul a volcano
that does not erupt.
O my dark pearl!
strange are the workings of fate
I am like one dying,
and you are a fresh, new birth.
Say that it is the moon.

Should I ask pardon
for the heart that has died
and in its stead a stone?
for the purity that has seeped away
leaving no trace?

Tell me
how should I ask pardon?
Do you know that words are
lies, betrayals, deceits,
a cover for ignoble lusts,
enslavers of mankind?
Say that it is the moon!

I came to you
illusions my companions
disease, suffering, weariness
Behind me years of life lived so ill
even the moon could not suffer it
Centuries of life so ill spent
every moment spells out the whole.
Before me lie in wait
the deserts of death.
O my dark pearl!
How can I be merry
and compose verses
that twinkle with the light of dawn?
My poems are better unsaid!
So say that it is the moon!

As for me, do not ask about me
My country is a rainless land
I sail towards a dangerous goal
My sea full of embers and flames
my days are full of agony
among the creeks and shoals
with other men, and the labour of verse,
As for me, do not ask about me
Enough for you these breezes, these melodies,
these dreams.
So say that it is the moon.

Tomorrow, speak of it no more!
Tomorrow the islands will call
to my ship
the festival of night
shall wither and die

and there will be no flowers
no sweet fragrances.
Say then it is the moon!

Translated by Sargon Boulus and John Heath-Stubbs

Your Loving

When I ask why is it I love you,
A thousand answers spring to mind:
One is because you are fairest among women;
Another, you are my shelter from the storm;
Because you are the voice of my conscience, threatened with silence;
Because you know I am a hurt child, who needs comforting;
Yet another, because you are the essence of tenderness,
Sweet modesty, wanton pride of existence.
I alone know the answer: because birds sing,
Because perfume allures, stars shine, tears flow;
Because if I didn't love you, you wouldn't be you,
And I wouldn't be I.

Your love is like the sea –
The sea where we glimpse a different world,
Where mountains vanish, and pastures disappear,
Where there is heat and cold, tumult and wind,
And the patience of harbours awaiting a Sinbad.[1]
Since my childhood I have loved the sea,
Laid its calm in my heart, like a rose of tears;

1. See note 2, p. 76.

And so for the sake of your love I have entrusted
My poem, my heart and my memories to the waves,
And sailed in search of treasure, knowing that life
Is beautiful when it is touched with courage,
And he who sails into love will never die.

For love is like night, when it comes down on the little birds,
And seeps under eyelids, touching the hidden cells of the soul,
For night is unending – it is always born anew.
We journey for improbable things. In the night of your love
I play with stars, or touch the crescent or plenilune;
So also, like night, it abolishes
Those false shapes which the hand of day has fashioned,
Peacefully striding onwards to things that are sad and strange.

I cry that your love is like water to me
In a dreary desert of sand and thorns;
Your love is the truth – when, amid cheap verbiage, truth is
                                 hidden and lost;
Your love is the light of my eyes, piercing the barrage of mist.

Translated by Sargon Boulus and John Heath-Stubbs

Qasim Haddad   **BAHRAIN**

The Sea has its Transformations . . . Make Way

Whoever saw a sea so narrow
narrow narrow
        like the pupil of an eye
I mean – who
I have seen
and it's narrowing still
hardly space enough for the sputter of a strange gull
small fish can find no space in which to make a turn

Turn the discourse around
Language alone discards the images and disperses them
It is not me
        language alone
So the sea invades the alleys
tinier than the gurgle of snails
as they suffocate

Hardly enough of it to make a hat
for the island, solitary, standing
in the cold
The solitary island remains
head bare and alone
The wind dispatches news to it
the storm, which is coatless, does not arrive

Narrow
We don't have enough of it to make a shirt
        for a child

Smaller than a handkerchief waving goodbye
A narrow sea like this
what am I to do with it?

A sea that has claws and is fiercer than
        a bird betrayed
He who knows the tiny narrow sea
has the right to set sail for weeping
for the island is bigger than the sea
                the sea

Bigger, bigger
        more spacious and glorious
open to the heavens and to names
        and to secrets not to be revealed
and the sea is narrower than books and prison cells
more constricted than the meetings
        between a prisoner and his wife

Is the sea a harbour?
Is it a peg for the tribal tent?
The teardrop of a land ringed by desert?
And where do the ships go?
How do they cast off
with the travellers, the messages
the sails and the ancient fishes?

A sea?
It doesn't even wash over the first letter of the word
It doesn't even wake the mountain up
Funeral feasts have no special place in it

Its messages are kept by it
Its messages are meant for it alone
What close-fisted sea is this?
It doesn't come to rescue the drowning man
It doesn't hear or see
A tongue but it doesn't understand languages

Turn the discourse around
Let the sea reject

make it rise up
Give it a spaciousness
and a plentitude of shores.

Translated by Lena Jayyusi and Christopher Middleton

Dominion

Before
        the paper
I stand amazed.

Who dares
        to breach this
Beauty, white.

Translated by Lena Jayyusi and Christopher Middleton

The Children

Those many children
        who frolic around you
Have you chosen names for them
        or will you leave the naming to the gardens?
Those green children
Will they ascend from depths
        or topple from heights?
Those very tiny children
Now I see them –
        iridescent fishes
                bottled in time –
Their water, you.

Translated by Lena Jayyusi and Christopher Middleton

Two Lines

Better to quarrel with the wound
Than be intimate with the knife.

Translated by Lena Jayyusi and Christopher Middleton

I Do Not Bow

Naked I stand in the chilling wind
Alone
      like the letter A
                and I do not bow
I mutiny against all the idols
                and I do not bow
I emerge from one raging fire and enter another one
                and I do not bow
I believe in the meeting of opposites
                and I do not bow
I mingle with ashes
                and I do not bow
                        except to you

Translated by Lena Jayyusi and Naomi Shihab Nye

Happily He Entered Death

That was he
He was my friend

whose body opened to receive the blade
He was neither mad nor rash
He was one
    who would conquer the world with words
He placed a signpost for the procession of palm trees
  saying
    It has come to an end
This was no misgiving he expressed, nor anticipation
He established a climate for his words
and threw his body into the path of brass feet

He said
    I will end with the palms
He heard the rain weep,
    the earth sob
He imposed his village on the city
binding stones together with grass
His timeless eyes merged his beloved with the homeland,
    He set up for her a palace of words

He would charge in, move directly,
his conversation was a language teaching speech
and he was also my friend.
      Enamoured with conquering
        distances
        and differences
He moulded his creatures rapidly
rapidly he would proclaim   rapidly act
            and rapidly die
When he turned to ask, the blade struck him
He opened wide his body and the murder rushed in
    as though he could not bear a deathless dying
        and so he died

That was he
my friend who was still young
for love, for poetry, for his homeland
still young for death
but he died

That was he
whose friend I was
and still am.

Translated by Lena Jayyusi and Naomi Shihab Nye

The Rider

Welcome Rider
Highwayman
   ragged with hunger and cold
   frightened by winds
Come, retreat to my tent
Rest awhile, lay down your sword
This fire that warms the soul is for you
This dew-washed robe is for you
and the wine stored in the tent,
the mare poised to charge,
the lance made of lightning, are all for you
and yours is the pillow
     but don't let sleep swallow you up
for those caravans
    filling the horizon come for you
    they come for you, for you, for you
              they come for you.

Translated by Lena Jayyusi and Naomi Shihab Nye

Ibrahim al-Hadrani   **YEMEN**

Fountain

My love, we passed by this fountain once,
when our love was flowing freely,
we came back to it when the grass
was dry, so was your heart's longing.
Nature spoke thus to us: This,
this is what we are: first we meet, then we part.
My love, the grass shall be green once more
and other lovers like us linger here,
and the birds will sing on the hillsides
Fragrance, flowers, leaves.
But say: Our spring, now departed,
will it ever come back again?
My love, even the ashes of past days
are fragrant still,
Put them on the wound only for a minute
they are an antidote for pain.
All time is gathered into this moment
the past holds no sway over it, and
there is no unbearable future.
You are not guilty; if the grass has withered and wilted
and the streams are all dried up.
You, who are you, my soul's companion, and
who am I? We are no more than smoke
blown about by the savage winds. It is the winds
not us who are guilty.
I asked my heart that it should forgive you
You whose very existence is atonement.

Translated by Christopher Nouryeh and John Heath-Stubbs

Beauty

You are not like the supple bough
You are not like the fair-faced moon
Lovers describe beauty so many ways
All I want to say is, 'I Love you!'

Translated by Christopher Nouryeh and John Heath-Stubbs

The Streets of Rome

Even the walls ask who I am
as I roam these squares
'Whose is that strange face
that lean spectre?
As he walks, phantoms of the past surround him
There is a baffled look in his eyes
and a nervous anxiety.'
O cradle of the Roman stock
This is what our faded time has brought about
From the times of Himyar and of Cheops,

fear still comes upon us
the wound that bleeds in our hearts
is the wound the oppressor gave.

I walk in this city with faltering steps
my ears are almost deaf.
I feel the words like a blind man
astray in a wilderness
This place is estranged from me
but I love those who dwell here
I sing, but my song is alien to these skies
The roofs of the city cast my song back at me.

Translated by Christopher Nouryeh and John Heath-Stubbs

Muhammad Jabr al-Harbi   SAUDI ARABIA

Drinking from Her Eyes

Before I was born, before the horse neighed,
    before the dove called, cooing,
before the rainbow was painted,
    before the rainbow answered
the colours of the essential poem,
before the northward and southward
    migration of birds,
before the birth of the alphabet,
before I could stand on two feet,
        you came . . .
With the sun you came to stand
before me and I never doubted
what it was that makes music
    for the dance, nor what
answered my blood nor what said
    no to my tribe.
Woman of wheat, colour of wheat,
your eyes touch me like fingers.

I crossed road after road
where your name fell across
my forehead like a shadow.
I stopped, whispered, ran, cried
    I love you.
Love's heat is warmer than
the tremor from open windows.
Love's heat is warmer than
this epoch shaking the gate
    of the village.

As if just wakened I reach
    to touch your hands.
And you are there standing
at the portals of my eyes
fixed into the alphabet.
Your colour is my colour.
Your hand, my hand, you are
my journey and the movement of time.
    Why, how, who
are those people who claim kin
    and surround you?
They are immobile, but you come,
    forward, approaching
        like a poem.

I knew you.
We were young.
How did you discard your old shoes?
How did you make women jealous?
How did you make them angry,
make them nurture resentment
    like children?
Are you an adolescent? A nun?
And will perfume from Paris define
    The passion that fills
the air I inhabit when your voice
    reaches me?
I talk to myself because talking
to you never reaches, even though
my voice stretches toward you and
    I escape toward you
and I escape through you, from you,
to you. You choose the steps,
the distance, the size of the caravans,
the dress; the colours of the rainbow
    which you wear remind me
of chains, remind me of
disobedience. And I repent.
    I paint a palace without
windows, a house, fenced in
    with double walls.

I dream I am the flight of a wing,
   the light beam
refracting light from the threshing floor.

Child, desired to the point of tears,
   embraced by the eyes
of men and whispering girls,
I crossed the roads and
my heart fell in shards
where again for the second time
I found the image of my mother
and the accents of my father's voice –
you for the second time,
for you were with me
before I was born.
You stood with the sun
and I never doubted
which of you would be the
essence of the poem.

Diana Der Hovanessian
Lena Jayyusi (first translator)

Hufuf[1]

I see Death preparing a place
for my soul. But I cannot see my soul.

1. Hufuf is the name of a town in al-Ihsa, in the eastern part of Saudi Arabia. It is the poet's town.

Come, Hufuf.
I want to give a souvenir
of my heart to you
while I whisper secrets
while I break down in tears
while I wash in waves of sadness
across your ankles,
while I snatch at the waves,
and pour them into your lap.
Let your sands and
these waves come together.
Let them approach each other.
Come, do not be afraid.
I want to give you a souvenir
of my love.
I want to tattoo my name in colour
across your arm and let you
penetrate my ribs and
enter my heart,
let you keep a part of me
on your body, Hufuf.
Now I am powerless
and falling
down, down until
your sand wakes to my cry,
begins to moan.
The sands remain in turmoil
Until they are waked up,
Hufuf.
I have a soul that does not tire
although it grows impatient,
even weary,
but it does not tire or give up.
Tormented,
it climbs seven measures,
descends seven measures
to acknowledge its mistakes
and then my soul leaves,
Hufuf.
How long will
I discard one sorrow

for another and go
to another span of life,
Hufuf?
As for him,
the one who lies between us,
embrace him, then.
Ask nothing except
his name.
Memorize it.
The earth has turned
from yesterday,
and settled on your wrist
gives you advice:
Take him.
Give him your greetings of peace
Give him my greetings of peace
Hufuf, let him have peace.

Pray long and hard for him.
Do not leave him to the mercy
of air as your palm trees were left,
with neither earth nor people
to mourn,
Hufuf.
Sprinkle dew into his hand,
under the soil,
over the soil.
Should birds fly over
they will pass by. They will
pray for him.
Let them fly by,
one after another
with a song which sadness
has shaped.
Hufuf,
without hesitation
I cast off my soul for him.
I did not falter
although I weep.
My life and its time
rushes ahead of me

and I lag behind chasing
and never quite reaching
while it rains
inside my ribs.
My tears shed me
lamenting my life.

Oh, town
called Hufuf.
My brother
My child was school,
the sky,
the sidewalk,
mixture of mud and reed,
loss and the lost.
He was song,
and conversations
that stretched through time
and contracted time.
He was the river that flowed
into the first compass
of the heart
to stop the heart.

The bellies of the Island[2] beckoned him
    as though this Island were extensions
of his own hands.
He wandered far from home
    looking for work, not love.
Pursuing a shadow, he would rush from each place.
    No home could keep him. No walls could
hold him. Neither could wind. The Island would
call him to hold him.
Then in some lowland
        it would discard him, forget him.
He would turn to others
This Island, this land submitted its riches to others
    but would resist his touch

2. 'Island' here is a reference to the Arabian Peninsula spoken and written of as
'the Island' rather than 'the Peninsula'.

but would close doors.
He would smile at discovering water,
    then find it was mirage.
He would reach for the star
but would plunge into the pit.
    I shall weep over his robe,
    his shroud which
we shall yet wear.
    That is the way of life.
But it is exile, a life of exile
not the approach of death that makes me weep,

Hufuf.
Embrace him
    embrace him
        embrace him
The letters of my alphabet have been dispersed
and, as you know, my tired body
has stooped.
I am resigned to mortality,
Hufuf.
I am resigned to my weariness,
Hufuf.
Do you know weariness, Hufuf?
Do you know how the mountains stoop with care,
and how aches surge out of earth,
no longer concealed,
aches that no one suspected
until sorrow detonated them?
Now all have made peace with weariness
having forgotten their own departed pains.
Fire bursts from combustible earth,
and from my heart,
that fire that destroys your face.
When the face laughs, it discourages
wanderlust.
You bend and embrace the child
saying 'I love you, Hani.'[3]
'I love you too' is the uncertain reply,

3. Hani is the son of the dead man, the poet's brother.

because your face is already fading from his view.
Of course you know child's love, and
you knew, didn't you, the voice that asks
Has Father gone?
Is he still in the hospital?
Where is my father?
He laughs thinking I am laughing
as I caress him and the rain of tears
washes the heart.
The heart is the warrant
that confines us, Hufuf,
imprisons us inside grief.
Now go out into sunlight
and apologize for this gloominess
to that child who waves
beyond my lifescape.

Diana Der Hovanessian
Lena Jayyusi (first translator)

Muhammad Ubaid al-Harbi   SAUDI ARABIA

Bedouin Lament at the Gates of the Equator

i   BIRD AND WIND

1
Who has sighted the melancholy bird
   in the palm tree?
Who has beheld her rainbow plumage?
Who has watched her counting children
   in the courtyard,
   counting the women
of the house, who?
Who has witnessed her filling her wings
   with clouds, and folktales?
She said: Tell me who has died
   and I will tell you who lives.
He answered: Roses.
She said: Yes, the roses and the river
   of green foliage.
Who has seen the red honeyed planet
   deep in her eyes at dawn?
Whoever has seen her will inherit
half my heart and half my house.

2
We still ask:
   Who has recognized
   the one who was first,
   one who died

115

on the slope of the hill?[1]
Was it you or I?
If the wind wished, it could chisel
the face of the rock.
If it wished, the wind
could fertilize the sprouts in the field.
When it wants, the wind
can be wind
but we will still ask:
  Who has seen the one
  who died on the road?
  Will he come or will he
  stay behind?

ii SONG OF THE SLAIN

Beirut invades the mind.
She is the moon set loose by war.
Beirut is in the blood.
She is the wild mare that wakes
  whenever I sleep.
She was Shatila's[2] child wearing
her slain father's shirt,
the one with his last bullet
My desert is giving birth
to a bigger desert.
She was Sabra's[2] child, nurturer
of roses, suns, wedding songs.

1. The 'Hill' is the Tel al-Zaatar Hill where thousands of impoverished Palestinians and Lebanese lived prior to their brutal massacre by the Phalange Lebanese forces in 1976. At least 15,000 people were slain, mostly Palestinians. The camp was levelled to the ground after its capitulation.
2. Sabra and Shatila are the much publicized Palestinian refugee camps in Beirut where a heinous massacre (again, by the Phalange Lebanese forces) took place in September 1982, when Beirut was under Israeli occupation as a consequence of the Israeli invasion of Lebanon which began in June of that year. Whole families were wiped out. The two camps became a symbol of atrocity.

Every morning my hands helped
to carry my corpse from shelf
   to shelf
while I asked: Whose body is this?
Who has died? And who has died without dying?
Who is left alive?
Beirut is the blood inside the blood.
Each time my corpse steals into Beirut
it comes to life so that death can sleep.

iii   TATTOO OF THE WORLD AND THE HEART

Why do you lean against my heart?
How can you rest against a heart
   that holds the empty quarter,
   the empty half
   the empty whole
Let the world laugh.
Let the night stretch on endlessly.
I was the furnace, the fuel, and the embers.
When I was born the tribal rifle
was lifted and two shots fired into the air.
Then, another shot when I screamed.
Between then and now
an empty quarter,
half, an empty whole.
How can you laugh, leaning there?
The world laughs,
the night stretches endlessly.

iv   SONG OF SOUTHERN ANXIETY

All that remains inside us
is unadulterated anxiety.
Whoever wants to share can share it.

We will share.
Our lords come from the north.
What remains at the bottom
of the glass now is not worth repenting.
All we carry is pure anxiety,
  small conflagrations,
  excessive goodness of heart,
  and the ruins of Beirut.
Whoever wants to share can share
We will share.
Masters of the earth,
this is the stubbornness of our blood.
This is the flower of our anxiety,
that rises in the dialogue
  between wind and rock
in the southern dialogue
that never ends, never tires.

Diana Der Hovanessian
Lena Jayyusi (first translator)

Saad al-Humaidin   **SAUDI ARABIA**

A Poet's Confession

Do you want me to spread
a flying carpet on the wind
or spike my breast with a dagger,
Play a tune on my flute
to make a serpent dance?
I am no Indian *fakir*
to gouge out my eyes with a nail
or stick a dagger in my breast
I am a wound crawling with maggots
The living clay dies in my hand
and sorrow lords it in my heart.

I have been rowing
till the oars snapped
my boat runs aground in the sand
my mouth is a gravid leather bottle
my tongue is a hollow cane
poetry a crooked staff
in a blind man's hand
a worn-out shoe
on a beggar's foot
The poet is a bridge of cobwebs.

And the windmill turns
and turns
Here are corpses
          Here are dismembered limbs
                    Here are shattered stones

The windmill's rumble
digs deep
into my ears
Here is a bridge
                a shoe
                        a staff

Do you want me
to vanquish the wind,
stick a dagger into myself?
Play a tune
            tam tam
        from Zalfa
tick tock
        from Sāmir
to make a serpent
dance in the square?

I am no conjuror
gentlemen
I am a poet
and, as is well known,
the poet sucks up everything like a sponge.

Translated by Sargon Boulus and John Heath-Stubbs

What is Left for Me?

I wonder what is left for me?
The crow's harsh call
that tears me

120

apart
at daybreak?
While a flower blooms
I plant my dizzy head in mud
and smash it.

Beneath a tar-black umbrella
silence seethes and knocks me off
my chair
where I congealed
and questioned the distance
behind the wall
of a café filled with smoke
and the sound of a languid song.

I scatter what is left
'the phantom image of a comrade
        the book of a friend'
A dusty path that stretches onward
in whose maze
my steps wander and echo.

My steps faltered
like one bewildered
searching for love in the unknown
my harvest was nothing but dirt
A knapsack filled with slime
that flaps when the north wind
blows a vision in my path.

A boy choking with tears
a mother weeping
These are all that remain
The pain of those
who had lost their country
as though the land had never been
as though they had never been its people
its agony and its want.

Translated by Sargon Boulus and John Heath-Stubbs

Abd al-Rahman Ibrahim   **YEMEN**

On the Road to Jerusalem

I weep and I weep
Proclaiming to the Holy City
that the coming into her arms
will be nearer than the neck vein.
I have tears enough and to spare
for everybody
Yet each day I also strut
with a fresh kind of pride
on the road to Jerusalem
The road approaches me
and I approach the road
endlessly
I alter my gait,
my name and my image,
but the vastness of the distance
to Jerusalem
defeats me,
and my words are bigger than I.
I weep and I weep
Will anyone cross
the bridge I build with my tears?
Peace upon you, Jerusalem, I said,
This is my apology
in the name of my remote homeland
the Yemen that has bred me
I am now a new name in the land of Prophecy
and I lift up a laudatory voice
proclaiming to Jerusalem
that the coming into her arms
is nearer than the neck vein.

Translated by Sargon Boulus and John Heath-Stubbs

122

Muhammad Fahd al-Issa　　　　　　　**SAUDI ARABIA**

Rebellion

Break these fetters, my soul,
I am bored with life
In the shadow
Of unanswered wishes.

I'm tired of
Living this way –
Contrite humiliation,
Sorrow, injustice.

Today I don't care
If I am alone,
Suffering the pains
Of aloneness.

Just let me break
My bonds,
Let me dissolve
The walls of my cage.

Is it wrong
To have no more desire
For love or wine?

No.
I have drunk
Till I am intoxicated,
Drenched in sighs.

All my life I sang
Hoping to meet the beloved,
I filled the world
With my poetry and art.

I shed so many tears
For the sweetheart
Who disappointed
All my dreams.

When I complained to people
Of this love,
They felt
Nothing but suspicion.

Even the flow of nights
Did not heal me.
My moaning and weeping
Were useless.

My melancholy song
Even bored the birds
Who missed
My older happier tunes.

I am alone.
So let me smash
The memories
Of love, delusion, and weakness.

Translated by Issa Boullata and Naomi Shihab Nye

Abdallah Muhammad Jabr   SAUDI ARABIA

The Bursting out of Summer

When summer comes, why
does the dove of poetry depart?
Why does verse desert me, and
the hedgehog of prose wake up?
Why does every rhyme
look askance at me?
I toy with them, but they play the coquette
and come only shyly
as if I were a hunter of ghosts
on the swing of boredom.
Like a bird of Hijaz
in the grip of an eagle's talons.
I quest and quest for them in my distress
but I come back empty-handed
Luck does not favour me,
the whole world shrinks
the doves of inspiration
laugh and sneer at me;
Am I not their passionate lover,
did they not dance at my command?
On my fingers and on my lips?
and fields of roses blossomed.
How could I live a stranger now
in this land of thorns.

Tell the heat to spare me
until another day
its searing waves beat

like sparks on the asphalt
and every bend of the road
becomes a rock out of hell,
or like a face of a treacherous friend
who shakes my hand deceitfully
and attacks without warning.

Tell the beautiful girls of our town
if they are about to set forth
to fly with all their riches
to the lands of delight and feasting:
'When your cups of joy
overflow with delicate fragrance
and delight lifts your companions
to the sphere of the moon
when the youthful festive nights
pass by so swiftly,
and each pretty girl
sways her gypsy breasts
and goes to and fro clothed in
her teasing charms,
then ask where is our poet
where are the gems which only he can bring?
Where are his rhymes that sound
like the twanging of a plucked string?
Where is the skilful hand
that fashioned exquisite images?
And how could we have pleasant company
without his graceful speech?'

We left him behind
gathering the cobwebs of despondency.

Translated by Christopher Nouryeh and John Heath-Stubbs

Muhammad Saeed Jarada

Space and the Goblet

Here I am in darkness
with its grim face
stretching desolately
The newborn crescent is robed
in illness like a youth
weeping for his distant lover
The shipwrecked stars a funeral procession
led by stillness
I touch the goblet
that stings my palm
as if I'd placed my hand in flame.

Translated by Sargon Boulus and Naomi Shihab Nye

Trivialities

What do you seek, O poet,
wasting your life in meter and rhyme?

You have lived in a selfsame universe
when your bewildered eye
seldom lands on anything new
All around you, mere contentment
or wrath, the pursuit
of objects, mortal and base.

Translated by Sargon Boulus and Naomi Shihab Nye

Junaid Muhammad Junaid   **YEMEN**

Identity for a Prophetic Body

Call it what you want.
Give it any name.
We have gone beyond
those things which
inhabit us,
those names for
green moods that blossom.
Flammable
new meanings are born
out of the silence
that throbbed within us.
Definition and language
would obscure it now and
hold back the solution.
But rising toward the answer
and meaning we see a fragile
strange form, weary, but
trying for, reaching toward
perfection.

Scattered over
the circle of horizons,
adrift,
sailing out with the arrow of the dream
that takes us, aims us
at the secret target,
we pick the goal.
How long have we been on

this secret journey?
How many cycles has the heart yet
to travel through regions
where no grass shines with dew,
no colours shimmer
in the rose of the soul?

O soul that mourns, yearns
there is still in our hearts
a virginal anima
gathering dreams into her heart
dreams of a divine place,
dreams leading to dreams,
while reality points to exile.
All we own is sight,
the vision of what is,
stillness and storm,
unfinished images which dance,
woman trapped by man
old images which the woman
wipes away.

A wall divides material things
from emptiness
but the heart can slip free
to slide over the wall.
We press forward trembling
through barbed wire,
past fragmented places and
past times from which we have
become estranged.
We press forward into exile
that unrelenting exile.
Rising toward definition
and meaning we see
a strange and vulnerable form
fragile but trying to
become perfected.

We ascend our first ladder
that totters, stretches

to the point of silence
leading to violent
exercises inside the mind,
to explosion.
O wick of silence
burn us.
The first kiss kindles the flesh
and we are two lovers
invited to submit to life.
Days, our days,
turn green,
        they pale
then turn green again.

They live,
        die
            and live.
Days are bouquets,
flowers curved into wreaths
for the living dance.

We set days on fire
so they kindle
the inner explosions.

We ascend the first ladder.
But who accompanies us
to the land of wonder?
We ignore those who cower
in the dark of madness.
Now in silence
the ladder takes us
beyond immaturity,
beyond our time,
into netted air.

A mood, consciousness
beyond defining
dominates us . . .

This is how we march
toward the explosions.

A vast horizon above
a vast horizon below
both friendly.
But wherever we are
earth resounds with
unfamiliar tales.
The heart listens to
strange tales.
No address confines us.
We are scattered over
four horizons that stretch
even within us.
Hail, O endless space.
Will you teach us the chant
of broken storms, winds,
tearful stars, prayed-for rains?
Will you offer an oracle
confirming our faith
in our only love?
Will you be our ally;
revive us if we die?
Slake our thirst,
with heavenly elixir?
In the blinking of an eye
in the gleam of a glance.
will we find what we seek?
O horizon stretching within,
love alone and only love
is what we seek.

We rise above limits set;
we hold up incandescent signs.
But the question remains
strange
like a fragile form
reaching out

waiting to be perfected,
waiting.

Diana Der Hovanessian
Lena Jayyusi (first translator)

Fawziyya Abu Khalid   SAUDI ARABIA

Poem

Without paper or pen
  into your heart I reach
Listening is more poignant
  than any speech.

Departure

You must have seen me from the window
  of the departing plane
Looking as small as the toy you broke once
when you were little
and then cried over it.
I was alone and all the city
  was leaving
I could not understand why people should run away

on the evening of a feast
You have never known the desolation of a king
    discrowned on his coronation day
Nor the sorrow of a city with decorations taken off
    on the evening of a feast
Nor the grief of a fair young bride
    widowed on her wedding night
Nor the bewilderment of a child who is told:
    'Your mother has departed westward,'
Who, when he takes a dishwasher's job on a ship
    that would carry him to her
    finds only the sailors' drabs.

Translated by Salwa Jabsheh and John Heath-Stubbs

A Pearl

This Pearl
Was a gift of my grandmother – that great lady –
    to my mother
    and my mother gave it me
And now I hand it on to you
The three of you and this pearl
Have one thing in common
    simplicity and truth
I give it with my love
and with the fullness of heart
    you excel in

The girls of Arabia will soon grow
    to full stature
They will look about and say:
'She has passed by this road'
and point to the place of sunrise
and the heart's direction.

Translated by Salwa Jabsheh and John Heath-Stubbs

Distances of Longing

When you go away and I can't
follow you up with a letter,
it is because the distance
between you and me
    is shorter than the sound of Oh,
because the words are smaller
than the distance
    of my longing.

My Friends

On a winter day, I went to you
and came out taunting my friends
over the shawl of suns you had woven
    for me
from the fire cocoons
    within your breast.

Butterflies

When you abandoned me,
I didn't need an elegy
because you had planted
a flight of butterflies in my heart
whose path I follow
like a bedouin who knows
how to perfectly trace the footsteps
   of his truant mare.

My Grandfather attends the General Assembly

When we were at that formal assembly
and all those attending were practicing
the rites of protocol with piety and reverence:
   there was
      a button for clapping
      a button for smiling
      a button for constant approval
I found myself emigrating from this world
      fleeing from those seas of mercury
      following you to the equator
         to the jungle of snakes
         to the burning spices
           and
the glittering daggers under your skin
      without rites.

Translated by May Jayyusi

Ahmad Muhammad Al Khalifa   **BAHRAIN**

The Lost Mirage

O mirage, do you not complain of weariness at noonday heat?
You appear like water on the vast horizon
goading the traveller to lengthen out his way,
You seem like one of the streams of paradise, nourishing life with its virtue,
like the mist from the light of a censer that kindles perfumes at the altar.
In the waste you are like a lost dream in the eyes of a girl,
ever moving, as if in love with the wilderness
Have mercy on those a-thirst in vacancy, the caravan comes near to agony.
Always you waken longing when the caravan is lost and the rain clouds are
    sparse
You whose essence baffles man – you are the mystery of all the ages.
Did you come down from the clouds above, rise from the earth below?
Are you the dream of the waterless desert when noon heat blazes upon
    the hills?
We are alike, lost in this life, and both our fates are dark.
But I, unlike you, you deceiver of travellers,
am lost in my own country, and among my friends!

Translated by Christopher Nouryeh and John Heath-Stubbs

My Mother's Grave

I came to the cemetery searching
in black night for my mother's grave.
So many years had passed that I had forgotten the spot
I stood there at a loss, despairing
looking at so many gravestones, baffled,
peering at every ancient, crumbling tomb.
Opposite me I saw a figure
walking there, muttering and whispering to itself.
I called out, who is that? Softly came the answer:
Who comes at night but the keeper?
I am the keeper of the dead in the darkness of the night,
the graves are always my assembly hall.
I cried: Do you remember the grave
of my mother close by a withered tree trunk?
He stared at me. Then answered: these
graves have confused my thoughts
So many dead! So many graves! I no more know
one ruined grave from another.

Translated by Christopher Nouryeh and John Heath-Stubbs

The Deserted Valley

I came to it when the valley flowers were withered,
and the wind among the leaves of the willow were crying,

Scattered sand and piled-up yellow
leaves were blocking the course of the stream.
For a long time upon its shores the blossoms had been withered
rough gales have driven away its song birds.
There is no place left for men to shelter in
except rocks which slope compassionately,
and a few branches which bow their
heads like one who prostrates himself.
Wherever I look memories of past happiness
come back again to my mind.
O how the dawn once shook my
heart, how the sight of it blazed upon my eye!
Only yesterday the valley was green
and beside its stream the shepherd sang his songs.
But now it is desolate and its present
weeps when it recalls its past.
By day the crows flock to it
at night the owl haunts it.
I never thought that drought could come upon this place
where once the shepherds sang its lushness.
A valley where beautiful girls walked gracefully
where wishes bathed among its streams.
Nature's enchantment had made this place
a bright dream we cannot interpret
Where the eye saw nothing but a pageant of greenness
enthralling the visitant with its grace.
Why today is it nothing but wilderness
its pastures do not gladden the shepherds?
I stood there with straying thoughts,
like a lover whose hopes have perished,
saying to the birds: return
do not abandon the place where once we were happy.

Translated by Christopher Nouryeh and John Heath-Stubbs

Ali Abdallah Khalifa   **BAHRAIN**

A Window for Longing

There, on the highest shelf, you will rest.
Be careful, I want you to settle
between the perfumes and graceful antiques
till the day my hands can reach you
to dust you off,
sweeping the longing from your cheeks
and all that waiting may have done to you.

Dazzled lover,
the road of love has changed.
The concerns of this strange age become
a cross on which the beloved dies,
a token for those of no invention.
Wrap yourself in a grave-like silence
and the solitude of a melancholy night.
Tell your soul: these days, emotions are hard as wood,
and you are merely a small concern among many.
All you are is a swing where one rests a moment,
or summer fruit, unexpectedly come to us in winter.

Why then, out of the blazing furnace,
do you exert yourself each evening,
    emerging from the moment of fusion,
to coax dream-buds into flowers
and throw open a window for longing,
    a window for longing.

Translated by Lena Jayyusi and Naomi Shihab Nye

Sorrow of Laila: Tuful

Over the shoulders of the sea's blue expanse
stand two little girls.
One child kissed me and slept,
sad fields of papaya in the lap of meadows.
One child tormented me long, so long, and never slept.
I rose from her side, wounded,
aged by flames.
Fire was my exit.
Fire was the entrance gate to her
I rose from her side, wounded,
accompanied by harbours
and the darkest daisies, cloud-wounds and thunder.
Weary, her braid kissed me,
entrusting me to the little birds.
Laila's heart was tearful, she carried within her
the sorrows of vagrant birds,
    a bird faced by rifles,
    a bird bleeding and scarred.
Laila's heart was tearful. I was a lover
chased forever by hounds of the tribe.
My love surged to her in waves, stringing death to life,
interlocking with the tremors of stars, the flights of meteors,
and eruptions of the hearts.
I wanted to dissolve within her
To believe my vision, for space is reddened
    by the blood of roses surprised by rifles,
by the heart of the bird which kept its feathers
and did not sell its song at the auction.
Believe what the eyes of Gulf oysters say:
'She whom I did not betray, within whose tumult
    my arms grow stronger,
will be neither the continuity nor conquest,
if all of you do not keep faith.'

Laila's heart was tearful: I was combing Tuful's hair
as she called for her father, whom they had killed and buried
and wiped the tears of the innocent jasmine
as dry sands sought water
springing into grass in her lap.
Summer delivered its rains on the balcony of waiting
as Tuful called for her father, drawing a sun in the sand,
a palm tree,
and a single arrow, pointing towards a fifth direction.
Her mother realized her little bird's wound would be
saddled like a daring horse, to carry her from the
    defeated age of fear
across all the bridges, wholeheartedly.
Within it the ripe winds of presence struck root,
all the wounds wore its scars.
The roads shed oils to turn coat-threads
into candles and flames.
So be rested now, Gulf soil,
    drink up these blazing fires.
One day the baked brick of buildings
shall shed sun-froth and jasmine
and glimmers of lightning.
Be rested now, Gulf soil,
    and wait for me.

Translated by Lena Jayyusi and Naomi Shihab Nye

Dhabya Khamees   **UNITED ARAB EMIRATES**

Schizophrenia

Because things are not alright
I break my mirror, I renounce make-up.
Because things are not alright
My beloved does not embrace me,
He offers me no roses.
Because things are not alright
Children wear black,
They burn the grass
And turn their wooden horses
Into guns.

Because things are not alright
Death – and escape from death –
Are the only professions of the East.

Translated by May Jayyusi and Naomi Shihab Nye

Don't!

The sun lives in a small forest,
The branches and shadows suffocate the sun –
But after they suffocate it,
    they burn.

A Truth

And now, after nothing,
and everything,
I realize I knew you,
and never knew you.
Sadly,
   I continue to look for the you in you.

Happy New Year!

On the last day of that year
I did not celebrate or bid it farewell, as usual.
I remained sleeping at the edge of my bed.
The year had robbed me
   and it was not affectionate.

Translated by May Jayyusi and Naomi Shihab Nye

Love Poems in Times of War

Tonight I shall stage a wedding for your poems
Kindling my memory, I offer the sacrifice of Abraham
to those inflamed prayers,
handing you the book as on doomsday
   the Great Book is handed over.

Tonight is not like other nights,
It is not raining,
No moon shines over the desert,
No stars fall, reflected on the window pane
Tonight you and I and the long road of poems,
and a window overlooking the end.

The sky is still blue,
earth is still the earth,
asphalt streets still carry their dead
and the mosques are full of worshippers.
Even migrant birds are returning.

So why did you take on the whole city,
   sealing your love off below the heart
and bidding goodbye to your face in the mirror of my eyes?
(It used to drown in my blood like love, like sorrow)
   Now your face no longer contains
     the language of questions,
     the smile of newborn love
     the glow of the old warmth.

I closed my eyes, which I never did before
               I never did before
               I never did before
You used to look out of my own eyes at me.

When summer came, you had hidden in it two wings for love.
The summer was long and encompassing.
The summer lured me, pulling my feet to the foam of the sea.
It used to be the arms of a lover and now has become
    a winter in the heart of warm months.

Translated by May Jayyusi and Naomi Shihab Nye

In My Ribs the Orchard Grows

Come, teach me,
take my hand and open my eyes.
Inspire love among the entrapped ones,
speak to the air, sky, and vibrant green,
sing to the waters and give me the first dance.
Come, let the birds twirl their melodies,
let the sun weave,
let all living beings escape hibernation.
Our axe will slash away those demigods choking
                the sky –
Let us destroy all weapons and create trees,
roses, gazelles, we will build a temple
        where love is prayer
Oh, let this face crouching before me
        be lit with joy!
Away with indolence, away with mechanical war games,
and minds defined by the ruler and coin.

In this time of crucifixion, where is love,
and why do trees run away from us?
To where do flocks of squirrels disappear?

Translated by May Jayyusi and Naomi Shihab Nye

The Poet Dies

(TO HAWI, FODA, DUNQUL, ABD AL-SABUR, BASISO, HALLAJ
AND TO THOSE WHO WILL COME)[1]

Wild is the day
Laden with the unopened buds of drying plants

Its breezes carry me towards a voice
in which I embrace words I have never seen
I cry for one who came like a sun, and disappeared
A sun
Another sun, and another . . . are extinguished.

They become dust
But the space they opened remains a dream
Their absence extends, stretching forth bridges,
suitcases for us to carry on
our journey toward truth.

Translated by May Jayyusi and Naomi Shihab Nye

1. The poem is dedicated to five contemporary poets who are dead but whose
names are linked with the fight of the contemporary Arab poet for freedom; and
to al-Hallaj, the medieval Islamic mystic who was crucified because he refused to
compromise and stood up for his convictions.

148

Hamda Khamees   **BAHRAIN**

Very Much Alone

(Julie: Do you believe in me?
Danton: How do I know . . . we know very little about each other, we are
thick-skinned people, we stretch our hands out to each other but in vain
. . . so we make do with scratching each other's thick skins. We are . . .
very much alone.   Georg Büchner)

We lived together
for seconds, minutes,
hours of eager longing . . .
You were an unchecked madness
and I, a madness longing for release.

You talked about yourself,
said much of love, of longing . . .
how a yearning clamours within you.
You said you were a wandering sail,
a voyager of the heart on an anchorless journey.
You were a sobbing child
adrift from his safe harbours.
Then when we met, you lay down to rest,
folded the sails of departure,
sought refuge against my breast
and I became your fuel.
Still, you were a lighthouse
a safe shore,
the green of budding foliage
embracing yourself
when you embraced me.

You said many things, repeatedly.
  'I love you a million times over.
  I worship in you a god I had lost.'

I talked of myself,
about the sorrow of the years,
how I was born a stranger
and lived estranged,
but when I found my path to you,
I was fulfilled.
My spirit rested.
I engraved my face on your chest,
offered a thousand prayers,
bowed down in homage,
declared you the shade beneath which I found refuge.
You were such a fountain of light and love
that I spilled all my cups at your feet.

I did not really get to know you
when you talked about yourself.
When I talked about myself,
I remained a stranger.
We were lost in each other.
Though we embraced tightly,
our skins mingling,
we remained
very much alone
very much alone.

Translated by Lena Jayyusi and Naomi Shihab Nye

About Love and the Impossible

When I met her
I had been travelling that famine so long,
parched earth of longing upon my lips –
I stretched out my hand, and she blessed me.
My lips became blessed
and from my emptiness
a sea burst forth . . . I crossed over it
towards that one who suddenly inhabited me
and I set her between yearning and madness,
between my veins and my blood's desire.

She spoke to me – I smiled and
offered my ribs to her.
I said, They are waiting for you
to arrive like a wedding or a birth.
They await the season of threshing,
the singing fields.
In each heart, in each grain of sand is an embryo –
for you, blood gathers its banners,
colourful rifles are raised . . .
But a shadow of sorrow flickered across her face.
When I beckoned silence, it came.
I approached her, leaned against her breast,
and she broke into tears!

You flowed all around me.
I told you I had bathed in the river of my blood –
Our weary caravans, travelling famine's roads,
bathed in a truthful glow.
I begged you not to open the balconies of tears.

Love is a judge.
Between my murder and the sword of tyrants
hover the dates of reprisal.

You said, 'You all come without the passion of daggers,
no earth kindling the fire in your spears,
and you fall defeated by the wayside.
Does it scare you that time waits for me in the distance?
Does it terrify you?
You plan to depart on the wind's saddle
but my saddle is sharp as lances.
For him who comes singing to my door,
I will spin a wedding of love,
I will feed him the desire of the impossible.'

The sea tells me of you,
the palm trees confide in me.
My country, you rest in the cradle of our arms . . .
I have tattooed you onto my child's delicate breast,
inscribed you as a language in my mind,
and a secret in the words of the sea.
My country, are you sleeping? The shores are wakeful,
the stars are kisses.
Will you rise? Put on your dress, the wedding has come.
You arrive as a volcano spewing fire.
We write love in your name,
with fire we purify your aches.
You said, Enter from her closed windows.
    – We have entered.
Read me!
    – We have read you.
Break the bounds between hesitation and entry.
    – . . .
        We are broken!

We have snipped the distance between you and our death.
My heart throbs in your sands.
My far-reaching dream dismounts from the
    saddle of the unknown
to ride the saddle of impossibility.

My language shatters the impossible in Tel al-Zaatar.[1]
In that famine, fire hones its teeth.

1. See note 1, p. 116.

I let loose its volcanoes upon you all
for you to bathe in.

They said, 'Give them no bread[2]
so their hungry lips become paralyzed.
Human arms beat the ground angrily.
Amidst pain the axe is broken
but the famine is two-edged:
   terror and a flailing whip . . .
It is a time-bomb.'

Translated by Lena Jayyusi and Naomi Shihab Nye

2. The poet's quoting of the notorious sentence: 'Give them no bread . . .' is a reference to a phrase used by the Phalange Lebanese forces when referring to the inhabitants of the besieged camp on the Hill, i.e. Tel al-Zaatar.

Hasan al-Lawzi   **YEMEN**

The Book of Dream and Revolution[1]

(The dream is one of lightning's secrets
igniting from the forest's flame
into the minds of the poor,
growing gradually to the point of sudden eruption,
when the sky begins to flare.
The dream completes its cycle
at the moment of fulfilment.
If it subsides, it may bury the dreamer
    beneath its ashes.)

1
I hunger for you
My bitter hunger grows voraciously,
piercing the body and blood,
penetrating without fulfilment.
You are the shade and the dew,
The fragrance kindling the heart with love and desire.
You are the distance between two pulsing bodies
    at the moment of union.
You are the mesh of the joints, the gap between my death
    and resurrection.

2
I am weary of writing, of hunger, of balancing on
the knive-edge of beginning,
of gathering your face each evening at the core of my mind
and dividing it equally among the hungry like illusory
    mirrors.

1. See note 3 of 'The Journey' by Z. M. Dammaj, p. 361. It is clear from the
poem that al-Lawzi has participated in some way in the revolution.

It dissolves into a star at night's beginning,
a lush cluster of palm trees at night's end.
And, at the banks of thirsty death, a rivulet of water.

I am tired of the phantom that provokes my country's hunger
but offers nothing to eat.
Till when will the hungry embrace nothingness?
All the signs point to you,
leading to the forest of palm trees in your heart,
to the time of fulfillment.

3
How shall I protect myself from you,
from the searing pain of our separation?
Each time my skin is stripped off, I lose you in anger.
The forged history of my grandfather stands implacably
    between you and me.
And this bandage which I am swaddled in,
how can I remove it?
How to be free of the sands they pumped into me,
    the nights of siege?
A cloud spreads its heavy mantle over the plains
and leaves me torn with impatient longing,
torn between that part of me scattering cornstalks
    of refusal, blood roses growing
    in the earth's womb,
and spiders of fear emerging from their webs within me.

I choose to be cocooned in the gleaming light of martyrs,
refusing to feed on the ashes of their death.
And when, in future, the distances between us shrivel,
our reunion will be sweet . . .
the wind will scatter me into all the trees that will shade
    the poor,
then dance over my far-reaching branches . . .
the wind will begin to write its native history,
painting across the sun's forehead
the new face of my country.

Translated by Lena Jayyusi and Naomi Shihab Nye

Creating Words between Two Ages

It is time to write with light about the passion of
   coffee-brown bodies,
      to write of my love for the gentleness of this stricken world,
      but virginal silence fails me, that brute silence,
      the tendons of my tongue become immobilized
      by the weight of surprise.
Passion enters me painfully, multiplying like infection,
my cells become crowded with gunpowder, laughter, and flame.
The law of impetuosity governs me.
I prepare myself for the celebration of change
when the earth will undo its straw shirt
   and don the waving grass of revolution.
Then I shall clasp the ecstatic keys and achieve dominion
   kindling the passion of those who approach
      with humble chisel and hammer –
Into them I shall breathe my avid aspirations.

It is time to write with the desire of coffee-brown bodies
of what rises from the pulse in my wrist.
To write of the thousand blue dreams stored in their moth-eaten coat,
to spread my passion among people, and across the stones
   of the earth.
In my passion the fury of a suppressed fire
fuses harmoniously with water, love merges with
   the gunpowder of hatred.
As my wound grows, I grow, but I am caught
in the deadly blood-letting between revolution
   and counter-revolution
between the boulder of counter-revolution and revolt.
The key is lost to me and I revolt against myself
For I am both rebel and tyrant
Before my eyes the wind's footsteps grow silent
I fall into contradictions,

for I am the manifest and the mysterious,
and I am all the expressions of wakefulness,
the last fig leaves to cover the nakedness of this dead age.
Hallucinations invade me as I write poems
in which light exhales old pains
like golden bubbles of nothingness.
Despair invades me, then hope, then despair.
Fishes without names or hearts
    devour me
    in time's wide dish.

Who are you? To think you could erase the errors of mankind
    in the blink of a single dream?
Who are you? Becoming the other within the multitude
    that is yourself . . .
My limbs are still raw, not mellowed by the sun.
As I enter the vast arena of patience
intent on uncovering secrets hidden in each heart,
with the humble chisel of the poor I kindle the passion of men
    advancing across their homeland.
I grow tired and sleep,
    my slain body lying beside me.
When I wake up I shall ask it:
    Has the time arrived?

Translated by Lena Jayyusi and Naomi Shihab Nye

Abd al-Aziz al-Maqalih   **YEMEN**

Lament

(TO SANAA, CITY OF HOPE AND REVOLUTION)

He was here yesterday.
Yesterday he loved this land,
each stone, each street, each lot;
worshipped the rain, drank in each drop
with his eyes. My name was his name
and he bore my face. I knew his secret.
Today I turn this way and that way
and cannot find my face reflected,
cannot find my voice echoed,
cannot find my shadow.
If he has died where is his grave?
If he has died when will I also embrace my death?
I am tired of wandering, of cries and silence.
I am tired of the days' brilliance and pigments.
He who loved them,
he who prayed, and sang praises
is gone and I remain
dull and colourless as soil.
The winds of exile have eaten
yesterday's glitter from my eyes.
In my blood the bitter clouds of winter
rain and spread fog, and raise
a mirage of trees
in my deserted heart.

Will he return,
he who would laugh at the hills,
he with my name
and my face? Nothing is behind the clouds
except the call of ravens,
the hoot of owls, the weeping of widows
of drowned men, weeping, waiting
for them to come down from the stars
and push back the walls of dark.
Will a door swing open for those who return?
Will I see *him*, hear his voice
tell him of my longing
confess the secret
run barefoot again as we did yesterday?
I have been shattered, my shadow dispersed
swept off the sterile road
and the fragments of my past scattered.
They lie abandoned across long passageways.
My body dies. And
My life laments its dying.

Diana Der Hovanessian
Lena Jayyusi (first translator)

Beirut, Tel al-Zaatar,[1]
Night and Bullets

1
Who will stitch up your wounds?
Your wound spreads across the map of the world
It batters the forehead of the sun with blood

1. See note 1, p. 116.

Rises, sinks,
Inhabits the colour of embers and the flesh of death
Your wound
Enters the sea – the waves
Emerges from the eye of a mountain baptized with blood
Runs after the bullets of the trees which stand in the night
After the tears that flow from the face of the wind
From the voice of the river
The fire of ice
The flowers of thyme.

2
Every morning I take off my eyes so that they shall not see the
                                            talons of death
Every evening I take off my ears so that they shall not hear the
                                            tidings of death
I dissever myself from the language of traitors
From the age of man the murderer
I kindle my poetry into a fire over the mountains of grief
I weave it into shrouds for the swallows over the water
A handkerchief for the mute river
There are thousands of the slain within my eyes
In my words
And in my verse
Where can I emigrate from the age of murder
From the age of sorrow – this renegade age?

3
Your face contracts, expands
Your dream expands, contracts
Your blood-stained rock has grown larger
The grief sprouting in the sockets of the eyes
On the trees of the heart
Have grown bigger
Your children are not your children:
This face with the thorny shadow
And this hand with the poisonous fingers
This grief in the hollow of the eyes
This language of mongrel words
This suppurating breast
Are not yours

Not from the homeland of that rebel
That steadfast sage Gibran.[2]

4
Who spreads over the wearied body the table of murder?
Who blots out the last chapter of love and writes the first
                                        chapter of blood?
Who presses out the sap of words?
Who quenches the fire of lips with the water of silence?
City, you who once spoke for all
for the murderer and the victim
tell me . . .
Who is it who makes
From the ribs of the cedar
From the skin of Zaatar children
Clothes for the invaders
And shoes for barbarous soldiers?

Translated by Lena Jayyusi and John Heath-Stubbs

From 'Yemeni Thoughts'

i   SANAA IS HUNGRY

One who had witnessed said to me: Sanaa is hungry
and the minarets go shamelessly begging
Aiban[3] carries his children, the coffins of his dead,
and migrates

2. This is Gibran Kahlil Gibran, the famous Arab-American poet, writer and
sage who wrote in Arabic and English.
3. Aiban is a mountain near Sanaa.

Where is the path to the water?
The river's thirst torments me
the thirst of the sea torments me
Every place on earth is a home except my house
All of them carry their notebooks
all of them lug their skulls to the dwellings of exile
The earth's womb has dried up
Time's bursting womb is dry
My footsteps stare at each other
and the road is my cloak.

Translated by Lena Jayyusi and Naomi Shihab Nye

ii   MELANCHOLY

Melancholy has sprouted
struck roots within us
Blessed are its branches
its supple tendrils unfurl in my lungs
I have become like the water's edge
Neither silence nor writing can heal me
Neither rose garden nor clouds
I knock reverently at night's door:
O Night! Merciful screen,
you have erased the tedium of the day
cleansed my spirit from its hell
Its fruitless longing
washed from my eyes the black umbra of light
washed from my lips the uncertainty of questions.

Translated by Lena Jayyusi and Naomi Shihab Nye

iii SEASON OF SLEEP

– It is the season of sleep
He said, his eyes open, searching their depths
                    for some stray remnant of sleep

– It is the season of sorrow
I said, the echo diffusing behind me
        and all the passageways were closed and cold.

The dagger of glowing insomnia in the breast
        scratches out the wound
When day's forehead was sinking
A sigh, traced into the sun's core, escaped
– It is the season of sorrow
Yellow, the colour of sighs, are the trees of the field,   ,
and the graveyards,
and the grass is yellow, black
and black is the place where we meet.

– What season of the year has come upon us?
– This is . . . the face of all seasons.

Translated by Lena Jayyusi and Naomi Shihab Nye

iv   FEAR

I walk behind its voice
It walks behind mine
At times I become its shadow
At times it becomes mine
Who is this that lies awake in sleep?
– Fear is the bridal of fire
It springs up from yesterday's ashes
Glides out from today's sands
Dances within tomorrow's frost

– Earthen joy, where are you?
Fear inhabits my blood
It chews on me
I chew on it
We devour each other
We drink each other

When will we part?

Translated by Lena Jayyusi and John Heath-Stubbs

Ahmad Qandeel　　　　　　　　　　**SAUDI ARABIA**

Death in Life

Can it then be true that it is Death that holds you,
and that the cold and hungry grave enfolds you?
You are a memory only which, in its pain,
the anguished heart still struggles to retain.
While you lived you were a stranger to my heart:
I too am diffident, lonely, and apart.
But I was your father – and you, my daughter, were mine;
Now, as my life's clearest beacon, you shine.
But within my heart, though it had never known,
of all my stars you were the brightest one.

Within the same house we lived aloof
like two strangers dwelling under one roof.
My love to you as a father you never knew,
nor I descant the secret way to you.
Till one morning Death took you, and by the word
that brought those tidings my hidden love was stirred.
The moment I lost you seemed your real birth
and all my love, suppressed before, broke forth.
A creature of flesh and blood you then became,
overflowing with life, kindling my grief's flame.

How many times your mouth, so rosy and small,
kissed me, tenderly, lovingly – but never at all
The shelter of my fatherhood you knew,
Or tasted a father's sweetness as your due.
Your spirit now has to eternity flown –
One backward glance to my poor phantom is thrown.

Daughter, in what was I guilty? – Deep in my breast
There lies a sorrow, never to be expressed.
If I had been a father – more than in name,
Knowing my spirit's torment, there would have been no blame.
A wavering thought, a hope, withered and thin,
Is all that I am, all that I've ever been
I dwelled apart in a world of phantasy,
And made myself an alien from humanity.

My daughter, death took you without giving warning,
And made for me a desolate world of mourning
I feel the pain still, yet in my heart is descried
New life – life of the beloved one, who died.
I spent the night beside your body there,
Like one who, in a shrine, kneels down in prayer
Though the grave engulfs you, daughter, still lingers on
The grief in my heart, whence it had never gone.
I hold back my tears, for in you I find
My living love, within my breast enshrined.

Translated by Christopher Nouryeh and John Heath-Stubbs

The Poet and the Moth

She came at dawn, a brilliant moth
like light, like the dawn of life,
like my heart astray, driven between two sorrows
    one open and one concealed.
She said, 'With love's wakeful eye, I saw
your window still open at dawn

and the dim light of your lamp
still burning low like the fragments of a dream
I saw scraps of paper scattered on your bed
some scribbled over with unfinished lines like a bird
about to take off;
and in the air of your room the echo of a melody
its tunefulness a rival to the lute'
And I said: "This is where I want to dwell
nearer to the solid earth.
Neighbouring houses have locked me out
They are as dark as my dark fate
Only you, poet, are here
poet of tears and rain."
I said: 'Welcome my sweet little neighbour
I love you, moth, for what you signify
You sacrifice your life for life's rising tide
so that we never see its ebbing away!
Companion of light! In the whirling of your wings
Poetry is the richer for your being
Winged phantom, child of night and wakefulness
A ray of your spirit vies with the dawn
in the dream of the dawn's bright tresses!'
She knew her enchanted universe and exclaimed:
'Will you not then tell the world about me?'

Translated by Christopher Nouryeh and John Heath-Stubbs

Maysun Saqr al-Qasimi   **UNITED ARAB EMIRATES**

Cycle

Now I am the empty landscape
which is stripped of trees,
willows, valleys.
Now I am the settler
of empty spaces, open
places
praying wherever
prayer settles.

The city repulsed me,
stoned me,
ravished me.

I became mute,
fearful for the virgin
in all things,
guarding
with hell's silence
against hell.

I allowed agony to
overtake my soul,
agony without refuge.
I delivered my soul to
silent sorrow,
to broken song,
to the winds.

My body, the banner of many wars,
keeps within me the god

who is a child. He is decked
with bracelets, his eyes
burnished by anger,
his hands, two orphaned doves.
He comes from the age
of nakedness.
He runs inside me,
gushes, spurts like
an open vein.

My love, you were not here
with me when weakness was
crushed by the forces of sin,
when deprivation led to my defeat.

How could I resist when
my dagger was weak and rusted?
I admit I did not resist,
but waited for, expected you.
I had memorized you.
Inside out. Outside in.
You who are fragrant with
the aroma of smoke,
where in you
the harbours of tranquillity
lie broken, where laughter
is gone. You, full of mirth
who runs toward your becoming,
vanquisher of grief,
but who showers sorrow.
You, who are both discordant
and harmonious,
migration and settlement,
being and negation,
stillness and startling move,
you, my love, blessed and blessing,
your love was my fortress, ally,
and my choice.
You demolished a castle within me;
you established a castle within me.
I was freed from the guilt of defeat,

freed, and my innocence liberated.

Now I sail across water's
wound, rising above tears
groping for roots, grasping for migrating roots
And amid sands, amid the furnace
of other eyes I hide my longing
amid tree trunks.
As I listen to the day speaking,
my future approaches
holding in its hands
my ancient elegy.
My love, the future is coming.
Tattoo your emblem,
on my wrist, the image of
a sad child with birds, flowers.
I have flung myself over
the clouds of passion
and have emerged
with cloudless colours.
Like the seven phantoms
I gave birth to desert chants
to the ardour of virgins,
to the dreams of infatuated young girls.
This is the essence of my being,
that never was. And this is my heart
that used to run breathlessly
over the waves to dwell inside storms.
It has become a burning silence,
a blossoming fervour,
a dagger, unsheathed.

My love, my love, with whom
the children of my love are
nurtured, a woman has died within me.
A woman was born within me.
And I have come full circle like
spring turning toward spring.

Diana Der Hovanessian
Lena Jayyusi (first translator)

Hasan Abdallah al-Qurashi   SAUDI ARABIA

A Poet's Prayer

Disturbed by troubles, I lay them before You
You who created me
For I am wearied out with this stifling world
Which overwhelms me with pain I would not suffer
And perplexes all my faculties
I am wearied out with the people of this age
They are fell as wolves in thick darkness.
Worn out and wasted, I
Would hasten towards You seeking liberation
To Your clear fountain of light, oasis
of tenderness eternal
Pulsations of bright hope
There I'll seek out the pleasures of my lucid soul
There shall my visions be full of excess of sweetness
Breathing forth a lingering perfume
I shall swim in a vista of dreams
And gaze towards a world of delight
There I shall cast off my consuming pains
Your gate shall welcome whoever knocks.

Illusions have torn my sail, they are twisted,
They are awry in stormy darkness
I need You, O God! Take my hand in Yours
Be my Helper, You who created me,
I am a stranger and an exile
Let my estrangement take flight to my heavenly home.

Translated by Issa Boullata and John Heath-Stubbs

The Fleeing Phantoms of Humiliation

Until the armies of liberation descend,
And their banners stream over the battlefields;
Until the eyes of morning shine,
And the volcano trembles,
And the deluge dislodges the rocks;
Until tragedy veils her eyes,
And the river of victory
Waters our desolate gardens each evening;
Until the names of martyrs blossom,
And the face of night is seen no more,
And the phantoms of humiliation are routed;
Until the wings of the ravens flee away,
And the death shrouds fall off from my Arab body and my soul;
Until the cavern of silence falls in,
And the snows of desperation melt,
And the phantoms of death lie down for good;
Until the wounded dawn shines brightly once more,
And eyes are radiant with happiness again,
And the sorrowful dead rise up;
Until the manacles are shattered,
And the blood the executioner sheds is dry;
Until the darkness that veils history dwindles away,
And the ink of our words is proud,
And we, the exiled,
Return to the soil of our forefathers –
The hills and valleys of home must cry out,
The walls must collapse on the house rats; the pawns and the eunuchs
Must be swept away by the wind of time,
Ground into the earth by the hurricane.

O my weeping homeland! My Arab homeland, stooped over your wounds:
Rise up, do not remain distressed!
The morning will come, O my homeland!

Translated by Issa Boullata and John Heath-Stubbs

The Altar of Love

In Paris I experienced the smouldering embers of love's sickness
I came to detest the sub-uvular 'R'
That is trilled behind the mask of a beautiful *djinn*
Or manifest in the whisper on the hysterical lips
Of a call girl
For I am a poet – not enough for me
Mere beauty of form
That which I love in woman is the spirit
of the green East,
The feel of a land that is suckled on sunshine
The sense of the beauty of human love
I am a poet who sees a snake
Striking at the humanity of all sex
As I watch a girl loitering in a café
Or in a passing limousine
Or waiting in the prison of a dark alley.

In Paris treachery is heavy in my breast
Like a child deprived of his parents
I saw the hunting dogs that rushed at me
Licking the causeway underfoot
The hunting dogs run and pant
To feed on the heart-beat of a dark-skinned stranger
Who is seeking an inspiration for a poem.

In Paris I felt the alienation
Of a bereaved soul,
And I sensed the death of all my dreams.
Paris, your daughters are drunken
They cannot delight in my melodies
In the hasty moments of love
In the arms of black and white pirates
And of soldiers thirsty for the Seine

Who have finished with the killing fields
And the slaughter of the innocent
Who come from the throes of battle
To rowdy nights of drinking
And to women whose trade is lust
Who know no sense of human tragedy
In this their country of rowdy nights
On their faces is a sneer of contempt for passionate feeling
And for the tears of the East they bewilder

I walk your white streets washing away
All my despair in cascades of light
Like golden nereids, the four fountains gaze at me
I wipe away rain drops from lenses over sleepless eyes
Is that what a poet receives
In your shadow, O Paris?
Is your gift to my thirsty soul a hungry mouthful
a mirage, an abyss?
You, who are a myth and a song
That has inspired the deprivation of my country
Whom poets have embellished with images of love.
Your evil enchantment has blasted the flower of my years.

I return alone, a poor shadow
Groping my way to the Metro
And merge with the throng of humanity
Going back to my inane hotel
Alone
Like an exhausted spectre.

Translated by Issa Boullata and John Heath-Stubbs

Abd al-Rahman Muhammad Rafee^c   **BAHRAIN**

Voice and Echo

When I'm in bad shape
I tell myself:
Look at those others
how many there are

      and still
they make me feel
like crying in pity
their fortunes hastening them
to their ends
after all the bitterness they drink
It crushes me
to see this
Even dumb rocks
could laugh
though humans are struck mute
I keep my gaze fixed
I scream noiselessly
without uttering a syllable
In a lush garden where
others are offered roses
before my death I die
But my mind says,
Come, wake up,
the heart can never despair
You are led by your senses
and won't be satisfied
as long as a drop

is left unsipped in the glass
Your complaints will never end
in a world where you want
charity to reign
In our land injustice
is tailor-made
and there's no other robe
to be worn

Once I was more hopeful
hope dallied with me
intoxicating me
But now
the hours repeat themselves
over and over again
their light cursing the darkness
I feel death's legions rushing towards me
breaking open the jail of this life
Do not be shocked, friends,
if one day my boat
drops its anchor forever
It is not that I lack courage or determination,
It is just that I hate this bankrupt world.

Translated by Sargon Boulus and Naomi Shihab Nye

Sayf al-Rahabi   **OMAN**

Blooming Tree of Suicide

That day we were not singing.
Only the streams sang
with the joy of a sky
surprised by madness.
Grasses did not cower bashfully
when they heard the gasps.
A tree was lit like childhood.
Gloom drank from the river's pure water
and swam in our bodies.
O moon waking up in a young girl's lap,
O fields of emerald stretching in our souls,
O nights of raw suffering!
Bound in the chains of pleasure that day
we were free to cry,
to knock on the tropics of clarity.
O blooming tree of suicide,
return us to the loftiness of destruction.

Translated by May Jayyusi and Naomi Shihab Nye

A Pencil and a Noose

A cloud over the desk,
a pencil and a noose.
From the garden of the house
sprout miniature birds
and executioners wearing coats
with gilded collars.
I await the waves
flowing from my interior shores
where old hostilities sleep
peacefully together.
I wait to write
something about my childhood,
the bird accused of history's crimes,
the children spreading terror among sparrows,
mothers who murder their infants
for fear of discovery,
beasts born from the wombs of roses,
and the crimes which shine like moons
on the braid of the night.
A breeze, a cluster of stars,
and nightingales pass through
the cracks of this door.
I put them to sleep in my bed
while I remain sitting,
a desk in front of me,
a pencil and a noose.

Translated by May Jayyusi and Naomi Shihab Nye

Far, Far Away . . . Over the Hills of the Corpse

The day should have cut off its fingers
at the threshold
The hawk should have soared high, high
over the hills of the corpse
And you, priests of the poets,
should have been loyal to the thunderbolt of treason
The murderers should have lit up
      with the strength of storm clouds
      or charms
The lakes should have rippled
  like their ancestors, the springs.
But there will be born another day
  Light will be the midwife
  which will birth an army of probabilities,
  for a well-studied massacre.
There is talk of oppressed nations
and those which are not oppressed
Talk opening its windows wide onto the void
And I feel your pulse, impossible to kindle,
a spirit spilling rivers of blood,
fluttering eyelids that cause doves to moan
when caught redhanded in criminal acts
like when you walk alone
in a forest where the jabber of fish rises
and a slain man's head
The vision of your shotgun suicide,
is offered by the laughing wind
After the first shot
you shall laugh and laugh
when you realize you are the master
of this futile massacre
You shall laugh as your death rises

like a tower of bells
in a procession led by a tree
Maybe you dreamed this tree
when you walked in the streets of your vision,
a slumbering childhood adrift
on a sky of blood.

I am compelled to confess
the guilty history of butterflies,
the savage deeds I did not do.
As a first step towards justice,
the judges will shell us
with paper airplanes,
Their verdicts bloom in the strangely lit eyes
of the multitudes,
a torrent of tremors on the braid of a child
who died in Beirut.
An eraser, weeping pencils that a wolf
carries to a dead gazelle.
I confess my political ignorance,
I am only a poet killing in the company
    of another poet who died for strategic reasons
in a public garden.
Who can prophesy what shall arrive
in this eclipse of strangeness?
Carnivals of the dead are plucking off
the roses of the dawn.

I became a nightingale
devouring fifty dawns in one meal,
then dipping itself into a lake.

Let me blind the time that is slipping through my fingers!
Let me blind the eyes of this furious moment,
become a new Oedipus loitering in the streets of Beirut.

I need time for all this too,
time for the fall of cities, armed with fire
and desperate guns,
time to pave all distances with a knowledge of destruction,
    and godliness,

time to push the cart of madness to the farthest end
   of the pit.
I am not a fool, I will not bandage the wounds of doves.
This finger stretching like the limb of an angel
lacks courage to probe the regions of ruin
in my guts.
I am the great destruction, the huge fatigue.

Translated by May Jayyusi and Naomi Shihab Nye

Muhammad Hashim Rasheed   **SAUDI ARABIA**

The Exile's Return

The exile has come home to you, embrace him,
And let him slumber in the visions of his past
Let him sleep his fill drenched with fragrance and with love
Among his comrades and among his children
Longing has left nothing but a flicker of passion
Almost snuffed out on the straying path of exile
Let him rest now, enjoy peace and content
Love will kindle its light and will protect him.
When the storm in his soul has died away, his lips
Begin to murmur a gentle tune
He's ceased from wandering, but his eyes are fixed
On a light beyond the skyline drawing him onwards
For when alienation grips the soul,
There's no place a man can call his home
All images of beauty now become
Hints of an unknown truth holding him captive
Happy is alienation then, it opens a path
To a new sunrise through the wilderness.

Translated by Issa Boullata and John Heath-Stubbs

Abd al-Kareem al-Razihi   **YEMEN**

The Need for a Second Heaven and an Additional Hell

O sky vaulted with the glass
of myth and bones of ancient legends
sprouting out your stars
those welts spread beautifully
over your blue skin, reborn
each evening from the germ of original sin,
they climb all over your face
like a graceful herd of
glowing smallpox

There is something dirty inside me
I want to get rid of
and toss into your basket
woven of the sufferings of saints
and fronds of mystical love
I wish I could bury my burdensome guilt
in one of your gaping black furrows
where the ancient pagan gods
used to live
but my guilt is actually too big
for you – it is deep and high
and in need of a second heaven
and an additional hell

O sin that stands like a primitive
beast at the gate to my soul
O rock of fear blocking my way
to God and evil
keeping me imprisoned
in dark resignation
move over a little and let

a thread of smoke rise
from my soul's blazing hearth
let it drift outward
to reconnect me to the worst worm
that crawls under the earth's skin
and to the greatest being residing
behind this cover of sky

And you, fear, what remote place
did you come from?
What strange unknown planet
dropped you down?
Out of what bottomless pit
did you arise? How did you find me
with your dense and dreary nature?
O freak created of dung
and beauty's lowliest obsession,
how did you rush forth
with such enthusiasm,
to be embodied in this awful way?
What made you exaggerate
your interventions, unloading
your heavy burdens
in every quiet corner of my body,
every angle of my soul?
Stepping with your stony, pointed
feet on the dove of my heart,
here you are reshaping me
in your broken, terrible image

O fear building its kingdom
over this pile of wreckage and corpses,
establishing its throne upon
this vast terrain of stolen lives,
I am one of your subjects
I will become a good citizen
in your kingdom
I will not incite anyone
against you.

Translated by Sargon Boulus and Naomi Shihab Nye

Suad al-Mubarak al-Sabah   KUWAIT

A New Definition of the Third World

Because love with us
Is a third-rate emotion
And because women are third-class citizens
And volumes of poetry are literature of the third rank
They call us the peoples of the Third World.

A Thousand Times More Beautiful

Because in long black hair you take delight
They let it down like curtains of the night
Those Eastern girls, to greet you, prince, they say
We would not have those tresses shorn away.

Because you love a countenance sun-burnt
To bathe in the sun's rays those girls have learnt
To bid you welcome these things they have done
You who on love's steed come riding on.

Because you love my face simple and plain
They bathe in rose water and tropic rain,
Because you love my beauty's simple dower
Simple as is the morning lily flower
God, to honour you, has given his grace
To Singapore, perfecting its bright face.

The world is larger for your loving me
The sky's more wide, a deeper blue the sea
The birds are freer flying in that sky
A thousand times more beautiful am I.

A Covenant

1
Come, let us sign together
A covenant of peace
Whereby I reclaim my days under your sway
And my lips besieged by yours
Whereby you reclaim your fragrance
That courses beneath my skin.

2
Write down whatever form of words you choose
Whatever terms you deem right
And I will unconditionally sign
Draw up what covenant suits you best
So I be eliminated from the numbers
In your notebooks
From the furniture in your office
And you depart from the glass in my mirror.

186

3
Come, let us try to play this impossible game
If only for a day
So I will go to my hairdresser to kill time
And you to your smoking room to play cards.

Translated by Salwa Jabsheh and John Heath-Stubbs

Sojourn Forever

I deliver to you all the keys of my city
And appoint you its governor
Expel all its counsellors and take the chains
Of fear from off my wrists.

I have worn my robe woven with threads of care
And have made from the light of your eyes my eye shadow
And in my hair I placed a sprig of orange blossom
You once gave me
And I sat waiting on my throne
And asked to sojourn forever in the gardens of your breast.

Your fragrance drifts in my fancy
Like a sword of steel
It pierces the walls and the curtains
And it pierces me
Annihilating the fragments of time
And annihilating me
        Then you leave me to walk barefoot
On the broken glass of mirrors
                        and depart.

Translated by Salwa Jabsheh and John Heath-Stubbs

Free Harbour

Many ships have asked for sanctuary
In the harbour of my eyes
I refused asylum to all of them
Your ships alone
Have the right to take refuge
In my territorial waters
Your ships alone
Have the right to sail in my blood
Without prior permission.

You Alone

You alone . . . control my history
And write your name on the first page
And on the third, and the tenth,
And on the last.
You alone are allowed to sport with my days
From the first century of my birth
To the twenty-first century after love.
You alone can add to my days what you wish
And delete what you wish
My whole history flows from the palms of your hands
And pours into your palms.

Translated by Salwa Jabsheh and John Heath-Stubbs

Ali al-Sabti   **KUWAIT**

Regret

When I see your mouth
With its bright smiling
summon me back
My weary heart overflows with joy
And a tingling in my veins tells me
However far I am from you
And however long we have been parted
I shall always be with you despite the distance
Then I hear spring passionate in your fresh voice,
Its song a forest of dreams to remind me
Of a time when I was a knight among dream-people
And of the oath that we took to stay forever
Enchained by love; to remain
On the road with our love for a torch
And our faith unyielding
The desert unable to baulk us,
The stinging wind of no avail against us
Because, enchanted by love, we tamed all hardships
Broke down all barriers,
Kept a candle always flickering in our hearts.
I remember how, on cold winter nights,
The old crone Um-Hameed
Told the story of the fisherman
Who caught a whale one day and found
Ambergris in its belly
And thenceforth became a rich man
With ships roaming the seas
And a house packed with merchants and hangers-on

Every evening
Then one day he found himself alone
On the verge of starvation
And no one sought his company
Except the cold
That day I wished I had that whale
With ambergris in its belly
To make a present of it to you
One that will make you proud.

And time went by, year after year
Not even the phantom of your image in dreams
Not even a smile, or word
Forgive me my love:
I was a stranger in a ghoul-haunted night
My only solace was that I was a man
Of my word, who atones for his faults
By his return
Still resplendent as ever before.

And I am crushed by your question: how
Did I spend that bitter time?
I had no time, and my past is dross
A time without you is no time at all
I lived in a black night that left
A taint in my blood
Leaving you I saw the sunlight of my days
Turn into the darkness of catacombs
Where only ghosts stirred fear in my soul
Scattering my songs to the wind.

Translated by Sargon Boulus and John Heath-Stubbs

Dismounting from the Dream-Saddle

(TO THE MISTRESS OF FERTILE SEASONS IN THE YEARS OF DROUGHT)

1
Marvellous you are when you sit between my sadness and remembrance
Marvellous are you in silence, like the palm trees of Qatif[1]
. . . she teaches me to sprint . . . robs me of all other women's names
   teaches me to sprint . . . bounding inside the compass of the heart,
                            this maiden,
leaping like a rabbit
              one step . . . two steps . . . three
and Fairuz[2] waters the orchards of the heart . . . cries out
one step for the birds . . . one for weariness
           and one for the eyes of Damascus the beautiful.

2
She grows up before my eye, this imp, she grows up
               inhabited by vines and almonds
I shut my eyes, crying,
Plum of the heart, Pelican of the soul, bathe in my vision!
    your hair is weary, let it down!

3
I passed by her house . . . sparrows were pecking at her window
and all the birds were wandering in the streets

1. Al-Qatif is a small town in Eastern Saudi Arabia.
2. Fairuz is a famous Lebanese woman singer.

I passed
   the panes reflected the curtains
the palm trees embraced the face of my love
   one palm tree . . . two
        and the beloved was asleep.

4

I passed by, knowing my love blooms when she sees me
     that I shine when I hold her
that sometimes poems encircle her face
     I know that . . .
I passed by her house . . .
Sometimes I call it the heart's capital . . . other times I call out,
'Homeland – peace be upon you!'

5

I passed by her house
A tryst the hue of palm trees possessed me
and time was horses racing in the blood
I nearly dismounted from the dream's saddle, and a voice said,
  – Have I really stepped down?
Ask her
      the panes reflected the curtains
the palm trees, enfolding the face of my love

6

Ask her
for she has long inhabited me
her face possessed me for two nights
    and on the third she emerged from the rooms of my heart . . .
     she stole the poems from my lips
we would stay up till doves returned to a morning coloured with
        greetings . . .
Now I know how my love excels in passion
       Ask her then
a ghost named 'promise' dwelled within me
nothing in the heart but passion –
    Ask her.

7

For Damascus has estranged me for so long,

streets and store-fronts have occupied me . . . military transport
buses . . . women who sell their love . . . orchards and desire . . . hotels
and trailer-trucks . . . bookshops and the songs of distant mountains.

8
Two years she dwelled within me,
      and Sham[3] was embracing Nejd
      I would give her my hand,
      she would clasp it, crying out, Son!
    Nejd will give you her secrets,
    the poems will leave their colours,
and your love will one day come, launching the luminous ships
      of embrace,
      in a kiss of the birds . . . one for fatigue . . .
        and one for the eyes of Damascus the beautiful.

Translated by Lena Jayyusi and Naomi Shihab Nye

Fiddah Learns to Draw

Invocation:

Alone here
the pretty lass has left me
This hallway flung wide its doors to her

3. Sham is the area of greater Syria.

she took two steps . . .
decided to return, and did.
Now she emerges from my arm.

Fiddah is drawing women and a midwife, a nose, an ear, an eye,
now she draws a school and beds, draws two lines
and a bird between the line and the eye

Do you see me?
– Yes
ever since a radiant fragrance drifted
            toward shuttered skylights
Laugh . . . laugh
Between us there is tobacco, wine, a labyrinth

Fiddah now draws fields and a skull
asks me about my father
– He was a river of light and questions
He used to love this Peninsula's mud till he wept
and spoke of the approaching waves.

Now Fiddah sits between me and my silence
the pretty lass jumps up, removes her anklet, tucks it away
then draws a barefoot child
    – This is a courtroom!!
The room turns into a judgment hall, a hall for those accused of
subversion, for those who remain silent, another for those who
talk without speaking, a last one for the witnesses.
– The witnesses – the witnesses!
    A gesture toward the crowd from a boy who sold news, gossip,
Arabic papers; voices of women, a clamour rang out from the end of
the rows, rosary beads rolled down from one of the lines . . . an old
man cleared his throat, bathing himself in incantations . . .
– This is a courtroom!!
Today's session is adjourned
    Remove your robes
– Do you see me?
– Yes
    or I see a fragrance in the bed
the space is tiny . . . tiny
                not wide enough

Fiddah now draws a glass and raises it, 'To your health'
Can you see this glass or this stubborn wild mare?
    I galloped on it – where were you?
        – in the fields of love last night.
Fiddah etches her secrets onto my arm
        and munches an apple for fun
Ah, how lovely you are, how lovely you are . . .
She turns into a mare whose hooves gallop in my blood
        then breezes into seasonal laughter
Holds a glass of fire up to my lips
– Do you see me?
– Yes
        a leafy corner, horses immersed in silence
Now Fiddah draws a sea, sails, a small space,
becomes evasive when I bargain with her:
I will buy your gypsy sea and give you a field full of neighing,
        a basket of mud,
I'll set free my sparrow in the tiny space
– Now Fiddah draws a child and asks him about his aching palms
    She sends him to class
– Do you see me?
– Yes
The child carries his notebook, spells out the streets and the
inhabitants, wears a *kufiyya* and a gold-braided *igal*
– Do you see me?
– Yes
Flaming lips, exhausted song
The child runs inside my weariness and revives me
– Ah, Arabian Fiddah,
    Talk to me, for morning's faces are confused
    Talk to me, for the clouds have often drenched me,
    and the streets usurped me . . . swallowing me and
    oppressing a child with his school notebook,
    wearing a *kufiyya* and a gold-braided *igal*.

She stood up!
The pretty lass asked about her shawl
She sat down, braided her hair,
asked for a glass of tea and a cigarette,
placed her face against my arm, and wept.
At high noon a mare kissed her pony,

asked me of suspicion, how it comes.
– If fear should seize you, woman of fear: if it should mutter
into your child's breast, and its faded cloak
        envelop your obstinate face . . .
– Do you see me?
– Yes
A silent language, her shawl lost
When did she lose it?
She asked me for a glass of water and a cigarette, took refuge in
        tears
– Do you see me?
– Yes
Pains have united us, Arabian Fiddah. The indifferent language
of those who lagged behind has worn our lips like slippers.
Betrayals launched their journeys
    in Arabian blood
        The caravan is lost
She drew a cat with two wide and seeing eyes,
a dish of milk, a string with which to dally
She cried out, Do you see me?
– I do not see.
I become a rose in the cities of this land,
I transform my eyes into racehorses and bread that has the flavour
    of the poor
I bargain with those who would sell the essence of poems
so I could buy it
    I become
a chant of praise for the land, an incantation for travel.
– Ah, Arabian Fiddah, how am I to see?
Now she draws a door and shuts its wooden blot tight.
She draws a house and erases it
    a house and erases it
    a house and erases it
Lost in morning mist are the features of our Arab house
And lost in the evening, women stitching a veil against the light –
    How am I to see?
Now Fiddah asks me to stand and sing
– I shall open a window for the orchards' weeping
one for the face of my homeland, departing with me
Do not ask for my voice
The distances have confiscated it

Stay with me now, Arabian Fiddah,
  'so we may weep over what has passed'.[4]

Translated by Lena Jayyusi and Naomi Shihab Nye

4. Excerpt from an old folk song.

Ahmad Salih al-Salih SAUDI ARABIA

How Fear Dies

Bassam Shakaa[1]
Children in the alleys
know you, a bright star
And so do the olive trees,
and patient peasant women.
Mothers in Jerusalem
sing of you
by their suckling infants' cradles
bless your glorious name
in their dawn prayers
You, who best know
how Nablus has been orphaned,
how the homeland has been widowed,
and how tragedy has been born.

Bassam Shakaa:
Your torn-off limbs
are an ever-growing symbol
of rejection of injustice,
They are an ever-shining beacon
of infinite resistance
of crying out, 'No!' a million times
in these days of darkness.

1. Bassam al-Shakaa is the mayor of Nablus who was the victim, together with several other mayors in the West Bank, of Zionist terrorist acts. Al-Shakaa's legs were blown off in a car bomb blast.

Bassam Shakaa
A chivalrous ambition
flashes in your eyes.
Your people wait
for Jerusalem on the march
You wax great in the eyes
of your companions in anguish
and they grow taller than despair.
Your voice resounds
and theirs rises high in turn
making despicable those
who only speak in whispers.

Your blown-up limbs are mingled
with the earth of this land
Your voice has awakened
even the seven sleepers.[2]
Welcome to you, hero,
hoisted on the shoulders of men.

Look:
This is the way victory comes,
This is the way fear dies.
Who shall declare to the world then
'Bassam Shakaa
Begins the march onwards.'

Translated by Issa Boullata and John Heath-Stubbs

2. The 'seven sleepers' are the martyrs of Ephesus who took refuge from persecution in a cave where they were supposed to have slept for 100 years. It is both a Muslim and a Christian legend referred to in the Koran in the chapter of 'Al-Kahf', XVIII.

Habeeb al-Sayigh   **UNITED ARAB EMIRATES**

The Sniper

A wall illuminating the sky
and the ripe shots –
this is my hand. It is as old as my grief,
which knows no ebb or flow.

So have pity on it.
Now that it lives in fear,
it has submitted.
Be gentle with my questions!
I shall not argue with you after my death
or provoke your streams,
the girls swimming between my veins and prophetic eyes.
I shall not barter new moons
to a year that has robbed me of my time
and left with the caravan,
king-like, surrounded by chanting.
I shall not buy a shroud,
sell the pure air,
cross out the balconies with a faded chalk.
Glory to my skin! It shall not be flayed.
Glory to my songs!
My blood is nobler than purity itself,
nobler than those murderous corpses –
My face is more true.

I wear the scum of the sea
and am caught in the old wars.
The horses of my people
gather their hooves from rotten mud.

Here is my copybook lighting up the grave
like a dim candle,
and my foot, stretching and limping.
Sometimes I feel the edifice of civilization
hounding me like a beautiful dog
while I grip the leash,
my eyes on the dog's shadow and mine.
And I follow, follow, follow,
desolate in the shadows
till it pulls me out of my own hands.
I find my hands melting like rain,
my forehead growing smaller till it melts
into rain.
Abandoned, I face the howling of rain.

All the houses became mine; the earth
vibrated under my footsteps,
but I did not care. April
was considering its history,
applying its make-up.
But I did not care.
My homeland was the cold night
where I took my lonesome refuge,
robbed of room and blanket.
I wilted like a branch.
My face melted away under my mask,
but I did not care.
I huddled over myself,
searching for where my heart used to reside.
Autumn's whistling tore at my ears
but I did not hear it.
All I owned were my glances scanning the sidewalk
and my lost soul.
I was the only singer caught between
wilted leaves and reckless kisses.

My voice intensified inside my skin.
I was planted like a malignant cell
in an amorous body.
My voice was a wall
separating me from my song.

I aimed at you all,
I drank you down with poisons and soldiers,
you jumbled my thoughts like a mass of torn palm fronds.
I drank you with death,
I left you at the harbour
only to find you in the seas.
Do you witness?
    I aimed at a star, but it travelled farther away.
    I chased it until it lost its light.
    I looked around, stars were embracing one another
    as they went dark, and I was all alone.

Never forget –
I aimed at all of you.
I am the first witness:
    'I witness to my death and slash your skins. I
    suspend them in my room like a ceiling. I carry
    them on journeys like a suitcase. I preserve them
    like the beloved's fragrance. And whenever the
    night surprises me simply by coming, I wail like
    a blind cat that was seared in a fire and crashed
    against a wall.'

Now the house is deserted
and here I am.
Here is my sword, gallant
in its dreams.

I am the nectar of the Pleiades, I once apprenticed
to the river and learned to spill blood behind
demarcation lines in a regular flow. I was, and I
was, and I was . . .
But now my death approaches,
my jugular vein entices me.
I aimed at you all,
I shall not retreat from the thick dust
surrounding me, so hold fast to our rendezvous
and accept me when all the elegies are ignored.

Translated by May Jayyusi and Naomi Shihab Nye

Shawqi Shafeeq **YEMEN**

Dancing before the Queen

1
Tonight the earth
walks upon my eyelashes
and I live among her beloved ones
Starting a fire,
I light up a woman's face
hidden inside my memory
kneeling till I link
the roots of trees to my arteries
feeding this soil with my blood
till it connects
to the shining fabric
in reflected light
from the sword of the river

2
You who are branded
into my flesh
tattoo and love-testament
you who approach while fleeing
the earth turns now
making us turn
Tonight it walks
upon my eyelashes
to offer joy, a love poem,
to share in the dance

3
Just a few more steps
and we reach the summit

4
Tonight lovers congregate
becoming one
with your splendid body
They approach you
O princess of the heart
guided by the divine body's glow
and the earth shares
their dancing
Every false lover falls away
and the flame of passion awakens
in the faithful ones

5
Just a few more steps
and we reach the summit

6
Tonight my heart dances
to golden light streaming
from this lustrous body
and faithful lovers share
in my dance

Lie down, beloved, inside my blood
and rest
This glow will spare me
from the chill of foolish days
Rest inside
where a glow will be fed
by the heart in its madness.

Translated by Sargon Boulus and Naomi Shihab Nye

The Body, the Joy

Two shapes for the body
at its wedding:
to stretch inside a joyful waist
or be scattered
throughout the body's geography
and I seek both
taking refuge in the page
So stay a little distant
lest the mornings overflow
in abundance of pleasure
the soul's agony overflowing from its vessel
and the body swept away
in a cloud of chemistry
Wait till I finish my song of you:
the rain writes its poem
and I hide my final pain
in your grass-coloured eyes
lest my childish passion be revealed
Two shapes
the vast body
can take:
piling up of volcanic poetry
within the silence of stone
or the expansive rituals
of the sea
And I choose the final forest
for my explosions
the one worthy of me
and embrace the distance
so at least a single spot
of purity
will colour the whiteness

Two shapes for the body
at its wedding:
entering the furrows of self
or celebration at the luminous gate
The poem seeks its champion
who will not be silenced
for silence is a sign
of folly, of the heart's disgrace
The body advances in the gasp
of proclaimed histories
and the looming spring of ash
sharpens the appetite
of the reticent rose
Two shapes the body takes
at its wedding,
and I only know this:
how sweet the body is,
and how murderous
The body filled with perennial song
and luscious joy
Come closer
to make mornings overflow
come close . . .
before the soul
departs.

Translated by Sargon Boulus and Naomi Shihab Nye

Ahmad al-Shami   **YEMEN**

Blind Minutes

How I count the slow and tedious hours.

They pass as though each minute
Towed on a rope
Were blind.

I live alone, astonished,
The seconds all around me
Stumble. Old
Disasters moan, I hear them

Cry, like me, for time.

Translated by Sargon Boulus and Christopher Middleton

Defeat

Ride, ride the horse of your despair;
Do not hark back to what you left behind.
The land you cross, love will not be there,
No fated meeting, no melodious air,
No welcome waits for you, and hope is blind.
Once and for all your halcyon days are gone;
All those ghosts behind you! But ride on,
Scatter the dust in phantom faces. You
Who failed in love, never its champion,
Dare now the dark to eat the light you're riding through.

Translated by Sargon Boulus and Christopher Middleton

Ali al-Sharqawi   **BAHRAIN**

Presence

At night's end you arrive,
a bird chosen by morning,
alighting on my shoulder,
and I sprout leaves like lightning
amidst these winds.
They redden like a promise before it ripens,
broaching the thought of departing from worry to dream.
Laughter of lighthouses echoes
across the spacious darkness.
You arrive like sails
journeying across my lips.
As distance expands with you,
I expand.
Your mast extends across the day.
I am a bud seamed by a country
where wishes blaze and songs collapse the walls.
You are the gem of my soul,
clarity of love that shimmers in palm trees.
You arrive in everything,
the words passed from bird to prisoned bird,
the wind's child migrating from one homeland to another,
the dream, venturing into untracked territory –
In everything you come,
the radiant foliage of the spirit
embracing the feast of seasons,
the bride's passion as she hangs up
    her wedding dress.
You arrive – it is enough

that your presence is a sea,
    my heart is a sail,
        and there is no coastline.

Translated by Lena Jayyusi and Naomi Shihab Nye

What Keeps the Innocent Wakeful?

Who is this strutting upright through the marketplace of sorrow
wearing his maize-tinted spectacles
carrying a bag full of lightning
and gliding like a sail through the sea of people?
        We do not know him!
Who is this, weathered from long exile,
self-absorbed, emitting thundering words
that swim in the rain of weddings and pleasure?
        We do not know him!

1
Water disclaims you, and the words that drift from your lips.
Melodies abandon you, and your woven dreamlike cloak.
Anxiety mutters within your eyes.
Fool! You are defeated, pure as you are,
so will you rise up?

If only you would feed the child of the Bedouin alphabet
the milk of uncertainty,

or inhabit the doubts of the unknown . . . Innocent fool!
How terrible that one who contains the four corners of the world
shrinks to the size of a meal and the confines of a shirt!

2
How can the innocent ones of the earth fashion the branches
    of the sun?
The road changes from day to day
while rabid night hungrily gulps at our bodies.
And I who loiter in the hallways of the present
am consumed by the mundane.
Will you tell me
which path enters the labyrinth of the self?
So I may touch the world to my lips
and speak my fears –
ah, if only you knew what this head carries!

3
Hospitality of this sterile age!
Soothe the day's troubles with olives.
Oil your alphabet with the voice of waves.
Children of the neighbourhoods now circle, chanting:
    'The black one munches the worker's shoulders
    The red one was suffering from anaemia
    The green one did not understand the grass's dream
    The yellow one prayed to the stone
    The other colours were lost in the well!'
And you, the white one, roll forth,
swing the children of the Bedouin alphabet high on your ropes!

4
I perceive the eroding anxiety of daily bread.
I count and count, then go back and count again.
What has the innocent one done with this day?
I have eaten
    What else?
I have drunk
    What else?
Nothing
No one recollects my days, moist from the petals of love
No one recollects my searching child's feet

looking for moments of joy
No one recollects the laughter of the house made warm by
    lightning's sweet tea
No one recollects my heart, wider than all directions
No one remembers me.

5
Living withdrawn with his little girl,
he lifts her above the harbour's song.
She touches the core of his olive-green heart
and laughs.
Withdrawn, struggling with unformed words,
words feeding on the lisp from his lips,
he lets them out to fly like a festival dance
on the branch of the moment.
Withdrawn, he weeps.
A lifetime has passed
    and triviality destroys him.
He shouts at the world –
    Can someone who bears nothing new emerge into the streets?

6
The speech of my hands is forbidden,
forbidden the play of my mouth.
The road is changed since yesterday,
and this cloak woven from the alphabet's downpour,
from the shoulder of towering labour, eats its own substance
                          thread by thread.
Even whispers are forbidden in the street –
who knows now where a climate of springtime exists?
Who will unfold the spell hovering over this soil?
My heart grieves –
I wander about steeped in wistfulness
looking for a new mirror.

7
You who gather within your facets the world's day –
all colours return to you.
He is ignorant
who does not measure time
by the silence inhabiting your lips.

8
You import dreams
      and distribute them freely.
Can anyone import his own complexion,
        the voice of his father,
          the laughter of a childhood lost to poverty?

9
You joke about things yet you are the opposite.
They said,
      Fool, when will you come to your senses?
Did you tell them
      the sensible one is made sensible by the grave?
But there's only a dream left in your cloak.

10
Inhabited by palm trees, the mundane filters through me
        again and again
So I escape
   Who will cloak the sea?
Between the darkness of the womb and the grave, time is short.
I possess no memory –
Darkness beckons me with its blade.
Even my name disclaims me.
I am the innocent fool, knower of the unknown's secret –
I was born an antithesis
I lived as antithesis
Am I to continue this way?
The mundane has widowed me.
A bird misses the dawn's song by sleeping.

                    Translated by Lena Jayyusi and Naomi Shihab Nye

Warmth of Blood

You said:
   Prison cells are cold
   I shall send you a woollen garment
   Wrap yourself up
I said:
   The chill is warmed
   by songs of comrades,
   memories of love rising
   in the branches of embrace.
And it is warm
   when you appear in my dreams.
Your longing voice, a stoked and radiant fire . . .
I wrap myself in your words like an ember that says:
   Freedom.
I clasp my vision, reined in by the mind
curb my flowing sorrow.
Do not send me a woollen garment.
   only
     come to me
       with the dream.

Translated by Lena Jayyusi and Naomi Shihab Nye

Hamza Shihata   **SAUDI ARABIA**

Night and the Poet

Poet, whose high music sings
The universal frame of things,

Whose heart's ensnared within love's fire,
And all the hazards of desire,

Shunning love not lest he fail
But unjust ways in love prevail,

Surely he was never sated
By beauty that he contemplated,

But the toil of love's harsh way
He does not wish now to assay.

To purity he would aspire
Shuns the sick vileness of desire,

Will only to himself complain
Of his affliction and his pain.

He sits with downcast head and eye
Yet marks all things as they go by

There is no single whispered word
He's not, in his alertness, heard;

While all the world's at rest he lies
Wakeful – sleep eludes his eyes.

Oh night, who like a hermit, dwell
In darkness bidding home farewell

Unending, always journeying night
Giving the caravan no respite;

Bound to march on eternally,
When shall your bondage loosened be?

Those wakeful stars in wheeling flight
Do their eyes not tire of their own light?

The busy world holds us in thrall,
Whether we wake or sleeping fall.

None can withhold his debt, none's free
To shake off this world's tyranny –

This profligate world, beneath whose skies
Walk hand in hand both fool and wise.

Oppressors, who devour the weak
To weave a shroud for them would seek,

And in this world the naked can
Find no help from the well-clothed man,

Nor any pity for their plight –
Why have we come here then, Oh night,

Where he, who his own dryness slakes
No care for him who's thirsty takes,

And he, whose hunger's satisfied,
Exploits the hungry in his pride?

If a good man seeks what's right and just,
False dealing fells him to the dust.

This world is one great battlefield,
Where all to evil passion yield,

And we betray as wrong rides high
Even the apple of our eye.

Translated by Issa Boullata and John Heath-Stubbs

From the Road

He swears at me
and I at him
With no previous knowledge
we curse one another
Then when we are introduced
he offers his hand
gently, respectfully
and we shake hands
A nice fellow
We embrace and kiss
This is my brother
It is the way I feel
and I regard him accordingly
But when did it happen? When?
Yesterday I told him
I forgave him
But when did we
become enemies?
When did we meet?
Here we are shaking hands
as if he were
my real brother
my real friend
I wish I had had
the same tongue
when I cursed him
I wish to God
I could understand him

well enough
to say
Was there ever
a problem between us?
Once my mouth condemned you
brother
I feel like a criminal
because I slandered you
whom I did not understand
But I've heard
that you, brother, also
slandered me
shredded my honour
trampled my name
without knowing a thing
about me
Should I say
in case you are looking
for a problem
you and I
are the problem?
But my heart hesitates
even my hand withdraws
I want to be kindly,
utterly candid,
to have this out
in the open
But where is my courage
for insult? Where is
my courage for
sincere generosity?
I don't really know him
He might feel ashamed
if I were honest
or shun my insolence
then turn around
to slander me again
and I him
What has happened?
Why this muteness
in my tongue?

How easily
it cursed yesterday!
I catch my breath
as if waiting for something
I cough to break the silence
and our awful meeting
is over
our nerves frayed
We go our ways
the same as we did
before we met
separate paths
We wander days and seasons
shovelling dirt
cursing clouds and stars
looking for a name
to trample
to bad-mouth or burn
Our tongues are poised spears
insatiable
tireless
inventing new curses
without reason or cause
I wish I were
a pair of scissors
travelling among my brothers
shearing off any tongue
that talks behind backs
or dances over someone else's bones
I'd clip it out
from the root
to prevent its lengthening
and that would be
my happiest day.

Translated by Sargon Boulus and Naomi Shihab Nye

Husain Sirhan   **SAUDI ARABIA**

On Time

Fortune, I find you my enemy
Fortune, I do not care for you
A vast distance separates us –
the road to you impassable!
I want from you what cannot be had
Night's long darkness wearies me out
No star on the horizon, no light anywhere
My songs are incandescent with sorrow
My desires are aborted dreams.

Vagabonds seek your favours
sooner or later you give all they ask
But you show your sharp teeth, your rock-face
to the noble and the great-hearted
those whom disasters make resplendent
like a sword burnished with emery
You seek to enslave free spirits
but they break loose from your chains
Evil only will languish in chains
It is slaves that you put in manacles;
they sing of your bounty. Let you be glad
        of the base and the foolish.

                Translated by Christopher Nouryeh and John Heath-Stubbs

The Last Worm

Worms swarmed upon a corpse;
it was wrapped round with a web of their bites
They drew from it the last remains of goodness
and destroyed the last vestiges of its life.

How often this body lay on a soft bed,
how often it took its fill from the fount of joy,
retaining a vast retinue where
the oldest vied with the youngest to oblige.

These countless myriads of worms
found in it a rich banquet

If a man beheld this corpse in its grave,
through sheer horror his nerves would fail him
comeliness reduced to such foulness
what joy is there in life if this is the end?

Myriads of worms were revelling in this, their garden.
heaven never devised anything better;
they harvested whatever they wanted
from among its fruits and flowers.

Here ruler and ruled are equal
here, the master and slave likewise;
and he who is haughty and proud
will be brought low by earth and the tombstone.

Now the worms, having finished up the corpse
are quite alone in the field
and now a strange battle ensues which
shatters every cherished illusion.

Now the worms rage one against the other,
and the strong kills the weak and feeds upon him,
like people – witness human nature
wherever in the world you observe it.

After the battle, the destruction, the carnage,
two worms are left for the final act; both
wish to go on living – O foolishness, for
what they imagine is all illusion.

And now hunger strikes, one can
hardly wait, the other is impatient likewise,
both desire to live – that desire indeed which
plagues all peoples here on earth.

And so the battle grows more intense,
it flares up in cruelty and rage – O what a
picture, though only a miniature, it yet
depicts the wider reality of life:

What is the difference between human war
and war in the earth among worms?
Any creature who seeks to preserve his life
will fight to the very end.

Finally one worm weakens and collapses
the other pounces on him and devours him
– say, how many worms had he devoured
before he became the last survivor?

Now he became the victor in the grave,
his kingdom is a kingdom of mere dust –
monopolist of life and wholly convinced,
of life's infinite potential.

What remains after victory in the field
where the vanquished and the vanquisher are both alike?
The cup of death must be drunk in the end
even by the most unconquerable of men.

The conqueror may see the morning shine auspicious
but does he know what the evening hides?
How often an army wins victory in the morning,
itself to be wiped out when evening comes?

Hours of agony have passed,
and the worm was tortured by devouring hunger.
This is the misfortune which succeeds happiness –
but is there any state that lasts forever?

The worm in the throes of death, strives
to sustain himself from his reserves
gnawing at his own entrails to fend off death
from his precious life.

But his long lesson is now over – no wonder
the most eloquent speaker must be mute in the end
Is it not him who died willy nilly
the devourer of the corpse and all its worms?

Translated by Christopher Nouryeh and John Heath-Stubbs

Muhammad al-Thubaiti   **SAUDI ARABIA**

A Page from a Bedouin Notebook

What is it that you want?
Certainly not my flags.
Those are unavailable and
you shall not have them.
Nor will I spread my oasis
across your hands.
Do not be deceived by the dream
blazing in my eyes.
No one goes beyond that dream.
My dream points back to me.

If I sailed into your eyes searching
for spring, I have not cast anchor yet.
My camel is still waiting, standing
at the gates with eyes still unblinded
by the airport lights.
My song still lives in desert dreams
lulling old passions in the pastures
of my sheep.

I am that ancient stallion whose blond
mane is sprinkled by the sun with morning light.
I am the rebellious stallion untamed
by the vine's confessions, untouched
by perfumed moments.
I came here at a gallop with the desert
at my heels, the alphabet of sands
spraying from my running hooves.

I came riding past the horizons
leaving my pain with the horizons,
searching in them my beginning.
You can never remove the touch of sand
from my shoulders even if you pour
the full moon over my soul, even
if you flood my soul with the waters of the seven seas
you cannot remove the scent of lavender
from my cloak.

The prints that cling to my soles
are poems inscribed by the pulse and throb
of the vast distances I travelled.
This thirsty smile on my lips
is a river of wind telling untold, untouched
tales.

What do you read in my palm? Do you read
the history of pain? What do the lines tell?
Night's weddings? Promised joys?
Do you see a conflagration? A giant
striding closer and closer in the
season that comes?

Diana Der Hovanessian
Lena Jayyusi (first translator)

I Spelled out Dream
I Spelled out Illusion

It is the fire of passion
that scorches my face;
the incense of passion

intoxicates my senses.
The time of ill-tempered
happiness and the time of waiting
  unite within me.

I stole out from the dark
  of empty questions,
  of sterile questions.
I bathed in the clouds
  that emanate
  from Laila's braids.
I climbed the distant face of cliffs,
  the face of distance,
to stare into the eyes of my beloved,
  even as she slept
  in the nest of many
  rendezvous.

I spell out a dream.
I spelled out an illusion.
I read the story of her tears
  page by page.

For her dreams I silenced voice,
slaughtered words, slew
the question
when she wrapped herself
in my memories.

How much more night? How long?
  One year? Two?
How much remains of life? How long?
  One hour? Two?
I said
  My lady wears the mountain
  narcissus.
  My lady's night ends
  at the gate of waking
  when a sprig of sweet basil
  springs on a mountain of patience,
  when a whirlpool swirls out

from living blood
from living absence.

I said
    the ship recognizes in me
    some of her old harbours.
I said
    the ship sails through my voice.
I said
    seasons arrive, startling away
    fear.
I said,
  and I said,
    I spun out bones from the memory of dust
        and returned without memory.

Fields.
The fields,
a palm tree on the edge of water,
the sun on her braids,
telling the secret of her tall figure to the air,
stripped naked on the shore,
casting her image into the water,
into the ocean.
And drums, the drums.
A dance of ecstasy in simple camel songs.
The milky way begins within me
and I, mingled with sands,
    become seed,
    become root,
    become incense,
    penetrate the ocean's pulsing heart
    while thoroughbreds rear
    and wander inside my heart.

Diana Der Hovanessian
Lena Jayyusi (first translator)

Ahmad al-Mushari al-Udwani   **KUWAIT**

The Year that has Ended

It wasn't a matter of numbers: twelve months
gone fleetingly with the revolving stars,
but a year of flesh and blood,
a chain from our life that's been unstrung
and slipped into the void.

Ever anew the sun will dazzle,
the constant moon quiveringly allure,
but our lives, our pains, our aspirations
are folded pages,
the dispersal of life
counted by a beginning and an end.

I wish we were like the months
which revolve with the stars,
all through the year,
and after each month to return again
and revive lovely memories.

Translated by Jeremy Reed with the help of the Editor

Waiting

Two desires conflict in my heart:
the impetus to find a shady tree
with dense foliage and honeyed fruit,
and a deep terror growling like a volcano
destroying where it goes.

Thus I sit on a shaky planet
waiting for the sky to illuminate my soul
and free me from this blind sorrow,
so that the road will suddenly blaze out with light.

Can I depend on the sky, and how long
will I wait for this realization?
Or will I encounter life,
    a prisoner in my own home?

Translated by Jeremy Reed with the help of the Editor

A Tale

Those knives
that lacerate my heart continually,
are the remnants of a tale,

I wrote on dust
with my shed blood:
'I am a stranger on this earth,
I have sown my doubts across the world,
and have lived in certainty.'

Translated by Jeremy Reed with the help of the Editor

Song of Departure

I left you a long time ago,
Yes, sirs, yes
I departed,
    and carry on departing every day.

I went off in search of my comrades,
those who had become wise before me,
and preferred to seek out horizons,
rather than live among shadows,
and chose a place whose singular quality
is that it's neglected.
Yes, sirs, yes
    I departed
    and carry on departing every day.

I left you to demolish walls,
to interpret secrets in clear daylight,
to witness life, the universe
free of imposing barriers.
Walls hinder me,
dams block my vision,

the laws of darkness
govern me,
even in the playground of dreams.
With every footstep
I was killed and killed again.
Yes, sirs, yes
    I've departed
    and go on leaving every day
for endless adventures,
danger's ecstatic challenge,
affording me brisk wings,
that fatefully flap in the wind.
On every road they salute me with banners,
they incite me to the brink of rebellion,
the abyss yawns like hell,
and conceive endless new goals for me,
schemes I had never anticipated.
I left you, so that each moment of my life
would have the immediacy of birth.
Yes, sirs, yes
    I have departed
    and am forever departing.

Translated by Jeremy Reed with the help of the Editor

Ibrahim al-Urayyid   **BAHRAIN**

Why

Why does our meeting foreshadow departure,
and my ear turn from your lute's persistence,
and the loving-cup we sipped ecstatically
leaving it kindle fire in our dead hearts,
    still hovers over us?
    Why should we close our eyes,
    deny that fire,
    and still the heart's resounding bell?

Hasn't life's flux created in us waves
which only made contention for a while?
The murmur of the wind soon scattered us,
and we found generous lightning, quick flashes
    illuminating our world
    from horizon to horizon,
affording our life the briefest meaning.

How is it passion lives on after us,
still kindled in the universe, but we
can know it only fleetingly,
and how it expires like a breath of air,
and only lasts through one briefly voiced prayer,
    and why it possesses such power to hurt,
    yet allows us the chance to rejoice,
if only for a moment we gave all to love?

You spoke of a melodic tune that touched our lips,
and sought its meaning from darkness to daybreak.

Why then the nights, those starry witnesses
impress on us our lives are wholly void?
      This edge of darkness
      in which our dreams
are transient like the moon's mutable face,
retreats with us into a forgotten past.

She who has touched the stars shouldn't feel cold,
and she who time in turn has glorified,
how can she ever be engulfed with fear?
Suppose we're strangers, lacking harmony,
then aren't your flowers art held in my hands?
      Enter my prayers then,
      for life's an ever-renewed spring,
fiercely revivified by us, two birds,
you'll be immortal so long as I live.

Translated by Jeremy Reed with the help of the Editor

Fragrance

Beautiful woman! So many join me in loving you,
      but misinterpret my feelings,
they see beauty in the colour of the rose,
      for me it's in the fragrance.
They hear spring in the canary's voice,
      I feel it in nature's vibrant heart.
They find life in the ecstasy of wine,
      I see it in the cup itself.
I trust in my own singular vision
      and not in how others see the world.

I love you truly, for in you alone,
my spirit achieves harmony.
Everything's revealed in your eyes, beloved eyes,
at once intimate and trustworthy.
You hover round me, and my love for you
is like a fragrant rose; claim it fearlessly.
And when you lie down my love is revealed
like moonlight gently overtaking you,
a love that flows like the clearest water,
that sparkles in descent from mountain tops.
I love you truly, and in you I see
the rose and myrtle that live in my soul.

Translated by Jeremy Reed with the help of the Editor

Sterility

The star went on dying
       horizon a requiem
Night a tomb
       on a barren shore
Ships waiting for wind
       me this crazed sailor
Brandishing an oar
       left and right I struck
Water heavy as clay
       I called to the sea
Take me, give me
       that piece of the land
Nobody knows of it
       It is far away
'Go back,' the sea said,
       'poor man, what
Were you waiting for?
       Why did you come
In the twentieth century?'

Should I bite on my dagger like Brutus
And sing, love, of your demise?

It's the cities unbuilt I'm asking about,
A word still to be given a meaning,

A string to give me a melody,
A face I know, but where?

You, wind, with onset of winter,
Can mow down all the trees.

Earth is a barren woman
Grumbling that the rain is impotent.

Translated by Sargon Boulus and Christopher Middleton

Ismail al-Warith   **YEMEN**

Prayer to the Beloved

I open up to you, my heart unfolds like a storm
You enter
I do not know if my depths
contain your hidden secrets,
or if you are like me.
I have tried many hearts and found them
too narrow to preserve my covenant
I have entered many cities which
filled me with wonder, but finally
exiled me
With you I offer my skull on my palm,
I walk briskly at times, and other times slowly,
never knowing where my feet will lead me
When you are distant, your image shakes me
My longing tosses me onto the waves of your memories
bitter when I am in you, beloved when I am far

I travel to you through the eyes of my friends
When I see the scars you have left,
I travel away from you.
You are that exhausting journey,
the anxious ploddings toward the impossible.

Do you remember the child who used
to enter your ancient doors filled with joy?
Now he stands at your walls
with thorns in his feet
observing your birth

Though he awakens from the tempting dream
which is you, you throb in his heart
and shine in his eyes
Still he embraces your gloomy shadow!

Forever my lips are yearning for you
But you dissolve in a nightmare
while I wear the night and go knocking
on the doors of longing, searching for you.
Are you with me?
No, you are not.
You arrive and sorrow erupts in clouds of smoke.
I go to you, but the angry sparks of your eyes
deflect me.
I am lost on a strange road,
a traveller whose cane broke
from too much nervous tapping
on the trips of endless waiting.
I watch for you in the eyes of those coming
from beyond the seas.
I speak to you of ships that have not
set sail
and ask returning ships about you.

In every invisible port,
sorrows nip my eyes like snakes.
I do not know how many barren years have eaten into me
while I dreamed of your fruitfulness.
History passes by me, wrapped in
clouds
smiling like an old man to his
tiny grandchild
Death laughing within earshot
and I
lamenting your life as new as spring

But you have not died yet.
You grow leaves, like a coffee shrub
over the sorrows of your little children
and the tears of your orphans, you spread
branches of lavender

The soothsayers claim your hair
is tinged with white
How can you grow old before you were ever born?
There are signs of your coming which mothers recount
to their children before they sleep
signs of your coming: the desert
turns green
From the parched rock
fresh water gushes forth

I see you in dreams as a loaf of bread
a protective cloak
a hut that shelters the frail
but this endless journeying tears at my feet.
Come down, come down from the cave
of blissful love!
Teach me a new alphabet,
remove those coloured masks!
Your Yemenite face is beautiful
and needs no make-up.

Translated by Sargon Boulus and Naomi Shihab Nye

Presence in the Sacrificial Alphabet

Usually I step over
my enemies' heads
crossing the boundary
separating fear

from fearlessness
Holding the sword
of words in my hand
in the dark I proclaim
that the light will embrace the deprived
But when I saw the idolators
praying before the palace
barefoot, heads covered
with slime
beseeching the Wali
in beggar's voices,
'O to be those horses
that carry you
when you travel
and guard your tents'
I slandered the idols
and threw in the lying poets' eyes,
the drunken scribes of wooden words,
a handful of sand
that whizzed past the jailer
(if you lower your head before him
and ask for forgiveness
he might consent)
I would not be angry
if my friend sent me
to the stake
but he who waits for rain
in the name of the barren desert
and calls to children
to sharpen their picks
or tried to plant
the slim trees of his rejection
what is his guilt?
Now I shun the stage
where frogs read their poems
where crows are cawing
I hide my grief-stricken face
and lower the curtain

If my death gladdens you
If one foot slips

while the other
still clings
to my destined earth
then I invite you to come and die with me
until we are resurrected
and our words illuminate –
I don't mean the soiled ones,
the frivolous, rotten, lowly ones –
But the others. Sanaa, I offer
the sword, the torch of rebellion
I raised in you
I scare off the night-bats
and the ghosts that creep
in haunted valleys down below

Your walls lock me in
your doors knock me about
I wear your terror
cling to your skin
and I open cracks for light
finding your face sometimes smiling
sometimes sad
I inhale the legends
of your mystery
in the eyes of your beautiful girls
and unknown alleys
The scent of history mystifies me
I disappear in the dream
which disappears with me
Looking for a foothold
I find a land
where piles of gold await
Then I see the knife blade
and step over the knife

Don't be scared and write
with blood-soaked letters
Either you choose your path
or you join the chorus
The music is loud
The dance is a sham

Take my head and hang it
from a lamp-post
along the warring street of
merchants and night-brokers
The flood of poetry
flowing from the sufferings
of the deprived
from the body of revolution
will not stop

I tried diving into myself
and found your dreams
bleeding, shot by hunters
drowned in desert oil
I found you looking for a map
drawn by a sword
pinpointed with horses

How hard it is
to journey inside ourselves
only to find
the spillage of your blood.

Translated by Sargon Boulus and Naomi Shihab Nye

Khalifa al-Wugayyan   **KUWAIT**

Tattered Sails

When I suffer, it's for those who drift,
Drift in the night, as if drowned
Broken oars on the sea, tattered sails – ships
Astray in the darkness, eastward or westward sailing
The pilot has lost his bearings:
I'm tired of correcting his errors.
When I was young I wrestled with fate,
Bet my life's experience against it.
Each step he takes upon the road
The traveller is hemmed in with fires.
No tyrant has struck fear in me,
Nor his dungeons blotted out my vision of truth
I came back, in my mind, on my lips,
That which, for horror, cannot be spoken
And if I were to say: 'How many are still slaves?'
That would count as incitement to riot.

Translated by Sargon Boulus and John Heath-Stubbs

Estrangement

Coming or going, I am a stranger;
Whether near or far, remote
I quiz the people's faces,
Searching the streets as I pass.
Each man there has somewhere to go to
I alone do not know what I seek
As if, wherever I went, I stood still –
The road with its wayfarers turning around me.
An ardent longing for I know not what
Tears me apart.
The winter of loss and desolation
Blows me onward.
All ports I've visited, all roads I've travelled,
Perhaps desire will bear me far away
Towards horizons passionately sought.
A fresh fountain I am
Others I give to drink:
But my own thirst was never satisfied
I was a guiding light,
But I myself had no lode-star.
My soul I suffused in every cup –
Vine for drinkers, but myself not joyful.
Am I to be on every road
A lamp in the night without oil?

Translated by Sargon Boulus and John Heath-Stubbs

Tahir Zamakhshari   **SAUDI ARABIA**

At the Door

Beauty's very image at love's open door
She stood – seductive was the charming dress she wore

With an inviting smile upon her countenance
That wore bright threads in which was fancy stirred to dance

Guards are set about her, though she allures all hearts
Glances sharp as swords, and keen as pointed darts

Shyness shields her face that is so bright and fair
Breathing forth a fragrance to the ambient air

I stood before her threshold, a favour I would claim
To quiet my throbbing heart that is with love aflame

More than I hoped for were the promises she made
They were just a mirage and so, like it, away must fade

Sufficient gift it was only her eyes to see
Although they gazed elsewhere and were not bent on me

Cautiously I gazed, for fear had gripped me still
Lest arrows from her eyes my own heart's blood should spill

Passion for her fetters my tongue, and I raise
those fetters up to her and would this question phrase:

Shall I then find with you the key to set me free
from fetters of love's sickness, growing grievously?

Translated by Ishaq al-Khalifa Sharif and John Heath-Stubbs

Coquetry

Looking at her maddened lover
She's beguiling at their meeting
With that swinging walk of hers
Yet will not return his greeting

Coquettish charm is yours, your face
Drives away the shades of night
From your languid body breathes
Lavender, in soft delight.

On your lips is fiery wine
Honeyed eloquence and craft
That string the words in song's array
Pouring in melodious draught.

How long will you still be coy
Cheating me of proffered joy?

Translated by Ishaq al-Khalifa Sharif and John Heath-Stubbs

Khalid Saud al-Zayd   **KUWAIT**

My Son

My image is imprinted on his face, if only he knew
And in his eyes flash echoes of my roots
The brush of beauty strokes his lips
As a breeze caresses my chest

A sweet huskiness defines his voice
A singular melody to my ears
He repeats my tunes and shows them off
For his listening peers

It bothers him if I do not respond
When he calls, or if I do not hear
Oh, how he hits me, proudly, playfully,
Pushes me onto the floor, and watches me fall

Should someone provoke me
He punches him, with tearful eyes
What swift little fists he boasts,
Protectors for my dreadful old age

And when he calls, 'Papa!'
I answer, 'Yes, heart of my heart,'
And he smiles and swells with pride,
Pearls shining on his lips.

He acts coquettishly,
Wittily commanding at his whim
At times I stand between him and his whim
Other times I consent without pretence

If he cries out with pain in the night
I cannot rest
I speak to him from my worried heart,
And press him against my aching chest

I kiss him sometimes on his forehead
Sometimes on the tender neck
I toil just to bring him joy
And clown to make him laugh.

Translated by Sharif S. Elmusa and Naomi Shihab Nye

The Stranger

Wearing his frail body,
He staggers with lowered head,
Not knowing which turn leads
Away from trouble.
He no longer believes in hoping,
But wishes hope had never crossed
His path, for it wounded his good heart
And stunted his will.
It left him living and dead.
Glimpsing any shadow, he starts,
For fear of being noticed and censured,
He cloaks himself in darkness,
Wishing it were eternal.

Once he lived in ease
Under his parent's canopy,
Singing of Saada's love.
She spoke to him, as if in secret,
Enchanting him with her honeyed words.
Such memory flashes and fades
As spring fades behind a sultry summer.
Soon he will ascend to heaven
Where doors may open
To all hearts wronged in life.

Translated by Sharif S. Elmusa and Naomi Shihab Nye

Muhammad Mahmoud al-Zubairi   **YEMEN**

Moments of Illumination

I feel a breeze like that of Paradise
That breathes within the depths of my own soul
And then I feel the rhymes, they seem to creep
Like ants that creep within my consciousness.
One rhyme eludes me as it flits away
Others there are that serve me willingly.
One parts from me and I despair of it
Another's full of promise to return
From these I write about the life of men
And wage my war against their murderers
It is with these I write about existence
Revealing what is fine and exquisite
And of these rhymes some flash as lightning does
Revive the dead, refresh the barren earth
If they should only softly touch my soul,
My heart would leap up then within my breast
Among them there are those which are most rare
And never dwelt before in mind or heart
And if they should descend on me charge on
Just as a beast that finds a fertile land.
And some are dromedaries which, led on,
Conquer the sky and lay bare the unknown
And some are untamed camels of the desert
Only a prophet has the skill to mount them
Most of these rhymes escape out of my hands
Vanish away although against their will
There is a rhyme sought in the depth of ocean
You find true pearls and a rich hoard of treasure

251

And there are measures bearing the weight of mountains
That in the mountain's heart dissolve away
There's meaning that will straightway find the word
And words that run spontaneously to meaning
Each of them has its own appointed place
And with precision it will find it out.
As if my mind were like a garden, where
Every lover finds his own beloved
I give myself in wonder to these rhymes
Jealous not to lose them in my joy
Sometimes in silence I will listen to them
At other times I cry out in my rage
My mind has never been a slave to them
Nor have I sought from them mere worldly gain
But it is my resistless fate decreed
I be a poet – and indeed I am.

Translated by Ishaq al-Khalifa Sharif and John Heath-Stubbs

Fiction

Muhammad Abd al-Malik   **BAHRAIN**

The *Hazeen* was Singing

The *Hazeen* was singing . . .

The lights, red, yellow and lilac, were all lit, and all the women were made up with the greatest of care. It was the night of Salem Khamis al-Wardi's wedding. All the men were standing outside the house, and even the newborn babies were attending, sleeping in the laps of their mothers. The wedding drums had been prepared, and men and women were busily carrying them outside, while Maryan was skinning the lamb, with all the boys gathered round him, watching him as he took out the entrails and put them in their special place. The big transport cars were weaving in and out of the crowd like great armoured vehicles on their way to the front, for the bridegroom was Salem Khamis al-Wardi from al-Muharraq and the bride was from al-Hidd in the North.

And the *Hazeen* was singing . . .

Sharifa cut a path through a huge crowd of people – the whole neighbourhood had been brought together – carrying the tray of sweet-meats and nuts, and said mockingly:

'The *Hazeen* is singing!'

She laughed and swayed her big waist, so that her plump body quivered beneath the large, tight dress.

The *Hazeen* was standing in the middle of a group of boys and girls, all under ten. With his hunched back, and his mouth open as he sang out the notes of an old folk song, he looked shrinking and downtrodden. Any moment now, the voice of one of the bridegroom's family or the bride's family might be raised in curses, as had happened at previous weddings, silencing his own voice. Or it might be the voice of some woman guest at the party, irritated by the intense heat of the night. His yellowish mouth was open, showing two back teeth missing on the left and a third decayed on the right; a dark-brown colour had crept over the rest of the teeth so that they looked like the inside of an old, much-used teapot. His eyes narrowed as they took in the light, and the old gown which he'd kept specially for Salem Khamis al-Wardi's wedding was patched on the shoulders. He hadn't folded his *ghutra* over his head, as he usually did, but left it draped over his left shoulder. His hair was meticulously arranged over a forehead that was worn with care, a forehead creased with deep lines that spoke of humiliation and poverty and a life of wandering from house to house and mosque to seashore and dwellings to roadside.

Sharifa came back, bustling and happy, went round serving drinks and tea and nuts; she sprinkled rose water on people's hands and faces, or into the air, sang the traditional ululations and wiped the perspiration that flowed down her broad forehead. The perspiration didn't worry her, because tonight was a once-in-a-lifetime thing; Salem Khamis al-Wardi was her cousin, and there were other prospective bridegrooms outside and inside the house, stealing glances, and . . .

'Sharifa!'

Um Saad had called her, nudging a woman who was sitting silently next to her.

'Patience is a virtue.'

Sharifa walked on, smiling and coquettish. Her waist no longer kept its familiar form; it swayed away, quivering, from the rest of her body, moving now to the right and now to the left. She darted constant glances at the *Hazeen* and the group of boys and girls, repeating, with a note of protest this time:

'The *Hazeen* is singing.'

It was all very well for the *Hazeen* to sing at a small local wedding, in some small, obscure corner, lost among all the people and the noise. But for the *Hazeen* to sing on the night of Salem Khamis al-Wardi's wedding, into the microphone, that he should go on singing for several minutes together in the middle of the great courtyard, with no one raising a voice in protest or having, apparently, any intention of protesting – the strangeness of it struck her, for all her preoccupation with the guests and the young men who'd crept in among the women and were standing in hidden corners.

The *Hazeen* was singing with great feeling, his eyes filled with tears. The women were talking busily about the bride and bridegroom, who were sitting close together on two seats brought specially, for this occasion, from the houses of dignitaries in al-Manama. They were wiping their perspiration with a white handkerchief that grew damper as time went on.

The band and the singers were having an interval for rest, which meant that this was the time for gossip and winks and nudges. You could see an ear moving towards some face or mouth, or a mouth moving towards some ear, and one hidden face greeting another. You could see lips moving hesitantly, anxiously, saying things no ear could hear except the one they'd sought out. Every face had placed itself close to some other face nearby, and hidden smiles met returning smiles, or else faces that were on the watch too – on the watch for a possible satisfying conversation they'd missed and were going to try to decipher now through the faces and the cautious glances sent here and there among the black cloaks and long dresses and veils. Meanwhile the coffee cups went round, lightly and gracefully; you might have thought they were moving under their own power, were it not for a hand that would appear lightly holding a cup, with a woman's body weaving and twisting behind it. The children were jumping about in the little space to be found among the bodies, falling from lap to lap, happy with the noise and the crowd and the lights, shrieking in pure joy. They would go round a mat here or a cushion there, or disappear behind one of the women. The incense burners were working busily, and Salem Khamis al-Wardi was stealing glances at his bride whom he was seeing tonight for the first time. He'd wooed her, then become engaged to her, then married her on the strength of a photograph – a photograph taken without the knowledge of the bride or her family, which they'd brought him from al-Hidd wrapped in an old handkerchief. He wanted to make sure that his bride's face had no blemishes, but he was overcome with embarrassment, because no sooner would he raise his eyes than he'd be the target for hundreds of other eyes which felt like thousand upon thousand, piercing their way through his face and settling in his mind. He'd hurriedly lower his eyes to look at the floor, then, unconsciously, he'd repeat the attempt, and fail, and repeat the attempt again. The bride's head was bowed low, her hands were clasped between her thighs and she didn't lift so much as an eyelid. No one took any notice of the *Hazeen*; he was just an errand boy for weddings and other gatherings and special occasions, carrying water and incense and nuts and bottles of rose water, and dancing when his hands happened to be empty.

When Sharifa passed in front of the microphone, she walked deliberately provocatively, within just a few feet of the *Hazeen*. He glanced at her in a way that aroused the suspicions of those who saw it, then looked round to see what effect his glance had had on people; then his eyes darted rapidly back and met hers in a look that was full of meaning, so that he trembled and Sharifa laughed and made a pretence of modesty. Her shoulder shook, then she let her laugh trail off in a lingering, flirtatious way; and the *Hazeen* sang: 'Oh bird sent down from heaven!'

He beat the ground with his foot, enraptured, so that his hunchback became more stooped than ever, and he looked humble and defeated, as he always had been and always would be – a symbol of abasement and lowliness, an object of mockery in the neighbourhood. He'd wrapped himself in an old, patched gown whose colours had been bright once, but were faded now.

The *Hazeen* wasn't one of the singers from the band, so the group of girls and dancing women had moved away from the round area of floor which was the focus of everyone's gaze that night – the night of the wedding of Salem Khamis al-Wardi, the first male schoolteacher in the neighbourhood, who had wooed the first woman teacher in al-Hidd. The wedding was, after all, a town wedding, and the chairs belonged to important people, and the bride was wearing a white veil.

Whenever the band stopped playing, there was an interval for conversation; very short intervals at first, then, as time went on, they became longer and longer, till the conversation took over everything. Talk would meet talk, and voice would meet voice; one of the voices would try to dominate the other, and then a third would try and become dominant, and the whole place would become a to-and-fro of high-pitched chatter. The *Hazeen* would stay outside all this, as if he were no part of the place at all. And then the children would come, and the cushions would rise and fall; and sudden laughter would follow a passing whisper; and there was the smell of incense and Indian perfumes. Salem Khamis al-Wardi's sisters and mother and aunts and cousins constantly crossed one another's paths as they attended to the guests, giving out smiles to everyone, as well as nuts and glasses of sherbet and bottles of soft drink. Meaningful laughter would burst out from words and phrases which had more point to them now than at other times.

'Good luck to you, girls!'

The ululations would ring out from behind the women's veils and young faces blushed instantly.

The *Hazeen* was weaving his way through the opening of his song, guiding it, alone, from the pathways of love into love's open fields, then moving on to sing of a woman's face – he'd secretly dreamed of this woman, but he'd kept the secret concealed.

The *Hazeen* was singing. But only he was excited by his song.

The woman who'd captivated him now appeared before his eyes. The dream enfolded him and he surrendered to it like a fearless child, closing his eyes and moving off on the wings of a *mawwal*; and the *mawwal* itself was a wandering stranger come from Yemen to settle in his heart.

The *Hazeen* was singing . . .

Um Saad said to a woman next to her:

'The *Hazeen*'s really singing from the heart. He's in love!'

Her neighbour laughed.

'Poor soul,' she said. 'What earthly hope has he got?'

His eyes were still shut. Was the *Hazeen* singing or dreaming? Only he knew. The *Hazeen* lived in a small rented room in the neighbourhood, a room containing nothing but a wooden chest – which he'd made himself and painted with two crossed palm trees – a teapot, a pair of leather slippers and a mattress. He had no trade – or rather he was, as they say, a jack-of-all-trades – his livelihood was uncertain, he was always down on his luck, and he had no family of any kind. The only time he got a mouthful of warm food was at weddings where, at the end, he'd also be given some nuts and fruit and money. The *Hazeen* would be there at every wedding; he never enquired whose wedding it was, nor did the hosts ever ask who he was, or what he wanted there. His connection with them would start as soon as the engagement was announced in the neighbourhood. You'd see him carrying the mirrors on his back, preparing the wedding room, chopping the onions, washing the pots and helping the cook. He'd clean the rice, chop the wood, keep an eye on the fire and cooking pots, skin the sheep with Maryan and hang them up, then cut the meat and put it in the pots, gather the wood and build a fire for warming the drums, then dance into the middle of the circle of women and sing. What energy he had! Such energy that he never stopped dashing about, sitting down and jumping up, calling out here and there, dealing with requests from all sides from one sunrise to the next; energy that would wake him from his slumber, would surge out, as soon as a wedding date was announced in the neighbourhood. It was as though the *Hazeen*'s whole dream sprang into vigorous life on these nights, in these crowds, in this singing and dancing – the dreaming of loving as other people did, of taking his place, like other people, in a settled home.

Like other people, his arm was never still, nor were his legs, nor was his tongue, till dawn came – for a day like this was the *Hazeen*'s day.

And the *Hazeen* had fallen in love; that's how it seemed and what Um Saad suspected. He'd fallen in love before, but then his love had been shrouded in silence. This time he decided to do something he hadn't done over all those years: to declare his love and let people do as they liked about it. The *Hazeen* had fallen in love, but who was the object of his love?

It had happened months before, and he'd gone to the market-place, sat down on the pavement and said to the letter-writer:

'Write me a letter.'

He wished he could write like the people who'd been to school; he would have filled the pages with ink and tears. The *Hazeen* had fallen in love. He folded the small piece of paper carefully and placed it, first, in his pocket, then in his wooden chest. Every night he'd open the letter under a dim light and look at it until, as time passed, it became frayed in his hand and he kept it close to his breast. Months before he'd made the decision to send it to the girl, but hadn't done so. The *Hazeen* had fallen in love; and who'd intercede for him for this sin to be forgiven? Who'd rescue him from the torment of loneliness? And who was the one who held him captive, so that his heart and body yearned for her? Who was it? The nights flowed by like rivers and, whenever a friend visited him, he'd immediately lift the lid of the wooden chest, take out the letter and open it out on the floor for fear it would fall to pieces in his hand; then he'd read it out, without giving the name or place or time.

'Who is it?' his visitor would ask. 'Who is she?'

The visitor would ask again and again, and finally he'd reply:

'A woman . . . from around here.'

'Where did you see her?'

'At a wedding.'

And he would add:

'At the wedding of Jabir's daughter . . . one Friday night.'

Then he'd serve tea from his teapot, and he'd say:

'Shall I recite some poetry for you?'

He'd ask this because he wanted to recite at that time, in the quiet of the night, and because he was gripped by longing and anguish – an anguish that had made him oblivious to everything except his longing to meet her, so that he'd utter a long, deep sigh and gaze all around the little room. You could see him suffering silently, his chest heaving, then he'd recite in a voice that could barely be heard.

Um Saad said:

'The *Hazeen*'s in love.'

Her neighbour, thunderstruck by this, said:

'God is great!'

'The *Hazeen*'s a human being too,' retorted Um Saad.

Um Saad was a good-hearted woman, famous for her love of fine clothes and make-up, and also for changing husbands from one year to the next, attending every wedding without exception and dancing with the young girls even though she herself wasn't young any more.

'Is he really!' said her neighbour.

'And the girl's here tonight,' Um Saad added. 'At the wedding.'

260

'Here at the wedding?'

'Yes, here at the wedding.'

'Who is she?'

Um Saad declared, loudly and confidently:

'The boy's going to be found out tonight.'

The *Hazeen* was singing. And he was thirty years old.

'What about the girl?' said her neighbour.

'She'll be found out too!'

The *Hazeen* was singing.

His small eyes had become soft, glowing with the hint of a tear in the fading light of the evening of Salem Khamis al-Wardi's wedding. The *Hazeen* loved Iraqi songs, and now it could be seen, as he stood under the light, how a tear had left his dull eye, how it was rolling down his rough cheek.

'Look!' said Um Saad.

Sharifa was crossing the courtyard with a tray of nuts, gazing at the *Hazeen* with a mockery plain to see.

And the *Hazeen* was singing.

The tear rolled right down his face, from the little, narrow, inflamed eye down to his mouth and on to his chin. His voice sounded out more clearly, then poured from his lips in a warm, sweet stream. The women standing at the back turned their heads, while others crept forward; the chatter died down, the talk and laughter stopped, the yells of the boys subsided, and all eyes were turned on the singer they'd suddenly noticed. Suddenly, people's faces showed bewilderment and surprise, and the desire to understand what was happening, to absorb it without having to think about it consciously; for it had all happened without warning, springing from a source, unknown till now, which had power to shake them to the very depths of their being. The voice was the voice of a man who'd lived on the edge of people's memories, among them but unseen; there he'd been, rejected by alleyways and streets, and by houses, and by time itself, searching for the goal he never reached, however much he strove to approach it. What a voice it was! A voice that went to the heart with a sudden strange gentleness, a voice which first rose, then flowed unannounced through the unknown gates of the soul. The *Hazeen* was singing! His thick fingers were wrapped round the mouth of the micro-phone, covering its fine mesh, and tears were streaming from his eyes, while behind him stood the singers of the band, young and old. They cautiously approached and surrounded him, without realizing what they were doing, drawn by the inexplicable magic of his singing; then they passed slim hands across the drums and tambourines and, fresh after their rest, joined in the notes of the song. The young girls moved onto the dance floor and danced together like young fillies, and their veils fluttered like the wings of a butterfly. The people were all tapping their feet to the tune, and clapping and dancing.

The *Hazeen* was singing . . .

Sharifa stood bewildered in front of him, enraptured and entranced.

'The *Hazeen*'s singing!' she said. But this time she said it with a long sigh which expressed pain and boundless admiration. She ceased to sprinkle people's faces with rose water, and the *Hazeen* gazed after her with a look of sadness and dejection.

Um Saad said:

'It's love. You can see it.'

'Are you sure?' asked her neighbour.

'I know all about it, woman!' she answered reproachfully.

And the *Hazeen* was singing:

'Oh bear my greetings, you birds, on the wind!'

Someone or other said:

'The *Hazeen*'s fallen in love.'

And someone else added:

'Poor fellow!'

They all knew that the *Hazeen*'s love was like clasping the wind, grasping at emptiness and mirage, that it was unrequited love, with no limit and no meeting point and no end; all he would ever know was sorrow, loneliness, wretchedness and poverty in a small, empty room. The *Hazeen* was crying out both to the unknown and to a woman every guest at the wedding was now pointing at; and people talked about it in the neighbourhood long after that night had passed.

Sharifa, abashed, lowered her eyes to the floor.

Um Saad sprinkled her face with rose water, and it dried instantly.

The *Hazeen* was singing . . .

Translated by Lena Jayyusi and Christopher Tingley

Mayfaᶜ Abd al-Rahman   YEMEN

What Came between Aneesa and Me

'The mother herself is young – not more than thirty.'

My own mother was speaking to my father, but her eyes were on the ceiling. 'The daughter is just fourteen so how old was the mother when she was married? She hadn't reached puberty yet either, had she?'

Father didn't reply, but he raised his eyes to the ceiling where mother's eyes were fastened and brought hers down, looking sternly into them. Mother understood and looked dejected at the failure of her efforts. But Father tried to dispel her dejection:

'We have money, thank God,' he said quickly, 'We have a *qat*[1] plantation and livestock as well.'

I was aware that my father was trying to impress me with his power; at the same time I was also aware that my maternal aunt had gone off to the mountains (carrying five *dinars* of my own money), to reserve Aneesa as my bride.

After having spent six years (a third of my life) on the seasonal work circuit, being paid the minimal daily wage and suffering bitterly if any tiny mistake was made in the Accounts Section of the Department of Agriculture, I had been finally confirmed as an agricultural labourer. That was six months ago. During the last six months I had been able to save some money, the amount of which I have only an approximate idea, since my mother is the treasurer with whom I deal.

My father says he has money and, in fact, he is not boasting. He is,

---

1. The habit of chewing the leaves of the narcotic plant, *qat*, in Yemen usually takes place after lunch and sometimes through the early hours of the evening. *Qat* is usually chewed in company and the practice involves a great social and, in higher circles, cultural exchange which may include the reciting of poetry and anecdotes.

however, driving at something else which my mother and I instinctively understand. Thus, I am working and saving my money so that I will be somewhat independent. If I achieve that I can perhaps suggest to Father that he relieve himself of the burden of dominating us. That suggestion, of course, may not be received seriously in the shade of the tombs where the men of our village like to relax and chew *qat*, especially after lunch.

But still I had worked hard and saved, motivated by my desire for liberation from my father. From those savings I had taken the five *dinars* in order to reserve Aneesa for myself.

'Aneesa,' her father told her, 'a fine young man is asking for your hand.'

'Does my mother know him?'

'He's the one who bought cigarettes from you on Friday when I was at the mosque.'

'I don't remember him. Is he from Jihaf?'

'No, no – he's from al-Azariq, from a good family with a reputation for being well off and respectable.'

The days passed slowly after my aunt had spoken for Aneesa. I felt as though I was under a good deal of pressure, waiting for Aneesa on the one hand and, on the other, finding my head full of helter-skelter fantasies about other girls, the daughters of drummers and garbage men: Saida, Amina and Qabul – each of them less attractive and more available than the other.

'Here are fifty *dinars*,' I said to my father, touching his beard respectfully and adding, 'I want to get married.'

He shoved me away at first; then he took the money and added, as though divulging a great secret to me,

'You know, marriage costs a great deal. You're not marrying a drummer's daughter.'

He sold a cow and a calf, borrowed a hundred *dinars* and set out for Mount Jihaf accompanied by my paternal uncle and my mother's prayers. At Mount Jihaf he met my maternal uncle and aunt who had been the ones who spoke first for Aneesa. Aneesa's mother, however, made excuses. She didn't want to marry her daughter off in such a hurry, she said; Aneesa had not yet reached puberty, she said; she had not yet had her fourteenth birthday.

Later, I found that Aneesa's mother had said the same thing to my aunt earlier, but my aunt never told me, nor did she ever return my five *dinars*.

It had started this way. One day my aunt came as usual to visit us. Since I was at home I couldn't avoid meeting and sitting down with her, my mother and my two younger sisters. First she had talked about various topics but then she introduced the subject of marriage, in particular, recent marriages in her own village. I got up to leave so as to avoid the inevitable next steps in this discussion. At this point, my aunt would usually begin to make jokes about marriage and refer to our own family. If one of my sisters' names were raised, that unfortunate girl, the butt of the jokes, would find herself a wife whether she wanted to be one or not. In this way, three of my sisters had been married off. Because of this, I always rejected the idea of marriage in front of my mother and aunt. And since I, personally, did not want to obtain a wife through the machinations of someone else, no matter who they were, I pretended to shrink from getting married at all. My mother and my aunt, for their part, took my rejection seriously since such was the prerogative of mature males, but I used to daydream constantly of marriage wishing, if it were possible, to have all the girls of the village.

So that day, when my aunt began to joke lightly about the subject of marriage, I decided to leave immediately; however, she was ahead of me, squeezing me between my shoulder and neck.

'You've grown up and put on airs, have you?' she said in a tone that was both teasing and reproachful. 'Why don't you ever visit us? Do you think Jihaf is too far away?'

It became obvious to me that she had already carefully prepared the matter of my marriage and was about to get the better of me. I had to apologize for not visiting her and, of course, that led to my agreeing to visit soon – which really meant that I was agreeing to facilitate her goal of marrying me off, of solving my own growing preoccupation with the subject. In my boundless naïveté, I had felt I was above my aunt's sympathy. I was fed up with being single, fed up with myself and my stupid fantasies about marriage and choosing my wife in my own way, yet all this time my aunt had been preparing the whole affair in a manner one could only envy. No sooner had she extracted my agreement to visit than she began carefully to lay the yoke of marriage around my neck.

'When are you going to get married?' she asked me.

I smiled at her like a virgin girl, answering the question in practical fashion by going to visit her.

It was pointless to feign indifference and pride under the illusion that I could myself map out the way to the goal of marriage. For I am not such a unique person in our village that I could defy the customs by which it had abided for ages. Thus did I persuade myself to accept the yoke which my aunt was fastening around my neck; in her teasing way, she was reminding me both of my age and her plea for me to visit her, then making a connection between the visit and the prospect of my getting married. Thus did she make sure that the first inevitable step on the long road toward the goal of marriage would be attributed to her.

My aunt suggested to me: 'There is a girl who passes the house every morning on her way to school. You should sit by the lote-tree so you can see her when she goes by.'

It was half-past six. I left my tea and went out. I waited by the tree a whole hour for that girl. My aunt stood in the doorway of her house, signalling to me the direction from which the girl was approaching. But no sooner had the girl seen me, than she turned down behind my aunt's house as though to escape a wild lunatic on the road. I left my spot beneath the tree and walked in the opposite direction from the girl's so I could confront her face to face, only to be bitterly disappointed by her plain looks. Would to God I had never left my tea! Would to God I had never waited! Would to God . . .

But, somehow, the news spread throughout the village that I wanted to marry this girl whom I couldn't bear to see. I was filled with annoyance and rage. The rumour spread from village to village until it re-echoed in the mountains around our village of al-Azariq. This did not throw me into despair, however. I had come to a decision. I went to visit my aunt again, but this time of my own accord. I had made up my mind to get married and to ask my aunt to help.

This time, my aunt called me urgently to the rooftop. 'Do you see her?' she asked.

I could not see anything clearly, but I understood at once what she meant. 'What about her?' I asked.

'Do you like her?' my aunt returned.

'I can't see her clearly,' I answered.

But by now, I had become really serious. My aunt, however, was a resourceful woman. She had never been lacking in quick, spontaneous solutions to new situations, such as mine. She simply suggested that I go to the store owned by the girl's father and buy two pounds of sugar. My aunt said she was sure that the girl herself would serve me since the shop was parallel to the house, the father was at the mosque for the Friday prayer, the mother at the well to fetch water where she would no doubt be delayed, and that left no one at home except the girl and her little sisters.

So I went, and called out the name of the shop owner, the girl's father, just as my aunt had told me to do. After I had called many times, Aneesa did, in fact, come out. I was dazzled. I was completely taken by her, I found myself wishing for her, actually desiring her at that very moment. Forgetting all about the two pounds of sugar my aunt had asked for, I asked for cigarettes – five of them. Aneesa handed them to me, taking my money and, at the same time, my heart. The thought of leaving her dismayed me, so I tried to prolong my stay a little.

'Fifteen *fils* each!' I stammered clumsily. 'That's a lot. How much do you sell a pack for?'

Considering my aunt's previous attempts to reserve this girl for me, Aneesa obviously viewed my speech as flirtation, so it was not surprising that she should reply, harshly and firmly:

'Do you want your money back or do you want the cigarettes? We don't sell full packs.'

After this incident it was, as my aunt said, perfectly appropriate that I should agree without hesitation to follow my aunt's first step with a second step. It was then that I took fifty *dinars* from my savings and placed them in my father's hands, asking him to arrange my marriage with this girl, Aneesa.

The marriage contract took a very long time to work out, many times as long as the distance from our house to where the girl lived. The working out of the contract was characterized by the exercise of coercive pressure and power plays on both sides which, after a while, began to seem more important than the actual marriage. In spite of all our work, Aneesa's father resorted to evasion, refusing to make a decision on the grounds that his daughter was too young, that she had not even reached puberty. My father countered with the logic of one who didn't care whether the girl had reached puberty or not. Aneesa's father in turn tried to use his wife's opposition to the marriage as an excuse. But my father did not allow him to seek refuge in this feeble ploy, pointing out that a wife could not be allowed to impose her will on the husband, that the deciding voice in the marriage of both sons and daughters had always belonged to the father alone.

Why did my father go to such pains on my behalf, since the girl had not yet reached puberty? It turned out that the motive behind all this manoeuvring was Aneesa's great value in the kitchen, at the well and among the livestock – which I discovered only after our marriage. As for the children she would bear, I did not think about that at the time – there was something else involved between Aneesa and me, more important than any future children, something that could take place without them – that *had* to take place or else I was afraid I might succumb to the enticements of the drummer's daughters.

The girl's father then retreated and pushed forward in another direction.

'The dowry for my daughter will be high,' he declared. 'Your money couldn't possibly pay for all the milk she has drunk.'

I wavered momentarily between Aneesa and that cow which father had already sold; for a moment, I found I was unable to move a single step. The cow, after all, was expensive also and, in addition, gave milk rather than just drinking it. Father, on his side, proceeded to check this new move made by the girl's father.

'The amount you name is too much,' he said. 'Two hundred *dinars*! That's a large sum,' he added with irritation.

As for me, I found I was still fluctuating between the cow and Aneesa; that image of her which had dazzled and bound my heart to her had vanished from my mind. But my father said, almost defiantly, 'Such an amount as you're suggesting is against the law.' With this he restored Aneesa's place in my heart and erased that distorted image of her evoked by the cow.

Her father's face darkened but, suppressing his anger, he spoke again,

'And what is the sum which the law states I should receive if I should give my daughter to your son?' he asked in a voice strongly tinged with sarcasm.

His tone made me feel weak at the knees. But my father countered sharply,

'You're not going to give us your daughter for nothing,' he said scornfully. 'A hundred *dinars* are enough for you, and that's according to the law.'

'A hundred *dinars*!! Well, all right. We won't disagree. But come back after two years when the girl has reached the legal age.'

He rose quickly as if to leave the group, a group large enough to fill my uncle's house on this happy occasion, though my uncle seldom received guests at home.

As the girl's father rose to leave, I felt my mind begin again to confuse Aneesa with the cow. My father had sold his cattle in order to marry me off. He was very proud of those cattle from which he derived his power over us. Was Aneesa's father's stubbornness an indication of his pride in her too? Certainly, that was acceptable. But did he wish to use his daughter as a means of gaining power over my father?

All during these discussions the guests had cheered either for my father or for the girl's father – according to which family or village they belonged. Those who were related to my father agreed with him even if they were not from our village, and those from our village, even though they were not from our family, also supported him. The same was true for those from Aneesa's father's family and village. Now one of the guests, a man from Jihaf, intervened:

'What's your *final* demand?' he asked the girl's father.

'Two hundred *dinars*,' Aneesa's father answered emphatically.

'That's your final demand?'

'Not one *fils* less!'

The man turned to my father.

'And you, how much will you pay? How much can you pay?'

'What the law states,' my father replied.

'Why bring in the law now?' the man asked. 'The law is one thing and your son is another. You have to choose: either the law or the haven of marriage; either the law, then, or the girl.'

'But the law itself is a haven,' said my father. 'The law is for everyone, for me and for the girl, too.'

I threw myself into the heat of the battle. But the others shut me up roughly and blew me away as though I had no more substance than a feather. I shrank back, ashamed, and told myself I would be content just to watch and listen.

'I want him to chop something off the amount,' said my father finally, after a pause. 'He's better off than I am. He's got two *qat* plantations and a shop besides. And he has five younger daughters who'll bring in five more good dowries, with God's blessing.'

After a long argument, involving discussions between the members of each side as well as discussions within the larger group, the girl's father agreed to reduce the dowry by twenty-five *dinars* – if, in exchange, I would buy the bride a ring, a gold necklace and a pair of earrings. My father cried out in protest! I, myself, was amazed, wondering why the girl's father had laid down a new condition – the purchase of gold, directly after accepting a reduction in the dowry. I could not understand all this at the time, for everything was becoming mixed up together: Aneesa's father confusing her with the gold; my father, on his part, also confusing *me* with this gold. The members of the group on my father's side were confusing the dowry with the law, and those on the side of Aneesa's father were confusing his greed with the idea of married love. In this process, I found myself seeming to merge with my own father, Aneesa seemed to merge with her father, and marriage itself had become equated with all sorts of tactics and trickery. Whom was Aneesa going to marry? It appeared that it was my father. And for whom would Aneesa produce children? It appeared that it was for her father – this was all part of the strange confusion that seemed to be developing. It also appeared as though my father was going to marry Aneesa's father, and the one would produce children for the other. Now, because of Aneesa's father's last suggestion of my buying gold and the opposition to it by my father, the deal was put off once again.

'Let's exchange concessions,' said my father finally. 'I'll make one and the bride's father can make one.'

The girl's father took one step forward and another backward in front of my father and, grudgingly, said he accepted the idea of both sides making concessions.

Then it was my mother's turn to put her foot in it, along with the multitude of other feet that had been involved on the road to my marriage to Aneesa. My mother decided to prepare two sets of clothes for Aneesa, according to her own taste. She took the first lot over before the wedding: two dresses, a head scarf, a *meyzar*, and a pair of stockings.

'The stockings must be expensive ones, because they're the first thing a man's eyes fall on,' my mother explained to me matter-of-factly.

Thus, in her turn, she had participated in the overall confusion: the stockings, the gold, the cow and Aneesa on the one hand; and men's eyes and money on the other. Money. Yes, money! High prices, the cow and the cow's udders; high prices, gold and the guaranteed value of gold; high prices, the stockings and my mother's ideas; high prices, men, my mother and Aneesa, the gold, the cow, the stockings, the eyes, the feet, the udders, and people's ideas. All of this blended into one flaccid jelly-like mass mixed with the juice of *qat* – and it rolled back and forth from one pair of human jaws to another as the men sat chewing *qat* in the cool shade of the graves, both on the flat plain of al-Azariq and in the high mountains of Jihaf.

For the afternoon of the wedding day, we had reserved two full rows of *qat* in one of the *qat* plantations near us. That cost us twenty *dinars*. It happened that the day of the wedding coincided exactly with the time to pick the *qat*, which guaranteed its freshness. But so many extra guests arrived that we were forced to raise the sum spent on *qat* that day to thirty-five *dinars*! That sum constituted the last step but one on the road towards Aneesa. But it had been preceded by a great many other steps, all lost now in the whirlwind of my anxiety and fatigue which had accumulated during the six months following our first speaking for Aneesa – six months I had spent suspended between waiting and preparing for Aneesa on the one hand and, on the other, contemplating running away from the increasingly heavy burden posed by Aneesa, to the daughters of drummers and garbage men. Still, on the night preceding the wedding, I stole nothing from the drummer invited especially to play at my wedding, except his drum. I wakened my two younger sisters and banged out joyful tunes on the drum for them to dance. My joy was like a tall green tree growing and flowering in my heart. My heart itself was a broad plain, ploughed, planted and irrigated with happiness. The mountains surrounding this plain of my heart were my own veins alive and filled with hot blood that pulsed strongly with the melodies of my joy, melodies loud enough to waken the whole village and the surrounding villages as well. I could hear different voices full of emotion echoing here and there: a woman's ululations, a child's crying, a dog's barking and the crowing of a rooster – all of them sharing my emotions in different ways.

We had slaughtered a cow and two lambs for the wedding day lunch. This, minus the cow we had sold, left us only two cows and a suckling calf, though we did still have a good number of sheep and lambs left. We had also killed a goat which one of my friends had given for my wedding, in return for a similar gift I had given him. The guests crowded in . . . and a dreadful malaise crept over my body, riddling me with anxiety, making me drag my steps heavily. Where had all these guests come from? And who had invited them? I had no inkling about that at all, just as I had no inkling whatsoever about how much money I had actually deposited in savings with my mother before the wedding. Perhaps it was my mother who had had something to do with these successive waves of guests – I say, perhaps, since it was only a possibility.

The cause of my nightmare of anxiety – the arrival of so many guests – in the long run, however, helped to bring about some relief and contentment in me. How? Some of my male relatives suddenly wanted to bring the bride away from her father's house, although it was still early for that, only three o'clock in the afternoon. This was a pleasurable prospect. But, on the other hand, I had just begun to feel at ease with all the guests during the afternoon *qat* session, so my relatives' suggestion about the bride disturbed me a little. I felt torn in two. The problem was that I did not know how to chew *qat* properly and how to get the most effect out of it in the shortest time possible; the anxiety was having a more powerful, numbing effect on my body than the *qat*. I kept thinking that if only I had time to get a proper fix of *qat*, I would overcome my worries and forget the huge amount of money we had spent on the *qat*, both before the wedding and now. The guests were distributed through several rooms in two large neighbouring houses in our village. I had to circulate among them all to make them welcome and create a relaxed and friendly atmosphere (and I had begun to feel content with this role). Still, my male relatives' suggestion to bring the bride early gave me a sense of pleasure.

271

It was completely in harmony with my longing to see Aneesa and to give myself over entirely to her after the long and tortuous road I had followed to reach her. This feeling of pleasure also coincided with my desire to break away from the nightmarish strain of the wedding. What a joyful moment that would be, I thought, after the long hours of anxiety and fatigue! But now my relatives suddenly decided to wait till four o'clock to bring the bride. I wanted her and did not want her at the same time, but I could do nothing but listen and wait until Aneesa, yes, Aneesa arrived at last.

She came well wrapped up – as is usually the case – covered from the top of her head to the soles of her feet. That bundling up of her and my own timidity prevented me from feeling any pleasure at all as I looked at covered-up Aneesa on her wedding night surrounded by an alluring accumulation of women's heads and breasts. I wondered if they had clothed her in one of the two dresses my mother had bought for her or the *meyzar* and the stockings. She had so many layers of wraps that I could not see what she was wearing at all. Even so, it was now quite clear to me that there was a tremendous difference between the cow we had sold and my bride Aneesa!

Aneesa's mother was calling on me to put incense in the incense burners in the bride's room. This, I knew, was not only to exhibit her pride in her daughter, but was specifically designed to exhibit me, the groom, to give the women of my bride's mountain town of Jihaf a chance to look me over. This little manoeuvre destroyed the rest of my self-possession. Picking my way to the incense burners among the women's covered-up legs – soft and warm legs, most certainly – which filled Aneesa's room, I nearly collapsed from sheer embarrassment. I felt as though my whole body was being pricked by arrows, suggestive looks, shots from the women's eager eyes: their whispers inflamed my fantasies and almost overcame me.

I did not have even a glance, however, for any other beautiful girl, even one ready to swallow me whole, clothes and all. I was concentrating only on Aneesa, my mind completely absorbed by, and blended with her. Together she and I stepped over the slaughtered body of the goat that lay on the threshold of our house.[2] This was the last animal but one which we

2. The practice of stepping over the slaughtered body of a goat or lamb is performed anywhere in the Arab world, not just in Yemen. In some Arab societies, particularly in the country or in the small towns, the animal is slaughtered as a thanksgiving for recovery from sickness or the safe return of a loved person or, as in the case above, for summoning grace. The meat of the slaughtered animal is usually, but not always, given to the poor.

had slaughtered for the wedding. After we had crossed over, I felt as though the greatest anxiety of my life had been lifted from my shoulders. That anxiety only gave way to a greater anxiety that began almost immediately, however, and marked the start of my life with Aneesa, the girl I had finally married after expending a huge amount of money, selling or killing a number of valuable livestock and purchasing an awesome quantity of *qat*, and after facing difficulties more frightening even than the expense! In the face of this new anxiety my joy receded and all that remained was a white cloth awaiting the sign of the bride's virginity,[3] that little bit of blood that would be shed legally; the glorious wedding shrank and became nothing more than a mishmash of the blood, bones and meat of slaughtered animals, of the twigs of the expensive *qat*, its leaves and its juice. I myself dwindled down to a mere male, a young bridegroom waiting for a bride to take off her veil and layers and layers of heavy wrappings. Aneesa herself seemed to have become nothing more than a black veil and a bundle of cloth. And the room shrank and became the hooves of the slaughtered cattle or the silver coins we had spent. Even the village of al-Azariq diminished to a shady tomb over which grass and weeds and thorns grew.

When we were alone in the room my mother had fitted out for us, Aneesa refused to take off her veil. She insisted on my paying up first.

'They'll demand the sign of your virginity tomorrow morning!' I reminded her, in a low voice.

She wept. To calm her down, I promised to pay and she stopped crying and held out her hand. I thought she had given in, so I took her hand, but she quickly and forcibly withdrew it. After a moment, she repeated her demand for fifty *dinars*. I realized then what strangers we were to each other and tried to speak gently to her so I could remove her veil myself. But she drew back from me in alarm.

'Don't forget,' I reminded her, 'tomorrow morning they'll demand the sign of your virginity.' I was distressed for her but also, by this time, for myself.

She started crying again, more loudly this time, insisting more strongly on the fifty *dinars*. I felt totally perplexed. It was a large sum, but clearly it was going to have to be paid. Then I realized that, with this fifty *dinars*, she would recover double the amount in the dowry her father had conceded to my father, the amount for which the gold jewellery was supposed to be a substitute. I pretended to be angry and made a quick

3. The habit of showing a white cloth stained with the bride's virginity blood (as proof of her good moral behaviour before marriage) has been prevalent in Arab society from time immemorial, but is now dying out in more urban circles.

motion to snatch the veil from her face. She jumped to her feet, which completely upset me. I realized I had to pay up and accept this as a *fait accompli* but, first, it seemed there had to be a bargaining session with my bride to get her to remove her veil.

Well, we bargained and we finally agreed upon the sum of twenty-five *dinars*. I stuck my hand in my coat pocket, produced the amount and gave it to Aneesa, who then removed her veil to reveal two cheeks wet with tears. I felt suddenly a deep compassion for her and the roots of my love for her stirred deeply in me, spreading out to fill my heart. I drew near in order to take her in my arms, but she shrank back in terror.

'They're going to demand the sign of your virginity tomorrow morning,' I repeated gently.

She looked at me with eyes as terrified as though I were a wild hyena about to devour her. At that look, I felt defeated, unable to demand any more of her. She appeared more distant and difficult to attain now than she had been before the marriage contract had been signed. But, well, that didn't last long. When I discovered myself actually beside her, I was soaking with perspiration and Aneesa was crying and begging and resisting me to the death.

Later, I could not even remember how the coverings and wrappings on her had all come off. The only thing I remembered was the terrible failure of my efforts – three successive attempts to finish off the marriage between the time we had come to an agreement and the break of dawn. This failure crushed me. By the break of dawn, I was so exhausted I fell asleep. And then my body was visited by fleeting nightmares – one after the other, of anxiety, fatigue, failure and the cool shade of the village tombs. Ah, Aneesa!

Translated by Olive Kenny and Elizabeth Fernea

Abu Rubbiya

A few raindrops were falling as I stood in front of the shop shivering with cold. But those drops did not bother me; what concerned me was, why was he late? Upon a wall I could glimpse his latest drawing, finished yesterday – the drawing smiled. How nice this Abu Rubbiya was . . .

I sat on the steps of the shop and collected my memories of him. Three years ago I had been sitting in the small square in front of our shop when he came walking up sedately, looking at the ground, kicking stones with his foot. He seemed to be in deep thought, as if something was bothering him. When he saw me, he smiled and said, 'May I sit down?'

I laughingly replied, 'Why not? This square is God's domain.'

He shook his head surprisedly, looking at the square and at me. 'Is anything in this world left for God? I am amazed to hear you say that. People have swallowed God's rights. This square is the government's property and you, here, represent the government.'

I laughed heartily – I, an elementary-school pupil, represented the government? What an odd idea!

'Sit down, Abu Rubbiya,' I told him.

'How do you know my name?'

'Is there anyone in Addis Ababa who doesn't?'

He sat beside me and his small cane began tracing lines that quickly turned into a comic drawing in the earth. He inhaled deeply, staring at it.

'Listen, what is your name?'

'Saeed.'

'Do you attend the community school?'

'Yes,' I said proudly. 'I'm in the fifth grade.'

Abu Rubbiya was thirty-five, dark-faced with deep-set eyes and a mysterious smile that seemed to mock people.

'Listen Saeed, can you tell what I've drawn?'

'It's a donkey.'

He tapped me on my back gently with his cane, saying, 'Look closely.'

All that lay in front of me was a donkey. When I stared harder, however, the head began to resemble a well-known person.

'That's Bajahsh!'

I laughed – the picture now looked just like him.

'But why is he a donkey?'

'His name is Bajahsh,[1] and he is also a donkey. He would not give me a *rubbiya* yesterday.'

He was silent for a while, then asked, 'What would you like to be when you grow up?'

I replied quickly, 'A merchant.'

'Ass! Don't you know that merchants are a bad lot? You want to be bad like them?'

'No, I want to be a merchant so I can help the poor.'

'Ah son, all of them said they would help the poor when they were young, like you, and today they all have lots of money. They have forgotten everyone else.'

Then he asked if I wanted him to draw me something else. His cane sketched quickly on the ground. Mountains, a sun, people and more donkeys began to appear, as well as other things which I could not identify.

'What's that, Abu Rubbiya?'

'Your country.'

He went on drawing and drawing as sweat poured down his face. Suddenly I saw a tear roll down his cheek. He was staring at his picture, then turned suddenly and gestured towards the distance.

'You know your country is out there? It's beautiful! Full of mountains and trees, sun and valleys. How would you know, you're too young . . . haven't you ever been to Yemen?'

'No.'

'Then how would you know . . . Listen, you must go to Yemen! What are you doing here in someone else's country?'

I did not answer him. I knew my father's country was far away. I had heard my father speak of my grandfather whom I had never seen, and of brothers I had never seen. I had heard my father's friends mention so many things – gold, newspapers, things I did not understand. I whispered to Abu Rubbiya, 'Listen, Abu Rubbiya, what do the newspapers say?'

He banged on the ground with his cane. 'Newspapers! They are all lies,

---

1. The meaning of 'Bajahsh' is the 'father of an ass', *jahsh* meaning an ass.

my son, don't believe them. They're greedy. If you have money, they'll honour you. If you don't, no one will even greet you. Listen, Saeed, why do all the Yemenis emigrate? They are cowards! They couldn't stay in their own country, so they ran away from it, left it to the bastards. Don't you see, they began emigrating a 1000 years ago, maybe more . . . they said the Ma'reb Dam was destroyed, and who destroyed it? A little mouse? See, they are liars, they destroyed the dam with their corruption, then failed to build other dams and ran away. God says, 'Saba[2] had in their land two wondrous Edens, one on the left and one on the right: eat from your Lord's blessing and thank Him. It is a good country and He is an indulgent God.'[3] Yes, Saeed, we had a good country. And haven't you heard of Balqis?[4] You're still young, when you grow up you'll understand everything. Balqis was the first woman chosen leader by the people. See how far our civilization had come? And what do we have now? All of us have run away, leaving our women at home.'

He sighed deeply and continued, 'Yes, we have gone to seek our livelihoods in other people's countries, when our own country is full of gold. God said in the Koran there was no place better than our country. Ah, a paradise . . . but it yearns for people, it yearns for its men.'

We became friends. Often we visited the homes of the rich, so he could draw their portraits on the walls. One person was drawn as a goat ramming a rock with his horns. We would sit back while the people examined the pictures, laughing, 'You know, Saeed,' he would whisper, 'if I were to go to Yemen, I would be rich.'

2. Saba is the Biblical 'Sheba', the region in southern Arabia which includes Yemen and Hadramaut. Its ancient inhabitants established a kingdom and a culture long before Christianity and Islam. Among their monuments was the Ma'reb Dam whose ruins are still to be seen not far from Sanaa, the contemporary capital of North Yemen. The bursting of the Ma'reb Dam is described in folk legend to have been caused by a mouse which made a hole in a strategic spot in the dam, causing it to burst. The Holy Koran blames this on the corruption of the people. Verse 16 of chapter XXXIV mentions this explicitly: having been advised by God to render thanks to Him for His bounty, they turned away, and so God 'sent on them the flood of Arim [the Ma'reb Dam] and, in exchange for their two gardens, gave them two gardens bearing bitter fruit, the tamarisk and, here and there, a lote-tree'.
3. From verse 15 of chapter XXXIV.
4. Queen Balqis is the Biblical Queen of Sheba who is said to have visited Solomon in the tenth century BC. Her visit is described in the Holy Koran in verses 22–44 of chapter XXIV. The ruins of her ancient palace are still to be seen not far from Sanaa.

'And you would forget the poor people?'

He would laugh heartily, saying, 'No, I wouldn't forget. In Yemen one is in his own country, but here we live in a foreign land. They can tell we are strangers. It's a shame how they say, "Look at that Yemeni walking barefoot in torn clothes." But what can we do? God has given rich people hearts of stone.'

And we would go our own ways.

Despite our friendship, I did not know where Abu Rubbiya lived. Each time I asked him, he would answer, 'My friend, God's land is vast.'

'But you said that people had taken God's land.'

'That's right, don't be upset – the Government's land is vast.'

Abu Rubbiya took pains to draw people he disliked in various ways. He once said, 'You know, Bajahsh gave me five *rubbiyas* today.' Then he added with pride, 'But I refused them, so they won't say I am greedy. I took only one *rubbiya* from him.'

Rain was still falling. The drawings on the wall looked like they were crying in the rain. The road was empty, save for a few carriages rushing by.

Where was he? Something must have happened to him. For three long years he had never been late like this. Only once had he been absent, when he had an illness. He had looked terrible then, losing weight till he was as thin as his cane. Next time I saw him, weak and pale, he had apologized. 'What am I to do? God afflicted me with sickness.'

I had once asked him why he didn't work at a regular job.

'You're still young, you don't understand. Don't I work every day? I thought you were mature enough to understand drawing as an art . . . listen, drawing is the best work in the world!'

'Yes, but it doesn't feed anyone.'

'Who wants to eat? The important thing is, people feel good when they see my drawings. People often wish they could describe this or that merchant as a donkey or a dog. But they can't. In my drawings I can and no one can tell me anything.'

'Why not?'

'You know how if you tell someone he's a dog, he gets angry? Yet you can draw him as a dog or donkey, people laugh, and he is not upset. This is human nature. When you grow up you will understand everything.'

But Abu Rubbiya did not return. A week went by and most of his drawings were erased from the walls. Only a small one was left, and it was one he had made for me . . . Once he had asked me again, 'What would you like to be when you grow up?'

I had answered quickly, 'An artist.'

The little picture was of me, with a brush in my hand. He had written my name under it.

Suddenly, I heard my father's voice. 'What's the matter with you? Every day you're out there. The cold will kill you, do you want to die? Come on inside or I'll teach you a lesson!'

But I was gazing out into the streets sadly. When I went in, my father sat at the table balancing his accounts. I asked him, 'Do you know where Abu Rubbiya is?'

'They deported him.'

'To where?'

'To Yemen.'

'Why?'

'Because he's crazy.'

Five years later I left Addis Ababa for Aden. Amidst the noise of a coffee-bar in the Shaikh Uthman area, I sat one day sipping a glass of tea. Suddenly I caught a glimpse of my old friend.

I called out, 'Abu Rubbiya! Abu Rubbiya!'

He turned to me but, before I could reach and embrace him, he had run outside. I ran after him, but he disappeared into the crowds. He wore tattered clothes, his feet were bare and his face looked miserable.

The coffee-bar owner asked me, 'Where do you know him from? He's called the Madman. He sits every day scrawling on the walls, making pictures of people that look like dogs.'

I said, 'He is not mad.'

'Then why doesn't he look for work and be kind to his own stomach?'

There was nothing else to say.

Translated by Lena Jayyusi and Naomi Shihab Nye

Brother, Pay Up and Get Out!

It was morning. I was feeling tired and did not go to work, especially since I knew for certain that the children were going that morning with their mother to their grandfather's house and I was going to be home alone to enjoy a normal day, away from their noisy playing and away from work.

No sooner had everyone left the house than I went straight to bed. It was winter and mornings were very cold, while the bed was warm and cosy.

A few moments passed and I began promising myself a wonderful day of calm and meditation, and perhaps even of reading. This was a privilege I had not enjoyed in many years. For how can a man read when he comes home from work always feeling tired, with four children around him, each one an edifice of trouble and disturbance?

Suddenly, I heard knocking on the door. It began calmly, then took on a kind of stupid insistence.

I thought at first it was one of the neighbours wanting something. I got up, cursing the failure of my one attempt at leisure. But the voice behind the door sounded harsh and sombre. A chill ran down my spine. I wished that my wife and children had not left the house.

When I opened the door he was standing there, wearing a long turban on his head. His rifle hung from one shoulder and his tunic was hitched up like a miniskirt. I noticed also that he was barefoot.

I was struck by the hoarseness in his voice.

'You must report to the police station!'

'Why? What's the matter?' I murmured calmly.

'Get over there and report, I said!' he answered without looking at me.

'But why? For what reason?'

'Don't ask why!' he shouted into my face. 'And don't get cagey!'

I felt the blood surge warm in my veins. My chill disappeared. I closed the door on him.

'Tell me why, and stop shouting,' I said. 'There have been no problems whatsoever between me and anyone else. Why should I go to the police station?'

The knocking resumed, this time vehemently. His voice roared and I felt he was about to break down the door. So I re-opened it. He was screaming so violently that I understood very little of what he was saying, but I could pick out some phrases here and there:

'He's reviling the Government! . . . He's insulted an agent of the State! . . . Everybody, come and see! . . . He has slammed his door in the Government's face . . .'

First children gathered, then women; then, some men began to watch us with curiosity. The policeman did not give me a chance to speak, but grabbed at my shirt and tried to drag me outside.

At this I abandoned my former calm and began to shout: 'Fellow Muslims, look! This man is violating my house! You are all witnesses! There is no more respect for people's privacy in this country!'

And he, in turn, shouted, 'You're insulting the Government! Who do you think you are? Who do you think you are?'

People interceded between us. Words flew this way and that, everyone trying to find a solution to the problem without really understanding what was happening.

After a short while I found myself completely uncertain of what to do. The policeman had taken the initiative and was acting as though he was the offended victim, while the bystanders pleaded with him to be good and kind to me.

Voices told me: 'Go with him to the police station.'

'Why are you afraid to go with him?'

'He does represent the State; you *have* to go with him!'

'*I'm* the one who's being oppressed, you God's creatures!' I shouted in their faces. 'There is absolutely no problem or quarrel between myself and anyone else to call for my going to the station. Yet this policeman comes banging on my door first thing in the morning without even telling me why!'

Now the policeman shouted, 'How dare you close the door on me! Who do you think you are? Who are *you* to disobey the Government? Or did you think there was no government at all? By God, if it weren't for these good people, you'd see what I'd do to you!'

People intervened again. 'Come on, man,' they told me, 'let's all go to the station together and see what the matter is.'

I found myself accompanying the policeman in my night-shirt. He walked ahead of me, his head proud and high, while men from the neighbourhood walked behind us, followed by the children, who were whistling and laughing all the while.

We reached the police station and I found myself in the middle of a group of the policeman's colleagues. As soon as they heard his story they began to buffet me about like some plaything. We did not get to the official in charge until I was in a most lamentable state.

'What's happening?' shouted the official.

'Sir, this man refused to report here!' the policeman said. 'Instead, he reviled the Government and insulted me in front of all these people!' He pointed at the people who had come with us to the station.

Without asking anyone, the official screamed in my face, 'Who do you think you are? Here, here – put him in chains and lock him up!'

One more time the policemen began to shove me around. Some of my neighbours now interceded with the official, pleading with him that I was a good man and the responsible father of a large family, that I had been out of sorts and had not meant what I'd said, etc., etc.

After I had already been put in chains and my clothes were all torn, the official called me back.

'What's your name?' he asked me.

'Fariᶜ Ali Saeed,' I answered.

'And why did you refuse to report here?'

'I did not,' I assured him. 'All I said was that there were no quarrels between me and anyone else, and that I was very surprised at being summoned without any apparent reason.'

The official turned to the policeman and asked, 'And what did you want with him?'

'Sir, it was you who asked that he be brought in.'

'I? Why?'

He started to think. Finally, he exclaimed, 'Ah!' and began searching among the papers on his desk.

'I asked you to bring in Fariᶜ Ali Saeed, the butcher, who people complain has been selling beef and calling it baby veal!'

Then he turned to me and asked, 'Are you a butcher?'

'By God, I am not a butcher,' I answered as firmly as I could, 'and have never been one. I have a haberdashery shop in the market. Everyone knows that.'

The official asked the policeman how all this had happened.

'Sir,' he explained, 'you asked me to bring in Fariᶜ Saeed, and when I made inquiries about him everyone pointed out this man's house to me.'

'But I told you he had a butcher's shop!'

'By God, I don't know!' the policeman answered. 'I asked, and everybody told me it was this man.'

Whispers could be heard among those present. I myself was about to drop from exhaustion.

At last the official ordered, 'Unfasten his chains and let him go!'

'And what about the fee, sir?' asked the policeman.

The official jabbed his finger at me and said, 'Come on, now . . . Pay the fee for unlocking your chains, and then you can go.'

I tried to protest, but one of my neighbours nudged me toward the door.

'In God's name, Brother,' he said. 'Pay up and get out of here!'

Translated by Lena Jayyusi and Thomas G. Ezzy

Abd al-Hameed Ahmad   UNITED ARAB EMIRATES

The Palm Tree Said to the Sea . . .

PRELUDE

I gave the palm tree my solemn promise I wouldn't tell anyone what she said to the sea; but today I must break that promise because it may be very important for you to know what it was she said. With nearly ten years passed, I don't think her conversation with the sea should stay locked inside me any longer.

Let me confess, first of all, that I ventured to break the rules of good manners by eavesdropping on the palm tree as she told her story. I kept the secret of what I heard for a long time, until the knowledge of it began to weigh on me and there was no way out but to reveal it. What spurs me on today is the feeling that death might suddenly strike me so that you'd never know what the palm tree said to the sea. There's no lack of death these days and it's cheap too.

A NIGHT AND A WITNESS

One night, when there was no moon or star, the solitary palm tree bent towards the shore and began to tell of the things she'd seen and heard and lived through. This is what she said, while the calm sea listened with dignity: 'The two of them would come under cover of night, when people were asleep and the life of the village was still, and they'd stand here beneath me, talking together and exchanging words of love. I listened to their talk with veneration and awe, thinking they must be two angels or *djinn*, and I loved them for their honesty. Let me tell you their story and entrust their secret to you, so that you can keep it safe in your depths.'

At that moment, I remember, some impulse had drawn me towards the sea and it happened that I was near the palm tree. I sat down on the sands, hidden by the night, and listened, even though I felt I was intruding on secret talk.

The palm tree continued:

'The first night they came, he said to her: "You know, Salma, how much I'm suffering. If it weren't for your love, which binds me to life like the roots of this palm tree, I'd be among the dead."

'And she said, her eyes wet with tears:

' "But things haven't gone well for us. I'm bound in marriage to another man, Salim; that's what they decided for me and, if I didn't love you as I do, I wouldn't risk coming to you every night."

' "You remember what happened," he said, "when I went to your father to ask for your hand in marriage. He wouldn't consider it; I was just a common sailor, he said, who owned nothing but his loin cloth. So you became the wife of the captain."

'Salma's heart was beating and her face was sorrowful. She said: "For all that, I and my heart are yours for ever."

'She wept, and her voice broke, as she added: "How could I ever forget the days we used to play on the seashore, you and I and Shaikha and Khalfan and Mariam and . . . ?"

' "Listen," he said in a purposeful voice, "we're setting sail tomorrow, with your husband as the captain. I give you my word, that one of us won't return."

'She trembled with fear, and said: "If you don't come back, I'll kill myself."

' "Last year," he said, "Khalfan hid a pearl, and the captain saw him and burned his chest and back with a flaming torch as a punishment. I can still see Khalfan writhing and screaming with pain. It was a dreadful sight, Salma!" '

DEPARTURE AND DEATH

'Salim embarked and they sailed to the heart of the Gulf. Salma still came every night to think of him, she'd feel he was close to her and burst into

285

tears. After four months the divers came back, but Salim wasn't among them. One day, so I learned from Salma, when he was ill and had no medicine, the captain had insisted he should dive down into the sea. So Salim plunged down and stayed under the water for a long time and, when they brought him out, he was only half a body. So the captain threw him back to the water and the fish, ignoring the entreaties of his comrades.'

Then I heard the sea break his silence, and say: 'I remember that. They threw him to me and I found he had no legs or eyes; so I embraced him down in the depths till he dissolved into sand and water. If I'd known there was someone waiting for him, I would have thrown him up onto the shore.'

The sea stirred, his calm turning to a tumult of waves. The palm tree said to the sea:

'Don't reproach yourself; you're not to be blamed for anything. I heard Salma one night, overcome with misery and grief, calling on God, and entreating him: "Oh God, take vengeance on my husband the captain, who forced my father's hand so that I was taken from Salim and given to him; and who then turned and killed Salim." But she didn't, sea, say anything about you. Her father, so I gathered from her, was deep in debt to the captain and, when he couldn't pay his debts, the man asked him for Salma in marriage and was given what he asked.'

BIRTH ON A NIGHT OF LOVE

I was so drawn to this story which the palm tree, in pain and anguish, related to the sea that I simply had to listen on to the end. The tree said to the sea:

'I'll tell you a secret, which I hope you'll guard in your depths and never throw up onto the shore.'

The sea grew calm again and lay smoothly at the foot of the palm tree. Then he said:

'Tell it to me. But for you, I'd know nothing of this world of land.'

'On the many occasions Salma and Salim visited me, their meetings weren't lacking in innocent exchanges of love. Then things developed between them as life might wish in its heart and in obedience to their curbed longings. Let me tell you what happened one night.

'The sky was clear and a bright moon shone in it, but Salma looked

286

grave and sad while Salim was angry and bitter. Desire, however, was surging within him.

'He said to her:

' "You're very beautiful tonight, Salma, like this moon; and sad too, like this palm tree standing alone here in the desert."

'She blushed, her lashes quivering, and answered:

' "Let me gaze into your eyes and dream of stars lighting other skies than ours."

'He took hold of her trembling fingers, then they fell, entranced, onto the earth; and she bore him a son who, as I learned from her later, she called Saeed.

'Salma was proud of him, and happy at what had happened that night – the night before Salim made his journey to you and never returned. Later she died, of grief and sorrow.'

THE PALM TREE READS INTO THE FUTURE

'They were wonderful days,' continued the palm tree, 'for all the cruelty and hardship that was in them. I came to love Salma and Salim very much, because of the passionate love they felt for one another, like my love for the soil which warmly enfolds my roots.

'But, sea, I'm afraid today, anxious and unable to find rest. The days of comfort and security are over.'

'Why?' asked the sea; and he gave her his full attention.

The palm tree said to the sea:

'Although the earth was thirsty, almost parched with drought, it was once full of palm trees and fruit. Then, after just a few years which flashed by like lightning, I found myself alone, with only those two tender lovers to ease my gloom. But all too quickly they departed too, like the palm trees that death had swallowed up. Sudden terror had struck us and we'd been made desolate.'

'Where did all this come from, palm tree? And how?'

'They found plenty of oil in you.'

The sea cried out, protesting:

'It's useful to people. It doesn't do them any harm.'

'It's useful or not, according to how they use it.'

There was a silence, broken only by the sea breeze and the sound of my own breathing. Then she said:

'I only came to tell you this today so you could think about what I said and remember it. You're strong, sea; they can't bring you to your death, as they've done with us. My heart aches for Salma and Salim; and what grieves me still more is that their son Saeed's become a stranger. I don't know him and I don't know where he lives. They say he lives in the city.

'I've presumed a good deal on your time, I know, and perhaps I've caused you distress. I'll say goodbye now and, if I don't see you again, you'll know that I've joined the world of Salma and Salim. Please keep what I've told you as a secret, forever.'

The palm tree began to shake her trunk violently until exhaustion overcame her. Then she grew calm.

WORDS BEFORE THE CONCLUSION

I've told you the story; now let me introduce myself. I'm a young man working as a salaried employee and I live on my own in a district of endless noise and hubbub. There are a lot of houses round me, scattered here and there, with Indians living in them and Pakistanis, and Koreans and other people too – I don't know where they come from. My life used to be pleasant and easy. When I'd finished work, I'd lie down and rest for a few hours in the afternoon, then at night I'd stay up till first light with a group of friends I happened to meet. I thought of getting married, but my finances didn't allow it, so I decided to stay single and enjoy my bachelor life – a life which was unspoiled by anything till I eavesdropped on the palm tree that night, and her words began to trouble my heart and conscience. When she found out that I'd heard the story, she was upset and made me promise not to repeat it to anyone. But what she'd said tormented me so much that I decided to reveal it, which I've done now for the first time. It may disturb you too, when you hear what it is I learned. It's a secret that ought to be revealed, even if the palm tree didn't think so.

I didn't understand why the palm tree was afraid and, although I've never seen a palm tree that was any use to anyone, I was still concerned about her fear. One night, when I was standing on the shore, I glimpsed a flame that was throwing its light from somewhere out on the deep, dark sea, as though a huge dragon had opened its mouth and started breathing out a mass of flames. Could this be the reason, I wondered? And has the sea been despoiled like the land?

DISCOVERY AND PROTEST

Before I end the story of what I heard and lived through, let me tell you what happened to me.

One night, totally drunk, I was leaving a haunt I'd started going to a little while before, to escape from loneliness and fear and to search for something or other that was stirring in my doubt-ridden mind. I know I didn't choose a good way to search for it, but the effort had exhausted me and I'd almost lost all sense of identity. That night I scanned people's faces, searching for myself. Their faces were strange and their voices rattled on meaninglessly, like things clattering in a tin box. Suddenly the palm tree's words came back to me, and then I realized. I was Saeed – Saeed, who was conceived on a tender, moon-filled night of love beneath the palm tree! Saeed, the sad and solitary stranger!

I ran frantically towards the sea, looking for her. The palm tree! I didn't find her. It seemed her prophesy had come true.

Bitter sorrow welled up in me as I thought of my parents, Salma and Salim, whom I'd never seen, and a sudden sense of terror flooded my whole being. I began crying out to the sea, which was spread out there in a deathlike calm, till my cries were scattered over the water and through the night air. I turned back, tired and distressed and alone, to be swallowed up in a night that was starless and inscrutable.

EPILOGUE

Note: 'I should have written this conclusion 100 years after writing this story, or 200, or 300, or more' – Abd al-Hamid.

The grandmother was sitting in a corner and the children were listening eagerly as she told them a story.

'Once upon a time,' she said, 'long, long ago, there was a people who built a civilization. The country was really rich for many years but dangers assailed the people, from inside rather than outside; corruption set in, boring into the proud edifice like woodworm eating into the trunk of a tree. And when the first blow came from outside, it collapsed and became a mere collection of relics, a place to which people made pilgrimage and wept.'

One of the children interrupted her:

'Didn't a mother tell her son, when the collapse was near: "Weep like a woman over the heritage you didn't protect like a man"? That's what they teach us at school, grandmother, if this is the same story.'

'Since you all know the story,' said the grandmother, 'off you go to bed, I'll tell you another story tomorrow, one you don't know.'

The children yawned and the grandmother fell silent.

Next evening she sat with the children round her as usual and started telling them a story.

'I don't know whether you children can believe that a palm tree talks; but one day a palm tree told the sea a story, and I'll tell it to you, so that you can pass it on to your friends.'

The children's interest grew.

'Go on, grandmother! Tell us!'

'Once upon a time,' said the grandmother, 'there was a solitary palm tree, and one night, when there was no moon or star, she bent towards the shore.

'The palm tree said to the sea . . ."

Translated by Lena Jayyusi and Christopher Tingley

Khlalah SEL

'Khlalah[1] SEL came.' 'Khlalah SEL's gone.' 'Have you seen Khlalah SEL?'

He arrives every morning, steps out of the car, his clothes dirty and his face taut and dark, eyes small and gleaming like faint embers that glow and fade in a soft breeze. He walks slowly to his familiar seat.

Khlalah SEL has acquired new qualities since the great change. Everything happened with amazing speed that not only astonished him but everyone else who had known the man and his former character. The children, particularly the school children, began to chase after him and call out his new name. In no time he'd become the current topic of discussion in every gathering, for some a cause of envy, of pity for others. As for him, he never understood what had happened to him; he had accepted it all with incredulous astonishment. His surrender had been like the surrender of a corpse at burial, or of a wounded bird caught in the trap of a cunning hunter. All of a sudden he found himself spinning in a new and different orbit, spinning at dizzying speed.

One day – a long time ago – the townspeople, particularly the old ones who knew Khlalah well, noticed that – contrary to what they were accustomed to expect – the man was sad and frightened; they'd never known him to be like that before. He'd always been happy in spite of his poverty. His small world held no secrets or sadness, and was open for anyone to see. But today they saw a different man in front of them. What had happened?

Moreover, where was Massoud? The absence of Massoud encouraged one of them to ask: 'Where is Massoud?' Khlalah looked at him with almost tearful eyes. In a husky voice edged with sorrow, he answered: 'Massoud! Poor Massoud, I don't know how I could provide for him.' And he fell silent, as did the others. Khlalah was sunk in a bottomless

---

1. A *khlalah* is an immature palm fruit, green and unripe.

pool of grief. For Massoud was not only Khlalah's best friend but his partner in life and work, and his only source of income. That was how folk saw the close relationship between them. Khlalah's compassion for Massoud was like that for a child; he cared more for him than for Khatoun, his wife. Khlalah never denied the true reason for all that care. With honesty he admitted: 'Without this donkey, I'd starve to death.' Of course everyone believed him.

In the courtyard Khlalah had built a tent out of palm fronds in which Massoud enjoyed warmth, plenty of fodder and date pits, rice and onions, to say nothing of the water that Khlalah changed for him every evening. Perhaps no other animal in the world was so well cared for as Massoud. Even his saddle was made of cloth stuffed with cotton to save his back from being galled. In the neighbourhood where they used to walk, the clatter of Massoud's hoofs raising a cloud of dust behind them, children used to run after them and hang on to Massoud's tail and annoy him. Khlalah knew how to protect Massoud from their mischief. He would stop, and so would Massoud, the picture of dignity with his russet coat, clear shining eyes and nimble body. And when they had halted long enough, Massoud like a statue with eyes fixed to the ground, the naughty youngsters would become bored and go away jeering.

The two of them would go out early every morning when the dew still hung in the air; in time they seemed to become part of the landscape. People could hardly remember a day when they saw the one without the other, as they roamed the streets looking for work.

Every morning, above the early call to prayer, Massoud's braying could be heard. Enchanted by his incessant braying, Khlalah would pray: 'You generous Provider, You who are merciful to all mankind, You who know what's to become of us, we rely on You.'

They were inseparable like a man and his shadow. People were used to seeing them together, Massoud leaving his droppings behind him in a straight line, his warm breath mingling with the cold morning air. They worked together, carrying people's belongings from the scattered houses to the main square, or bringing water, or doing the various other jobs that folk asked them to do. Even after Khlalah had persuaded the Balushi family to let him marry the bad-tempered Khatoun, and even after their children were born, he stayed loyal to Massoud; while Massoud stayed loyal and loving to Khlalah. In the evenings when they came home after a hard day's work, Khlalah – tall and slender as a lath – would stand at the edge of the well, bringing up water in a big pail to throw cold over Massoud. And when he'd finished he'd carefully dry his wet body and lead him to his tent where he would pat his head tenderly and bid him good night, after giving him food and changing his water.

So the sad heavy look that covered Khlalah's face one day puzzled the people. Some said:

'Maybe something bad happened to him or Massoud.' Others speculated: 'Perhaps one of his family is sick.'

But Khlalah kept silent, at times scrutinizing their faces, at times staring into vacancy. He was so sad he felt his heart was going to break. It was as if a nightmare or ghost was tearing at his heart to split it with a sharp poisoned blade. Still the folk round him insisted on knowing what was wrong. Then his eyes overflowed with tears, flowing like a stream in spate after a night of thunder and rain. Obviously hurt, his voice distressed, he said:

'You people ought to understand. I was working, so was Massoud. We were able to survive. But now! What next?'

One of them interrupted:

'We've told you that Massoud wasn't going to be any use to you from now on, why can't you believe us?'

As Khlalah trembled like one possessed, another added:

'Do you expect us to stop using our cars so you can carry our goods on your donkey's back?'

A third, trying to calm Khlalah down, remarked, 'Khlalah, the world is in better shape now, you will definitely find another job.'

Another observed gravely: 'The age of the donkey is over!'

But Khlalah sank deeper into his depression and fell into a fit of weeping; he felt as if he were being pulled deep into a bottomless pit, there to drown. He stopped listening to their talk, until a sentence pierced his ear like a bullet: 'The world has changed. Don't you realize that?'

Khlalah knew nothing, understood nothing, but the terrible new destroying sorrow looped around him like some fearful python squeezing at his ribs. All he knew was that after happy years which had passed as quick as lightning, all of a sudden he was jobless, his livelihood threatened; for the first time in his life he was afraid of starving. Massoud will starve and die and so will Khatoun and her children! And Khlalah knew no way by which he could feed them. Hunger and grief spread before him until almost all else was blotted out, like the legendary bird that spreads its wings to block the light of the sun, and so brings utter darkness. Then someone gave a parting shot:

'Do what all the others did, you might have luck finding a job in one of the government ministries.'

Khlalah's head ached as if bells were tolling in it. He stood there alone while darkness spread and formed shadows that increased his depression and bewilderment and fear. Work! Ministry! My God, how? I don't even know where the Ministry is! Then suddenly, having remembered something, he dragged himself off to his neighbour Khammas:

'Khammas! Do you happen to know where the Ministry is?'

Khammas laughed until the tears came. After a spell of coughing and sneezing he said:

'And why haven't you asked Massoud?' But, seeing that Khlalah was not his normal self and in no mood to bear with his usual banter, he felt his sarcasm was in bad taste, so went on:

'But which ministry do you mean, Khlalah?'

Khlalah's thin features filled with surprise, transformed into the face of a child caught doing the wrong thing by his father. Defeated, he said:

'The ministry where people work. Is there another one?'

The interminable conversations that Khlalah had with Khammas, and his later conversation with the responsible official he met at the Ministry, became the talk of the town and a subject for jokes. And when Khlalah took over his new job as caretaker for one of the schools, they asked themselves – and Massoud:

'What are you going to do now, Massoud?'

But this question was soon answered. In the morning, when the streets were full of cars and pedestrians and noise, Khlalah would ride on Massoud's back (he'd never done so before). Massoud would fight his way to the school through the traffic and noise with Khlalah resting upon his back. Khlalah would gaze at the shops on either side of the road, at the cars and pedestrians passing by, with eyes free of any kind of confusion or bewilderment – or, to be more precise, with eyes lacking any kind of reaction to any sight, whether common or uncommon. Massoud's hoofs played a tune on the asphalt. They, Massoud and his rider, were a pair of oddities, things from another world suddenly manifesting themselves among built-up streets full of people and shops and cars. Many who were curious about them to start with lost interest now that their daily walk to the school became familiar, and accepted them as a customary phenomenon. At first they seemed not to belong to this age but, later, they became a pleasant daily morning sight. Months passed in this new peaceful life till one day Khlalah was astonished to hear his old neighbours and friends asking him:

'We've heard your name on the radio. What are you going to do when you receive your compensation?'

He, Khlalah, compensated? He who had the reputation among his old acquaintances of always being full of energy? In fact he was named after the *khlala*, tough green date fruit that is ever young.

And as his head had begun to spin when haunted by fear of hunger, he was now frightened by this new mystery. What a time! Full of unexpected, odd and grotesque surprises! Khlalah had been encompassed by inquisitive looks when people found out about his earlier trouble, but now he was besieged with the news of a matter of which he'd been unaware. His mouth fell wide open like that of a haunted old well, enveloped by the silence of death. Compensation! Around him mad shadows of perplexity danced and jubilated. Idiots! Khlalah's peace of mind was lost; he was transfixed by worry and uncertainty. He asked, 'Khammas, what is compensation?'

Khammas answered jeeringly, in a tone not free of a touch of jealousy, 'They're opening a road where your old decrepit home now stands. You'll be compensated for it.'

Khlalah did not believe what had happened. His throat felt tight, as if he were to burst out screaming. His ears drummed; his peaceful way of life was under threat. He raised his hand and pointed to his house. 'But where would I live?' He heard a high-pitched laughter; Khammas was laughing sarcastically. Hateful laughter thundered in his ears. Khammas said: 'Don't worry. I'll arrange matters for you.'

But in Khlalah's ears the laughter kept echoing; it filled his days with uncertainty and fear of the unknown. But as it happened everything turned out quite differently from what he expected. He had never thought that things would be so much easier than he anticipated. To his surprise the bank manager came all the way to his home to see him, and told him cordially:

'We'd be pleased to receive the money on your behalf. It will be your money, and we'll keep it for you at the bank.'

Without thinking, Khlalah asked: 'Would it be 3000?'

The manager laughed. 'More like three million.'

Khlalah stammered like a baby. 'Mr Manager, what I really need is a house . . .'

Laughing, Khammas said: 'A palace, you need a palace, not a house.'

When Khlalah pushed open the outer glass door of the bank, wearing his yellowing *dashdasha* that had once been white, his old threadbare *ghutra* and worn-out shoes, the manager hurried to welcome him.

'Welcome, Khlalah, please come this way.'

The manager led both Khlalah and Khammas to his office. His employees rose from their seats and stared unbelievingly at them with wide open eyes. One whispered in a friend's ear: 'Can you beat that?' They could not believe that their peppery, short-tempered boss would get up to welcome a man who looked as poverty-stricken as Khlalah. Said one, 'It's a strange world!' The other replied, 'It's an age of miracles!'

When they returned home Khlalah was speechless. He looked round vacantly while Khammas remarked: 'Did you hear what the bank manager said? What a kind man he is, they're going to build you a house and buy you a car.'

However, Khlalah heard nothing but Khammas's thunderous laughter. He sank into a heavy gluey silence, his head blazing with turbulent thoughts, revolving round new, incredible, and seemingly insane calculations – confusing matters that he could not comprehend. And so Khlalah found himself drowning in new worries that tasted differently from those he used to have. He would begin counting – one, two, three, four – and then the numbers would get mixed up and he'd start counting again. People began to notice that the impoverished Khlalah, the ever-energetic, persistent and uncomplicated Khlalah, was turning into a confused worrier busily counting on his fingers, counting again and yet again.

While Khlalah was absentmindedly wandering around the streets like a tramp who'd lost his way, Massoud was roaming the new quarters of the city searching for food among the garbage dumped on the streets, sometimes pausing in front of the iron boxes outside the great entrance gates, often enduring painful blows from the angry inhabitants of the houses he passed by. He strayed far into the desert, where his eyes swelled, and tears mixed with dust dried on his eyelids. Boils and lesions filled with pus covered his body. And Khlalah, overwhelmed by new happenings, was stupefied by the strange unexpected events that swept over him like a torrential flood. His life was now organized into a new routine. One morning, just before the students went to their classes as usual, they were surprised to see a gleaming, luxurious car stop in front of the iron gate. Curious to see who was in the car, the teachers, students, and caretakers gathered together, wondering if it were some senior government official or perhaps a minister come to visit the school for some reason. An Indian[2] driver got down to open the back door of the car. Suddenly their eyes opened wide with astonishment as they recognized Khlalah. Their bewilderment spread like fog. But Khlalah, wearing the same old clothes and the same old shoes, thrust his way through that fog to his usual chair. That day there was no donkey to tie in front of the gate as usual. Khlalah sat silent, oblivious to the commotion he had aroused. His eyes turned in

2. With the oil boom, workers were admitted into the Gulf countries to do all kinds of jobs; they ranged from high-ranking bank officials to drivers and daily labourers. Many Indians were among them.

their sockets as if looking at vacancy. The headmaster had to tell the teachers and students to go to their classes. At noon the car returned, white and gleaming like milk in the sun. Khlalah seated himself in the back and the car sped off, throwing up clouds of dust behind it. One of the students cried: 'My God, it's a Mercedes 500 SEL!'

As the car drove along the streets Khlalah's eyes roved over the different things they passed, in dumb amazement. Buyers and sellers, shops and lights and stores and buildings, Khlalah found it all unbelievable. Sunk in silence, he could not explain what was going on in his head. All that he ever did now was that, before the sun had dried the dew, he would go silently every morning to his car from the top floor of his new house which was hedged round with magnificent trees and many coloured flowers. He'd take a piece of dry cloth, pour water over it and start cleaning the windows and bodywork until the car shone in the sunlight like a child's beautiful toy. Then Raj would come to drive it back to school while Khlalah sat tranquilly in the back seat, gazing stupidly at the streets and people. His eyes, once small and bright, were now like fading embers wilting in still air. Then he would walk slowly from the car to his caretaker's chair.

A cruel tedium now governed Khlalah's days. Time did not exist, he felt only the presence of these strange and surprising happenings, which to him were a fantastic new world he could not understand. Khlalah took refuge from it all in silence and bewilderment. A persistent worry filled his thoughts, just like the smell, the horrible smell that pervaded his bedroom one morning. It woke him up feeling drowsy and nauseated. The smell was coming from a new building being erected next to Khlalah's fine new house. Khlalah couldn't stand the smell. It filled the air, his bedroom and his lungs, until it nearly suffocated him. He hastened to find Raj and banged at his door to ask about the smell. When the municipal workmen came to check, Khlalah had begun his morning task of cleaning his white car with a damp cloth. Then he saw that the workmen had found from where the smell came.

It was a decayed corpse, squeezed in between walls that had been built so close together that it could not get out. So it had starved to death, which had resulted in that terrible smell which interrupted Khlalah's sleep that fine morning. As the workers began carrying away the corpse to place it on the garbage truck to throw away, Khlalah finished cleaning his car. Raj came up and told him:

'Guess what, they've found a donkey there.'

When the source of the smell that had disturbed Khlalah had been eradicated, the car sped on its morning route, heading for the wooden chair at the school entrance. Khlalah faced the morning and the people with the same glazed glance and silent absence of mind. He sat down on his chair in a silence like the silence of death, but for the children's repeated cry, 'Khlalah SEL, Khlalah SEL', and the derisive laughter that hummed in the air like the buzzing of bees – Khammas's high, bitter, derisive laughter as he recalled what someone once said to Khlalah:

'The age of the donkey is over!'

But Khlalah still sat dazed in his chair with glazed eyes, in silence like the silence of death, like the surrender of a corpse at burial, like the surrender of a wounded bird caught in the trap of a cunning hunter.

Translated by Salwa Jabsheh and David Wright

Muhammad Alwan   **SAUDI ARABIA**

The Bridge

The little girl coughed harshly, coughed until tiny blue veins stood out on her small dark forehead . . . she sneezed . . . she wiped her cold nose with the back of her hand . . . Her mother said her nose, always running, was like the nose of their cow.

Tomorrow was market day and there'd be fruit – figs and grapes. She wouldn't be able to buy them all, she decided. Yesterday she had stolen a lot of barley from the family stores. So far her father had not noticed. As she bent to sweep the floor, she smiled to herself. She had been so proud when she gave that stolen grain to her friends. They had blessed her and those words of blessing, which they had learned from their mothers, had filled her with happiness. Today God would help her to creep into the storehouse again, this time to take wheat. The women who sold fruits liked wheat better than barley.

She thought, yes, grapes, I'll buy them and I'll eat them all by myself. The sweeping was done. She straightened up, lifted her arms, stretching.

'Go and stretch somewhere else,' her mother yelled from beside the fire, where she was burning incense before her husband came home from the evening prayer.

'Go on; don't show us how lazy you are. The night's just beginning. Do your ablutions and pray.'

She stood on the threshold, forgot what her mother had told her and, without thinking, stretched once more.

'What!? Am I talking to you or to the wall? . . . Stop that!' cried her mother.

The night is passing by. There is the old woman whose stories she loves, the tales about her youth, when the world was a better place, she said. Yes, it was true that life was hard, filled with poverty, but it was good, too. The little girl lifts her head up: 'Does this mean that now it's better than it was before?'

The old woman hugs her: 'Yes, better and, yes, worse . . . the body's rested now, but the mind is restless, anxious.'

The coffee is brewed . . . the ashes of the fire pile up . . . the little girl smiles . . . the old woman is fighting sleep . . . it tugs at her head, her hair, heavy with glossy cream; then she gives a start, her eyes are red. The little girl understands this gesture . . . it's a signal of the end of the evening.

'Goodnight.'

'Goodnight!' She goes down with the old woman, a small light in her hand. The child can hardly close the big door; she has to rest her back against it and give it a hard push.

The door to the storehouse is ajar. She can take some wheat now.

Darkness filled the house. There was a sound of coughing inside, the dogs were barking outside . . . the little girl in bed looked up at the ceiling of the room . . . she imagined that the wooden beams closely joined together above her head were a bridge that would carry her far away to where there were cars, an easy life and beautiful clothes . . . far away from cold winter nights and early morning risings. Far away from the cow and the land, the sugarcane and the logs of wood. She sighed and fell asleep.

The market was filling up with people, but their small house was crowded with men . . . her father was there; her mother's face was flushed from the glow of the oven as she went back and forth with the hot loaves of bread.

The sun stood in the middle of the sky. Men in the market began packing up to leave, harnessing their camels and donkeys. The number of people in the market began to dwindle.

At last the little girl came out of the house wearing her new yellow kerchief. It did not go with her dress which had been black but now was the colour of earth. She tucked the wheat into a corner of her dress and pulled her skirt up to hide it, revealing two thin legs that ended in two bare feet . . . they were black too, from henna, dirt and cold.

In the village children were milling around a beautiful car that had just driven in, a car with children . . . children and women . . . little girls of her own age who were whiter and cleaner than she was.

A sweet dropped to the ground from the hand of one of the clean girls in the car. The village children crowded around. One picked up the sweet and, smiling, handed it back to the little girl who had dropped it. The clean girl in the car smiled in return, but the mother shouted: 'Throw that away . . . one of them has touched it.' The village children! Torn clothes, runny noses and dirty hair. Poverty has made one of them look even uglier.'

'Mama . . . Mama . . . look at him, look at the monkey!'

The children inside the car laughed together . . . the village children regarded their 'ugly' friend silently . . . then went back to looking at all the shiny things in the market.

The little girl came to the last stall, after going round all the others. The fruit was all gone; the last woman had nothing left but a bunch of sour grapes. She wanted to give it to the girl free . . . but the little one shook her head. 'You mean you want to *give* me the wheat?' the woman asked in amazement. The child nodded and took the grapes.

The car was still in the village and the passengers were throwing fruit to the hungry children . . . they crowd around . . . one boy's nose is bleeding, he laughs, wipes the blood, eats the orange including the rind. The little girl looks at them silently. 'Take some,' they urge her, but she refuses . . . she eats the sour grapes instead.

Her eyes fill with tears. She is not sure why she is crying, maybe in disappointment . . . The car drives off, leaving nothing but a cloud of dust behind. The little one sees the car go over the bridge . . . but it is a broken bridge.

At home she found her mother milking the cow. She kissed her . . . then kissed the cow . . . The mother looked surprised but went on milking.

Translated by Lena Jayyusi and Elizabeth Fernea

Love and Rain

The rain was pouring down . . . the streets were filled with mud. Nothing could be seen except cars and lost donkeys standing here and there in places where they were protected from the torrents gushing from the sky.

One of the pupils cried out: 'Sir . . . Sir . . . the water is getting into the room.' The teacher interrupted the lesson, yelled at those of us who were close to the door to lift the mat so it wouldn't get wet. We jumped up quickly.

We were all waiting for the inspector who would probably turn up any time now, to announce the closing of school. If the rainy season arrived while we were still at school, we would get a long break while the rains lasted. We were filled with glee although, of course, at such times our mud-brick homes were hardly places of comfort and security.

In a few minutes the inspector arrived and whispered some words into the teacher's ear. We knew what they meant. The teacher collected his papers, and turned to us. 'School break!' he announced.

Soon we marched out of the classroom to the large gate. It got too crowded as we hurried to get out and our clothes were getting wet. Voices broke out in unison: 'O compassionate one, O Provider – God, give us rain to drink, and give to all Muslims, O Lord, forget us not.' Windows in nearby houses were opened, heads of men and women peered out, their tongues wagged: 'Go home. Go home, for God's sake!'

We scattered, each to his own house. I knew the punishment that awaited me, so I walked very slowly. But there was no one at home. Where was my mother? Not here, thank God . . . I stripped off my wet clothes, went to the kitchen and put two large sticks of wood into the stove. They ignited and began to blaze. I dried my clothes before the fire. And then my thoughts carried me away. From one place to another, from the present to the past to the future. And in my travels I encountered many people and many things. I passed them by. I felt I had an uncanny ability to combine place and time and hold them for a few moments in my mind.

My mind stopped, however, at Hadba. Aah me, Hadba! Such a figure and such sweetness . . . and what manners! A jewel around the house, as my mother had told me. The only thing my mother cared about in a girl was that she should know how to cook and clean the house. Oh, Hadba! On top of all her other charms, she could read and write and now had a sixth-grade certificate. She was one year ahead of me in school. But this did not seem to matter. My mother had once laughed when I mentioned Hadba's studies to her, 'A woman is a woman,' she said. 'She will always end up cleaning and breeding.'.

'Aah, Hadba . . . Is it possible that she could love you?' I asked myself, 'when Ahmad and Nasir and Saad are hovering around her? They have fine clothes, the like of which your poor mother is unable to provide for you . . . and you refuse the clothes that people give to your mother as charity because you are, as she said: "Like your father. You won't accept charity even though you die of hunger." But, to tell the truth, when I utter Hadba's name, I feel warm inside. Why not pass by her house to tease the boys? I have nothing to lose. Perhaps they'll get angry, but isn't that what you want?'

This dusty garment is not good . . . this black one is the nicest . . . the best of your tattered possessions. True, it hasn't been washed for a long time. The rain has stopped, the water is streaming into the valley. Well then, wash your garment yourself . . . hang it out to dry till the time of the afternoon prayer. I shall put it on and try to saunter past her house as the others do. She stands at the door, so she will see me. Maybe I will attract her attention. My black garment will indicate my composure and, with it, I will wear the white *ghutra*. But the shoes – all I have are my gym shoes. Still, they will be more attractive in her eyes than black patent shoes. She will say to herself: 'This is an athletic young man.' Perhaps she really will admire me and toss me a glance or two. And after all that? . . . After that I shall return home. The Lord did not create the world in one day. God save us from expecting too much too soon.

I finished washing my black gown. I waited a long time until it dried. Then I put it on. Blast my luck . . . the thing is missing three buttons! I remembered I had a big collection of buttons in my school bag. Here they are, only they are grey and the gown is black. Still, she won't be able to see them at that distance. My sewing effort was a success, except for one small detail. I sewed the buttons on with red thread. I put on my *ghutra* and my shoes.

Then I strutted proudly down our street. How long the street is! Should I run? No, that's not proper! What if she met you in the street on her way to visit someone? Your dignity would be lost if she saw you. Take it easy . . . here's her house . . . and there goes your heart beating faster. There's no one here, thank God! You're close to her door now.

You feel happy, but she does not appear. Well, I'll try another time. I heard Saad yesterday saying that he strolled by her house dozens of times. But as I turned to go back home, I saw her. A strange chill invaded my limbs. My heart seemed to beat louder and faster than before. She was with her mother. I thought, I shall bid them good evening . . . after all, I know her mother . . . sometimes my mother visits the family . . . to wash their clothes. I was now passing by them. The road was full of muddy pools of water, left from the rain. I greeted them, my heart beating fast . . . I felt my back freeze suddenly and a sweet sensation came over me. At last Hadba and I were near each other! I wished her mother would ask me for something. I heard a voice calling me. At first I did not turn around . . . I thought I was dreaming. Then I decided to turn quickly toward what I fancied to be the source of the voice. Yes, it was true. Here I was face to face with sweet Hadba and her mother.

'Is your mother at home?' her mother asked me.

I looked at Hadba, only to discover it was not her at all, but her younger sister! Thank God, I thought, I will walk back to her house. She will be alone. I had no sooner finished that dream than I found myself flat on my back . . . I had fallen in the puddle and was covered with mud. My gown was wet and filthy. Hadba's mother and sister burst out laughing. Then the mother got control of herself and took me by the arm, 'Bless you, no harm's done,' she said, consoling me and trying to make me feel better.

I got up cursing those puddles in my heart, ran hurriedly to our house and banged the door shut behind me to face my mother:

'Okay! Break the door! What got your clothes so dirty? And your school gown is wet as well.' I knew I was going to have a taste of the usual punishment, not that which is lashed on by the tongue, but over the whole body, administered with a sturdy stick.

The rain keeps falling . . . the days roll on, and I sit at home thinking of Hadba. Could I try to stroll by her house again? But, even if I did, her sister would be lying in wait for me . . . laugh at me if she knew about my feelings for her sister.

That night, contrary to her habit, my mother tidied the house . . . prepared a batch of bread. She filled the pot with tea and the coffee pot with coffee. This was after we had finished the evening meal.

I did not ask the reason for this sudden activity because the answer came of itself. 'Go and ask the Massoud family for a couple of cardamom seeds,' said my mother, 'Hadba's mother and her daughters are coming to spend the evening with us.' I tried to hide my great joy by continuing to write in my notebook. 'Didn't you hear me or are you deaf, boy?' I got up grumbling . . . with affected slowness.

Then I rushed off like an arrow. Our house was at one end of the neighbourhood and the Massoud family house was at the other. The only thing that used to terrify me was the narrow covered alley between them. But there was no choice . . . I had to go through that alley, it was the only way to their house. People said the alley was inhabited by *djinn*. I walked into that narrow street, my limbs cold with fear. I began to recite Al-Fatiha[1] and then some incantations against evil spirits. I sang in a loud voice. (Such rowdy singing, people say, will frighten the *djinn*.) I passed through safely. I got the cardamom from the Massouds. I ran back through that terrifying place as quickly as I could, saying Al-Fatiha again, and the incantations. How I wish I could learn the Yasin and the Kursi *Suras*[2] by heart, that would help. Suddenly I heard a terrible shriek . . . it was the dreadful howling of a dog. I ran home, trembling with terror. I told myself the dog must have been a *djinn* in disguise.

The *djinn* take many forms, my grandmother had told me. But this time I had escaped, although I had dropped the cardamom seeds in my panic. How could I convince my mother that I did not mean to drop them? In her eyes I am a liar even when I am being truthful. But when I entered the house, a strong scent greeted me. Perfume filled the house and sweet voices. The guests had arrived. Thank God! It seemed I was to escape punishment this time.

'Salaam to you. May God preserve you and make your evening pleasant. Welcome, welcome,' I said.

After inquiring after their health, I sat in a corner of the room opposite the mother. Hadba and her mischievous sister, who could not contain her giggles, sat beside their mother.

'Praise be to God, Misfir – What grade are you in now?'

'The fifth grade,' said my mother, 'and the good news, let me tell you, is that he has a job with a foreign corporation this summer.'

Habda turned to me, 'You mean you know how to read and write English?'

---

1. Al-Fatiha is the first chapter of the Koran and is read in prayers, when an engagement is agreed upon, and on many other ritualistic occasions.
2. The Yasin *sura* or chapter and the Kursi *aya* or verse, a long passage in the *sura* of the Cow, are two of the most often memorized Koranic passages, repeated by Muslims on occasions particularly needing the grace of God.

'Yes,' I answered quickly, lowering my gaze. The conversation ended with me raising my head shyly . . . English . . . English.

Her mother said, 'Misfir, tomorrow we are having guests. I would appreciate it if you'd go to the market and buy some fruit for us; I'll make it worth your while.'

So it was arranged. The next day I walked to Hadba's house with confidence. Saad and his friends were walking to and fro in front of her door, but I did not try to greet them. I simply looked at them haughtily. I knocked at the door and turned my eyes in their direction, a small smile hovering on my lips. The door was opened . . . I went inside. The letter I had prepared for Hadba – where was it? Here in my pocket. I'll give it to her as I leave . . . but how? What should I say? I did not even realize, as I stood beside her mother, that my hand holding the letter was waving at her. Hadba's eyes shone . . . she smiled . . . aah, how beautiful she was . . . it was a simple matter after all to give her the precious letter.

I had thought she would get angry or refuse. But she simply said, 'Who is it from? Maybe Saad?'

I felt a stab of pain in my chest . . . a great pang in my heart.

'Is it from Saad?'

I rushed out of the house, tears streaming from my eyes, the letter still in my hand. When I got home, there was nothing but a gloomy fire burning in the fireplace. My dreams had been scattered to the winds. I took the letter from my pocket . . . opened the envelope . . . saw the English letters. I had not slept the night before, but had stayed up to copy those letters carefully from the side of the milk can. I had wanted to be something great in her eyes . . . a superior human being. It had all been a lie and the whole thing had turned bitter for me.

I put a match to the paper; the flames devoured the letters and approached the last line which was in Arabic letters, 'God preserve you! Your sweetheart, Misfir.'

Ah well! She was not destined to see it. I gathered the ashes as though I were getting ready to bury my sweetest dreams.

Translated by Lena Jayyusi and Elizabeth Fernea

Abd al-Qadir Aqeel   **BAHRAIN**

The Elevator

I stood at the building's entrance and lifted my head to see a looming skyscraper. How and when did anyone ever manage to erect such a building? I remembered King Kong climbing an equally tall building as he clutched his beloved blonde.

I entered and searched the lobby's information board for the name of the company that had called me for an interview. I had submitted my application to them hoping for a better paying job to ease my monthly budget. It was my own fault I was in such a jam: I had married an ignorant woman who would never be employable.

I waited at the elevator. Four men and a gorgeous blonde woman were also waiting for the door to open. When it did, each man paused to let the woman go first and she entered, self-assured and smiling. The rest of us rushed in after her. My arm happened to brush hers which made my heart pound and my face moisten with perspiration. What kind of an idiot am I? I asked myself. Why didn't I marry someone this beautiful?

The elevator stopped at the fourth floor. I stepped off, leaving the other men to enjoy the musky perfume emanating from her clean and tender skin.

At the company offices, the receptionist welcomed me with a smile and gently asked me to check with the employment office on the twenty-second floor of the same building. I thanked her and returned to the elevator.

The door opened and I stepped in. This time I was alone inside. After pressing the button for the twenty-second floor, I was overcome by a sudden feeling of panic: going up in an elevator alone always unnerves me. What would happen if it suddenly stopped, or the electricity was disconnected, or a fire broke out in the building?

I closed my eyes so I couldn't see the blinking numbers of the floors. Taking a deep breath, I inhaled the blonde woman's lingering scent. I remembered my wife in her unkempt dresses.

Floors number 20, 21, 22 . . . but the elevator didn't stop. It kept going up. I punched 22 again, but the elevator halted at the twenty-third floor. I felt irritated as I waited for it to go down, but it refused to move as if it were forcing me to get out.

After I waited and it didn't move, I decided to try the stairway. I stepped out and the door closed behind me. Then I heard the elevator's humming descent. I shook my head in amazement and turned to look for the stairs. The entire floor seemed to be deserted. Where was everyone? Up and down the hallway were empty offices. I kept looking for the stairs and felt safer when I found them. I hurried down. But I gasped to discover a cement wall in the middle of the stairway blocking my passage. Back again to the elevator I went, cursing my wife who was my reason for being here.

I pressed the button, waiting for it to arrive.

A nervous loneliness filled my chest. I pressed the button again and again but nothing happened. I banged hard at the door hoping someone would hear me.

Half an hour passed and I was still waiting for the elevator to come, but there was no sign of it.

What was I supposed to do? How would I justify the delay for my appointment?

I searched the floor for another exit and found nothing but the silent elevator shaft and the blocked staircase.

An hour passed and I was still waiting. I kicked the lift furiously, placed my mouth on the slit between the doors, and screamed as loudly as I could.

Another hour passed, then another. I was losing my sense of time.

Exhausted, I thought again of the cement wall, how impossible it would be to break it. I pressed my face to one of the windows along the hallway, but was horrified to see how high above the earth I was.

It gave me minor comfort to think that the elevator must be out of order for one reason or another and that someone was probably working on it right now. If nothing else, the night cleaning crew should soon be arriving. I simply could not believe I would stay there forever.

But when nothing continued to happen, I broke down in frustration. I was on the verge of sobbing like a small child. I wandered frantically to the window again, thinking only of rescue. The sun was a yellow ball rolling down to sunset, while I was still standing on the wrong floor waiting for a door to open. I sat down on the carpet wearily, wracking my brains.

Had I been King Kong, I could have escaped. I could even have smashed this damned building onto its tenants. But, unfortunately, I am only a weak man.

Darkness stretched across the floor so I hurried to find light switches and began pacing. I screamed wildly and kicked the wall.

Suddenly it hit me: why not go upstairs? So far I had only considered my need to go down, why didn't I try the other direction? Maybe, then, luck would find me.

I climbed the stairs. A strange mumbling sound was coming from somewhere. It grew louder as I climbed. Then I was on the twenty-fourth floor, standing dazed before a large open area. It was very dark but thick candles illuminated the scene. In the middle of the room sat a plump frog on an enormous chair, while around him a party of naked women were performing sexy dances, their faces convulsed with hideous contractions. They separated and formed smaller groups of thirteen women each, rubbing filth on themselves. It made me sick.

When they noticed me standing there, I shied backwards. Then I saw the blonde beauty from the morning approaching me. Her filthy body shuddered in rhythm with the boisterous dancing. A forceful hand pushed me towards her and I stumbled onto the floor. Now all the women headed my direction with lustful fires in their eyes. They were hissing like snakes! Their faces kept contorting and grimacing and I hated their looks. I tried to scramble upright and push them away, but the giant frog startled me by leaping onto my chest. He hopped quickly to my face and covered it, suffocating me with his disgusting smell. I felt many hands undressing me piece by piece. I tried to upset the frog that was smothering me, but I was not strong enough. After a few seconds I lost consciousness and could not say what else happened on the twenty-fourth floor.

When I opened my eyes, I saw the beautiful blonde again. Behind her were the four men from the elevator, staring at me disapprovingly. I realized I was stretched out on the floor of the open-doored elevator, so I immediately rose and reached toward the blonde lady's neck, as if she could tell me what had happened the previous night. Frightened, she withdrew, but the four men jumped at me and pushed me out of the elevator. The blonde lady stayed on with them.

I left that building slowly, dragging my feet, taking deep breaths. They made me feel alive again. I looked up at the skyscraper and saw myself as I truly was, a pathetic person, very feeble.

Translated by Salwa Jabsheh and Naomi Shihab Nye

Saeed Aulaqi YEMEN

The Succession

Morning rose over the capital and the great race began; suffocating crowds milling the aisles of the wholesale produce market, anxious living bodies of sweat and eagerness crammed together in the swirl of all their hopes. As the sun raised its head higher, throwing giant flames, the crowd intensified, cursed by the crush of routine.

Above this human mass, awash in the acrid odour of perspiration, loomed Haj Faríᶜ Salem, Emperor of the Market, standing on a raised platform, waving his hand. Gestures accompanied his ringing, self-assured tones and his hand prominently displayed its three gold rings. His expensive automatic watch reflected the rays of the sun against the faces of the poor, long-suffering peasants.

Into the mad throng slipped Fadeel, a peasant arriving from the countryside with his produce, trying to find a foothold for himself and trying to sell his produce. He merged with the crowd like an ant, the demands of his wife Khadija and her children cutting wide, crazed pathways through his brain.

But Fadeel felt hopeful, nevertheless, imagining a new set of clothes to replace his torn rags. His body was gnarled and brown from years of scorching rural sun. Pushing hard, he advanced slowly towards Haj Faríᶜ's platform which monopolized the wholesale distribution of produce. At the moment that Fadeel arrived at the platform, all the crows in the area were croaking.

For five years, the same scene had been repeating itself . . . the suffocating crush, the sweat, the eagerness, the unrealized hopes, the scorching, cursed sun, and the rings and watch of Haj Faríᶜ. Faces grew more sullen as time passed and backs became more stooped. Even smiles died more rapidly before they could choose the faces that would wear them. Days

310

passed and nothing was accomplished beyond regret and growing wistfulness.

But tonight was different.

Tonight, Fadeel would not sleep until he arrived at a resolution which would settle his accounts with Haj Faric, who bought his produce at one quarter the price at which he later sold it.

Fadeel rented an old wooden bed on the sidewalk, stretched over it in sweet relaxation and began to muse.

His whole life passed before his eyes again, rapidly, without order, strangely as in a dream. He stared at it hopelessly as though it were incumbent on him to account for everything leading up to this evening. His life formed, disintegrated and reformed anew ... a continuous reconstruction of events.

Before this night, Fadeel had not really thought of his children, the future, or the miserable life they all led. He was like a windmill, turning each time the wind blew. He was also utterly illiterate, enough reason, he thought, to curse himself, his father and mother and the circumstances that had led to this, every time he had occasion to review the reel of his life. But tonight he engaged in a deep dialogue with himself, attempting to shake off old dust and sketch a new path for himself.

He muttered sorrowfully, 'My life is a waste – if I could just take a sponge and wipe off all that is behind me, all that I have heard or seen, then re-enter the great school of life and learn its genuine alphabet – how different and enjoyable my new life would be.'

He thought of the practical steps he would need to take. 'It would be necessary to incite the poor peasants against Haj Faric so they could gain their rights. We need a collective stand in the face of exploitation! We must do something to stop the sucking of our blood and the theft of the fruits of our labours!' And he sank into dreams all over again.

He saw himself with all the peasants behind him, proclaiming in Haj Faric's face, 'Down with exploitation!'

Then he would sprint up and grasp Haj Faric's neck, which turned into part of a limestone statue in his dream. He would attack the statue with his pickaxe until it smashed and collapsed to the rhythm of the peasants' slogans. Then *he* would sit on the statue's pedestal!

Sometimes the dream was different. He saw himself walking through the heart of the city after midnight, while everyone slept, on the road leading him outside the city to the cemetery. He would dig up the graves of the dead and recite inflammatory speeches to them ... then a mad tuneless symphony would assault his ears. It did not emanate from any instrument. And his vision would blur: Khadija and her frizzy hair

311

would take over with the demands that shot out of her mouth like bullets from a machine-gun. He would feel himself rushing at her, gathering her hair into his fist, silencing her lips with a hard kiss like movie stars did at the cinema. But he could not bear the smell of garlic and onions, produce he grew himself, that wafted from her mouth. He lifted his head with a sudden vehemence that awakened him from his dreams and stared at the wooden bed beneath him, wondering amazedly, 'How can I dream so much on such a bed?'

He rubbed his eyes lazily, while the last traces of dream swirled around in his head. 'The day Khadija cried, her tears cut deep grooves in my heart until it felt like a blood-soaked pit.'

Dawn caressed the roofs of the houses. The sun had almost risen. In the city dawn had a tepid taste, like left-over food or a joke which gives no pleasure, like the smile of a woman on the fortieth day after her husband's death.[1]

In the countryside, however, dawn had a distinctly special flavour, like cultivated earth after irrigation, or a full stable piled with cattle manure, like the scent of a boy baby on the day of his birth, or stark eternal truth, lacking all complication. This was the distinction that made country folk genuine human beings. In the country everything was capable of being understood, everything, despite its quietude. That was why a peasant's love for the countryside was limitless. There, and there alone, he could sense the origin of creation's flowering and extinction, as well as his own place within it. He could sense this with indescribable certainty, exempt from the burden of logic.

But how could the love of the countryside withstand the temptations of the city?

This was not something Fadeel contemplated lengthily. He simply said, 'Do you know what it is to be a poor toiling peasant? It means, simply, that one is engaged in an endless war with the merciless enemy called exploitation.'

Fadeel entered the market by its rear gate, determined to settle accounts with Haj Fariᶜ today. The market was unusually empty, except for some stragglers here and there. When he asked where Haj Fariᶜ was, someone told him the Emperor did not work on the day of the feast, since it was his own reception day, 'something only the petit-bourgeois can enjoy! Poor

---

1. The fortieth day after a person's death is a day of ritual memorial. People flock to the family of the deceased for renewed condolences.

people never get such lush food'. Fadeel had forgotten the feast fell on this day.

He left, more determined than ever to have a confrontation.

When the promised day arrived, everything happened suddenly.

The crush of people inside the market was enormous. They gravitated rapidly to a bench where a simple peasant squatted, speaking in a loud, inflammatory voice. Ears that before had only been fed talk about prices, grains, transport and crops now listened to new words from a strange man. He was inspiring them with hopes for a better life. The crowd began to repeat after him, in a mad expanding roar, 'Down with exploitation!'

Before a real riot started, Haj Faric escaped through the back door, the voices of the crowd blasting his old corners. The throng pledged allegiance to Fadeel as successor to Haj Faric and agreed enthusiastically to obey him and follow his leadership . . . exactly as they had once done with Haj Faric. Now they saw in Fadeel the saviour who had come to end their exploitation, to take them by the hand and help them achieve their hopes, buried by the dusty years.

Fadeel's words did not truly express reality, but they tickled reality with a chanting, contagious power. He threw his words out with ardour, repeating them until their sweetness dissolved in his mouth.

After Fadeel began controlling the market, he quickly learned to enjoy the reception on feast days – good food became his great pleasure.

Nothing much was accomplished for the peasants, however, because Fadeel was suddenly comfortable. He had begun to learn the secrets of the market-place and became skilled at running its little empire. He abandoned all his former principles.

After a year he had become a bad copy of Haj Faric. A clique formed around him, set up a salon for qat chewing and learned the intricate games of the market, subject to supply and demand, based on the exploitation of the farmers.

One afternoon Fadeel awoke from a three-year sleep, came out of the salon as usual, and started wandering aimlessly in the streets. Deep inside, he was determined to enjoy his new life to the hilt.

After ten years of marriage to Khadija – whose tears used to cut grooves through his heart – her image in his mind was transformed. Her features dissipated with his tumbled thoughts. 'How was I ever able to spend all that time with such a woman? She is superficial, empty, naïve

. . . she cannot see beyond her own two feet. Yet each time I determine to take a new wife, I am crushed by remorse.'

He continued walking amid the threads of his own woven net. Suddenly laughter erupted from deep within him: it floated high as a soap bubble. Then calmly it burst, scattering glowing silver threads across the faces of the passers-by.

He wandered to the Idrus Road and found himself standing in front of Haj Faric's house, knocking calmly, yet eagerly, upon the door.

'I don't understand how I was able to talk to those people that day,' he began, 'nor how they accepted my words with so much simplicity. Everything happened so fast, as though I were a sorcerer displaying juggling tricks. From one day to the next I found myself forced into your place and, despite my great amazement at what had happened, I have just now found a plausible explanation!'

Fadeel was trying to win over Haj Faric, to open a gateway for his subsequent address.

Haj Faric replied somewhat cunningly, 'The one-eyed man is king in the land of the blind. Those wretches were waiting for someone to open the gates of illusory hope in their dull minds. By pure chance you were that one-eyed king.'

Fadeel continued, speaking thoughtfully, 'Since the day that I succeeded you, I have been trying to convince myself that I stood on the edge of freedom and a new life. Only security betrayed me as I stared into the unknown. I was suddenly filled with terror such as I never knew before. At last I realized that my loneliness was the cause, and the only solution for that was marriage.'

Haj Faric was rather perplexed by this declaration, and they were both silent. The pause was charged with expectation. After a moment, Fadeel cleared his throat and, with all his accumulated sexual frustration, almost hissed, 'The damnedest moments of life . . . night-time without a wife!'

It seemed that Haj Faric now understood his intent, because he smiled broadly. The meeting ended with the reading of the Fatiha[2] for Fadeel's betrothal to Wadiaa, Haj Faric's daughter.

Fadeel emerged happy, realizing he had crossed the narrow road that separated the dazzling clarity of truth from the labyrinth of illusion.

Marriage to a city girl was the greatest thing Fadeel could attain. Now he

2. The Fatiha is the first chapter of the Koran. It is short and is recited on important occasions of either joy or sorrow. Here, it is recited to confirm the betrothal.

hoped to find the peace of mind which he had promised himself. But it kept eluding him.

In desperate attempts to regain the equilibrium he had lost, he plunged deeper into exploitation. No longer was it possible for him to hide behind the mask with which he had won the battle against Haj Fariᶜ. One of his friends advised him to be moderate, but he answered, 'Do not encourage people too much! Don't tell them we are all equal, that we have the same rights, or they will trample on you, steal your bread, and leave you to starve!'

Surprise was voiced by another man.

'This was not your opinion at the beginning!'

Fadeel answered, 'Opinions change every day according to the circumstances and needs of their bearers!'

Another friend asked him, 'Are you really happy in your life?'

He answered falsely, 'For the first time in my life I know happiness and I understand the uselessness of education for, without it, I have been able to achieve all I ever aspired to. Besides, I am more experienced and wiser in life than those who just have education.'

He swallowed the juice of the *qat* which filled his left cheek. A surge of arrogance flooded him. 'How, I wonder, did I get so wise?'

An educated man replied, 'If the fool persists in his foolishness, he becomes a sage!'

Before the circle broke up, Fadeel announced the good news of his intention to perform the pilgrimage to Makkah.

After Fadeel had engaged in one of the fits of sexual frenzy with his wife Wadiaa which overcame him after he chewed *qat*, he sat in the calm of night, talking to her. 'I have triumphed over your father, but he also defeated me with his defeat – he left me to drown in the seas of restless anxiety. No doubt he is better off than I am now.'

Before the hour struck midnight, Wadiaa's delicate nightgown would be ripped open again, and all the legends would pale beside the curves of her ripe tall body; the legends of slave-girls and incense, the ardour of love-poets – Abu Nawwas[3] and Khayyam[4] would fall short and Abu Rabiaa[5] would rip up all his poems.

3. A great poet who wrote about love and wine (among other subjects). He lived in the eighth century AD.
4. This is the famous Omar Khayyam, Persian author of the *Rubaiyyat*, translated into English by Edward Fitzgerald and others.
5. This is Omar ibn Abu Rabiaa, the most famous love poet in classical Arabic poetry. He lived in the first century after Islam (seventh to eighth centuries AD).

Fadeel was berserk on these occasions. He lost the reason which distinguished men from animals. He would pounce upon her, burying his nose between her breasts. With his tongue he would lick the drops of perspiration that settled beneath them, savouring the salty flavour in an ecstasy of carnal pleasure during which he imagined himself reconquering Andalusia,[6] piling up its women inside a giant stadium, to drown in the sea of their femininity.

After he awoke from his passion, he despaired again at his unsuccessful attempts to feel peaceful. He wished all the beautiful women in the world would die on the same day he died.

'If I had raided a bank, or stolen a million dollars, or killed a hundred innocent persons and escaped from the police; if I had planned a military coup d'état which failed, and eluded prison, my peace of mind would be greater than it is now, seated on the throne of the market, successor to Haj Fari[c].'

He begged the night to end his sleeplessness, his anxiety and torment.

After his return from the pilgrimage, Fadeel was seen in the market waving his hand to greet those who welcomed him back. Three gold rings glittered on his fingers and a new automatic watch graced his wrist. A poor peasant emerged from the crowd to shout, 'You are worse than your predecessor!'

Someone else tried to beat him up and, out of nowhere, a chanted slogan grew louder, 'Down with exploitation!'

Chaos reigned until Haj Fadeel's assistants were able to impose order again.

Haj Fadeel wondered how long he could escape the attempts made upon him simply by ignoring them.

Days passed ... crowded, scorching, sweating days ... eagerness and fettered hopes continuously revolving. Each new morning the desire for change was renewed. Each day hidden wishes for rebellion surfaced in the frowning, grim faces of the poor peasants, only to be swallowed again.

But one morning, into the breathless crush slipped Mansour, a peasant arriving from the countryside, seeking a foothold and a price for his

---

6. The Arabs ruled Andalusia or parts of it for over eight centuries, losing their final foothold there in AD 1492. The loss has never been forgotten by the Arabs, particularly because a great Arab-Islamic civilization flourished in this region, the largest in Spain.

produce. Like an ant he merged into the crowd and, pushing mightily, was able to reach Haj Fadeel's platform.

At the moment he arrived there, all the crows in the area were croaking.[7]

Translated by Lena Jayyusi and Naomi Shihab Nye

7. The croaking or cawing of the crow is regarded as a bad omen in popular Arabic culture.

Salih Saeed Ba-Amer   **YEMEN**

Dancing by the Light of the Moon

It was morning, the sun's rays came creeping over the mountain peaks. He sat on the stump of an old palm tree and watched her bend and squeeze her slender body through the fence, stepping with bare feet, avoiding the main gate. With both hands she parted the palm fronds that blocked her path.

She was nineteen, with a fair, dreamy face, honey-coloured eyes, rosy cheeks and a smiling mouth. Above her upper lip was a delicate tattoo executed by a skilled woman. She wore a loose, embroidered gown gathered in at the waist by a silver belt.

He waited silently until she sat on the ground in the middle of the cornfield. Mechanically, she began collecting the cobs into her basket. When he was sure she was absorbed in her work, he rose quietly and approached her. He hid in the corn and stretched out his hand, catching at her hem. He whispered, 'Good morning.'

She froze. Some cobs fell from her hand, scattering kernels. She turned startled eyes towards him, her hand to her chest.

'Sweilem?'

Nothing was between them but the basket she clutched.

'Yes. Sweilem, who's been looking for you day and night.'

Sweat erupted on her brow. 'Go! Go away before someone sees you!'

'Why?'

'I have to tell you this. Please help me –'

'Help you?'

'Circumstances have changed. You have to consider my position . . .'

'Which circumstances? What position?'

She looked at him through narrowed eyes. Her mouth opened, then shut again. Somehow she looked older as she spoke.

'We have to understand the realities among which we live.'

'You're different today.'

She stared at him searchingly. 'It's over between us,' she said.

'What *is* the matter with you? Have you gone crazy?'

'You have to understand. We were living in a dream.'

He bent his head and frowned, playing absently with the fallen twigs. She balanced the basket on her head and stood up. She shook the dust from her dress. Sweilem followed. He blocked her path. 'I'll be waiting for you in the square after the dance.'

She was quiet for a moment. Then she said, 'You haven't understood. You'll never understand.'

He tried to look into her eyes, but she turned her face away. He gripped her arm and held it tight. He tried to embrace her but she pulled away from him.

Later, while walking, she recalled again the confrontation with her father a week ago. Returning home from the dance, she had stopped in surprise outside the front door when she heard the gurgling of his water-pipe. 'Heavens! He's still up! What has happened?' She paused a moment before opening the door and going in. She found him putting fresh tobacco into the pipe.

'Father, you're still up?'

'Your dancing kept me awake.'

'Oh, we've had such a wonderful night!'

He watched her as she began to prepare for bed. She froze when he said, 'I hear you only dance in Sweilem's circle?'

'Yes.'

'Why that circle particularly?'

'It has good dancers in it.'

'And the other circle?'

'I don't like it.'

'Why not?'

'I don't like the dancers. They're old-fashioned. There's no warmth in their movements, and . . .'

'And you want to stay close to him,' he interrupted sarcastically.

'Who is "him"?'

'I know everything.'

She bent her head. A smile of relief touched her face as if she were getting rid of a heavy burden. But her father continued:

'I have to warn you against them.'

' "Them"?'

'Sweilem and his friends. They are trying to trap you.'

319

'They are *my* friends.'

'They are rubbish.'

'That's all in the past.'

'No. They are still rubbish! Put your illusions aside. You are very young and all this dancing has kept you from noticing a lot of things.'

She looked away. A knife turned in her heart. Her fingers played with the straw fringe of the mat they sat on as she searched for words to appeal to him. But he continued, 'You have to realize who you are, put your illusions aside!'

'Who am I?'

'You can't understand it. But from now on you've got to be careful or you'll be in danger.'

'Danger from whom? Those people you think of as rubbish?'

'If we give them room they will become dangerous.'

'They're our brothers.'

'You would have them for brothers? Oh, they've really poisoned your mind. What is it you like about them?'

'Their kindness. Their truthfulness. Their loyalty . . .'

'Their singing. Their dancing . . .'

He mocked her. She was quiet as he continued, 'You have to understand. They are not of your level.'

Suddenly he buried his face in his hands and pretended to weep, crying out brokenly, 'When will it be clear to you? When? When?'

He peered at her through his fingers. She hugged her knees, puzzled. He left her to her thoughts. She closed her eyes and thought about Sweilem: his words, his love-talk, his playful endearments, his concern for her. She thought of their circle, its haunting music still ringing in her ears –

'I know you love him. But Salem will help you forget him.'

'Salem?'

'Son of the Mayor.'

'No, no! I hate him!'

'Why?'

'Because – because he –'

'Because he leads the other circle which competes with Sweilem's. Didn't I say they've poisoned your mind and made you hate the ones closest to you? I don't believe it. All I've done for you will come to nothing.'

There was silence. Then she broke down and wept. He held her to him and kissed her forehead.

'You have to preserve our reputation,' he said gently. 'If you must dance, you've got the other circle.'

He waited. She dried her eyes and whispered, 'Father, whatever you say.'

She stayed at home for days – sad, tired, confused, not knowing what to say to Sweilem. Finally, she decided to face him and his friends and tell them the truth.

In the vast square washed by moonlight, the hills and valleys of the village echoed with a moving tune. Palms rustled as the laughter and dancing footbeats of the young people penetrated the night. It was almost as if the valley welcomed these youths and maidens thronging to the dance circles. Sweilem, in his group, was surrounded by friends. They sang, danced, and stamped rhythmically on the ground, with such force they caused cracks to appear there, as if the earth could open up and offer a solution to Sweilem's problem.

The spectators surrounding the circle were ecstatic. The dust from the stamping feet rose in clouds among them, mixed with the scents of sweat and perfume. A girl stepped forward to dance. Jamaan and Alyan drew her in. She embraced them and twirled around the circle. Her braids brushed their faces, her silver ornaments tinkled sweetly, and her breasts heaved. But Sweilem was preoccupied tonight – divided between the circle and his look-out for al-Zein. He listened closely to the chatter of the women, alert for the sound of her voice, but it was not among them. He was terribly nervous – heart racing, hands shaking, mind swarming with dark thoughts. He stared at the crowd. Surely everyone could see this in him. Surely everyone knew what was happening. He stopped singing and merely carried on with the formal clapping. He gazed towards her house, but there was no sign of her. Sighing deeply, he whispered to himself, 'Will she never come? Time is passing. It's after midnight. What a moon! We'll have our nights again. But I'm worried. Al-Zein would not deceive me, but what she said today at the fence shows some sort of change of mind. Did she mean what she said? No, no, I don't think so. But the devil could be working on her. He's her father and he knows her weak points, but he doesn't realize his star is descending. I never paid attention to all of that, but I do now. There's still time. She's al-Zein and I won't let her go.'

Totally lost in his thoughts, he was roused only when the dancing stopped. Some of the dancers rested on the ground; others walked over to watch the dancing in the next circle. Sweilem drifted over with them and there, in the middle of the other circle, was al-Zein. His face darkened, a web of intricate wrinkles appeared at the corners of his eyes. 'I don't believe it!'

He broke into the circle to drag her out, but six young men blocked him and pushed him back. Salem emerged from among the dancers. He wore fine clothes. A rifle was slung over his shoulder and his belt was studded with bullets. A gold-rimmed *janbiyya* hung around his waist. He faced Sweilem, 'Stay away from her,' he ordered.

Sweilem turned to him in surprise. 'What's that?'

'Isn't it enough you've messed about with her in the past?' Salem asked scornfully.

'What business is this of yours?'

'I'm her fiancé.'

'Her fiancé?'

'I've been waiting for her answer and today I got it.'

Sweilem stared, riveted, the words dying on his lips. He gazed at the crowd of faces surrounding them. 'But . . . but, al-Zein . . .'

Before he could complete his sentence, al-Zein cut through the crowd, took Salem's hand and led him back into the circle. Sweilem watched her. He bit his lip and hid his face in his hands. He wanted to weep, but he fought for control and said, 'I've lost her. But I haven't lost my circle.'

An eagle glided above the square. Dawn breezed in and the palms swayed. Sweilem returned to his friends and found them even more enthusiastic, more determined to win. He felt good. He smiled and nodded. He took the centre and held out his hands.

With the sun's rising, Salem's circle ended their dance, declaring themselves beaten.

Translated by Ahdaf Souef and Naomi Shihab Nye

Fawziyya al-Bakr   **SAUDI ARABIA**

The Lake of Nothingness

'What is there left?'

He said it wearily, knocking the ash from his fortieth cigarette; he'd been smoking them one after the other. The music from the cassette sounded like shrieks of terror. The smoke filled the luxurious American car. Was there no escape?

Suddenly – it seemed to pass in less than a second – he almost touched a car that flashed by close to him.

He straightened up quickly, feeling as if the defector in his soul had been viciously slapped awake. He smiled bitterly. Behind his evening trips, he remembered, there were the elegant men with their leather briefcases and the representatives of the foreign companies with their fat deals – and their commissions, which were even more tempting and desirable. Oh God, have mercy on us, quickly!

For seven years he'd been running without stopping. The imported workers. The glittering financial deals. The expensive parties given by the businessmen. First-class hotels. Luxurious seats in the planes, flying in and out of the capitals of money and business.

He suddenly remembered he was already thirty-two. His waist and buttocks were beginning to get plump. His sleep had been uneasy, he remembered, ever since he'd started this kind of work, and he always woke up feeling anxious. It was months since he'd given his neglected wife a smile.

He called to mind one of the girls he'd been out with – the last young thing they'd arranged for him on his business trip. That was how those amazing deals were finally approved – even though some of them should never have been made. Was there no escape?

The roaring sea sweeps everything before it. The old traces of childhood were being destroyed day by day – like all the good things in this world.

He remembered, tenderly, the mud hut he'd lived in when he was a boy. He'd gone barefoot and things had seemed friendlier then, even the insects and the dirt. And the neighbours, those good people, used to exchange smiles and food with them.

He arrived at the company's head office and put on an artificial smile. He'd inwardly decided to pluck his depression out by the roots – the depression that came to devour him from time to time. He shut his soul up firmly inside his smart clothes. But he was still weeping inside, like a maimed animal that's lost one of its limbs. Here he was then, tonight, being silently crucified – like a broken-legged ladder on a lifeless table.

Smart ledgers. Trained fingers. His General Manager had decided to appoint a favourite to a sensitive position. He smiled at the protégé meekly, thinking that he looked even more stupid and self-important than most company executives – those creatures who are made to seem so glamorous by the newspapers and luxury hotels.

There's a new deal to be made in a cold country. He's expected to be there in twenty-four hours.

He'd promised to take his daughter to the exhibition of children's drawings. And his son Thamir was expecting a telescope he'd promised to buy him the next day!

Inflated contracts. They're a real lure; everybody gulps his share down voraciously. The same familiar accounts, and the cheques passing round and round the system. But everybody's withdrawing into himself; they're thinking, almost screaming: 'Isn't there any way out?'

It's the downfall. And getting used to the downfall.

The telephone rings.

'. . .'

'Yes, speaking.'

'. . .'

'Hello. How are you, sir?'

'. . .'

'Can I help you in some way?'

'. . .'

'Oh. Yes, I know, there's been a new invitation to tender. What about it?'

'. . .'

'My company's submitting an offer. Will you . . . ?'

'. . .'

'I'll think about it.'

'. . .'

'Trust me. I know the importance of men like you.'

324

The cramped muscles of his face were forced into a bitter smile. As usual. It's the downfall. It goes on and on, like a river. He tries to raise his head but his back, he finds, is too used to bending right down, too used to being hunched – more, far more than he'd expected.

His neck doesn't straighten. His fingers are sticky, like fruit that's just started to go rotten. The sun completes its daily course. He'd like to ask . . .

Why do the good sink into obscurity? Why do those sullied with crime dominate the cities, cities bloated with money and instant wealth? Why do our moral qualities, even the greatest, succumb and yield? Why do people rejoice in momentary victory and forget their real part in the game whose end is inevitable? Why do we fall so early into the lake of nothingness? And why are the streets full of dead men, foolishly jostling for the privilege of a larger grave?

He closed his eyes, inwardly cursing the gloomy depression that was assailing him yet again. He picked up his briefcase and fled from himself. It was time he started working out the forged tender for his friend. Outside all was well with the world. People were jostling each other. The sun lit up the whole universe. And the vicious power crawled on, mocking and murderous. At the main entrance, outside, the poor doorman was borrowing 200 *riyals* from a junior employee. He wanted to buy some books and equipment for his daughter, who was studying at the Medical School.

Didn't I say all was well with the world?

Translated by Salwa Jabsheh and Christopher Tingley

Hamza Bogary   **SAUDI ARABIA**

From *Saqifat al-Safa*

Hamza M. Bogary tells the story of a young man who grew up in Makkah during the period between the two World Wars, i.e., before oil had changed the whole tempo of life in Saudi Arabia. The novel, which has all the features of an autobiographical account of the life of Muhaisin al-Baliyy, the name the author gives to his main character, describes fully the educational and social life of Makkah at the time: the school system, the state of women and their isolation, the life of the freed slaves of the rich, and of Makkah's madmen, and the many customs, beliefs and superstitions which dominated the life of the individual.

The novel opens with the death of Muhaisin's stepfather, a loss that immediately gives the central character a better status in the household, now composed of his mother and himself. His mother's best friend is Auntie Asma, a frail but resourceful woman. No sooner was the legal period of a wife's confinement after her husband's death over[1] than his mother decide to take Muhaisin on a visit to Madinah and the Prophet's tomb.

As usual, my mother consulted Auntie Asma who decided to accompany us. Since at that time camels were the only available means of transport, she took it upon herself to find out which family in our quarter was going on a visit to the holy shrine, so that we could add our camel to their caravan . . . She did, in fact, find a large family intending to travel in a caravan of five camels . . . but, for some reason which I could not fathom, the timing of the trip did not please Auntie Asma and she lost interest in the whole affair. Her search started all over again until she found a

1. This is a hundred days, which would determine whether a woman was pregnant of her dead husband.

caravan intending to travel at a time that pleased her. Since both Auntie Asma and my mother believed in many of the traditional customs and beliefs of the time, Auntie Asma brought a man to our house the day we were supposed to leave. At first I did not concern myself with why he was there, particularly since he stayed alone in an inner room. Then, after he had settled down and the customary tea been offered, he began to chant in a sing-song voice while Auntie Asma kept moving between the window overlooking the street and the long corridor that ended in the room where the man was . . . Gradually, I began to like his voice and to recognize the words he was chanting, all of which either pertained to our coming visit to Madinah, or were prayers invoking peace on the Prophet. Eventually I geared up my courage and, pointing to the window Auntie Asma kept approaching and to the room occupied by the man, I asked her to explain the relationship between them, and also the meaning of the man's presence there. Anyone who was alive then will know that the chanter was the *muzahhid*,[2] a man whose job was to make people shun the world with his beautiful voice and kindle in them a longing to visit Madinah; while Auntie Asma's frequent goings and comings from window to corridor were to make sure that no one who frowned on such unorthodox religious practices would hear the *muzahhid*'s voice.

Although, when I grew up, I prayed to God for forgiveness for all the unorthodox religious practices which I had followed while under the wing of my mother and Auntie Asma, I have never forgotten – and may God forgive me for this – the *muzahhid*'s tender and gentle voice as he chanted . . . 'God's prayers and peace be on you . . . Prophet.'

That afternoon our camel driver, Atiyya, led out our camel with the *houdaj* on its back, the two women lodged on each side of the *houdaj* while I sat between them. The first moments were those of fear and prayer against the devil, for sitting at that great height on the camel's back – a traveller's first feeling was that he would fall at any moment. But, as the moments followed one another without incident, we began to feel calmer; our camel did not start with fear and nothing happened to make us feel that we were about to fall off. Moreover, the sight of the rest of the caravan when we met up with it on the outskirts of Makkah gave us a great feeling of security. What I did not expect was to find the *muzahhid* on the outskirts of Makkah, bidding us farewell with his tender chants, which went unnoticed by any observer, and wishing the pilgrims success in being accepted by God and His Prophet.

2. *Muzahhid* comes from *zuhd*: asceticism, abstinence, indifference to worldly things.

Despite my many trips later on in life through those plains and hills, the smell of the caravan at twilight during those twelve days we spent travelling between Makkah and Madinah was never so delicious in my nostrils. Suhail and I, the only two boys of the caravan, would run behind the camels, playing and hopping about before nightfall came down on us and we had to retire to our sedans in the *houdajs*. The dry grasses and the flying locusts around which we jumped represented the loveliest experience in any trip of discovery or any adventure of youth. Despite the many bruises which our sides received from sleeping on the backs of camels, and despite the mosquito bites which were inevitable at every single station where we stopped during the trip, no one ever complained or expressed vexation . . . and how could they do so when they were on a trip that would take them to the best of mankind?

Among the discoveries I made on this trip was 'The Terror of the Night'. According to Auntie Asma, he would intercept caravans in the evening and attempt to mislead them, guiding the camel drivers the wrong way. He would appear to them as a friend and try to give them advice, though all the while his real intention was to send the caravans to their deaths . . . he would even set up imaginary cafés whose illusory lights the caravans would glimpse in the distance and head towards, just as the Bedouin would head towards a mirage thinking it to be water . . . then, as the caravan travelled through the night towards these imaginary cafés, they would disappear and the camels and all they were carrying would be lost.

Auntie Asma recounted innumerable incidents about those who had met their deaths as a result of the trickery of this accursed 'Terror of the Night' . . . This was why she almost never slept while the camels were moving, but would stay awake for fear the camel drivers might be lured astray and lead us all to our deaths.

One evening – I think we were between al-Safra' and the Nar Valley – Auntie Asma's protracted, high-pitched screams pierced the night: 'The Terror of the Night! The Terror of the Night! Don't listen to him, he's a liar!' I was woken from a delicious dream and the fear the screams induced in me almost made me jump off the camel. In vain did my mother and the camel driver try to calm her; she continued screaming, warning us of 'The Terror of the Night'. And what a terror! The story continued until the caravan drivers stopped and made our camel kneel, then brought Auntie Asma out trembling and distraught and poured a jar full of water over her head. After that she was able to listen to them and learn that what she had thought was the 'Terror of the Night' was, in fact, no more than the owner of the café where we had spent the previous night. He had followed us – on a camel – when he discovered that one of our blankets had been left on a chair in his café. Fearing that he might be accused of having stolen the blanket when we discovered it was missing, he had followed us to return it to its rightful owners.

After that evening Auntie Asma stopped talking about 'The Terror of the Night', although she did not stop talking about more important things which together constituted a collection of surprises and exciting information for me.

During the eighth night and the eighth station of our trip to Madinah, our caravan reached Badr.[3] No one was expecting anything unusual that evening, and the caravan arrived just before sunset; the camels were made to kneel near one of the clusters of huts set up on the way. Mats were spread on the sands and the preparations for our meal began as usual. That evening our supper was to be a kind of *tharid* made up of dry bread, carried with us from Makkah, and cooked with a small amount of dry meat and water. After supper, Auntie Asma untied the bundle in which she was carrying her clothes, took a few things out and then sat alone away from the others. She began to comb her hair and to rub coconut oil mixed with herbs into it. Then, when she felt happy about the way her hair looked, she put a triangular piece of cloth which had two strings attached to it over her hair and fastened it in place by tying the strings at the back of her head. This was a *shanbar*. She also brought out a handkerchief called a *mahrama*, in which she wrapped her braid, then put a white head shawl with embroidered ends, a *mudawwara*, over her head. After that she pencilled her eyebrows and applied *kohl* eye-liner to her eyelids. You would think that she was going to attend a wedding.

When people were getting ready to retire to bed, she took me by the hand and headed towards the desert. When we were far enough from the cluster of huts, she sat down on a little dune and made me sit near her as she listened to what was going on around her. As the night deepened she began to move about near the bottom of the dune, slowly at first then, little by little, her movements changed into a quiet dance that gradually became more feverish. It seemed to me that the dance was keeping time to some tune coming to us from far away, some drum beat perhaps. She continued whirling and dancing as I sat, completely terrified, on the sand,

3. Badr is the name of a place where a major battle was fought by the early Muslims against Quraish, the Prophet's tribe, whose authority over Makkah and the Kaaba and whose superiority among Arabs were threatened by the rise of Islam. The Muslims lost some of their best men in this battle.

wondering whether Auntie Asma had gone utterly mad, or whether I was in a dream. Then, when the continuous swirling had tired her out, and at least half the night had gone, she sat down to rest next to me, then took me by the hand and headed back to the caravan. Mother was not surprised at our returning so late, nor at the sight of Auntie Asma with so much perspiration covering her face and forehead. I could no longer wait but asked, with a gesture of my hand, what all this was about. Mother indicated that I should wait, then, when Auntie Asma had gone to sleep, Mother explained to me something I had had no knowledge of before. First she asked if I had heard the noise of drums. I answered that I had heard some sort of rumbling noises that I could not fathom. She, God rest her soul, answered that these rumbling noises I heard were the drums of the fighters at Badr, the drums of the martyrs who fell in that battle. These drums are only heard there when the moon is full and only during certain months of the year. Auntie Asma was one of the few who knew those months and the exact days. This was why she had refused to go with the first caravan because its arrival there would not have coincided with these days. Mother finished by asking me not to reveal what I had heard to anyone, because strictly religious people did not believe in the existence of these drums and did not permit people to dance to their beat . . . Poor Auntie Asma, she and others like her did not know anything about the movements of sand in the desert!

As a result of her husband's death, Muhaisin's mother decided to get rid of the services of Misfir, the water carrier who brought water to the house in two tin cans suspended on each side of his shoulders by a bamboo rod. Her reason was that Misfir was a young man and should not now enter their house which had been left without a husband's protection. This meant that the extra services which Misfir had done in the house became Muhaisin's responsibility, for Amm Bashir, Misfir's substitute, was an old, half-blind man who lacked the strength even to kill a chicken. He belonged to the troop of freed slaves who frequented a bench known as the Bench of Slaves in Muhaisin's quarter. They had all been freed when they had grown old and weak.

With Amm Bashir's addition to our household, that bench became an object of curiosity to me and everything that happened near it was important to me. I discovered that the bench had a Shaikh or master who was also the Shaikh of a whole troop of water carriers, and that everyone who sat on or near it was a water carrier. The freed slave spoke an African language which I could not understand, he remembered a past which had nothing to do with the present but stretched back to some village or other in the Black Continent. His memory, moreover, involved a series of masters who had bought or sold him for one reason or another. Some of the freed slaves would remember a son or daughter who was sold one day and of whom nothing more was ever heard. They also recounted tales, some sad, some merry, about their experiences with their masters.

I also discovered that the bench had principles of conduct and laws for punishing those who violated them. Most of these offences were related to events which took place around the well from which they brought the water, as when one of them would take another's place unfairly, or swear obscenely. The trial always took place after noon prayers at the bench, where the Shaikh sat surrounded by the wiser men. The accused would squat on the ground. The accusation would be made and the witnesses would give their testimony. Then the accused would be asked to confess, which happened every time. He would be sentenced to be flogged and would be stretched on the ground to receive his punishment. This was done with a piece of leather which formed part of a rope the Shaikh had tied at his breast. In most cases the flogging was no more than three rather gentle strokes, unless the plaintiff forgave the defendant, or unless some busybody in the troop threw a green bunch of clover or leeks into the middle of the circle. At this, the 'court' would adjourn without inflicting punishment on the defendant, but not before the Shaikh had shown how annoyed he was with the person who had thrown the bunch into the circle. This was usually one of the vigilantes of the area . . .

I have never been able to find out why the punishment was annulled as soon as that green bunch was thrown. Of all the many people I asked, none knew the reason behind this.

On that bench, which I began to frequent whenever I had time, the stories of the 'masters' who had once owned those slaves and then sold or freed them were recounted, and on that bench many families' reputations came to grief. There I learnt that masters often covered up their relationships with their slave women as they regarded themselves as their owners. Many of them would, as soon as a slave girl became pregnant, marry her off to one of their slaves in order to avoid having to acknowledge the child as theirs which would mean entitling him to a part of the inheritance. Amm Bashir knew many stories like these. He would mention names like Mahsoun or Saeed or some other such name, all of whom were really the sons of their masters – rich men in the area – and not their slaves. Many other stories were told about the women in former masters' households, all of which were unpleasant to listen to.

When Muhaisin reached the higher grade at school, he could then borrow one or more books from the school library. It was the principal of the school who always chose the books for him to read, many of them books of poetic satire. Despite the unattractiveness of some of these works, however, Muhaisin was able to cultivate the art of avid reading, doing this in the evenings either in the Great Mosque (al-Haram) or in the street under one of the street lamps near his house. This was because the lamp at home was too weak to permit constant reading. His reading every evening at the corner of the street drew the attention of Ustadh Umar.

He was a strange and unique personality. He was probably the only grown-up man in the whole quarter who had ever read a book outside the usual school books, the only one who held a government post, maybe the only one who wore a cloak (*jubba*); he was normally the first to do anything – he was the first to buy a radio when radios were invented, the first to use prescription glasses; later on, he was the first to buy a car when cars were imported, and the first to hire a servant other than the usual servants of the Hijaz,[4] etc., etc.

On one of these evenings Ustadh Umar invited Muhaisin to visit him as he had a large collection of books from which he suggested the young boy could borrow. The visit proved to be the beginning of a long and fruitful relationship with this erudite man. Here Muhaisin is about to visit Ustadh Umar for the first time.

I told mother that evening about his invitation. She was silent for a few minutes, and I had to ask her again. She said that she did not want to prevent me from going but that she could not agree without thinking hard about the consequences of such a visit, since she said that it was rumoured that Shaikh Umar was a *farmasoni*, i.e., a Freemason. She insisted that this was something the whole quarter knew about. He went to the countries of the Christians and could talk a language other than the language of Muslims and he read huge books, the contents of which were unknown to anyone. Then she added, 'If you insist on going, I shall go with you the first time; I know his mother, she is a good woman although she has become very old and may not be able to recognize people; nevertheless, I shall go and visit her while you borrow the books.'

Shaikh Umar might indeed have been a Freemason or even worse, I

4. Hijaz is the area of Saudi Arabia which constitutes Makkah and Madinah and is the centre of the early Muslims.

thought, because the first thing I saw when I entered the sitting-room was a large picture of a bearded man who might have been his father or grandfather! Photographs were, at that time, as good as committing a sin, and you would not have been able to find a single photographer's studio in our quarter, nor in the whole of Makkah. No one would have imagined that he would dare hang a picture, any picture, in his house, let alone a large picture like that. Where on earth could he have brought it from?

I kept gazing at the picture without crossing the threshold. How could I? Didn't the angels abandon a place where pictures were hanging to devils and demons? When he noticed my hesitation he approached and stretched out his hand to greet me. Since there was nothing suspicious about that outstretched hand I took it in mine and he smiled and said, 'This is a picture of my father taken many years ago whilst he was visiting London.' London! What was all that? It was true what mother had said about him then! I decided to be very cautious.

The relationship continued with Muhaisin borrowing book after book from Ustadh Umar, then venturing to sit and chat with him sometimes. Eventually, a real bond developed between them, stemming in the first place from the older man's admiration for Muhaisin's diligence and avid appetite for knowledge. Later on, Ustadh Umar asked him to tutor his son, Jamil, who was not making any progress with his studies at school. It was a long, protracted attempt to enlighten a boy of Muhaisin's own age who had no aptitude for, or interest in, learning.

Then one day as I was leaving the room where I gave Jamil his lessons, Ustadh Umar stopped me and invited me to take a cup of tea with him. He surprised me that day by giving me a small book entitled *Common Expressions in the English Language*. I thanked him and was about to leave when he said, 'How I wish that my daughter Jamila were a boy. I would have asked you to tutor her, and it would have borne fruit. She is so very intelligent that it seems as though she has taken both her share and her brother's.'

I thanked him for his concern about the trouble I was having teaching Jamil and his worry about the amount of effort I exerted with such poor results. I didn't give the sentence about Jamila a second thought, for I regarded the whole matter as his way of showing me his appreciation.

However, the story of Jamila was not over, it seemed. For Ustadh Umar brought it up again on another occasion, saying, 'It is unfortunate that there are no schools for girls. Because of this Jamila has been denied the opportunity of learning despite the fact that she deserves it.' Then he fell silent. I asked him why he did not send her to the Kabariti *kuttab* for girls where she could at least learn the first part (the Amma) of the Koran, and come to know some of the Koranic chapters which she recited in her prayers.[5] He answered that she had been there and had learned most of the Amma off by heart, adding that that would not be enough, for she was capable of learning much more than that. He fell silent again and, since I did not know what to say, I fell silent too. But he again broached the subject, saying, 'Were it not for traditions I would have asked you to give her lessons as you do Jamil.' I was silent again; he left me alone and I left the house.

On my way home I began thinking about what he had said and, during the minutes that separated our house from theirs, I came to the conclusion that that Freemason must have had more on his mind than the mere wish that there should be schools for girls. And what I expected happened a few days later. He asked me, 'Isn't learning a duty for all Muslims, men and women?' I said, 'Yes.' He said, 'And how should one fulfil this duty?' I did not answer. At that he asked me point blank, 'Would you agree to teach her just as you do Jamil?' I answered, 'But . . .' He interrupted, 'She will come with her grandmother and Jamil, of course. The two of them will share the time between them.' I felt shocked and terrified. It was all like a bombshell for me. But he did not let me express what I felt deep inside myself, for he added, 'She will be veiled, of course, and during the first few lessons she will just listen to what goes on between you and Jamil, without participating, then she will start to take part later on. You may use the same stories and tales which you prepare for Jamil, until she perfects her reading; after that you can move on to teaching her the school reader which you have studied in Preparatory School.' Then he added, 'It is unfair to her to leave her ignorant when she is capable of learning.'

Jamila was younger than both me and her brother Jamil. I had not seen her for many years. I remembered her as a girl of five or six years old; then she began to wear the veil and all news of her had ceased. In fact, I had completely forgotten that she even existed, until her father started talking about her.

Jamila was a strange and unfathomable bundle with nothing to be seen of her, as she was completely covered by a *jama*, the large cloak worn by

5. Prayers are recited five times daily by the Muslims: dawn, noon, afternoon, sunset and evening. It is part of the ritual to recite some verses or whole small chapters from the Koran during the prayer.

women which showed nothing of what it covered. The only openings in it, from which the wearer could look out on the world, were the two small slits for the eyes.

Her body was small and slim and differed greatly from the much bigger physiques of Jamil and myself. At the beginning, she sat in a corner, with her grandmother at her side, and did not move at all throughout the lesson. When this was over, she would leave with her grandmother following her, silently, without having spoken or greeted us.

Then, when the time came for her to participate actively, Ustadh Umar himself attended. As he entered, a man servant, carrying the tea tray and a plate of the kind of cakes which housewives used to prepare during the pilgrimage season, came in behind him. Although Ustadh Umar did not participate in the lesson by so much as a single word, his presence created an atmosphere of confidence and calm for those around, and this made me insist that he attend the lessons that were still to come. He never did this in a regular fashion, but would come in once or twice during the lesson if he did not want to remain throughout. It seems that the grandmother became convinced after a few lessons that what we were doing, although completely unprecedented, did not – as she expressed it – represent any overstepping of boundaries. This conviction was reflected in the greetings which she began to give me whenever she came to the lesson. At first her entry had been completely silent. Then she began to say, 'Peace be upon you.' After a few weeks she began saying, 'Peace be upon you, son,' and after a few more weeks she started exchanging some words with me and asking after my mother, as well as showing admiration for me in my *jubba* and turban. The situation developed even more and she began to ask God to protect me from the evil eye; later, she went so far as to ask God to reward me generously for the lessons I was giving her grandchildren.

During this time, whilst the grandmother was undergoing this mild psychological transformation, two other developments were going on hand in hand. Jamila was really very intelligent, far more so than I had suspected. She devoured the stories I gave her to read, one after the other. She would, after reading them with me once or twice, revise them during the day until she knew them by heart without making any mistakes in their end-vowelling,[6] although she knew no grammar.

6. Like Latin, the end letters of most words in Arabic change their vowel endings according to the grammatical function the word is playing in the sentence: whether it is subject, object, or preceded by a preposition, etc.

The other development happened inside me, for I began to feel much at ease with that low voice with its soft twang. I felt so used to it that I would miss it during the day and try to remember how it sounded. There was nothing else of her I could remember, for Jamila had remained an ambiguous, unfathomable bundle of clothes. There was only that childlike voice which she began to raise little by little as her confidence grew with time.

The situation developed within my mind, and I began to draw a picture of that mysterious slim bundle sitting in front of me. In my fancy I relied on the three figures I knew: the grandmother, Ustadh Umar and Jamil. I would put this person's nose under that person's forehead, and then add to this Jamil's figure, after making it smaller and slimmer, so that a kind of complete, composite image of the girl who was sitting in front of me, completely screened by her clothes, would form in my mind.

Translated by May Jayyusi and Dick Davies

Zaid Mutee^c Dammaj   **YEMEN**

The Journey

The road was unpaved and neglected too; it had been left to a German
company which was doing the job slowly. The passengers were almost
choked by the dust, and the air was cold, with the sun still not up from
behind the proud summits of the mountains. The bumping was nearly
enough to break people's ribs and enough to drive them mad as well.
Discussions could be heard and silly, tedious intimacies.

The dust didn't grow any less till the bus began to climb up one of the
mountains; then people opened the windows. The bus crawled on up the
slope.

We'd left Taizz behind with its smoke-polluted atmosphere and
ingrained smells of restaurants and cafés; and the mountain air, wonder-
fully refreshing, began to wash the dust out of our clogged pores. The
farms teemed with farmers gathering in the drought-stricken harvest. I
cursed the road and its dust, I cursed the windows and the winds. I
wanted to open the window and see the simple peasants with their
women and cattle, and hear their voices ringing out harvest songs. I hated
the silly intimacies and noisy discussions, and I hated the smell of the
passenger sitting in the seat next to me – a strong smell of perfume which
I'd had to put up with since the morning. He'd been having a night of
love, maybe, somewhere in Jamaliya!

When we reached the mountain plateau, I opened the window and
there was the valley stretched out, with its people going about their
labours like ants. As I contemplated the scene, my neighbour intervened,
asking me to close the window, which I did. Perhaps his request had been
meant as a preface to conversation, for he asked me:

'Do you know this region?'

'Yes.'

He shook his head thoughtfully.

'I know it better than most people. It's full of rogues and outlaws.'

I lowered my head, surprised.

'You don't know it then?' he went on.

'Yes, I do,' I replied, and gazed again at the valley and its people.

'Don't let them deceive you with all this appearance of hard work,' he commented.

'It looks genuine enough.'

'Actually, they're rogues and highway robbers. They really are an ugly lot. If you don't get on top of them, they'll get on top of you.'

I was bored with all this, but he kept on talking:

'Did you know Shaikh Abdu al-Maddah and his whole family were slaughtered here, every last one of them?'

I didn't answer.

'They made them lie down flat on the ground. Then they shot them slowly, one by one . . . women and children too . . .'

Again I didn't answer, so he went on.

'They confiscated his land, his cattle and property were plundered and all his houses were blown up.'

Still I didn't reply, and again he went on. His face had changed and his voice had grown harsher.

'But he fought like a hero and they lost a lot of men.'

He fell silent for a while, then said in a calm voice:

'And if it hadn't been for Shaikh Ali al-Dareeh, with his men and money and power and influence, no one would have avenged him.'

Bright sparks glinted in his eyes.

'They hunted the murderers down everywhere. A lot of them were killed, and a lot of them were dragged behind moving vehicles until they died. Whole villages were destroyed.'

Seeing that I didn't answer, he broke off and shook me by the shoulder.

'Why don't you say something?' he demanded.

'I'm listening to you!'

'Didn't you know Shaikh Abdu al-Maddah?'

'I may have done . . . Perhaps I've heard of him.'

He pretended to be angry.

'You've spoiled my trip!'

'Why?'

'You didn't show any interest when I talked to you.'

'What do you mean? I've been listening for an hour!'

'Maybe you're one of them!'

He turned his head in my direction with a malicious grimace I hadn't expected.

338

'Who are they?' I asked.

'The rebels. The outlaws. All those bands up in the mountains.'

'I'm an ordinary civil servant.'

'Where?'

'In Sanaa.'

'Mm.'

He was silent for a while. Then his anger welled up again, and he said:

'There's so much corruption in the government.'

'Every country's got that.'

He seemed to realize how pointless it was bringing up subjects that just upset him and made matters worse, so he said no more.

The descent was a steep one and almost drove us to exhaustion. The dust was still rising and the hot sun had begun to beat on the faces of the passengers sitting on the right-hand side of the bus, so that they drew the curtains on that side. I opened the window and tried to persuade the passenger sitting directly in front of me to open his window, too. He seemed to be an ordinary farmer, in his late forties, slimly built with a pale face, and wearing a cheap sort of straw *kufiyya* with the lower part of it consumed by sweat. He'd covered himself with a coarse sleeping bag. Alongside him there was a stout, well-dressed man of thirty-five, with a suit and matching tie and an expensive pair of glasses; and next to him, in the extra seat in the gangway, sat an ordinary young man.

The wife of the well-dressed man was sitting with their children in the seat in front of him. Judging by the way her eyes sparkled behind the transparent veil as she talked to her husband, she was a beautiful woman, and you could see he loved her because he was so concerned about the way the dust and suffocating heat were affecting her. He was constantly shouting at the passengers to open the windows and frequently got up to open them himself so that his wife's soft hands, decorated with henna and gold bracelets, shouldn't be revealed.

I asked the slim farmer to open the window, which he did happily enough, but my perfumed neighbour insisted it should be closed; we should make do with the window next to us, he said. The well-dressed man stared at him contemptuously.

My perfumed neighbour said:

'We've reached Ibb.'

'Thank God for your safe arrival!'

'Where are you going?'

'To Sanaa. My job's waiting for me there, God willing!'

People jostled one another to get to a popular restaurant whose tables were crowded with customers. I found a seat after a lot of effort, and it so happened that it was next to the well-dressed man and his family. He didn't seem pleased to see me sitting there, but there was no choice; I wouldn't have sat there if there had been any other way.

I saw he was watching the way I glanced at his wife, who was eating behind her veil, so I ignored his gaze and concentrated on my food. He said nothing for a while; then he made an effort and remarked:

'This seems to be a good restaurant.'

I looked up and saw it was me he was speaking to, so I nodded my head in agreement.

'What an ignorant country this is,' he grumbled. 'People are afraid of fresh air, so they put up with dust!'

'That sort of ignorance has been going on for a long time!'

'Do you realize dust can cause dangerous diseases?'

'Yes. But it really was very cold.'

'It was just bracing. Fresh air never made anyone ill.'

I tried to reassure him:

'The trip should be pleasant from now on. The sun's risen and it's not so cold. The windows are sure to be opened.'

He shook his head in a gesture of hopelessness, and said: 'I don't think so. Didn't you see what happened? We were just beginning to cheer up with the sun starting to reach us, and the people on the right-hand side drew their curtains. They even closed their windows!'

'Perhaps the sun was beating down on their faces, especially after the cold.'

'If the windows were open, the sun wouldn't be so strong.'

There was a silence, during which he wiped his children's hands and scolded some of them because they'd dropped some crumbs on their clothes.

We got up and I went back to my seat in the bus. Some new passengers had replaced the ones who'd left us, and one of them was sitting next to me.

More passengers crammed into the bus and the reserve seats were set up along the main gangway.

The noisy discussions and silly intimacies increased, but the pleasant sound of music from a tape-recorder began to rise up from the front. The bus swayed on through a series of farms. Our stomachs were full and we had plenty of energy now for friendly conversation.

The man next to me had a friend sitting in the gangway. The two of them appeared to be prominent lawyers in the religious court, and they deafened me with their talk about a case one of them had, which had gone

340

before the Ministry of Justice and then through the appeal procedure, and about all the verdicts which had been overturned again and again. I preferred to say nothing. Throughout the account I could see the man in the straw *kufiyya* with the lower part consumed by sweat turning towards me and smiling, then shaking his head. I became curious to know what was going on in the mind of a poor, simple, good-natured peasant like that.

Perhaps, I thought, he's a lawyer at the Ministry of Justice, but he doesn't seem to have the money that goes with a job like that. Perhaps he just keeps a kiosk in the streets of Sanaa. No, his age and health wouldn't let him do that kind of work. Perhaps he's a simple watchman working for some hotel or company.

He took the sleeping bag from his back, then turned to me once more, and asked:

'Where's your friend gone? The man who was sitting next to you?'

'He got off in the city.'

He shook his head, and then smiled, which intrigued me.

'Do you know him?' I asked.

'No.'

He said nothing for a moment then, without turning towards me, he said:

'What he told you was a lie.'

'In what way?'

He turned to me then, and said:

'It wasn't true what he said about Shaikh Abdu and Shaikh Ali.'

'Do you know them?'

'Yes, and I know what the whole thing was about, too!'

He was silent for a while, which aroused my interest again, and I asked:

'What do you mean?'

'Shaikh Abdu was one of the worst tyrants on earth. He plundered and stole and violated every decency. He used to shut his subjects up in the latrine among all the filth, and he used to make them breathe in mace fumes until he got what he wanted.'

'That's unbelievable!'

'Why?'

I couldn't reply, puzzled as to how to argue the point.

'Everything that's happened up to now,' he went on, 'is the result of all those injustices.'

'Even so, some of the things the Resistance did seem pretty extreme.'

'You can't call it extreme. It's really just a reaction.'

I sensed that he was beginning to speak seriously and thoughtfully, so

341

I let him carry on.

'Reaction to the bad way the state behaves. The men it appoints aren't right for the positions they hold. It makes me think of what Haroun al-Rashid[1] said in his reply to the Queen of the Franks: "I choose men well." '

I smiled in astonishment, then said:

'But the state seems to deal with things as best it can.'

He laughed.

'The state seems to apply the theory of Ziyad ibn Abih[2] in al-Kufa,' he said.

I knew what he was getting at. Yet he said it as if I didn't know anything about history – as if he was speaking to himself. I leaned over and put my head on the edge of his seat, so he wouldn't have to turn his own head towards me, and gazed at him for some time. But he'd finished talking now and he was looking out at the valleys where the people were toiling away at the harvest.

'They're good people,' he commented. 'People whose minds are on earning their bread – and, of course, providing for the governor and the army officers and the rulers and the Shaikhs and all the civil servants and middlemen.'

'Perhaps things will get better.'

'I don't think so.'

'You can't be as pessimistic as that. A clear-sighted man like you!'

He smiled.

'The Yemeni,' he said, 'acts greedily and beyond his powers. He's addicted to alcohol and smokes from his earliest youth – and his politics and the way he oppresses people and the way he thinks are all in the same vein.'

'That doesn't apply to everybody.'

'I don't agree. Everything I've said's true. And why are things like that? It's the result of constant suppression and deprivation from time immemorial, and the lack of basic education – the education leaders give

1. Haroun al-Rashid: one of the greatest Caliph-Emperors of Arab-Islamic civilization. He ruled at the end of the eighth century AD and exchanged presents with Charlemagne, King of the Franks.
2. Ziyad ibn Abih (AD 622–673) was a great general and an invincible ruler. He was appointed by Muawiya, the first Umayyad Caliph, as viceroy of Basra, Kufa and the rest of Iraq. He imposed martial law on al-Kufa, threatening to seize the father for the offence of the son, the brother for the offence of the brother.

to the people under them. We're in a vacuum, we don't know where we're going and that's going to lead to serious trouble.'

His neighbour, the well-dressed man, moved towards him to open the window, and he said no more. The well-dressed man, for his part, had been so busy ordering other people about, and giving them advice about how harmful dust was and what terrible things it led to, that he apparently hadn't been following the conversation.

My companion opened the window before his well-dressed neighbour could do it. The bus began to twist and turn, whining painfully, as it climbed the dangerous bends of Mount Samara. The wind had died down and some of the curtains were opened so that people could gaze out at the *qat* plantations, the white villages scattered over the hillsides and the sheer drops. The tape-recorder was still blaring out gay folk songs. I hoped circumstances would allow me to meet this man again, even if it was on worn-out seats in a popular café.

'That's interesting,' I said.

'It has to be said. It's not the sort of thing you enjoy saying, but you can't stop yourself, and out it comes! This is a tiring journey, you know, and you have to say something.'

'Yes, although there are a lot of things spoiling it – all the shouting and yelling and the stupid songs from that tape-recorder. The man who's playing it must love music – and he must be madly in love too!'

'It's a girl who got on at Ibb.'

I was surprised at this, but he said:

'Where's the harm in her playing the tape-recorder? As long as she's veiled and wearing her *sharshaf*?'

His well-dressed neighbour had apparently heard the conversation and protested strongly:

'How can you talk like that? Can't you hear the cheap way she's chattering to other people and the shameless way she's laughing?'

The other man turned towards him calmly and with dignity.

'She's just behaving naturally!'

The well-dressed man turned towards me in disgust; then he turned to the man with the straw *kufiyya* and said, sarcastically and disdainfully:

'Ignorance still builds its nest in the brains of the peasants from these parts.'

I laughed at this, which offended him.

'Do you agree with him?' he asked.

'Yes.'

He scrutinized my clothes and said contemptuously:

'You seem to be the same sort of people.'

343

'What sort?'

'We've got to have decency and moral standards. Otherwise society loses everything worthwhile.'

'What are the worthwhile things in a society, sir?'

He looked at me as if he thought the question was much too big for me, and asked:

'Where did you study?'

'That's not important.'

After a short silence, he remarked:

'I presume you studied abroad.'

'Well, what's wrong with that?'

He was quiet for a moment. Then he suddenly turned, and said:

'Do you know why the sea's salty?'

'It's like that naturally!'

'No. The rivers are constantly taking salt into it from the mountains.'

'What about Lake Qaroun in Egypt? Where does that get its salt from?'

He didn't answer. My friend seemed to be enjoying the conversation and uttered a low laugh which made the well-dressed man turn towards him disapprovingly. To stop himself laughing, my friend said:

'Sir, I agree with what you said about opening the windows. The dust can cause dangerous diseases. Most of the passengers don't seem to realize that.'

The well-dressed man didn't answer. What he'd meant to do was to get a discussion moving so he could show off the general knowledge he'd acquired at university. After a moment's silence he turned to me, and said thoughtfully:

'Our country seems to make people rigid and ignorant.'

I asked him what he meant. He continued.

'You come back to your country with your mind full of marvellous, exciting ideas, but they only last a few months. Then little by little you lose them. It messes up all your expectations and careful calculations.'

He laughed for the first time.

'It even happens to the foreigners,' he went on. 'All the calculations and assessments and plans they make as a basis for their policy in this country, they all fail. And so we end up by going back to fate and predestination; what will be will be, and what won't be won't be.'

'Is that the solution?'

The smile was wiped from his lips. He said, in a tone of angry complaint:

'How's it going to end? What is the solution going to be? Shattered nerves, a gastric ulcer and diabetes?'

He stopped, then went on sarcastically:

'Don't you realize all the top government officials are suffering from diabetes? And I don't blame them. Nobody knows what the country wants! If you carry out reform, people call it tyranny. If you work to bring the country peace, they call it surrender. If you get aid for it, they call it throwing yourself into the arms of reaction and imperialism. The country just wants to be like a lake with the stormy waves lashing against one another.'

'And if the waves didn't lash one another,' said the man with the straw *kufiyya*, 'the lake would get stagnant.'

'Peace and quiet's a marvellous thing.'

'But stagnation, my dear sir, will rot the lake and kill the creatures that live in it.'

The well-dressed man didn't appear to be convinced and he looked at me in the hope that I'd say what I thought about it, but I preferred to say nothing and there was a short silence – at least as far as the three of us were concerned. As for the rest of the bus, there was still uproar everywhere. The tape-recorder was blaring out sentimental popular songs and the girl's voice was constantly ringing out, with a bunch of frustrated young men close to her, while the lawyers next to me were still going over past verdicts and rebuttals and appeals. And all the while people's shoulders were shaking with a monotonous, rhythmic movement which aroused the curiosity of a young man, a university graduate apparently, who was sitting behind me.

'Did you know,' he said to his neighbour, 'that riding in the back makes you giddy?'

'The back's always the worst part of everything, except that of a woman,' his neighbour answered.

'I'd love to be in the front, next to the woman and her tape-recorder!'

'I won't get the chance. I would have been happier that way too.'

Out of curiosity, I turned round to him and asked:

'What's to stop you?'

'I could hear your conversation over the tape-recorder.'

'You couldn't have. We were talking quietly.'

'I really enjoyed it, in spite of all the disturbance next to you.' He gestured towards the lawyers.

Meanwhile his college friend was busy watching the scene around the tape-recorder.

'We're a long way from all the excitement,' he said, 'and there are a lot of things in the way between us and them.'

He pointed at the reserve seats which had been set up in the gangway.

The educated, well-dressed man lost his temper and interrupted.

'Didn't I tell you they wouldn't open any windows?' he complained.

We showed our anger, too, by making gestures of displeasure so as to flatter him and show respect for his civilized appearance. The bus had stopped in the town of Dhamar to let off some passengers and he now got up himself to open the middle windows. We were longing to get out and have a rest and drink some mineral water, the well-dressed man being the most insistent.

I didn't try to get out from the rear door because I wanted to see the girl and her tape-recorder. Apparently all my neighbours felt the same way, so we jostled one another down the gangway.

The girl had turned her machine off. She was sitting in the seat right by the door and, although she was wearing a *sharshaf*, her veil was partially lifted; she'd left just the lower part of her face covered, revealing her sparkling eyes which reflected the street vendors as they crowded round the passengers at the door of the bus with their bananas and biscuits and cigarettes.

I took my time getting off the bus so as to give myself the chance of a close look at her. Her eyes were enough to make you fall in love with her and she'd allowed her fingers and arms to be revealed, so that love would turn to impetuous passion.

My friend prodded me from behind and I got out quickly, but the rest of the passengers definitely took their time leaving the bus! I made my way to the nearest café and gulped a drink down quickly, in the hope of getting back to the bus before the others did and seeing her alone. But they'd all beaten me back.

My educated, well-dressed companion was taking drinks to his wife and children who'd stayed in their seats.

'You haven't been long,' he said.

'There's no point hanging about,' I answered nonchalantly.

He looked at the girl and smiled in a meaningful way. I took no notice of him. The bus was crammed with new passengers again and there was yelling and noise and uproar; then it moved off and the loud shouting and boring discussions started up again. A close, thick dust was blowing because the soil there was very fine, and violent bumping became more frequent so that those of us in the back were suffering wretchedly. The emphatic voice of the well-dressed man rose again, sternly ordering the windows to be opened.

Suddenly a boy in the middle seat stood up and shouted at the well-dressed man to open the window by his wife's seat.

'What's the matter with you, lad?' asked the well-dressed man.

The young man's temper flashed out.

'You keep bothering us, you . . .'

The well-dressed man looked in my direction. Then he stood up and started arguing with the lad who, for his part, was still raising his voice in heated dispute so that it looked as if they were going to fight. No one intervened; it was as though the boy was exacting everyone's due from their well-dressed fellow-traveller.

The lad looked about thirteen. He had a dagger stuck in his belt and was holding a cigarette which was burning quickly, the smoke rising into our friend's face. The lad started yelling louder to show he was willing for a violent confrontation and his hand reached for his dagger. I realized that he was a soldier in the local army, the army stationed in the fertile villages which had been swept by disturbances. Perhaps he was on leave.

I got up from my seat and tactfully intervened, persuading my friend, the well-dressed man, to sit down.

'He's just a young boy,' I said, 'and he's lost his head. You must make allowances.'

'How can you say that?'

'Don't worry about it, my dear sir. Don't spoil the trip for your family.'

He saw my point and regained his temper, but the lad was still threatening him and making menacing noises. His neighbours were trying to calm him down, but all to no avail.

Then a sharp voice rang out, shouting at the lad with a vehemence that shocked him into silence:

'What's the meaning of all this insolence, lad? Sit down or we'll throw you off the bus, here, in the open country. Sit down and be quiet!'

It was the voice of the girl who was standing up and pointing at him. His face went red and he tried to say something, but she quickly turned on the tape-recorder so that it drowned everything else. The lad looked deflated and pulled furiously on his cigarette. Our well-dressed companion saw this and turned to me.

'There you are,' he said. 'Didn't I tell you?'

'It doesn't matter, my dear sir!'

'We're almost choking with dust and he's been smoking one cigarette after another ever since this morning. At his age too! What's wrong with this country?'

I didn't answer. I wanted things to calm down a little so that we could get some other conversation underway.

Many people were happy enough to enjoy the tape-recorder, although that didn't apply to our lawyer friends who were still engaged in an endless examination of verdicts and the way they'd been overturned.

I leaned forward towards the man with the straw *kufiyya* and asked him about his village and why he was making the journey. He took the coarse sleeping bag from his head and I again rested my head between my arms on the edge of the seat so that he wouldn't be forced to turn towards me. He was silent for a moment, with a gentle smile on his face.

'I have a case in Sanaa,' he said. 'It's about my son who's been killed.'

'Was he killed in Sanaa?'

'No.'

'Where did it happen.'

'In America.'

He sensed my astonished surprise and explained further:

'My son was a trade-union leader.'

'Were you with him?'

'I emigrated there before he did. I used to come back from time to time because of business in the country and family problems.'

He paused for a moment, struggling with his emotion.

'There are a lot of murders in America, I know,' I said.

'Yes, there are,' he said, trying not to let his sorrow show in his face. 'Crime really does have the upper hand in American society.'

He stopped for a moment, then started speaking again, in a calm, unemotional voice.

'My son was killed during a labour demonstration.'

I hadn't meant to make him sad again with my questions, but he continued:

'Two policemen killed him in the middle of the street. They were arrested and brought to trial.'

'So the case is over,' I said, wanting to bring the painful subject to an end. 'You won it.'

He smiled sadly.

'Unfortunately, I wasn't there when the incident happened, or for the trial.'

That meant I had to ask for further details.

'I was here in the Qalāa prison,' he continued. 'I was in the prison for a whole year.'

I felt that he was now twice as grief-stricken as before and reproached myself for embarking on a subject like that. Even so, I decided the conversation would relieve his feelings and forced myself to question him further.

'Why were you imprisoned?' I asked.

He laughed.

'It's a long story, my friend.'

I really didn't feel we should go into it again, but he continued.

'They found arms and munitions in my home.'

I was astonished at this and he gave me a reassuring look.

'Don't worry, I wasn't one of the people brought to trial. Things worked out differently.'

'How was that?'

'I sympathized with the armed liberation movement in the south of the country. My house was used as a hiding place for the guerrillas and their arms and supplies.'

'That was a sacred, patriotic duty.'

'There wasn't anything special about it, but it was certainly sacred, as everyone realized. Then the recent troubles started and, with things the way they went, I found myself thrown in prison, and I suffered a lot there.'

'Didn't you have anyone to clear things up for you?'

'Most of the people who questioned me knew about my old links with the Front and most of them had the same links. But personal questions took over.'

Our conversation was drowned by shouting and uproar at the front of the bus and people craned their necks to see what was happening.

'I hope it's not because of the girl,' said my friend.

'No, it isn't because of her,' said the well-dressed man. 'It's between the old ticket collector and a passenger. He seems to be a soldier and he won't pay his fare.'

'When did he get on?'

'In Dhamar.'

The yelling grew louder and the ticket collector shouted above it to explain what was happening.

'He can't stay on the bus without a ticket. That's the company's rule.'

'Let him have a free ride,' said one of the passengers. 'He's a soldier!'

'It can't be done.'

'Don't be so officious. You ought to be ashamed of yourself.'

'I'd get a quarter of my wages docked by the inspector.'

The ticket collector lost patience and yelled to the driver:

'Muhammad! Stop the bus!'

One of the passengers got up from his seat and took the old man by the shoulders.

'You can't do that, man. You can't put him off here by the side of the road.'

'Please don't interfere.'

The soldier shouted angrily, as if his honour had been insulted.

'I'm not getting off, you lousy swine!'

'Did you hear the way he insulted me? There's only one lousy swine and son of a lousy swine here, and that's you! Stop the bus, Muhammad!'

'You lousy old swine! We'll be meeting again!'

'Are you threatening me?'

'Yes. And your father too!'

'Muhammad, stop the bus or I'll report you!'

The driver stopped the bus abruptly and we all suddenly lost our balance.

'Anyone who wants to relieve himself can leave the bus,' he said. 'Be back in two minutes.'

This was the driver's pretext for stopping and we were glad he had, because it gave us the chance to move our stiff limbs and breathe in some fresh air.

We pushed and jostled our way towards the front door so as to get out. The quarrelsome lad accosted us, shouting into the face of the well-dressed man.

'Why don't you get out of the rear door, eh?'

The well-dressed man stopped dead in his tracks and looked at me.

'The rear door hasn't been opened,' I told the boy, with a laugh.

'That's not the reason.'

'What is it then?'

'You've never stopped bothering us. The windows, the air, the dust, the door! Huh, what stuck-up, pretentious people!'

The well-dressed man tried to start an argument and I took hold of him. But the boy barred our way even so and kept us there in the gangway so that we were the only people left.

The girl didn't get up from her seat. Instead she turned the tape-recorder back on, producing songs redolent of love and passion.

The passengers from the back of the bus got in again to enjoy the song and the conversation they were having; their words and laughter rose above the yells of the soldier and the old ticket collector. Then the soldier jumped down onto the middle of the road, an angry look quivering on his brown features.

The whole crowd was looking at him with interest but he didn't give them a glance, concentrating his angry, anxious stare on the two sides of the road.

A car came by and the soldier forced it to stop, standing right in front of it in the middle of the road. He climbed in, making threatening gestures at us with both hands.

His sudden departure was no solution. Instead, our feelings turned to deep apprehension.

'He's sure to make trouble for us on the road,' said one of the passengers.

'Why should he? The conductor was right.'

'No. He shouldn't have put the soldier off in this open country.'

'You're right, he should have put him off at the next stop.'

'That would have been the reasonable thing to do.'

The driver, as though he felt from the passengers' exchange that he was an accomplice in the crime, exclaimed:

'Do you really think I'd have left him here? I just meant us to talk the thing over properly.'

The old conductor was in a furious rage.

'I was just doing my job. The driver knows the rules.'

'You didn't need to stick to the rules as closely as that.'

'That's what you think, is it, Muhammad?'

The argument almost turned into a fight between the driver and the conductor.

The well-dressed man turned to me.

'There you are,' he said. 'There's no chance of rational procedure in this country.'

I laughed, but didn't comment.

The dust had almost turned us into phantoms and the worst off, it seemed to me, was the well-dressed man. He'd started by wiping the dust off his expensive glasses, then out of his hair, then out of his ears. Next he moved on to the suit he was wearing, giving it discreet, controlled smacks, then continued his work with his shoes.

The ticket collector came up to the well-dressed man.

'Did you see what happened, sir?'

'What?'

'Wasn't I right?'

'I wasn't paying attention to what was going on.'

The old man had reckoned the well-dressed man was an officer or official who'd be able to protect him from the soldier's vengeance.

'I'm really not in a state to judge anything any more,' said the well-dressed man.

The old man wasn't convinced.

'But I was right, sir,' he insisted. 'I'd have had a quarter of my pay docked by the inspector.'

'It's all over now. The soldier's left quite peacefully.'

'It's not finished yet, sir!'

'What do you mean?'

'He's sure to stop us on the road.'

'Of course he won't.'

The face of my friend with the straw *kufiyya* broke into a wide smile.

'I wouldn't count on that, my friend!'

The well-dressed man, bewildered, said nothing, but looked at me imploringly.

The driver and his assistant were now hard at work changing a punctured tyre. The old ticket collector, meanwhile, was anxious and dejected, fearing an unknown situation that was approaching him, bringing violence and possible insult which his old age couldn't bear.

The plain was vast, earth and dust whirling about all over it and the sun was beating down on the foreheads of the passengers. There was no shade or pleasant breeze, just great clouds of dust swirling over the old telegraph wires which dated from the time of the Turks. The wires stretched between poles made from small local logs, old and crooked, and supported in a makeshift sort of way by stones of different shapes and sizes. They sent out an intermittent whine.

I was unlucky this time, too – the girl didn't get off to walk about on her own in the open air. I again found myself drawn automatically towards my friend with the straw *kufiyya*, and our well-dressed companion joined us, leaving his wife and children in the empty rear of the bus. He anxiously described the fears of the old ticket collector and was absolutely convinced that life had become impossible in this country.

He was obviously deeply upset, unable to conceive of any reform or even of some improvement in conditions; and, being a pessimist, his convictions on the subject were strengthened by the smiles of the man with the straw *kufiyya* – smiles which seemed to me to reflect an exaggerated obstinacy.

There we all were then, scattered in groups here and there, but with no group far from the others – except for our lawyer brothers who'd ventured deep into the open country. They'd squatted down together and scattered in front of them were papers dealing with Sharia judgments and orders. Suddenly a piece of paper was caught by a treacherous, whirling wind and flew off amid the dust, joining the dozens of other bits of paper flying about. They got up and pursued it here, there and everywhere.

My friend with the straw *kufiyya* pulled me a little to one side.

'Let's leave our friend to work out his ideas,' he said. 'I've just had an interesting thought; let's make a quick tour round the different groups of passengers.'

'They're all talking about different things,' I said.

352

'No, they're all talking about the same thing – the girl!'

I liked the sound of the idea and we set off.

The first group we came across passed a sentence of death on the girl, a fate which my friend, judging by the taut expression on his face, found distasteful. He pulled me roughly away towards another group which was made up of people dressed in a variety of ways.

The conclusion we gained from them was that the girl was loose and longing for men and that every one of them was prepared to satisfy her desires out there in the open.

They only differed over details, some being generously willing to present her with some money in return, while others insisted that she'd do what she did for nothing, to satisfy her own desire.

All this annoyed my friend with the straw *kufiyya* who, as I was savouring the ideas they'd expressed, once more pulled me roughly to one side.

The last bunch contained most of the occupants of the bus.

There was a variety of fashions and colours and shapes and sizes; here a pair of trousers, there a turban, here a man with a fashionable European haircut, there another with a straw *kufiyya*, here someone wearing slippers and socks, there another wearing slippers with no socks. The groups included the university graduate, the civil servant and, most prominently, our foolish young friend, the soldier from the local army, the lad who couldn't stop smoking and worrying.

'If I got her alone, I'd leave her in pieces!'

'You savage!'

'You're not civilized!'

'I'd have every sort of sex and pleasure with her.'

'Then I'd leave her and rush off back to the bus.'

'I'd have to get her address afterwards.'

'And I'd live with her in Sanaa, and we'd have a life of constant . . .'

'I'd marry her so we could build a new, happy generation, one that was prosperous and moving forward.'

'If I had the chance, I'd take her and emigrate to the islands of the moon, away from the lot of you. We'd have music and sing all kinds of songs together to the rhythm of the ocean waves . . .'

This last thought swept us into a dream world, each of us dreaming the dreams his own particular imagination suggested. The vast, dusty plain became a blue lake and the mountains which circled us, arid and darkly desolate, became covered in woods and had summits gleaming with snow. The donkeys and beasts of burden disappeared and, in their place, there were boats sailing on the lake. The whine of the telephone wires turned into inspiring Beethoven symphonies!

Then, suddenly, yells and uproar broke out.

The tyre had been repaired and the jostling at the front door of the bus had begun. I saw the well-dressed man moving towards the rear door, a pained expression on his face.

I walked slowly past her, like the others, and saw two eyes overflowing with love and gaiety, a forehead that indicated firmness and courage. She looked at me with a generous candour that made me feel ashamed, and I lowered my eyes. There were so many things I wanted to know about her. Was she a student? Or perhaps she was a factory worker, a civil servant, or perhaps a nurse?

Was she married or not? Maybe she was a widow.

The engine started loudly; we were about to resume the journey. Then I remembered our lawyer friends, lost in the depths of the open plain, and I cried out to the driver to stop. He let out a string of curses under his breath.

We looked out of the windows. They were a very long way away, so far that we couldn't make them out properly; they were just little ghosts racing about in the whirling dust. The driver began to make an ugly noise honking the bus's horn, with varying loudness at first, then with such force it almost drove us mad. The girl spoke.

'Can't you stop that?'

The driver turned to her slowly, his hand still pressing savagely on the horn.

'What do you expect me to do?' he asked rudely.

'You and your assistant should get out and fetch them.'

'That's not our job!'

Realizing the futility of trying to teach him his job, she turned towards the passengers, then addressed him again.

'One of the passengers should volunteer to go and get them.'

The driver looked at the assembled passengers, but no one moved. Everyone turned a deaf ear and my friend with the straw *kufiyya* smiled.

A period of silence followed; then the silence turned to whispered conversation. Suddenly the girl stood up, opened the door and took off towards the lawyers at a steady run. Her youthfulness and energy were made evident by the whirling wind which caressed her black *sharshaf*, revealing feminine curves. She didn't call out but ran towards them without stopping.

All the passengers crowded against the left-hand windows of the bus to watch the scene and I tried to make out what they might be saying, but to no avail. There was a shameful silence with everyone feeling a sense of dishonour. She returned with the two men and we could see from their calm gestures that they were talking quietly together. Then she got on the bus with them, quietly sat down and, taking a small embroidered handkerchief from her handbag, began carefully wiping the drops of perspiration which were trickling down her smooth forehead. The two men were subjected to a torrent of rebuke and abuse from the rest of the passengers, with the voice of the driver, rude and insulting, ringing out above the rest.

Misery was written all over their faces – in fact, they were almost weeping. They'd lost their most important document, the document which was taking them to Sanaa with all their wonderful dreams, which would bring them victory over injustice. It was the document which might have put an end to the fines they'd been paying and the drain on the money they'd saved, and they finally burst into tears over their misfortune. Everyone was silent except the girl, who reproached them for the weakness they were showing.

'Life's wide open, full of opportunity,' she cried. 'It can't be blocked by the loss of a single paper!'

'But it means everything to us!'

'A paper can never mean everything to anyone!'

'It's the paper about some land we've been robbed of.'

'There's always hope for the future.'

'There's no future now.'

'Yes, there is! It'll put an end to all these miserable, meaningless papers, and bring comfort to a lot of people like you.'

They fell into their seats, in a state of nervous agitation.

The bus moved on in silence and my well-dressed companion started working his ideas out again, while a triumphant smile hovered on the lips of my friend with the straw *kufiyya* with the lower part consumed by sweat. Then someone broke the silence.

'When they reach the Court of Appeal, they'll find they've got the paper!'

'Never! It has disappeared behind the Anis mountains.'

Smug laughter broke out sporadically among the passengers, and this produced a response from the foolish, heavy-smoking young soldier.

'If I could, I would ask the Captain to check the matter out for them.'

The girl realized that his gaze was directed mainly at her and she screwed up her lips in disdain.

It was now two in the afternoon. The air was hot, dust was forcing its way through all the windows of the bus and everyone was obviously exhausted. Young and old were asleep and hunger had begun to induce a kind of dull lassitude.

Nausea started gnawing at people's stomachs and almost everyone reacted accordingly. The most upsetting sounds were the heavings and retchings of our lawyer companions and, as the sound of their vomiting rose above the rest, some of those who'd been fighting it back now started themselves.

This provided an opportunity for my well-dressed friend who, in spite of the surging dust, opened the windows for people to throw up. The driver started grumbling and his assistant joined him, quietly cursing. The old conductor was still gazing fixedly at the road, with obvious anxiety, as if the hangman's noose was to be seen in the folds of every mirage. The girl had turned her tape-recorder up to improve the situation a little.

I and my friend with the straw *kufiyya* managed to hold out, helped by the fact that we were broaching serious subjects. The silence following the bouts of retching gave us the chance to continue our conversation, and he became engrossed in it, before suddenly retreating into his own private thoughts. Nevertheless, he seemed to trust me – perhaps he thought of me as a member of the union his son belonged to before he was killed in the streets of New York – and the silence and total calm gave him the chance to tell his story: the emigration to a strange country; the initial hardships; the struggle before he finally became settled; the son he fathered who became dangerously embroiled in a bitter class struggle, fought out in another country, but spurred on by his accumulated experience in the home country; the failure to form a union when he himself came back to his country, because people here were only concerned with matters of religious law. Even his emigrant countrymen in America were only interested in flashy clothes and cars with all the possible trimmings, which they drove to death in two years at the most.

'The Yemeni treats his car like a horse,' he said. 'He saddles it, and decorates it, and . . .'

He saw my smile and paused for a moment, wondering if he'd said the wrong thing. Then he went on.

'If you go into a restaurant or café, you'll find him drinking his tea from the saucer in quick bursts. He's anxious and he's quick to show his anxiety.'

I remembered how I'd behaved like that myself when I was with my friends.

'It's all the legacy of Imam Yahia.'

'But he led the national movement against the Turks.'

He looked at me sadly.

'It was a nightmare,' he said. 'He ruled for forty-five years, years which were the beginning of the twentieth century and saw the developing nations start to wake. And he did nothing in them.'

'You've got to think of how things were in his time.'

'No, he had a backward, lousy, rigid mentality.'

'That's a matter of opinion.'

'That just sums you up! You just see what's on the surface and build it up into some grandiose idea that's got nothing whatever to do with the real situation. Imam Yahia wasn't a hero of national independence. It was the people who fought the Turks and made Yemen a graveyard for them.'

'But the people made him an Imam for forty-five years, and there was order and stability in the country through all that time . . .'

For the first time he interrupted me.

'And the Imam's stick reached everywhere. Isn't that what happened?'

He smiled sarcastically, then bowed his head like some brilliant, logical debater.

'If you'd lived during that time, you wouldn't think the way you do.'

'But history's what you see in front of you.'

'Didn't I say that people like you treat what's on the surface as if it had some deep meaning? The people kept up a long struggle against the Turks. They fought against an empire, just imagine that! An empire that overwhelmed the world with its vast conquests, even in the heart of colonialist Europe, was defeated by one small nation.'

He stirred slightly in his seat; then, having made sure that I wasn't going to interrupt him, he carried on.

'The people were exhausted by wars and famine and siege. They were ready to grasp any solution which would bring their trials to an end.'

'And Imam Yahia was the solution?'

'He came at a time when people were hungry. They were weary ghosts who just wanted to survive, and have safety and stability.'

'They put safety before conviction.'

'The Imam came with the mentality of a wealthy farmer. He'd collect money and grain and hoard it, so that he could buy more land and build more palaces and fountains, and he'd take out lawsuits against people, to seize their lands and get everything they had, old brass and rich furnishings and everything. He never left the capital of his kingdom, never built the smallest thing for the state, never founded any cultural institution for the people. In fact, he took all the schools and cultural establishments the Turks had left behind and turned them into palaces and dungeons! In the end his followers and everyone else got fed up with him, and he met his end. His end!'

357

'Leaving what?'

'A new Imam who was full of hatred.'

'Is that really how things were?'

'It's exactly how they were. Why not go right in behind the surface people write so much about?'

I didn't try to argue with him or carry on the debate because I could see he was beginning to suffer from his attempts not to throw up. I left him for a while and he vomited, without losing his dignity, out of the window. Then, for all my attempts at self-control, I had to do the same and thrust my own head out. It really is unpleasant, vomiting on an empty stomach; I felt as if my ribs and everything behind them was going to be forced up through my throat. You feel as if you're dying a painful, lingering death. Vomiting is a part of the final moment on the verge of death, the final breath of life. I closed my eyes and lay back limply, hoping that the painful, persistent retching would stop.

The sound of people vomiting alongside me was unpleasant to the point of revulsion and I wished the driver would stop for a moment, so that we could throw ourselves down somewhere outside the bus. I wouldn't have minded a bed of hot ashes – anything that wasn't moving! The constant motion churns your stomach up as if it was something used for whipping milk. The ascent of Mount Yasluh increased our nausea, and our giddiness became one with the winding movement of the bus.

The voice of the old ticket collector forced itself on our attention. It was the voice of some dreadful ghost in a dream, sweeping through the passengers:

'The soldier! The soldier!'

It was the soldier who'd been thrown off the bus; along with his companions, he'd blocked the road at the top of the mountain with empty, broken barrels. The bus had reached the summit with a long, sad whining sound from the motor which had filled us with a sense of gloom to add to all our other troubles. The place was a bottle-neck, a narrow pass between two elevated points from which the barrels of the soldiers' machine-guns peered down. It was very dangerous to stop at the entrance to the passage and a number of small rocks had to be put in place behind the rear wheels. This was done by the assistant, a young boy, who was obviously used to doing it.

Everyone craned their necks towards the empty barrels blocking the road. The soldier was standing behind them in full gear, with hand-grenades and a sub-machine-gun and a dagger, chewing angrily on *qat* and with a cigarette in his mouth which had burned right down to the filter. His comrades stood alongside him, their faces revealing the strong emotion their friend had aroused in them.

The soldier didn't move, but his comrades came up to us and spoke:

'We sit here on the top of the mountains with danger all round us, watching all the time so that the rest of you can be safe. We do it for a pittance and a few worm-eaten beans, when it's freezing cold and burning hot. And, in spite of all that, people always treat us with contempt!'

'It's because we don't get their respect by showing them what's what.'

'What a big, strong, solid bus!'

The last speaker kicked the floor of the bus violently with his heavy boots, and the seats shook, along with the people sitting on them.

'Isn't it funny,' he went on mockingly, 'that there's no room on it for a soldier? As if a soldier in his dusty uniform was going to drown the bus in the great, rolling waves of the Jahran valley!'

There was a logic about this which pleased my friend with the straw *kufiyya*. We all felt the tension of the situation and stopped vomiting – except for the lawyers. There was a dreadful silence, followed by urgent questions as to why we'd been stopped.

'It's a search.'

'A search?'

'Yes.'

Whispering began, rising above all the other noises. It was interrupted by a command from the soldier.

'Everyone out with their suitcases. The ones on the inside and the ones on the roof. Quickly!'

The tension grew. The insistence of the soldiers, together with the weapons they were waving and the hatred that was obvious from their violent gestures, persuaded everyone to go along with them.

How harsh problems can be to the weary traveller! Whispered protests began. Something had to be done, because it would take hours to carry out the search.

'This has never happened before,' protested the driver. 'You can't do it!'

'We can do it all right.'

The old man had sunk down in the back of the bus, fearful and agitated, like a mouse in a trap, with no way of defending himself and no one to protect him. He was swearing that, if he managed to escape with his life, he wouldn't stay in his job for another day. The soldiers proceeded to put up the reserve seats in the gangway, and take down the suitcases stacked on the racks, while their comrades outside climbed onto the roof of the bus.

The situation came to a head when it was found that one of the passengers had a weapon without a permit from the military police. He'd felt safe right through the journey, because the bus was never searched; if he'd known what was going to happen, he would simply have gone and taken out a permit from the nearest station we passed. There was a heated argument which almost developed into a fight, and he was the loser. He was a close friend of an expert in the entourage of some Shaikh, and merely mentioning his name would, he supposed, preclude the need to apply for any permit or licence for the weapon. He threatened a good deal, but seemed to make no impression on the soldiers whose inflamed state of mind had blinded them to all discipline.

The way they behaved struck some of the passengers as totally unacceptable and there were many voices raised in protest, the most prominent being that of our well-dressed companion when his wife's suitcase was thrown about. A bottle of perfume was broken and the smell of it wafted over us, adding to our nausea.

Some of the passengers had now had as much as they could take and were prepared to quarrel with the soldiers. Some repeatedly threatened to report the unit; they knew various officials and top people, they said. Another man said he was an officer out of uniform, and another that he worked in a minister's office, but it was all to no avail. The well-dressed man turned to us, and declared:

'This is the worst journey I've ever had in my life.'

'Quite the opposite,' answered my friend with the straw *kufiyya*.

'How can you say that?'

'Why not?'

'That's a funny question after all the things that have happened!'

'And what has happened, my dear sir?'

'You really amaze me! An unpaved road, quarrelling fellow-passengers, choking dust, sun, hunger, throwing up – and now military terrorism, going on at this very moment. And after all that you say: "What has happened, my dear sir?" '

'What's happened is perfectly normal.'

'That's enough, please. I wasn't speaking to you anyway; I was talking to your friend. Please don't make me feel more disgusted than I am already. Spare me that at least.'

I smiled in an attempt to tone down the disagreement but, needless to say, all I did was make it worse. Still, the situation was a critical one and, in view of the weapons and the tired, terrified children, I had to make friendly conversation; so I chatted pleasantly and calmed them down for a while, so that we could see how events developed. The soldiers were still bringing down the cases and people were shouting more and more loudly. My friend and I didn't have any suitcases, and he addressed me again.

'Do you know how many martyrs fell here, in this narrow pass?'

He didn't even give me time to shake my head, but went straight on.

'Dozens fell here, no, hundreds. During the siege.'

'It's been happening since the revolution[3] started, too.'

'In the glorious early days.'

'What memories!'

'I was taken prisoner here along with some friends. They'd emigrated, but they came back as volunteers in the National Guard. They took me to a cave in Kholan. There were a lot of caves there. The Royalist Commander asked me who I was so I said I was a *faqih* who taught boys to recite the Koran and that I'd been forced to join in the battle.'

He laughed, for the first time, till the straw *kufiyya* nearly fell off his head.

'Most of my friends were taken to a prison in Najran,' he went on, 'but I was kept in the cave and released after a few months. I escaped from the Najran prison because I didn't have any gold teeth.'

He laughed again, making me laugh as well. I asked him about the gold teeth.

'Anyone who had any gold teeth was taken to Najran,' he replied, 'because they thought he'd either be an officer or the son of a Shaikh. That was a lesson for some of our emigrant comrades who were always showing off their teeth! What honest, glorious days they were!'

Suddenly the sound of the tape-recorder rang out loudly, drowning all the arguing and quarrelling. Everyone stopped talking and some of the soldiers rushed towards the girl.

'Turn that tape-recorder off, girl,' one of them shouted.

'It's none of your business! You can't order me about!'

The soldier became angrier.

'If you don't turn it off, I'll break it!' he shouted.

'You can't do that!'

He rushed at her, but she faced him with defiant gestures. He looked at his comrades, then backed down.

'You're disturbing our work,' he said, trying to make his voice sound less angry.

She broke out in a mocking laugh.

---

3. This is a reference to the Yemeni revolution of 1962 which, after a fierce civil war which lasted until 1969, triumphed over the armies of the Imam, the traditional ruler of Yemen, and announced a republic.

'I'm helping you,' she countered. 'I'm hoping you might calm down a bit and stop behaving in such a childish way.'

'Childish?'

'Are we going to let her get away with that?'

Most of the soldiers moved to surround the girl. They were in a furious temper, but she showed no sign of fear. The situation had reached boiling point and each passenger had an uglier vision than the next of what might happen.

The man with the straw *kufiyya* sensed my anxiety.

'Don't worry,' he said. 'The Yemeni people are naturally civilized.'

'I'm not sure they will be in a situation like this.'

He smiled confidently – not to embarrass me on account of my disagreement with him, but to underline his own conviction. I felt alert and angry, ready to rescue the girl if she was subjected to any insulting behaviour. The soldier took the tape-recorder and threw it violently out of the door of the bus; it fell on the stony road but didn't stop blaring out the girl's favourite song.

Summoning up all her strength, she gave the soldier a ringing slap round the face, and he fell fearfully back into the arms of his comrades. No one had expected the girl to react so violently.

I began to persuade myself that I'd have to intervene, whatever the cost; there was no other course open to me. Then her voice rang out, as loud as thunder, silencing the cowardly whispers around her.

'You're not defending the homeland. You're just standing up for your own selfish whims.'

'You'll see!'

'I won't see anything worse than the way you're behaving.'

'You insolent woman!'

'No one's as insolent as you've been!'

'We were doing our duty!'

'What duty?'

'You were one of the people who let a wretched soldier be thrown off the bus because he was poor!'

'That was one particular incident. You passed the law and the old man carried it out to the letter.'

'You whore!'

'Whores are people who violate citizens' safety.'

I moved towards the girl, along with an angry group. The tape-recorder, with a persistence which matched its owner, was still playing the girl's favourite song.

It now looked to the passengers as if things would turn out worse than they'd supposed; for all their tiredness, and the hardness of the journey, and the hunger and sickness, they hadn't expected matters to come to this pitch of violence. They were prepared to tolerate hunger and thirst and vomiting and the discomforts of life, but the very thought of what was likely to happen here was unbearable. A girl confronting armed soldiers! What would their position be if they didn't go to the girl's assistance – thus exposing themselves to the soldiers' weapons?

My one concern, as I rushed forward, was to be vindicated against my friend with the straw *kufiyya*. But I was disappointed; he still held to his conviction that the Yemeni people were naturally civilized. I forced myself to think badly of him; a man who'd lived in a country of cowboys and Mafia gangs and Al Capone wasn't going to get worked up over a situation like this!

A terrible question arose in the mind of every passenger: what would the outcome be if the soldiers assaulted the girl? Some indicated that they were willing to sacrifice themselves, while others chose silence, and still others were attempting to intervene and solve the crisis by peaceful means:

'Look, you men, don't you fear God?'

'Patience is a virtue.'

'She's a girl, and you're men.'

'Men are above the way women act.'

'Women are small-minded.'

Personally, I wasn't convinced by the words of these people who were the sort who always serve their own private interests.

The solution was quite plain: either we had to defend her come what may, or else the situation had to be resolved in the girl's favour, even if it took some kind of miracle to do it. Some people supported my view that the girl was in the right and that we ought to defend her physically, while others wondered wearily whether the soldiers wouldn't defeat every possible solution – a challenge to those who were willing to sacrifice themselves.

The bunch of cowards in the party began to make themselves heard.

'A poor girl.'

'Soldiers who've been provoked.'

'An ordinary incident. People with extremist ideas shouldn't exploit it.'

What happened next brought back the old student enthusiasm, tickling my feelings and the feelings of some of the others. How the faces of the soldiers startled me, as they flushed with a shame which seemed ready to explode out of them! The clatter of their boots rose above all the suppressed whispers; the tape-recorder, still playing the favoured song, was thrown into the bus, the door was closed and the broken, empty barrels were removed from the road, to reveal heads bowed low in shame. The bus passed through, with the old man's jaw dropping, and we began a frantic descent towards Sanaa.

All the passengers collapsed into their seats without a word; the dust started rising again, and the trip resumed its normal course. I fell back in my seat, trying to ignore my friend with the straw *kufiyya* whose lower half was consumed by sweat. He consoled me with a sympathetic smile meant to dispel my sense of defeat. Then sleep descended on me and, for the first time, I felt I needed it; it took control remorselessly, responding to my wish to escape from reality. I slept soundly, with disturbing dreams that I'd never had before, like the dreams of a guard sleeping on the Naqeel Yasluh or al-Haima road, or on the besieged Wall of Sanaa. After an hour's rest, I woke up to find myself the only passenger left. There was no one there at all, not even the driver.

I darted through the heavy traffic, cars and fast motorcycles, looking for my friend with the straw *kufiyya* whose lower part was consumed by sweat – who'd perhaps taken pity on me and left me alone. I hurried towards the Yemen Gate and the crowded Freedom Gate in the southern part of Sanaa, and found many people wearing similar *kufiyyas*, but I couldn't make out my friend.

I got onto one of the motorcycles that were there for hire, sitting behind a boy who drove expertly and at a mad speed, and wore a straw *kufiyya* with its lower part consumed by sweat.

Translated by Lena Jayyusi and Christopher Tingley

*Khalil al-Fuzay*ᶜ   **SAUDI ARABIA**

Scattered Voices

The peace-loving village keeps a hold on hope at all times. When the men set off for the pearl-hunt, the women send them off with prayers; and they welcome them back with sky-piercing ululations. The traditional diving-songs place no value on composure: at the return of his son, the old man dances; the mother sings at the return of hers, while the wife's happiness is such that it brings tears to her eyes. This happens when they come back with plenty of pearls, but also when they came back with nothing. Reunion was always a joyous occasion.

After sunset the men gather in a semi-circle. Their dark faces flicker in the light of the fire at which they warm their drums and tambourines. The communal singing begins. It is exquisite in both its joy and its sorrow. The dancers dance themselves into a frenzy. In the pauses between songs, you can hear the sounds of the Gulf waves as they enfold the golden sands of the shore.

Jaber, a singer-sailor prevented by poor health from going to sea, whispered to his neighbour:

'His father, God rest his soul, was a good man . . .'

He did not wait for an answer, but raised his voice in song with the rest. The other man went on clapping, but at the first chance he said,

'I've never known anyone like that hypocrite!'

'Stop talking about him – curse him!' joined in a third.

The singing continued:

> Allah, hope of all ships,
> Vanquisher of the enemy's horses.
> Never accuse an honest woman, and woe to him who does so!
> Fear your punishment! Watch out for God and fear!
> Keep secrets in your heart and never tell your secret, fear!

Beware the conceited, ignorant man whose mind is shallow
And take care, today you'll see, the guardian is himself the thief.

The singing stopped. Among scattered groups conversations sprang up, conversations that all began and ended with the village and the sea.

'As long as we've known him, he's never done anything good,' said Jaber.

'How can we just let him spread misery in the land?' asked another. 'Piling up his ill-gotten wealth, persecuting the weak, robbing, even murdering . . .'

'Is he not the *Umda*?' answered Jaber. 'His father was a good man. Once, when I was preparing for a diving trip, the old man sent for me and said, "Jaber, if you need anything, I'm ready." But I'd already got what I needed from the captain, so I just thanked him for his generosity. We stayed away a long time and I was worried about my family at home. When we got back, I learned that he had helped them out without even being asked. But as for this one – before we'd got to know him for what he is, I left some money with him and, to this day, he denies ever having received it. He swears he never saw one rupee!'

Everyone listened to his voice ringing in the night. The music of the waves bore dew and promises.

Another sailor, not a native of the village but no stranger to it either, asked, 'Why don't you bring him to trial?'

'How can we?' Jaber replied, frustrated. 'He only strikes after setting things up so that he will necessarily seem to be in the right.'

'How many times have we tried and sentenced him?' said someone else. 'But *he's* our authority. Who will force him to carry out the sentence?'

The talk spread infectiously among the men. Each had a story about the *Umda*: how he had bought pearls from one man but then refused to settle the balance; how a dying friend had made him guardian over his children, whereupon he had robbed them of their inheritance and left them with nothing. A man with a large scar on his face told shyly how he had stood up to the *Umda*, who had then sent unknown thugs to beat him up. At the end his voice was quivering with rage and frustration.

The sea started to make a wailing sound. The water ebbed a little from the shore. A star shone, then vanished. Everyone was bored with the hopeless topic, and the old singer's voice rose in a song. Suddenly, a tremendous response to the music was generated. The night re-echoed the tune of the bitter-sweet voices. A man stained dark by the Gulf sun rose to his feet and entered the dance circle, beating out with his feet on the earth a rejection of all falsehood and pain. His body, in ecstasy, became part of a brilliant and happy world. The sounds of the drums and the singers seemed to be born of his rebellious body. Now his hands flailed out, joining with his feet in an eternal wrestling match with a phantom enemy. The men were transported beyond this world; they soared in fantastical realms of shipwrecks and the remnants of drowned bodies ravaged by sea-monsters. They roamed all the known seas and anchored at the shores of yearning where waves opened up to swallow everything: the green and the dry. The men pushed their singing, step by step, towards worlds that were even more violent and primitive, but the final stage of their dance expressed a resignation that was out of tune with their earlier defiance.

The light of a gas lamp revealed a figure hurrying towards them.

Jasim panted out his message: 'The *Umda* is dead! Murdered!'

The men gazed at each other in surprise, bewilderment and regret. This was something they had never expected. Not one of them had liked the man, but to hate him was one thing; that he should die murdered was another.

Some hurried to the scene of the crime. Others turned to go home, while yet others stayed where they were, waiting for the dawn.

Translated by Ahdaf Soueif and Thomas G. Ezzy

The Storm

Today is Saturday[1] – the beginning of the week and you are bored already. But you shouldn't be. Everyone says they come back to work full of energy after the weekend. Your work needs energy, mine doesn't. I'm the one who should be bored with this work, not you. All I do is clean the Director's office and wait for his orders. As for you, your work is always new; lots of people come to see you every day; you can deal with any case you choose and, if you don't like someone's looks, you can tell him to come back tomorrow. Don't be offended – isn't that the truth? What? Some truths are better left unsaid? You're right. But I didn't mean to offend you – you know that . . .

What? No, I don't want to sit down and chat. I know we have lots of time because the Director never gets here before eleven, but you always want me to talk about the past – about the pearl-diving days. Why do you always insist on this? You know very well there's nothing I'd rather do than reminisce about the old days, but right now I just don't want to. Why do you keep insisting?

Oh well, it seems there's nothing I can do. I'll sit. But, with your permission, I'll go and get some tea so we can enjoy the story . . . What? You've already ordered some? Well, in that case, there's nothing for me to do but talk. But what about your work and the people who are coming to see you? You can't just shut the door in their faces – a chat can be postponed. Ah, here's the tea! It's hot and delicious . . .

Right, well, now that you've taken care of your clients . . . No, no, don't close the door, I have to keep an eye out for the boss . . .

Pearl-diving stories are full of sorrow . . . But money ran through my hands like water then: diving brought it in in heaps. And now look at me

1. The Muslim holy day is Friday and the Muslim working week begins on Saturday.

– the Director's office boy! What a world! Praise be to God the Unchanging . . .

I had a big boat and on certain days we'd set off on our trips to the heart of the Gulf. Since I was the captain and in full charge of everything, I didn't have as hard a time as the divers. It was the men who did the work and suffered: the diver who hunted for the mother-of-pearl, his mate who kept watch for the slightest sign to pull him back to the surface, the boy who served and assisted everyone – even the singer who came along with us: they all worked harder than I ever did.

Sometimes we'd come back with plenty and sometimes with hardly anything at all. But whatever we got was usually enough to hold us until the next time. I used to have to lend money to some of the men and get it back after the next trip. No, no, I never charged interest. I didn't want to exploit my sailors. Some captains charged interest, but I never took back more than I had lent. Yes, you're right. A captain does live a good life but not as luxurious as you might think. He has his problems, too, and it's he who's responsible for everyone on his boat . . .

One afternoon, everything was running smoothly. All our men were on deck, busy splitting the mother-of-pearl, and I was sitting there enjoying my water-pipe and quietly watching them work. Then, suddenly, the sky darkened and the sea rose. The boat lurched and everyone lost their balance. I dropped my pipe and found myself huddled in the stern with my men. Some of them were gripping the sides and voices were raised in prayers and exclamations. Water was filling the boat. I shouted at them to bail it out, grabbed the nearest bucket and started bailing. So did the others but we could not keep up with the sea. We were desperate. In those anguished moments I was not concerned for myself as much as for my men. Through the noise I realized that some had been swept overboard and were, at that very moment, battling the waves. Something told me I would lose some of them . . .

You're letting your tea get cold, drink it. What? You don't want your tea? You want to know what happened next? Well, what happened next was enough to turn your hair white. We fought bitterly against the sea. The faster we bailed, the faster the boat filled up. The closer we came to death, the more we wanted to live. No one was speaking any more and Death himself could not have told the difference between the captain and the humblest of the men. At first I'd been thinking of my men but, in the end, I was thinking only of myself. I fiercely wanted to save the boat – not because I owned it, but because it was our only hope of survival. You know the proverbial 'straw in the wind'? That's how we were. The waves played with us cruelly, tossing us here and there. One huge, monstrous wave came at us. I thought we were done for but, suddenly, we were riding it, looking down as though from a mountain-top. Then we were flung into emptiness. The boat spun and we were all beyond the point of exhaustion.

But the will to live is stronger than any storm, so we fought. We saw those who gave in being swept away to God-only-knows-where. There was a moment when I was on the point of surrendering but the image of my son Jassoum sprang into my mind and I forgot my despair. In the midst of the terrible sounds of the storm you could still hear voices raised in prayer. These urged us to even greater efforts: surely, our Maker would not desert us? Those who lost faith vanished and were swallowed up by the waves.

The storm lasted maybe an hour. It was the longest, most terrible hour in all time. Then, as suddenly as it began, it ended. The sea was covered with bodies and wrecked boats. Men were hanging on to anything to save themselves from the death they had come so close to. We finished bailing out the last of the water and started rescuing survivors. We lost some men and saved others and, as sunset approached, the world was filled with silence. All tongues praised God and that night we slept as we had never slept before . . .

What did we do then? We did what everyone did: we went home to comfort our families, who had heard news of the storm. What? You say your own father died in that storm? God have mercy on his soul! You never told me that before . . . So that's why you're so keen on sea stories . . . But tell me, why are you always looking so bored? Don't you like your work? It's a comfortable job – Oh, oh. I have to leave now. The boss is here.

Translated by Ahdaf Soueif and Thomas G. Ezzy

Muhammad Hasan al-Harbi   UNITED ARAB EMIRATES

An Ordinary Death

He contemplated his barren world, and murmured:

'God damn it, what a life I've had!'

He put a cigarette between his dry lips, then, with his two hands, began searching for the lighter in the pockets of his threadbare jacket. He slowly eased his body downwards and squatted on the ground. 'The problems of life!' he murmured. He arranged the edges of his jacket, contemplating his grey feet and leather slippers. 'Everybody,' he thought, 'everybody except me! I'm the only one who's never made it!' He took a deep puff from his cigarette and it was as if the nicotine gave him energy for a moment. 'If I'd married Hussa,' he murmured, 'if God had shown me the right way, my son would have been as tall as me by now.'

He looked to the right: there were modest houses there, and women and the smell of baking bread. Then he turned to look to the left, and saw children playing. 'If I'd married Hussa that year,' he thought, 'my son would have been playing with them now, and I'd be calling him: "Fahd, Fahd!" and he'd answer: "Yes, *Yubah*." What a lovely word! I'd call him again: "Fahd, come here! It's getting dark, son. Let's go home, you've played enough." Then he'd hang about, and say: "Let me play a little bit more, just a little bit more, *Yubah*." Then I'd run after him and catch him, and I'd hug him and love him and hold him tight to my chest. And I'd say: "You lovely boy, my own father's grandson, you're the dearest of all to me!" That's what I'd tell him, and I'd feel a great sense of calm flood over me. But what's the use of being sorry now?'

The flow of his thoughts continued. He straightened his headband, pushed his *ghutra* down and touched his rough moustache. He felt rather weary. He bent his head, then decided he ought to change his position. The moment his backside touched the floor, he pushed one leg out, keeping the other bent; then he took off both his slippers, placing one

371

over the other and set them down in front of him. He stared at them and smiled sourly, and his nose looked like a dry raisin. Then he went back to his daydreaming: 'Couples, everybody's in couples! Life may be vast, but it only accepts couples. My God, it was only created for married people – a man and his wife.'

He tried to break the vicious circle. 'Suppose I borrow some money? No. Or, what if I went to work in another country? Maybe God would give me a chance. You know what they say: "There's a blessing in movement." '

He slipped back into his delirium, his thoughts whirling, swirling dizzily. 'Nuwayyir – I wanted to marry Nuwayyir. But people won't leave you alone. She was intelligent and solid – even if she did sell *bajilla*. They say her mother was a *bajilla*-seller too, back in the days of poverty and pearl-diving. Well, what if she did sell *bajilla*? Is there something shameful about being a *bajilla*-seller? I wish I had the chance to sell *bajilla*! I'd stand on the road where the schoolchildren pass, and sell it. I'd even sell on credit – they could pay at the end of the month.'

Delirium opened up a wound in his soul. 'God damn money! Wherever you go, all anyone ever talks about is money! I didn't have any money, they said. What business is that of theirs anyway? People are going crazy, God, they're crazy! I'd like to see them look round for some money, and not find any, ever. God, let them all go to bed hungry! Amen.'

Delirium drained him, dehydrated him, and things were made worse as he continued to cough and spit blood. He coughed, shivered, went back into his memories. 'Nuwayyir!' Cough. 'Hussa!' He spat more blood. 'Fahd! Money, *bajilla*, poverty, pearl-diving, money. You've played enough, Fahd.'

He felt around him, searching for his packet of cigarettes; then he stretched out on the ground, panting and delirious. 'If only I'd married her – I'd have – I'd have . . .'

Sudden, loud noises. An ambulance arrived. A boy carrying a pair of slippers was panting, and shouting: 'My uncle's dead! My uncle's dead!'

Translated by Salwa Jabsheh and Christopher Tingley

Kamal Haydar

A Man of No Consequence

'You're a fool!' my wife yelled at me at the top of her voice. 'You're a nobody!' . . . What could she have made up about me that would be further from the truth? . . . It is true that I feel the flame of my life dying down, and that I am becoming insignificant, and soon I'll be counted amongst the dead. But fool? 'Fool' is a little word, yet in its true sense can mean a lot. . . . Am I really one? Or is my wife just being vicious? . . . I just don't know . . .

This is what *Ustadh* Omar ibn Omar was muttering to himself as he left his small, narrow house in al-Amasir Alley on his way to the primary school – the same school to which he had given, as a teacher, the sap of his youth and the essence of his modest intellectual ability. As he walked along, he carried his students' exercise-books in his left hand, which he held firmly pressed against his sagging paunch to help support the load. His face was lined with anxiety. The spark of life had gone out of his eyes and had been replaced by dull resignation, along with drowsiness from having corrected the stupidities of seventy-two copybooks by the light of a kerosene lamp that danced to the sporadic music of the roof of his creaky house.

– Am I horrid? No, of course not! But . . .

His meditations over his wife's words were brought to a halt by the yowling of two cats, embroiled in a bitter, bloody struggle in a narrow, foul-smelling alley. He stooped over them with his bulky frame. Careful to keep his right foot, which was encased in a tattered shoe, from stepping into a fly-infested heap of human dung, he gave the cat that was getting the better of the other a good kick . . . Just as though he were kicking himself – his trivial self! Both cats scampered off, but one of them turned around to snarl at him angrily.

– Even this cat confronts me with my triviality . . . But no, no, I'm not a fool!

He was saying this to himself as he passed from the drab alley into the street, where he saw cars speeding by in a reckless frenzy while the crowd of chattering pedestrians jostled each other on the pavement. Some of them were talking about a football match that had been played in the city stadium between the Independent Sports Team and the Young Men's Islamic Association team. Others were arguing about some of the characters in the film *Antar and Abla*.[1] Still others were telling how bored and exasperated they'd been at a delay in getting their *qat* leaves the afternoon before . . .

Omar gleaned snatches of the assertions made by the passers-by. Then suddenly he thought – They say that teaching is a good, respectable profession! What a profession!

He let out a laugh whose bitterness he could taste in his mouth, and went on talking to himself – Words, empty words . . . Just like our lives!

'*Ustadh* Omar . . . *Ustadh* Omar!'

The insistent, loud voice of a child, calling him by name, struck his ears.

Turning towards the voice, he saw a child who had raised his hand in greeting, his face wreathed in a buoyant smile. The boy's father was hanging on to his son closely; on his face Omar caught the ghost of a grudging smile, a smile bestowed with condescension. Omar bared his teeth and nodded his head to return the greeting, while his mind told him:

This child is happy to greet me because he is in my class. Presently, however, he will leave this school to enrol in another, and in the end will pretend he doesn't know me. Soon, once he's finished with the Middle School, he will ignore the teachers from there also, and so on . . . There will be no greeting, no rejoicing in an encounter, no tiresome accosting . . . It's as if we teachers reminded our pupils of a horrible period in their lives, during which they lived and breathed with great difficulty . . . Or as if we were nothing more than human nonentities, who deserve no appreciation or gratitude from either our pupils or society . . .

He became aware that he was standing on the edge of the pavement, on the point of crossing the street. He had scarcely taken two steps when he

1. Abla and Antar were two lovers in pre-Islamic times. Antar is the famous poet, Antara ibn Shaddad, from Southern Arabia. The son of an Ethiopian slave woman, he was refused marriage initially to his lovely cousin, Abla, but eventually won her hand through the great valour he showed in saving his tribe from defeat in the raid of another tribe.

heard the screech of a car slamming on its brakes. With alarm showing on his face he turned around, as the chauffeur of the car heaped all sorts of unrestrained abuse on him. Then Omar's weak eyes caught sight of Ahmad Salih, who was occupying the back seat, wearing expensive sunglasses and watching with malicious joy and extreme insolence.

Omar proceeded on his way, subdued by the taunts of the man who had cursed him and the scathing comments of the passers-by. His teeth chattered with anger as he muttered emphatically:

– He's one of my pupils . . . He has returned to Aden from abroad, brandishing a university degree . . . We always see him with his chest puffed out, his head almost touching the sky . . . He has his own business here, and is making a profit from it that my limited imagination cannot even conceive of . . . He drinks every kind of beverage and satisfies his stomach with the best food, while he has put this learning on a shelf in his large, luxurious home . . .

Omar spat vigorously on the ground, as though he were spitting in the face of his former pupil, then continued talking to himself.

– How wicked he is! . . . Hard times and very bad circumstances made me need his help, but he made me taste such bitterness, and showed such ingratitude towards me that I could not bear it! If only he had been satisfied with that . . . But whenever he meets a government employee he starts spitting out words of complaint against the lives of us brainless, indolent people.

He discovered that his hand was in the process of extracting a cheap cigarette from his pocket. He put it between his lips with difficulty, his hand shaking. Then he sluggishly put his hand into the pocket of his frayed overcoat, searching for his box of matches. It wasn't there. Standing still to shift the copybooks to his right hand, he thrust his left hand into the other pocket. Then he remembered.

– My wife took it from me when she was preparing the tea. She didn't give it back, the simpleton! She has not learned, and never will learn, that this is the twenty-ninth day of the month, and that the shopkeeper has been asking me over and over for the payment of our entire account, along with the price of what we've consumed during this long, accursed month!

Taking the cigarette out of his mouth, he shoved it angrily into his pocket and made his way towards the school. Then, he thought of his lesson-plan book, and a shudder ran down his spine.

– I believe I did prepare today's lessons! he whispered to himself. Yes . . . yes, I did make my mechanical, boring preparation! When it comes to the need for a preparation, there's no getting around the arrogant directives of loud-mouthed school principals! What a joke! I have taught reading all my life so that now I know the lessons by heart. If it weren't for that bunch, my pupils' monotonous reading would put me into a sweet, blissful sleep!

His feeble smile bespoke an obscure, malicious joy.

– And who are these preparations for, I wonder? For the pupils? In Primary School, all they're interested in doing is causing a disturbance and making an uproar. In Middle School, their sole interest is in reading detective stories and arguing about what happens in them. And in Secondary School, as I've heard, they are mad about the cinema or crazy about girls. Only the small minority show any desire for the life of a university graduate, as something that will enable them to fill their bellies and pockets, and enjoy a life of ease . . .

Finding himself in the school, he sauntered into the staff room where he found the teachers preoccupied, as usual, with their rambling, pointless discussions that had neither beginning nor end. They didn't hear his greeting; so, placing his copybooks on his desk, he flung his balloon-like body onto his chair and listened, as usual, like a child, trying to understand what they were saying.

'But, my dear chaps,' Salah was saying, 'they sent him and they succeeded! Gagarin went up into space and returned safely! And he, or someone else, will be going to the moon and then to the rest of the planets, while we get all worked up and wear ourselves out with thinking about finding a secluded, private spot to spend an evening in!'

'Alas, how true!' said Ahmad. 'The Russians put this brave young volunteer into an experiment which, if it had failed, could have cost him his life. I wish they had, when they wanted to undertake this trial, chosen a man from southern Arabia. But, I believe, we wouldn't have been up to that, either.'

'True, true . . . I'm of the same opinion, my dear fellow,' agreed Salah. 'Our life is pointless.'

He said this with bitterness, sighing deeply. However, Jalal cut him off:

'Have you read today's issue of the *Independence*? It's embarked on a real slinging-match of name-calling and vulgar insults with the *Struggle*!'

'There's nothing strange about that,' stated Murad. 'It is a mirror that truly and honestly reflects our life. We start out seriously debating an important topic, only to turn to disparagement to conceal the emptiness of our minds.'

Jalal changed the subject. 'Have you heard that our colleague Yusuf Ahmad has died, leaving his family with no one to support them? Don't you believe that our position makes it incumbent on us to offer assistance

376

by making a generous offer towards the support of this stricken, respectable family until a solution is found to their problem?'

'What made you think up this strange solution, you big philanthropist?' asked Ahmad. 'What concern is this family of ours? Do you think we're God's messengers on earth?'

He seemed proud of this last statement and he turned around, laughing, to see what effect his words had had on his friends. On discovering Omar's presence, he hastened to ask, in words that dripped with malevolent gloating and stinging scorn: 'What's your opinion of surrealism?'

– I taught this young fellow the rudiments of reading and arithmetic, Omar thought to himself. I used to cover his belly with pinches and his cheeks with slaps, because of his absent-mindedness and his antics. Now he enjoys ridiculing me, to amuse himself and his colleagues at my ignorance. What a mean fellow he is!

As he was thinking this, he heard his tongue resonating with these words:

'Are you trying to entertain yourself, boy, by making fun of me? *You* tell me the meaning of sur-sur-surelism![2] What is it? What use is it to us?'

The bell rang, the school seraph blowing his trumpet. Omar stopped, panting with nervous energy that exhausted him. He got up, feeling disgust and nausea for those he was looking at. For the first time in his life, he saw them in their true light. Now he must come out with this truth, which he had just unearthed after it had lain for so many years of his life, hidden by his attempts to pretend it wasn't there. Yes, he must proclaim the truth! Perhaps it would send a new life through these young men – a life he himself had aspired to and now desired for them. His voice rang out like a peal of thunder:

'Yes, yes, I *am* an ignorant, trivial man! But what have *you* done, with your great learning and hot-blooded youth, I wonder? What? What, except talk – all this never-ending talk? Shut up, Ahmad! Shut up all of you! We are all equally trivial! All of us are fools! All of us! All of us!'

Translated by Olive Kenny and Thomas G. Ezzy

2. The misspelling is intentional to simulate the mistaken pronunciation.

The Imprint of Blackness

In the distance rose the lofty peaks of a wide circle of mountains. From the core of these mountains issued relatively high hills that stretched across the intervening space. Numerous valleys opened into one valley in which the torrents that poured from the high ground when it rained collected and were channelled towards irrigation-outlets for extensive farm lands.

This was the natural world on which my eyes first opened. By the time I was just over three years old, I had not grasped its true nature. I observed it simple-mindedly. The abundance of the milk I drank, which came from the udders of goats, depended on rainfall and the flourishing of the pastures; the little bits of bread I was used to eating came from the earth; when rain did not fall and drought prevailed, the ground became arid, and widespread famine and destitution was the result: all this I came to comprehend at a later date; but, at the age of three, I was concerned only with having enough to eat. I paid no attention to the natural environment of which I was a part.

Our village was a collection of box-like houses, one or two storeys high, that lay at the foot of one of the hills. Some of them resembled, architecturally, fortified citadels, while others were made of clay or goats' hair. These architectural distinctions did not reflect the tastes or desires of the occupants; rather, they gave clear testimony to their varying material and social conditions. Wealth called for the building of fortresses and two-storey homes, while poverty dictated clay and goats' hair. The village had not been set up this way originally, for our people, tribal in nature, once possessed rights over equal amounts of property. Need had forced some of them to sell or mortgage part of their land to those who, anticipating times of famine, possessed money or seed. One outsider, for example, had come to our village with money and cunning, and had made it a practice to lie in wait for those in need. Thus, he came to dwell in a large, castle-like house, and owned scores of acres of fertile land. I was not aware of these facts at that time.

When I was four years old, violent rains fell on the mountains and slopes, sending heavy floods down the valley. It was my first experience of this natural force. People rushed towards the fields with a joy and energy I had not noticed before, and I did not understand why they were behaving this way. I found myself and a band of village children racing along with the people, each of us holding on to his father's or mother's gown, paying no attention to the threat of injury in this rushing tide of humanity, and joyful in this happy, boisterous procession.

Our childish joyfulness, however, disappeared, followed by shock, at our first sight of the colour of blood. The red drops that flowed from the head of one of the men jolted our tender and innocent sensibilities. Two men had been arguing fiercely at one of the sluice-gates; one of them had struck the other on the head with a stone, and the latter had drawn a knife and buried it in the former's back. Blood gushed out and he had fallen unconscious into the torrent. People gathered to lift him out before the rushing water carried him away.

Instinctively, I hurried toward my father, who was busy repairing an outlet through which the flooding water had broken. The owner of the adjacent land was widening this outlet and taking away the mud which my father was putting back in place. It was a ludicrous sight.

People were intervening to prevent what had happened a few moments earlier from happening again, when some men who were wearing coarse, unfamiliar clothes came on the scene. They carried long wooden rods with holes in the upper ends (I learned later that these were rifles), and some of them were leading the man who'd stabbed the other. One of them pointed at my father. At this, cries arose and hands reached out but, finally, my father was led away, while the owner of the neighbouring land was left free. Angrily, I hung on to my mother's skirt. I felt an overpowering urge to go after my father as he left, but my mother held on to me tightly. Meanwhile our neighbour, paying no attention to the armed strangers, widened the outlet as he wished, until our own land was left completely without water.

I became tormented by an inner compulsion, an urgent need to understand the meaning of what I'd seen that afternoon: my father's leaving with the armed men and his failure to return. My mother's anxiety and sorrowful silence gave me no rest. They doubled my bewilderment and kindled my desire to get to the bottom of what had been taking place around me. As she was preparing supper, my mother noticed my anxiety and wondered at it. By the time supper was ready I had gone to bed. Amazed at my going to sleep so early, she woke me up. I said I would not get up until I knew what had happened to my father. She tried to mollify me with a few words, adding that the time had not come for me to know, that I would understand it later. I refused supper and pretended to go to sleep. A demon raged in my mind – a sudden insomnia kept my nerves on edge.

I heard my mother talking to herself and understood that she was giving vent to her anger:

'It's like this every rainy season! The land can't enjoy the rain, and now my man has been taken to prison! The authorities are hypocrites! They give judgements that favour whoever pays the most! They won't even give us a chance to feel happy at the rain – they snatch the joy out of our hearts! It is a tyranny that never ends!'

An unfamiliar agony took me over: my little frame trembled, and tears poured from my eyes, but there was no insight to help me understand the situation. All my efforts to grasp precisely what was going on were in vain; they were like speaking into a void. My brain was wrapped up in a dark, mysterious cloud, which left an imprint of blackness on it . . .

The wizened face of the mountains and rolling foothills vanished, covered by a mantle of green – a glorious display of our natural environment's radiance and splendour. My mother would go out early in the day to take the flocks of sheep to high ground, leaving her small baby on the floor. I pitied the little one's condition: swarms of flies gathered on his little mouth while he slept and, when awake, he would cry ceaselessly. He would eat dirt and whatever else fell within his grasp.

I saw children somewhat older than I taking on the task of shepherding the flocks, often at the insistence of their families. I no longer remember how I came to the decision to follow their example. My mother was startled when I told her that I was going to do the shepherding in her place. She disagreed on the grounds that the time had not yet come for that. When she saw she could not dissuade me, she entrusted me to the rest of the children.

In time I became accustomed to it, and learned to love deeply my fellow-shepherds. We would go out together in the morning and, at noon, would divide up the dry, round loaves of bread and make tea beside some stream. Before evening we would be on our way home to the village. Those were days of cloudless happiness. We wore only a knee-length garment (most of us had only one) for months on end. On moonlit

380

nights we would get together, late into the night, and play various games. Then we would sleep and set out again before dawn . . .

Time imparted a severity – or, more accurately, a stubborn patience – to my mother. The lack of news of my father gave rise to uneasiness in the village, in my mother and in myself.

One night, when the village was peaceful as usual, with no sign of life other than the faint glow of lamps that issued from the narrow windows and died out one by one, and while we children were playing as usual, a company of armed soldiers encircled the village. Having left their vehicles at the bottom of the slope, they invaded the village on foot. Groups of them took up positions at the entrances to the village, while others surrounded our house. Carrying a light in their hands, they knocked loudly on the door. We youngsters scattered amongst them. The door opened and there stood my mother.

'Where is he?' one of them asked, several times.

Close up, I could see my mother's astonishment. Mindful of the soldier's irate arrogance, she pointed to me and said:

'I have no man except him, and a suckling infant inside! As for my husband, *you* took him by force – you, or others like you!'

'You're lying!' retorted the man sharply. 'He is hiding inside!'

All together they burst through the door, almost knocking my mother to the ground. I was seized by a furious anger. I thought of picking up a stone to crash down on the head of one of those roughnecks. My mother put her arms about me and looked at them in amazement. She was truly baffled that they should be searching for a man they had put in prison.

The soldiers withdrew and those who had blocked off the entrances to the village went away with them. They left, however, a huge unanswered question in our home. We could not settle down all night, plunged as we were into a wide sea of anxiety and confusion. The impact of these events on my limited imagination was to thrust me into a whirlpool that seemed truly impenetrable. But all this translated itself in my mind into a protest against a wrong, that I did not understand, being perpetrated on us.

Gradually, this undefined resentment would advance towards a more precise awareness of its object. In retrospect, I later came to realize that such a quest for awareness is an element of basic intelligence which, if a child acquires it early in life, will have important consequences: resentment, hatred, even love, should not be allowed to subside into the unconscious without having been subjected to the ordeal of a long and exhaustive examination, which may take years, in order to find answers to the question of *why* we resent, or hate, or love. This, along with just reasoning, ensures the soundness and legitimacy of one's emotions, and results in stability and constancy . . .

My ordeal increased in severity. I became more and more concerned about my father, felt more attached to him. In my imagination I pictured him as a great man and listened in on various conversations to learn more about him. I decided to go to the city, where the authorities and the prison were located. I did not know how to begin, but no one would listen to me, for in our tradition, no one pays any attention to what children say: the general rule followed by grown-ups is to brush them off harshly.

Leaving the narrow confines of our village for the city, which seemed to me another world despite the fact that it was only a country town, was my first venture. I then decided to break into the prison, but the difficult question was, how?

As I was searching for a means to this end, somehow my feet led me up to the prison wall at a spot where I was able to climb up to look in at a window. I fell against it, however, and smashed the glass. I ran, but could not evade the guards. Powerful blows fell on my face and I was put in jail where I was greeted with great surprise. One of the inmates told me that my father and a few others had escaped from the prison and had probably headed north.

The setting sun was tinging the horizon with yellow when the door opened and I was released. My ear was pinched several times and I was threatened with some very forceful advice.

I wandered through the city as darkness fell. Ordinarily, a child my age would not dare to undertake the long distance between the city and our village while night ruled the highway. But I was feeling strangled by the strangeness of the city and it would have been unbearable for me to remain there.

Fighting back my fear of what the pitch darkness might be hiding, I decided to take the risk and left. The trees took on frightening shapes for me, which made my imagination run wild. From time to time I lost my way, bumping into a tree or boulder or falling into a ditch.

My mother, anxious as she'd been, met me with a painful beating, even before offering me any food. But her anger did not last long for, once she knew everything, she realized her error of hastiness. In her joy at my escape from the wild animals which, it was said, prowled the valley under cover of night, she had a ram slaughtered.

The meat was very tasty.

We had not finished supper when we heard a light knock on the door.

'Who's knocking?' she asked, in a loud voice.

Bidding her to keep her voice down, he opened the door.

It might not be possible for me to describe our feelings exactly, so I shall content myself by saying that the warmth of our joy compensated for the lack of burning coals in our hearth on that very chilly winter's night.

Father did not pay much attention to us or to news about the land or the people. Most of his concern was focused on the little one who had been born in his absence. A fountain of love had burst forth inside him: he examined the baby's features as though to engrave them on his mind, in view of possible future eventualities.

Before I went to bed, he embraced me:

'Plant the seeds of jasmine and sweet flowers in your soul for the motherland,' he said. 'Water them constantly with the life blood that flows through your veins so that they may blossom to spread a pure fragrance within you for the sake of our land, honour and freedom. Let your heart be a skilful and vigilant gardener, tending the motherland's flowers inside you, watering them lest they wither away. You must show yourself mature, for you are the man of the house and of our land. You represent me to others.'

My young breast swarmed with fervent emotions so that I could not speak.

'My little son, we have dedicated ourselves to the motherland.[1] We have taken our lives into our own hands and do not know whether we shall die from one moment to the next, or whether we shall live to a ripe old age and see our struggle crowned with shining success. I am entrusting you with everything – with my weapons and the convictions that lie deep within me. I am telling you all this now because I will be leaving with the dawn, while you are still asleep. Goodbye!'

Conflicting feelings, which I had never before experienced, struggled deep inside me, along with a powerful love for the man who would be going away in a few hours and who possibly would never return. This generated a powerful insomnia that kept sleep away.

In the following days, things seemed different to me. I possessed the germ of a strong conviction which was, inevitably, to become clearer to me: through it, the rancour that had appeared as a small imprint on my mind was transformed, took on new dimensions and a rational character

1. He is speaking here of the long political struggle in Yemen against the Imam prior to the 1962 revolution. For the Yemen revolution, see note 3, p. 361.

which justified its existence. I dared not act except in accordance with his parting admonitions, because his shadow dominated my movements and thoughts. I conducted myself as though he were present among us.

And when the news that he had been killed in a cruel fashion finally reached us, I was not filled with fear or grief for a single moment. Instead, I fired several shots from his rifle – a resonant kind of weeping which was, at the same time, an expression of pride. I kept my father's admonitions before my eyes, feeling them in every cell of my body and putting them into practice with scrupulous attention. And at their head I added another principle of my own, defined by my initial 'imprint of blackness': namely, that no piece of land should ever, under the protection of armed soldiers, have its fill of water while another piece of land remained thirsty.

Translated by Lorne M. Kenny and Thomas G. Ezzy

Mansour al-Hazimi   SAUDI ARABIA

The Nightingale's Triptych

She left, tears shining in her large eyes. I don't think she will return. Traces of her perfume still lingered everywhere. She had really gone, leaving nothing behind her but the fragrance of scent that would soon fade and vanish. Sooner or later all things, even the throbbing of the heart, come to an end. The heart can't go on palpitating forever in a state of turmoil. Of necessity, it must return to its normal, calm, monotonous beat. The universe is calm, monotonous and orderly. Night and day are followed by night and day as long as God wills. When the order of the universe is disturbed, life will end. Forgetfulness is the salve for suffering. When a relative died, the women would weep over him for days, then forget him, taking up their former way of life, eating, drinking, begetting offspring and singing. So why grieve over her departure, since she hasn't died? We shall probably meet each other again by chance on the pavement as we did the first time.

'Sir . . . sir . . . please.'

'Yes, lady, are you speaking to me?'

'Yes, please . . . Do you know . . . Street?'

He accompanied her to show her the way. They did not touch each other. It was a difficult beginning, all pain and effort, just like the path the Sufi novice follows. Night fell opportunely and brought the two strangers together amidst the crowds. Then, risking it, he drew close to her and took her hand in order to cut a way through the throng. Thousands of feet hastened in all directions. The lights of shop fronts flashed their insistent appeal. There were only two more days before the feast: the season for merchants and tradesmen. On feast-days people are the sacrifice; they spend a year's savings, if they have saved anything.

He didn't concern himself with gazing at her: but the sadness in her eyes had appealed to him as, in her shoddy green uniform, she sought perseveringly for the street she wanted. She could be a victim of the glorious war in which the Arabs won a brilliant victory over the Jews. That dark bruise under her chin might be either the result of shrapnel or a stray bullet! Her plain, sombre suit spoke of discipline and austerity. She might have been one of the remaining female recruits in the support army, or else a former housewife before the houses became rubble and deserted ruins.

He didn't let go of her hand and she didn't resist. It was a small, cold, lifeless hand. It slipped suddenly from him, however, when they came in front of a show-window full of children's clothes. Her eyes gleamed with a strange glow as she stood contemplating some of the samples meticulously fastened on the display board. He noticed how her eyes, glistening with tears, reflected the lights. No doubt a mother, and wretchedly poor. She didn't say anything but that did not concern him. Instead, taking the chance offered by her absorption, he looked her up and down with hungry eyes. God damn that ugly tunic, how thick it was. Loose and flowing, it revealed nothing. He was reminded of the London bus conductresses: masculine women, some of them, with long hairs on their chins that quivered emphatically whenever a passenger annoyed them, or whenever they called out 'Tottenham Court Road, next stop Oxford Street!' What a dreadful crowd.

Having given up hope, his eyes climbed to her neck. The dark bruise was there under her chin, its edge extending to her lower lip and part of her throat. That white blossoming lily-of-the-valley had been blemished. Hers was not an unfamiliar face. He had seen faces like it in the Pharaonic Museums. Seven thousand years. A deep-rooted civilization indeed, very ancient. A little warm water would remove the marks; the blow wasn't serious. The stem of the flower was green, but one doesn't look at the stem; what concerns one is the blossom.

His eyes besought her. An attractive smile hovered on her lips:

'What do you think of this dress? She's six. It would just fit her.'

He pulled her by the hand and they went on walking. It was a long street; no place for loitering – perhaps she was a pickpocket or a tramp, who could tell? When the feast-day drew near, the beggars, thieves and sham cripples multiplied. And, no question, he was valuable prey. Anyone could spot him without trouble, his face tanned by the desert, his suit of pure English wool, his French tie made of fine genuine silk, his Italian shoes of best leather, and his expensive Swiss watch. The Bedouins attach great importance to absolutely genuine articles. He was strutting along as if he were a walking showcase of the industries of the entire world. Everything he had on him, from head to foot, was imported. Legitimate catch from the land of petroleum. If not, why was he the one she had picked on to ask the way? She could have stopped any of the hundreds of passers-by.

Was she really lost? Or was she just pretending, in order to trap him? Inquiring about a street as an excuse to chat up a stranger, to become acquainted with, then fleece him. Al-Hamadhani had pointed a finger at this in one of his assemblies:[1]

> When I was in Baghdad
> I craved some *azad*
> But not having the wherewithal
> Went out to find the stall
> In al-Karkh[2] was a Sawadi[3]
> In his loincloth a knot,
> That's where he kept his money!
> Trying to drive his donkey.
> So I said, 'There goes my quarry,
> And may God preserve you, Abu Zayd.'[4]

I was the Sawadi then! What a laugh! I didn't have a donkey, but what difference between that and my luxurious American car? And asking the time – 'What's the time, please?' Or, 'Please give me a light.' There are many ploys, but the objective is the same.

He was quite sure of his judgement – they think we are simple: that we are still living in goat-hair tents, and ride camels. How stupid they are. They don't believe in progress. They don't yet realize that the world has changed. The desert Bedouins are no longer Bedouins. They penetrate the universe in their aeroplanes. A new invasion: they might be creatures from another world. For thousands of years they have been living on the margin of history. Neither king nor emperor gave a hoot for them. They had one awakening in their history, then they went to sleep again and the

1. The assemblies or *maqamat* (pl. of *maqama*) is a fictional genre, unique to Arabic literature. It is a kind of story or episode, written mainly in rhymed prose, which embodies the personality of a trickster. The two main exponents of the assemblies in classical times are al-Hamadhani (AD 967–1007) and al-Hariri (1054–1122).
2. A quarter in Baghdad which has existed until modern times.
3. *Sawadi* is a man from the country. The word is derived from *sawad*, the area around the River Tigris which stretches from Baghdad to Basra on the Gulf, which was very rich in crops in medieval times.
4. Abu Zayd is the main character, the trickster, in al-Hariri's assemblies. See note 1 above.

world forgot them. Now came the day of reckoning. An invasion is inevitable: London, Paris, Las Vegas, Bangkok, Manila, the shores of the Riviera – dazzling victories everywhere. One after another the great cities of the world capitulated. One by one their keys were docilely surrendered.

'I'm tired,' she told him. 'We've walked a long way and you haven't led me anywhere.' He turned to her as she walked beside him and saw that she was out of breath. Beads of sweat gathered on her forehead, running slowly down and evaporating on her cheeks.

It seemed she really was tired.

Now he saw her in subdued candlelight. People were speaking in whispers at their tables. Evening, gentle breezes and the river. The world was sleeping silently. On every table stood a candle; a gentle gust of wind played with the flames, making them dance, bending them right and left, almost extinguishing them. Then the breeze would suddenly drop and the candle flames flare again.

That evening he could only see her eyes sparkling in the faint light. A band of pure gold gleamed around her brow, and a string of pearls encircled her long white neck.

How wonderful! She was transformed. He had not seen her looking so pretty and glamorous earlier. As if a mummy had been resurrected from its tomb and reclaimed all its treasures. Here she was tonight, adorned with her rare jewels. That was all there was to it. Most likely she wasn't some ordinary woman, one of the crowd. She was either a queen or a princess or some great beauty. At any rate she had definitely been someone of unusual importance thousands of years ago. In bygone ages gold had been a sacred substance, locked in coffins and buried in temples, and out of which were made statues of gods and priests –

O daughter of Pharoah: pardon me . . . I took you to be a nobody. At first I didn't know who you were. Your shabby tattered garments fooled me. Your voice held an echo of grief, there was humility in your eyes. I was in doubt about you until tonight, when you shone so brilliantly and established your true identity.

Doubtless you go disguised, perhaps for fear of thieves. People would recognize you if you appeared in your true form. Probably they would hail you by name and, carrying you on their shoulders, return you to your ancient throne. But you don't covet power; you crave love. You were sad, the prisoner of tradition, 3000 years ago. You gave him your body but withheld your soul. Your heart was given to an obscure youth at your court. Roused like a wild beast with jealousy, the other tore him apart with claws and fangs. You swore then to revenge yourself.

And here you are returning to me trembling, rebelling against your shroud and defying the years. Time has made no change in you. You are still in the fresh bloom of your youth; your rosy cheeks, flushed with the warm blood flowing through them, exude a sweet perfume; your eyes, the colour of honey still, sparkle with the joy of life; if an ant so much as trod on it, your tender burnished skin would bruise; a lover's glance, even a zephyr, would wound it.

> I have come to you . . .
> Running, O temptress, into your arms
> And in my hands a heart that was never born
> And is on the point of dying
> Unlike you I was unlucky with the priests
> They did not put a talisman on my coffin
> They did not hold a vigil round my body
> Or read the *Book of the Dead*
> And so I went on enduring
> Swarms of moths and worms
> And the vaults of decay
> But I wrested from the corpse
> The part of my heart that still beats
> And longs for you
> I never grieved for anything before you.

Nervously looking at her watch, she said, 'Oh – I'm very late. I must go.'

Watching her as she prepared to depart, he was astonished: neither the gold headband nor the string of pearls were to be seen. They had suddenly vanished and, with them, the glow of life from her cheeks and eyes. The stump of candle remaining was about to go out. It sputtered vigorously, then died. Darkness reigned.

Ibn Hazm[5] says, 'In the beginning love is play but in the end it is serious. Because of their sublimity, its implications are too subtle to be described. They are apprehended only after strenuous effort. People have differed widely concerning love's essence and have debated it much and at great length. What I hold is that it is a union between souls that are separated in this world as far as their original numinous elements are concerned, but it

5. Ibn Hazm (AD 994–1064): a renowned scholar and writer of Muslim Spain and one of the greatest of the Muslim religious Imams. His book, *The Dovering*, is a famous treatise on love.

is not, however, as some philosophers have maintained, that spirits are divided spheres, but rather by the relation of their powers to each other in the celestial world, and the similarities in their composition.'

Al-Jahiz[6] says: 'The ardour of love is a disease whose advance cannot be controlled. Because they are so intertwined it afflicts the soul and pervades the body. Seldom does the lover declare his passion without infecting the other with the same malady, leaving its mark upon the spirit and infatuating the heart. This is due to similarities between people: the response of one nature to another, the yearning of one soul for another, and the closeness of spirits.'

Thus says Abu al-Faraj,[7] Ibn al-Jawziya,[8] Ibn Sina,[9] Ibn Rushd,[10] al-Tawhidi[11] and others, and yet others. How many stories and poems have been told and recited? How many huge volumes about love, passion, slave girls and lovers? Our heritage is redolent with the fragrance of women. And we are heritage worshippers, aren't we? We love the past and live in history. In the days of conquests, girls were sold for a *dinar*. How cheap they were then. Had he lived in that heroic age he could have bought a hundred of them. Not all of them were cheap. The beautiful ones sold for ten *dinars* or perhaps twenty. Peanuts. A hundred for twenty would be 2000 *dinars*. There are ten *riyals* in a *dinar*. It's not worth more than that. The pound sterling has fallen these days. The total sum would be 20,000 *riyals*. If he sold a piece of empty desert he would collect three million *riyals*. The rest of it would buy a mansion in al-Ghuta,[12] servants, an entourage, horses, mules and hunting dogs. His investors would send him the profits. It wouldn't cost him anything. He would live in luxury, his mind at ease.

6. Al-Jahiz (AD 780–869): thinker, scholar and prolific writer who covered a wide range of subjects from literature, nature studies, the comic portraiture of misers, to religious topics, etc. He lived and died in Basra.

7. Abu al-Faraj al-Asfahani (AD 897–967): Abbasid author of the huge compendium, *The Book of Songs*, a basic and early work on the life and experiences of Arab poets and singers up to the time of the author.

8. Ibn al-Jawziya: this is Ibn Qayyim al-Jawziya, the famous theologian and writer on theology and religious law. He lived in Damascus (AD 1292–1350).

9. Ibn Sina or Avicenne (AD 980–1037): the famous philosopher who wrote on medicine, logic, nature and divine studies. He was also a poet.

10. Ibn Rushd or Averroes (AD 1126–1198): a great philosopher of Muslim Spain who also translated Aristotle into Arabic.

11. Al-Tawhidi, Abu Hayyan, d. AD 1010, was a philosopher, man of letters and mystic.

12. Al-Ghuta is a fertile stretch of orchards and greenery surrounding most of Damascus.

But they say love is not bought with money. Spirits are divided spheres. If this is true, then the torment is greater. The problem cannot be easily solved. Therefore each of us is like a broken ripple, a broken circle. Thousands mill around in airports in summer every year. Summer is the season for love. They mill and mill around, spreading out in every direction, faltering because they are not whole, searching for the other half. It is something built into our nature, an instinct in the human spirit. We are bound by the laws of nature and passion is an irremediable disease, just as al-Jahiz says.

Why do they blame us, if such is the case, when we pack and spread abroad throughout the world? The world misunderstands. It is Zionist propaganda. Why not stop the birds from migrating from Europe in winter? They are looking for food and warmth in Asia and Africa. That is all our desert birds are doing, when they migrate in summer. And ruffians hunt them down. Knowing their schedules they waylay and kill them treacherously while they are still plump and prosperous. Villains! God damn them.

He had been led to his other half after long years of searching, deprivation and despair. No matter if it were a true or counterfeit half. The waiting had so exhausted him that his emotions had almost dried up. She made him feel that he was a human being. Weeping, she said, 'I love you and can't live without you.' That was enough for him. Hadn't al-Jahiz said, 'The lover seldom declares his passion without spreading the contagion, leaving its mark upon the spirit and infatuating the heart'? He need not look for further proof.

The time of departure was at hand; the return of the migrating birds. She pressed his hand, choking back her tears. 'I'll expect you in the spring. I can't wait until next summer.'

But he could not keep his promise. He came to her in autumn when the season of love had passed. The flowers had withered, the green leaves turned yellow, beginning to fall, to be scattered by the wind and trodden underfoot. The world was wrapped in a funereal cloak.

'It's too late, it's all over,' she said. 'You were a long time coming.' The tears pricked his eyes; he would never search again. He was exhausted . . . The illusion was so much more beautiful than the reality. If the theory of the broken circle was right, she would inevitably return. Perhaps after 2000 years, when the seas have dried, the wild beasts perished, then the fountains will gush forth and spring arrive. Love will only flourish on the banks of a river.

Translated by Olive Kenny and David Wright

391

Husain Ali Husain   **SAUDI ARABIA**

The Arrival

He became aware of the wheels of the train as they began to moan, then screamed piercingly as they came to a standstill in the station. He glanced anxiously at his watch. 'Ten o'clock!' he noticed with vexation. He felt apprehensive. The sun blazed outside and he said to himself, 'Well, at last you are going to face the city. Its dust will caress the features of your face, you are going to inhale to the fullest the fumes of diesel engines, and your cracked throat will taste filtered water; so prepare yourself now for a confrontation your body may not be able to bear!' He collected his few belongings from under the seat, reassured himself that the packet of cheap cigarettes was resting in his pocket, and checked that his *igal* had not slipped and was still firmly in place. He took a deep breath and prepared himself for the struggle to move out of the train through the long column of people winding like a snake toward the exit of the station. What drives these people? he cried voicelessly, as he moved within the throng, the human mass at the exit doors. Without knowing how, he found himself standing on the pavement outside the station: he was out of breath, his *igal* and *ghutra* gone. What kind of city is this?!

He crossed the street and stood in the shade on the pavement opposite the station. He inhaled the hot air. Events collided in his mind, repeating themselves like a melody on a cracked record. He had a deep yearning to see the sights of the city, to roam through its markets, looking at fine clothing, perfumes, oils and incense. But they had said to him, 'Take care. The city is like a coquette, a flirt, everything about it is deceptive and false, so don't fall in someone's trap' . . . What traps did they mean?

His suitcase fell from his hand onto the ground. The scorching wind was beginning to penetrate the corner where he stood. In a few minutes the noonday heat would cover everything . . . You are going to be buried in the noonday blaze, he told himself, the only thing that will save you is to take shelter in one of those deeply shaded cafés, cafés that are filled with rice, with tea, with the talk of men . . . What men? Have you ever had the pleasure of meeting such men? Anywhere? This city has a cruel heart so don't rest your head on its breast right away, stay aloof, for if you don't you will lose everything. He choked, and felt something like a thorn rising from his chest into his throat. His throat was dry. The sweat poured from his forehead making him feel dizzy as if he were in a hot shower, full of sticky vapour and mist. He felt the world swaying around him. Hundreds of multi-coloured phantoms seemed to be dancing in front of him, imposing themselves upon him little by little. Standing there he seemed as out of place as a fragile tree, assailed by the wind and the fine yellow grains of sand. He felt as though the sweat and viscosity were invading his body. He stretched his arm out. Then he relaxed it and the protruding veins began to swell. His hand jumped, his fingers twitched, he tried to relax and picked up his suitcase from the ground. Then, asking himself why, he put the suitcase down again and sat beside it.

The sun had imposed its presence totally. It stood straight over his bare head, beating down among the locks of his hair until he felt as though small pins and needles were pricking the whorls of his brain. He was going to have a headache, he thought. What to do? The disk of the sun is blazing especially for you. What will you feel like when the sun is full and round like a burning iron ball? Escape! This place is for wild feet, but your feet should return to their original place. And no taxi has come; the place is empty, there's nothing around except the blazing sun and your own fear . . . why don't the taxis come?

Pleading, he asked a taxi driver:
  'Do you know the way to a sleeping place?'
  'A hotel?'
  'There's no difference, is there?' he answered wearily.
  'I don't know!!' the taxi driver replied, and drove away . . . then another one . . . and another – all of them ignorant of the way to sleeping places. Now it was afternoon and still no one had stopped for him. The shade saved him from the feeling of dizziness, stickiness. The desert breezes blew over his hair and entered his body: he felt what seemed like tons of salt within him begin to thaw. He felt refreshed. After a short time the station emptied, the workers and porters went away and left him alone. He leaned against the trunk of an ancient palm tree in the middle of

a road full of dust, empty cement sacks, rusty bars of metal, old tin boxes and covers. What is this city?

A taxi driver examined him with his eyes,
 'I'll take you to a hotel for ten *riyals*,' he said in disgust.
 The desert cautiousness about money flared up in his weary body.
 'Ten *riyals*? All at once?'
 The cab driver turned down his mouth and said nothing.
 'How far is the hotel from here?'
 'God knows.'
 'Is that a secret?'
 'Does it matter to you where the hotel is? Don't you want to find a place where you can rest? I'll take you there for ten *riyals* . . . Well? . . . Will you pay or should I look for another fare?!'
 'I'll pay.'

It was five o'clock in the afternoon. The taxi had cut through the traffic jams. It stopped in front of a hotel. He got out, paid off the driver, carried his suitcase through the door. At the reception desk, he asked for a room.
 'We don't have any vacancy,' the receptionist replied haughtily. 'Check us tomorrow.'
 'Are there other hotels around here?'
 'I don't know.'

Ten o'clock in the morning. Harsh and bright, the sun was moving toward the centre of the sky. He stood in line at the ticket office of the station. Just as he had struggled to get off the train, so he struggled to get on. When he had safely arrived at his seat, he pushed his suitcase under the chair and plunged into a deep sleep.

Translated by May Jayyusi and Elizabeth Fernea

The Song of the Hunted Man

The night is a low, drawn-out song, the stars a flaming red forest in the heart of a deep black cloak. The tall water-pipe with its hose, proudly and strongly entwined as if it were a glittering stream upon whose banks swims the goddess of love and ecstasy, the thermos of fragrant green tea, the cravings of those coming back from a tiring journey, and I, lost, parched with thirst, sinking my two weary, weak feet into the depths of the soft earth. With my feet I embrace the dust and the rotted waste. I feel the pavement below my feet a moist sponge over which countless other feet, heavy with cares and hardships, have trod. I sink, I sink, I feel as if thousands of worms are sinking into my flesh. Heat flows over me, an equatorial heat that pulses inside my body and, in the face of this heat, I have no will. I am only a worthless person possessing nothing but wishes, nothing but countless years stretching back through life's journey without any achievement. Feeling the drops of sweat sinking down inside me, I stop suddenly and ask myself: am I perhaps in the heart of the African jungle? The only thing I need to see in order to be sure of this is a few elephants, some tusks and ostriches. Violently I scratch my hair. Two months, perhaps three, and the barber has not touched your hair. You've become so used to filth that it is now what you prefer.

My hands move, stretching like the smooth tentacles of an octopus into my pocket, feeling for the tobacco box. Big shots won't move without a secretary in tow; I won't move without a cigarette pouch. One can give up everything except cigarettes. My body used to be made of iron, but now I am worn out, returning from a wearisome journey. A fire! A fire! The smoke blocks the view ahead.

People surprise me by gathering close, suddenly, as if the earth has split open and amassed them around me; only God knows how they came to be here. The fire engines do not come. The people try to stop the fire, they come up with sand and a pail full of water, yet the flames fan out and block the road. With all my strength I withdraw, I withdraw.

A dangerous curb. Last night it rained heavily and all the roads were blocked. The rains made the ground beside the curb a deep ditch, yet I manage to cross it. One leap and you are in the isles of Waq Waq.[1] Why are you standing fixed? The cigarettes, matches and I are in the ditch. Suddenly I find myself floating on the surface – my clothes are soiled with mud, but never mind. Mud covers me on the inside and on the outside, so why should I care? My feet come to a standstill in the middle of the road. I put my hand in my pocket, my handkerchief is full of dirty water. I spit forcefully. The café must have closed, what's the time now? A question with no answer, for there's no one around to ask. The place is empty as a graveyard. My feet move a little; they used to be the fastest feet around. But now they are stopping. What's going on? Cats, dogs, mice and a watchman too? Where am I? I'm afraid, as if all the glue of the world was stuck together underneath my feet and had stopped them dead in the middle of the road. My hands grab a stone, several stones. I go on the chase, until the dogs scatter and the cats and mice die, also the mosquitoes and flies. The man seems to have got rid of that weight hanging on his chest, something he had been powerless to throw off. He thanked me but I did not reply even with a single word. A man devoured by insects? He infuriated me; I felt insulted. Without thinking I went back and slapped him. Even the night seemed to be helping me against that man. He cried copiously and withdrew into a corner of the desolate street. I walked away quickly, then stopped. An open grocery, with many lights; the faint beams leaked out to various parts of the winding sandy road. But everything had fallen into that cursed ditch, the money, the tobacco and the handkerchief, so how can I go to the café? I am tired. I am tired.

Translated by May Jayyusi and Elizabeth Fernea

---

1. Legendary islands mentioned in the *Arabian Nights* and other Arab folklore.

Ismail Fahd Ismail   **KUWAIT**

4 + 1 = 1

The noise from the machines was overpowering; if you needed to talk to
the man working alongside you, you had to shout at the top of your
voice. The few workers manipulated the machines with swift, disciplined
movements. The cleaner was sweeping the floor with a long-handled
broom, his head bowed as he concentrated totally on his job, unaware of
anything that was happening round him. But when he was just underneath the fan, he stopped for a moment and leaned on the broom, smiling
as he let the breeze from the whirling fan cool him.

'I'll have this corridor finished in a few minutes,' he thought. He took
out a handkerchief. One of the workers squeezed past between him and
one of the machines, and he moved slightly, without saying a word to the
man. He mopped the sweat from his face.

'Only the next corridor left now.'

He put the handkerchief back in his pocket.

'There's the director's office too, of course . . .'

He grabbed the broom halfway down the handle and moved back a
step to pick up the pile of dust from the floor.

'What on earth's happened?'

A cry of panic almost shot out of his mouth. The broom-handle had
crashed into something, the broom was shaking in his hand. There was a
muffled sound amid the din of the machines.

'Why didn't I look behind me?'

Pieces of broken glass all over the floor.

'I'm an idiot!'

Electrical contact. A flashing spark.

'We'll all be burned to a crisp!'

The shock of it all paralyzed his senses.

'What have I done?'

397

Puffs of smoke. Power failure.

'Now what's happening?'

The machines begin to slow down.

'Are they going to stop?'

They stopped.

'It was the broom-handle! It . . .'

All-pervasive silence, except for the fan which started to slow down too.

'What's happened?' asked one of the workers in alarm, from behind the row of machines.

All the workers came over to the spot where there was broken glass on the floor.

'Who broke the regulator?' one of them asked in disbelief.

' . . .'

The workers exchanged glances; then they all stared at the cleaner. He turned as white as a sheet, his lips quivering.

'I don't know how . . . how it . . .' he mumbled.

'You broke it?'

All he could do was blink.

'You're the one who caused all this . . .'

The worker said no more. Several seconds of silence.

'I wasn't paying attention,' the cleaner muttered.

'Do you realize how much that regulator costs?' one of them asked.

' . . .'

'You'll have to work for the factory owner for ten years to pay it off!' commented another worker.

Now the oldest worker spoke, in the tone of a man who was used to supervising production. 'The thing that's really important,' he said, 'is that the machine's going to stay idle until the regulator's repaired!'

'What are we going to do then?' the fourth worker asked in dismay.

The cleaner looked at them all in despair.

'If only that stupid broom-handle hadn't . . .' he thought.

The oldest worker took a look at his watch. 'The factory owner's going to be here in half an hour!' he said.

'You'll have to pay for it,' said another worker, pointing at the cleaner with a bit of a grin on his face.

The cleaner didn't say a word. He felt he could almost hear the factory owner's footsteps. Then his voice. 'Why aren't the machines working? Come here, cleaner!'

He was brought back to reality by the worker who'd asked what they were going to do. 'What are we going to do now?' he asked again. There was a serious edge to his voice, and something of an imperative quality as well.

The four workers looked at one another again.

'That's right. What *are* we going to do?'

'We're supposed to . . .'

The second worker tried to take it further. 'We have to . . .'

The cleaner moved his weight from one leg to the other, thinking of the factory owner.

There was a tense silence.

'Perhaps I could reconnect the current to the machines,' said the oldest worker.

No one said a word.

'We must hurry!'

He headed over to a large iron fuse-box that was attached to the far wall.

'Get me some wire,' he called out. The order wasn't directed at anyone in particular. One of the workers hurried over to a side door. The oldest worker spoke again.

'Unplug the broken machine!'

Once again the order wasn't given to anyone in particular, and the two other workers collided as they rushed to carry it out. The cleaner stood there stupefied, the broom feeling heavy in his hand.

The electricity was restored and the machines began to work, slowly at first, then faster and faster. After a few seconds they were working at regular speed.

The cleaner looked at the broken machine. Its very silence rose, ever more loudly, as he imagined the factory owner shouting: 'Who was it? Come here, you!' A shudder went through him. 'You'll have to work for ten years before . . .'

The fan started going round again, slowly at first, then picking up speed until, like the machines, it was back to normal.

He looked around him. The factory owner hadn't arrived yet. One of the workers came over to him.

'What are you standing there for?' he shouted at the top of his voice.

The machines were making such a noise that his shouting was almost inaudible. But he went on even so. 'Finish your job!'

The worker's face seemed to swim before his eyes.

'I . . . I . . .'

He lost his grip on the broom and it fell to the floor. He hurriedly bent over and picked it up, and the worker moved away. The broom seemed reluctant to slip across the floor.

'My hand's trembling!' he thought.

He could feel a moist warmth in his eyes.

'Why am I going to pieces . . .?'

'This blasted dust! Why doesn't it pile up properly?'

'My whole body's shaking!'

Sweat was pouring down his face.

'If only I'd looked behind me!'

He stopped working and took out his handkerchief.

'The broom-handle doesn't need to be as long as that!'

Maybe he took a long time wiping the sweat off his face. He felt a hand placed on his shoulder and he turned round. The worker who'd shouted at him a short while before was now giving him an encouraging smile. Then the smile vanished. 'What are you hanging about round here for?' he shouted.

'. . .'

He looked at the broken machine, but the worker pushed him away with a friendly shove.

'It wasn't you who broke the machine,' he shouted into the cleaner's ear.

Translated by Roger Allen and Christopher Tingley

Abdallah Ali Khalifa   BAHRAIN

The Bird

Year after year finds you staring at this gloomy street. Your heart is slowing, exile has become both a hammer and a storm. How did you happen to come here and become a fugitive?

Your body is stretched on the bed, your skin covered with scratches and poison, with the dust of construction. Outside, laughter sounds in the streets. Inside, the room is small and suffocating. The ceiling seems to look at you intently, to close in slowly on your presence, day by day. The smoke rising from your cigarette seems to sketch slim ghosts in the air which rise up to clutch the ceiling and turn into demons.

Your friend holds his suitcase. For months he has been dreaming of an imminent return home. Snow has dusted his hair. His chest is a continent of longing and moaning. Hey, friend, you don't have a passport to travel even to your own country. They expelled you, handcuffed. These vultures here nibble away at your body, and the torch of exile is a flame in your hand. Your flesh melts down but the flame of the torch is constant.

Grey images seem to gloom in the ceiling and are bedecked with various colours. There are the mountain houses, the Persian village living its long and terrifying night, whose stars are made of skulls and blood. You manage to make it to the other side of the Gulf. Your father, the builder, has passed on to you this staggering occupation.

Hey, builder, who no longer builds homes. Your hands have turned into stone, they can no longer hold stones. Why then does blood ooze from your fingers?

Here, on the ceiling, you see the image of a youthful builder, a robust cheerful man doing his job through the cold and the summer sun with stone and cement. With the building of things comes the debilitation of the body. Here you are toiling among strange teams of men who have come from faraway villages in Persia and Oman. They work and they learn together.

Hey, builder, who can no longer build, what a wonderful occupation it was! How good and simple the men were. Singing while working was another kind of wine I got accustomed to. Singing while working is an experience of real community feeling. The expatriate labourers, the paupers, the hungry, the stupefied were all a single band singing as you led them. Words and melodies emerged cheerfully and freshly from their stalwart chests, glowing with sorrow and joy; the songs made the men move their bodies in unison, mobilized them, made them merge into a single being, singing of fatigue, exile, love and travel, made them dream of the mountain village and the tangled city, the oil well, the blue mountains, the river laden with floating corpses.

At night the gang gathered around you. Questions were asked about tyrants, exploiters, lice. Where were those beings? They ought to be burned, banished. We are the builders. The earth should be ours and the sky as well. The questions, the answers, the hatred, the covetousness, all dissolved in the wine of community and filled men's chests with fiery liquid. One of the gang once said:

'Comrade, goodbye. I'm going back home. I'll write our songs on the walls of the village house.'

You, everybody, looked at him, and no one tried to hold him back. They hugged him, and he carried his luggage and books and went away. Others came and went, while the rivers (and the hatred) poured into the Gulf. Oh, when will our dates ripen?

Suddenly, like the rain, like a wedding song in a spinster's house, rose the voice of Fairuz, the Lebanese singer, coming from the blind man's shop. 'Back to my home,' she sang, 'take me home even as a flower, spring.' A careless hand changed the station. The light went out. Ah, you blind man, let me hear the song a little more. My home, you are far away and I waste away in exile. If I only could see you for a moment, then I could die.

A sinister laughter sounded in the street. They were going back. The train arrived at the station carrying the longing of the passengers; and the ships' longing to the kerchief-waving shores. Flocks of birds flew back to spring and to rosy horizons. The migrants returned home to the wretched alleys expecting their footfalls, to the women's colourful dresses which were omens of a world about to be reborn. The men went back home. Only you stayed behind, wasting away. Nothing is left for you except dreams and angry words. Look at yourself, your once muscular body caving in, your fingers unable to hold anything but your books. Sooner or later the gravediggers will come and inquire: 'How long has this man been dead?'

Your friend is still holding his sweat-soaked suitcase. He puts it down for a moment and puffs at his cigarette. The room suddenly shakes with his voice: 'How come we've been robbed of our right to live on our own land, in our villages? Why is it that lice roam freely in people's hair? Why do rats run through the houses of the poor without anyone stopping them?' He stands up, closer to you, tears sparkling in his eyes:

'Ali, I have a little daughter, as you know. I left her four years ago. She was young then. She wouldn't recognize me now. She must wonder where her Papa is, who is only a picture hung on the wall. Yesterday I received a letter saying she's slightly ill. Who knows, they may not be telling the truth so as not to make me anxious. Imagine if she . . . ? Imagine. What would I do in this case?'

You look at him sympathetically and hug him, but the tears coming down his cheeks do not stop – what's the use of words in moments like these?

'Ali, how can I live like this? Am I going to wander in exile all my life? What difference is this life from being in jail? Ali, you know how much I miss my family and friends. I'm always afraid that something bad might happen to them. But I do not have a passport, I do not have a single piece of ID that would enable me to go to them.'

'Calm down, man, you'll be leaving this prison in a few seconds.'

'But what if they don't show up?'

'Don't worry, they will.'

Soon I'll be all alone, a giant tree trying to survive the storms. Soon the last man in the gang will be gone, and I'll be here by myself, wounded but faithful.

An image appears on the cracked wall, a ship cruising through the Gulf, the Gulf a pool of mud and blood. You're handcuffed, they've deported you from your little homeland to your large one. You're nothing but a fugitive, an infiltrator, and they are simply returning you to your own country where, on the shore, an officer is awaiting your arrival. The seamen on the ship watch you and the ship's owner is keeping tabs on everyone. But at night you'll find that the ropes have been cut, the handcuffs removed, as you and your freedom lie in the belly of the beast. Eventually the harbour will take you in its arms and shroud you in its mist. You'll become an old sailor, a fugitive on the run, running always from the guillotine. And you will live in a small room whose walls seem to close in on you day by day, a room buzzing with flies and heavy with smoke.

'Ali, what's the matter with you? Why are you so absent-minded? I feel as if I'm conversing with a person suspended from the ceiling!'

'I'm thinking of a story I once lived. Such memories have become my sole entertainment.'

The ceiling's cracks seem to widen, images flourish in the smoke; I seem to see the builders gathering in a new building and my own voice hollers, 'Look, look carefully at this magnificent structure. We've built it for a man who traffics in prostitution. In a few days he'll decorate it with precious pieces of furniture. They'll cover up our blood and sweat. They'll drink their wine filled with blood and boredom. And, as for us, we'll have to rent rooms as narrow as graves.'

On another occasion a policeman approaches you and suggests building a few prison cells. The men looked sarcastically at him, and one said, 'Do you know anyone who puts out his eyes with his own hands?' Everybody guffawed and the policeman left in amazement. Another man said, 'Don't you see that building a boat would be beneficial to everyone? We could all run away, together!'

Your friend suddenly shouted:

'There, there they are!'

His words hit you in the belly. You plunged at once into a terrible loneliness, you imagined yourself alone, with no companion, with nobody. But how strange! You should have been elated for your friend now going back to his own country after years of exile. They were only a few years, but they had torn him apart! As for you . . . !

'I've got to go, Ali.'

He found him crying and they hugged, mixed their tears of sorrow and joy together.

'Why don't you come with me? No one knows you now there.'

'. . .'

'Come. You're an old man now, the police there do not know you any more.'

'I really cannot imagine my life alone . . . I have never tried being completely alone . . . I shall see.'

'Let's go, Ali.'

'No, you go on and let me stay and think a bit. At least I carry a valid passport.'

'Farewell!'

He was gone.

So, at last, you are all by yourself. Sleep, that dear nightwatchman, takes you off to his garden. Now you are in the streets of al-Manamah. The back alleys embrace you, 'Ali is back, he's back.' Then sleep, the nightwatchman, takes you to the far edge of the city where the cemetery rests, and with morning come workers, children, real flowers and warm songs. 'Good morning, pal, good morning, Ali.'

The clear light of dawn came gently through his window, and he woke up.

'Yes, I will go. My country calls me. Shall I spend the rest of my life in this rotten room, surrounded by these cracked walls? But isn't trying to go home like the unrealistic whim of an adolescent? Ah, let them do what they want with me. I'll go home, even if it's only to go to the scaffold.'

He collected his clothes, packed them in a small case, and went down the stairway. In the street he passed the houses battered by age and grief, but there were also white birds migrating north. Hope. And he sang aloud, the song of Fairuz. 'I want to go home now, even as a flower, spring.'

He smiled to himself and walked on.

Translated by Sharif Elmusa and Elizabeth Fernea

Muhammad al-Murr　　　　　　　　**UNITED ARAB EMIRATES**

Why Fattoum al-Ward Hit her Neighbour

First the tale must be told.

This story is related with great gusto by the poor to their friends, the poor. You will not find a rich person to tell you this tale. The story concerns two neighbours, the wife of a rich man, a merchant, and the wife of a poor man, a porter. The rich man's wife notices that the poor man's wife takes a bath every day. When she asks why, the poor man's wife explains, blushing with pleasure, that she must perform her ritual ablutions and bathe daily because her husband is filled with ardour and energy every single night.[1] The rich man's wife becomes depressed because her husband stays late in his shop and, upon returning home, is so busy counting his money that he hardly ever gives her a reason to take a bath.

FATTOUM AL-WARD'S CIRCUMSTANCES

Fattoum al-Ward (her family name means, literally, 'the rose') is a young woman in her mid-twenties. She got married when she was fifteen and has borne eight children. Not a single year has passed when her belly was empty of child. Her face is the face of a woman of forty. Her husband is a carpenter. He earns a daily wage working for a shipbuilder who makes him labour from sunrise to sunset. The house of Fattoum al-Ward is actually two shacks made of palm fronds.

1. Muslims are commanded to pray five times daily, and couples, if they have engaged in love making, must take a bath before standing in prayer in front of God.

THE CIRCUMSTANCES OF THE PEOPLE IN THE BIG HOUSE

The largest house in the neighbourhood belongs to a rich man named Hamid Hamdan. The size of the house sets it apart, for it is the only house built of cement; all the others are made of mud and rocks or, like Fattoum al-Ward's, of palm fronds. The house is so vast that, from its upper floor, its owners can look out over all the owners of the houses made of mud, rocks and palm fronds. Fattoum al-Ward went often to the big house. She even worked there, but not regularly, because of her repeated pregnancies. The rich man's wife liked Fattoum because the two women were the same age. She liked listening to Fattoum al-Ward's stories about the other neighbourhood women, stories which Fattoum stuffed full of exaggerations and enormous lies. When the rich man's wife laughed, showing her regular white teeth, Fattoum al-Ward wished that her own yellow teeth would turn white on the spot. And when, green eyes gleaming, the rich man's wife showed off the new golden jewellery her husband had bought her, Fattoum al-Ward wished that the glittering gold would be whisked like magic out of the big house and into her own wooden jewellery box, filled mostly with the bits of silver ornaments her husband had given her when they were married. The first refrigerator to make its appearance in the neighbourhood was in the big house. The rich man's wife gave Fattoum al-Ward a great deal of ice which Fattoum al-Ward took home and made into lemonade; all her children drank that delicious lemonade, even the youngest who was still nursing. The first house to have electricity was the big house. Not one, or two, but ten electric bulbs, all switched on at the same time, transformed the big house into a mass of bright light. Among the little houses of mud and stone and palm fronds, barely lit by yellow kerosene lamps, the brilliant flare of those electric bulbs practically blinded the poor eyes of Fattoum al-Ward.

HUSBANDS: A SAD COMPARISON

Fattoum al-Ward would become very depressed whenever she compared her husband, the carpenter, with his short skinny body, his constant wheezing and his weak eyes, to the rich merchant Hamid Hamdan, with his tall frame, his body full without being stout, his round, rosy face and his thick, lustrous moustache. Hamid Hamdan was about the same age as her husband, but he looked like one of her husband's younger brothers. His clothes were always ironed, perfectly, without a wrinkle (the first iron to be heated with coal was to be found in the big house). Hamid Hamdan never left the house before mid-morning and, when he did, he went perfumed, smelling of the fine scent of incense. His wife would see him to the door of the big house and every day she took two baths, one in the morning and one at dusk.

HOW THE INCIDENT HAPPENED TO TAKE PLACE

One autumn day Hamid Hamdan's wife, laughing loudly with joy so all her white teeth gleamed, told Fattoum that her husband had bought a movie projector. Fattoum should come that night, she said, to watch the film they were going to show. So, after dinner, Fattoum al-Ward came and sat near the door of the sitting-room where Hamid Hamdan, his wife, his semi-paralyzed father, his fat mother and his old-maid sister were seated in leather armchairs in the centre of the room. The light was switched off. In the darkness, Hamid Hamdan began to work the movie projector. The film was a romance, a melodrama. Fattoum al-Ward noticed that Hamid Hamdan would take advantage of the rapt attention of his family, whose eyes were nailed to the wall of the room where the film was being shown, to steal quick little kisses from the mouth and cheeks of his wife whose green eyes, Fattoum thought, seemed to gleam with enjoyment in the dark.

When Fattoum al-Ward returned home that night, she found that her husband had cut two fingers of his right hand. She put on iodine and bandaged the fingers. But she couldn't sleep all night because of his constant moaning and the crying of two of her children. When one fell asleep, the other would start up and when *he* would finally quieten, the first would begin all over again.

The morning after the movie, Fattoum al-Ward was worn out. After her husband went to work, she started to set the bread out for her children when her neighbour Osha dropped in to visit. Osha drank five cups of coffee, complained of the thick morning mist which was delaying her shopping trip to the market and mentioned in passing more than ten topics. After that, and for some unknown reason, she began to relate the tale of the happy poor man's wife with her lusty husband and the rich man's wife whose husband hardly ever gave her a reason to take a bath.

Now, although Fattoum al-Ward had heard that story countless times from the lips of Osha, this time for reasons that are unknown to this day, she could not contain herself. With one hand, she took up the hem of her dress and wiped the sweat that was pouring down her face from the heat of the oven. With the other, Fattoum al-Ward snatched up the coffee pot and flung it violently at unsuspecting Osha's head.

Translated by May Jayyusi and Elizabeth Fernea

Muhammad al-Muthanna   **YEMEN**

The Kiosk

Hadish Hasan settled back and sat down on a pile of rocks. He was exhausted. But when he looked up at the new kiosk, he felt a spark of energy stir within him. He had just put the final touches on that kiosk. Now, for the fiftieth time, he inspected it carefully: the wooden struts that framed it; the smooth counter; the metal band that held it together – all were feasts for his eyes. Such a fine kiosk had never before been seen in the village of Jabir, and certainly not by the neighbourhood street sweepers, of which he was one. Hadish Hasan recited, somewhat brokenly, some phrases of praise to God which he had learned from the religious Shaikhs; then he wiped his face with both hands in the same way people do after finishing their prayers.

Above him, in the distant sky, dark clouds shaped like serpents, foxes and ships, approached each other and touched as if in tentative reconciliation. A thin fog covered the neighbourhood street and the houses, shacks really, patched together from broken pieces of wood, sacking, metal from the bodies of junked cars. A soft damp breeze seemed to lull the village of Jabir. Hadish Hasan, his eyes fixed on his precious kiosk, felt himself also lulled into a mood of communion with the world.

The last rays of the sun brightened the grey afternoon fog. The kiosk seemed to be illuminated, clad in transparent colours. Hadish straightened his dark body. He had, after all, finished the kiosk; proud of his handiwork, and soothed by the calm afternoon, he no longer felt the ugliness of his face, of his life.

Aiysha, too, had just passed in front of him, dancing one of her magical, devilish dances. She had never found Hadish attractive, that mocking, carefree Aiysha. But now . . . in any case, he thought, she's the prettiest girl in the village. At that moment, Hadish felt as though he could embrace the entire world.

Fog was gradually enveloping the street sweepers' neighbourhood in a thick cloak. Yet Hadish Hasan's kiosk, with its new white wood, its graceful supports, shone through the fog – a radiant landmark in the midst of the chaos of makeshift huts and junk metal. Even before Aiysha had come into view, many hopes had stirred within Hadish Hasan. Not the least of these hopes was that the new kiosk would be filled with attractive goods, with bright light, and would be visited by all the neighbourhood girls, including Aiysha. He envisaged her kneeling in surrender before him.

The clouds shaped like serpents, foxes and ships completed their union in the sky and stood still, as if fully reconciled to each other. The breeze blew even more softly and Hadish Hasan felt he was finally in a position to reassess his own situation, both the frowning face of the past and the bright promise of the future. The sky seemed to sigh with gentle lightning. In the flare of the swift flashes, the roof of the kiosk glimmered and the metal support shone. The eyes of Hadish Hasan sparkled too. He lifted his hands upward to the sky, to receive the few drops of rain that were now falling, noting the cracks in his fingers and his palms with some bitterness. But today the bitterness was not as sharp as usual; it was calmer, a feeling which he believed might soon be dissipated.

Hadish Hasan remembered his father, a street sweeper like himself. As he had aged, the old man had grown hunched, his back bent, his eyes close to the ground, unable to see more than a few feet. He remembered a time when his father had actually lifted his head and stared in Hadish's face. As though delivering a brief sermon, he had said, 'Look here, son, look at these brooms, they're still quite strong. Your mother, God bless her soul, made them when she was a bride. They've always reminded me of her.' Half-closing his eyes, he had continued, 'Hadish, I see that you are a man, one of the finest.' He had looked down again and said no more.

When death struck his father in a back alley, that dark forehead refused to submit and fall flat onto the pavement. The old man had struggled not to do so; he had propped his chest up with the brooms. And when his father was carried off, the brooms were lying flat at his sides, as though weighted down by the death of an old comrade. These days, Hadish felt as though his own back was bending, was about to become hunched like his father's.

Hadish Hasan had inherited the broom from his mother, the bride, and his father, who had struggled without falling until he died. And Hadish felt he had done what his father wished as well as an obedient son could do.

The clouds shaped like serpents, foxes and boats clung tightly together, forming an immense mass in the sky; the wind began to taste like wet mud. The dark mass loomed over the neighbourhood, with its makeshift huts and junk metal scattered in confusion. But the kiosk was different, Hadish thought, a unique bright landmark in the village of Jabir. What was to happen now? Hadn't the time come for that farce they called parental legacy to be buried in a pit with the broom, once and for all? Hadn't the time finally come for him, Hadish Hasan, to experience a bit of joy?

Hadish Hasan was one of the army of illiterates who had been prevented from getting an education by the harsh realities of life. He had had to carry a broom instead of a pen, and had been unable to find a single course of action that might have offered some possibility of happiness. He hated the street sweepers, though he was one of them, and his hatred was too heavy for the whole village of Jabir to bear. Now, as he eyed his kiosk, the fruit of his own labour, he thanked God and acknowledged that he had been favoured by Sidi Jabir.[1] Hatred and bitterness, after all, had not stood between him and his ambition.

His hands were wet from the light rain. The fertile odours rising from the damp earth caressed his nostrils; flickers of lightning illumined, almost playfully, the strings of rain falling around the kiosk. Hadish Hasan gazed once more at the circle of light surrounding the kiosk, and he envisaged a crowd of street sweepers, men and women, young and old, shining in the darkness, disorganized, noisily buying flour and wheat and rice from his store. He saw himself filling the orders with a contented smile and joking with the children who came to buy sweets.

A car hummed in the distance, its headlights casting light on faraway buildings. Hadish followed the movement of the vehicle with his eyes, as thrilled as though seeing a car for the first time. Today he seemed able to find a reason for rejoicing in everything. Then came the roar of thunder and the pounding of heavy rain. Darkness descended on the neighbourhood and on the village of Jabir. Yet even through the rain and darkness, Hadish Hasan, lying back in the rusty car body where he had taken shelter, could still see the radiant landmark of his kiosk.

Then, for a moment, he could not be sure what was happening. First he thought he saw a crowd of street sweepers ordering wheat and rice, and children blithely demanding sweets. Then the rain came and flashes of lightning in which his kiosk seemed to flicker and burn. What unjust power had decided to sweep away his new kiosk?

1. Apparently, this is the village of Jabir's saint (*sidi* means 'my master', or, as here, 'my revered master or saint').

When the sun reappeared, the makeshift shacks of the village of Jabir emerged from darkness and stood out clearly in the light. The water lying in great puddles gleamed. But Hadish Hasan remained transfixed in the old car body, like a battered cloud. He felt as though life was once more pushing him out, rejecting him as a raging sea rejects dead fish. He stood spellbound, gazing at the ruins of his kiosk which floated on the puddles like bits of a memory, a dream. His eyes refused to believe what had happened.

Translated by Sharif Elmusa and Elizabeth Fernea

Ibrahim al-Nasir SAUDI ARABIA

Disappointment

The road before him seemed long, twisted and filled with hundreds of furrows and deep holes, caused by rain and the erosion of the seasons; the ruins of mud huts lay strewn in the middle of it. It was a grey and repulsive sight which reminded him of the face of an old hag. But this road was dear to him. Would it safeguard his steps and his secret dreams?

His heart was pounding. It strained like a bird whose eyes dart to the left and to the right, searching for a way of escaping its captivity. He felt like a warrior returning home after a long absence, drained of his life's blood from the violent battles he had fought. He was coming back with a strange and wonderful feeling; his very being was exhausted by distance and separation, yet he was filled with a longing whose nature he was unable to define. Was it a feeling of triumph, after all the cups of bitterness he had had to drink from? Or was it that his exile had brought his dreams closer to realization? In fact, these dreams had not changed much from their modest beginnings in the time before he had journeyed from home – namely, of marrying Khalida, his childhood neighbour and the sweetheart of his youth.

The thought of her triggered off a stream of speculations in his mind. Would he find Khalida the way he pictured her, her smile a radiant moon breaking through clouds and lifting the gloom from the face of the world? Eight years ago, she had hidden behind her slanted door every morning and waited to watch as he left his house. He had been able to have a glimpse of her golden braids streaming down alongside her head as she peered, partly in trepidation and partly in awe, through the narrow opening of the door and 'fed' him with a smile from her round, wine-red lips. Her black, wide eyes had been fixed on him, their eagerness bridled only by her shyness. And when he had directed a similar gaze, hungry and thirsty, at her, she had quickly withdrawn and once again ensconced herself in her confinement.

Often he had invented excuses to return to the house when he missed her, although he never knew precisely why he was attracted to her or understood the feelings clamouring in his heart. All he had known was that Khalida had become his daily bread; the sight of her each morning was like a night-lantern, without which he would not have been able to pass through the alley . . . Yet, why had she run away each time she spotted him? Why had she been so afraid, when she knew how much she meant to him?

And his father . . . Did he still walk with that agonizing slowness of his? Did he still lean on his spiral cane, thrusting it into the earth or knocking away the pebbles in the winding alley that was his customary route to the market-place? . . . Ahmad would never forget how that cane had bitten into his flesh, and how his feet had burned every time his father flogged him. Back then, even his name had been different: his father had always called him Ox, or Ass, or some other such honorific title. But now, everything had changed. In letters, his father addressed him as 'My dear Son, Ahmad'. Have you developed a new esteem for oxen and donkeys, Father? Or is it the hard-earned money I've been sending you that has altered my name? May God forgive you, Father. You must have been suffering from some kind of sickness.

And what about his aunt? he continued to wonder. Would he find her squatting cross-legged on the worn straw floor-mat, a smile beaming on her lips, refreshing like water from a well? Would that sharp tongue of hers, which she had used against her brother, his father, in Ahmad's defence, have been dulled? Ahmad had loved his spinster aunt very much: without her, living with his father after his mother's death would have been inconceivable. She had turned into a second mother and Ahmad thanked God for having sent such a sympathetic guardian; but he could not understand why she quarrelled with his father whenever he broached the subject of remarriage? Shouldn't she just have let him marry like everyone else? He remembered her replies to his father, the implications of which had gone by him unnoticed at the time: instead of marrying, she had told him, he ought to be dedicating his life solely to his son . . . But which son had she meant – the Ox, the Dog, or the Ass?

One day, the Ass had mustered up all his courage, entered his father's room, and said, 'Father . . .' But then he had begun to stammer and would not have been able to complete the sentence had his father not asked him, in his customary hostile manner, 'What do you want?'

At that question, Ahmad's face had reddened and his will had abandoned him. He had lowered his head, his eyes fixed on the rug on the floor, and

415

said, in a barely audible voice, 'Father, I want to get married . . .'

'Get married?' His father had sneered and answered with a sarcasm that filled him with confusion. 'Where will you get the money from? Or do you want me to finance your marriage and then support you and your wife and children for the rest of my life? You . . . Ox!'

Ahmad had smiled to himself at his father's uncertainty as to which name to call him. 'No, Father. I intend to move to the Eastern Province where I can build myself a more promising future, as Masoud, the son of our neighbour Abu Sareeh, has done.'

His heart had pounded as he mentioned Abu Sareeh. He had come close to declaring that it was Abu Sareeh's daughter he wanted to marry, but he well knew the consequences of letting his tongue slip. He had been satisfied at the time in persuading his father to allow him to move. Nevertheless, he had been compelled to leave the room staggering in defeat as his father made his pronouncement, which Ahmad had never forgotten: 'Let me think about it . . . What can an Ass do?'

Eight years had passed since that episode, during which many of Ahmad's ideas had been turned upside down. True, he had suffered; yet, he had also tasted life, as often happens when a man plunges into its midst and struggles to live it in all its robustness and afflictions. However hard he'd had to work, whatever pain he'd had to bear in order to earn his bread, none of it matched the cruelty and humiliation he had suffered at the hands of his father. He had found himself in a new world – a world he could never have foreseen in his village, closed as it was upon itself. Who there would believe him, if he told of the wonders which had opened his eyes to the world? Or if he told of the hundreds of foreign women, naked but for transparent dresses which revealed more than they concealed of graceful legs, round backs and soft white necks, parading provocatively in the city streets and sending flames through the bodies of thirsty men like himself? Who would take his word if he said that buildings in the city touched the clouds and that their lights rivalled the light of the stars? And, if he described the dazzling scenes of life and secrets of the universe shown every day in movie theatres and on television screens, would he feel safe afterwards walking in the village streets?

Eight years, and a new life which he had absorbed thoroughly. And now, he had to come back to the village: his aunt had begged him to show up in person, so that he might resolve the chronic disputes between herself and his father. Although Ahmad knew nothing about what had prompted their feud, he had recognized it was his duty to intervene – especially for his aunt's sake.

Ahmad set aside, for the moment at least, these dark thoughts and experienced a surge of joy at the visions they had interrupted of a future with the sweetheart of his youth, and of the love, fidelity and understanding they would share . . . Often he had been awakened by urges to return to the village to make sure no one had stolen her. But such thoughts had been pushed aside by the need to go on working to secure the means of supporting a family. No doubt, she was still hiding behind her slanted door and awaiting his return. Khalida . . . what a special name! He envied his very lips for pronouncing it.

Eight years. How had he managed to survive them? He recalled the train accident in which he had almost been killed, and the fire that had blazed through the oil-well while he was installing equipment, his clothes soaked with oil. These accidents had taken place at the beginning of his employment with the oil company, while he was still 'raw material'. Soon after that, he had been transferred to the company workshop where his skill and hard work had won him the respect of his superiors; there had been promotions and handsome salary increases. The 5000 *riyals*, the bulk of his savings, which he had sent to his father ought to have been enough to smooth over the father–aunt feud. His father might have saved the money for his son's own wedding expenses; or, if the quarrel had been over the choice of a bride for Ahmad, he would easily dispel it the minute he made public his plans to marry Khalida . . .

'Who is it?'

'It's me, Ahmad.'

The door opened slowly and a face, not unfamiliar to his eyes, peered through the narrow opening and emitted a faint moan.

Who could she be? Aiysha? Fatima? . . . Ahmad cursed his forgetful memory. She must be . . . Oh God! Impossible! It couldn't be! And yet, how could he not recall those golden braids and that smile? . . . But her youth and grace were gone and this withered smile was quite different from her old one. Time had wasted away her vitality and disfigured her virginal beauty . . .

'How are you, Khalida?'

'Fine, thank you. Welcome . . .'

Dear God, how *different* she looked! Her waist bulged and her face was overflowing with melancholy. Didn't she know that he had come back solely for her sake? Why was she standing so cold and uneasy? Had she forsaken their promise?

'Is my father inside?'

'No. I'm alone in the house.'

God damn the Devil! Who had let her in? Why was she there while his father was out? Was this the right house? . . .

417

'Tell me, isn't this my father's house?'

'Yes, but I'm by myself now. Please come in, if you'd like . . .'

By herself ? . . . Was this a riddle?

'Where is my aunt? What are you doing here while my father's out?'

'Your aunt is angry with your father. Now she's staying at a relative's house.'

'And you?'

'Me? I'm in my own house. In my husband's house . . .'

Ahmad lowered his head as if dodging a fatal blow. The shock was heavier than he could bear. Then he returned to the road, which a few minutes before had been witness to his illusions of happiness. Now it was a long road indeed, filled with furrows like the tombs dug in his heart by those withered dreams.

Translated by Sharif Elmusa and Thomas G. Ezzy

Abd al-Majeed al-Qadi   **YEMEN**

The Final Ring

The first time the alarm clock rings it is early in the morning. I reject it. I struggle between waking and sleeping. I wait. I do not want to believe my ears. But, in seconds, the alarm rings for the second time. Reluctantly, I open my eyes but a languor, delicious and unending, closes them again. Oh, how I wish that the night could be extended for another hour. The alarm rings for the third time. No hope. The noise is insistent like the hum of an obstinate fly.

I mumble, open my eyes. Darkness still struggles with the dawn. I try to move. But I find myself unable to: I'm a small fish, gracefully enfolded by an octopus. Oh my beloved octopus. Between your arms and thighs I am really small, a small person, my love.

Cautiously, I pull myself together. I raise my head, tighten my waist, try to pull in my behind. No use, no use. Your closed eyes and the half smile on your lips pull me to you. I try to resist. I implore you, I appeal to your compassion but, oh, you plant your thorns in my breast. In the heat of passion, I find my being dissolving. My limbs seem to scatter and burn. The ringing of the alarm becomes the echo of a wedding ululation, coming from far away. Oh my love, no sooner do you turn away than you come back to me again.

When I pull my damp nightgown together, torn in half in front, when I get up and leave the heaving bed, you stretch out your arms and legs and cover both sides of the bed.

Never mind, it's your right, after all. You have another hour to sleep, so sleep my love. As for me . . . me . . . well, the kitchen is my responsibility, and the laundry . . . then, of course, we have the results of all our love . . . You share the pleasure with me. But you have nothing to do with the work and the unpleasantness.

At six o'clock I come back and find you still asleep. You've turned over and crossed your arms under your broad chest. I run my thin fingers through your curly hair but you don't move . . . With a mother's tenderness I caress your broad sinewy back. My hand looks like a small butterfly, fluttering over the trunk of a fallen tree. Suddenly I find I'm weary of waking you up and I give you a pinch. You raise your head, you groan, you bellow – Leave me alone!

I whisper to you – Everything's done. All your things are ready. On the clothes rack, as usual, you'll find your shirt, your pants, your belt, your handkerchief, your socks. Both shoes are under the bed, waiting for you. They shine like mirrors. As for that growth on your chin, my love, in the bathroom you'll find the soap, the towel, a new blade for your razor, all in their regular place. What else, my love?

As for Shadi, our baby, I've washed Shadi. I've changed his clothes, I've already breast-fed him, I've put his little things in the bag. He'll have everything he needs. I've got him in my lap now. In a minute I'll take him and his bag to my mother and then rush off to work. My poor mother is in a lot of pain these days . . . What? Are you still asleep? . . . No . . . there's no time for more. Work begins at seven. Wake up, my love.

Dizziness, nausea, I'm sick at least six times a day. These are symptoms you couldn't possibly know about. They're hereditary, passed on to girls by their mothers since the beginning of time. Give and take. Forgive me, I am not to blame for what happened. The doctor forbade me to use contraceptives. You know what happened to me before when I ignored his advice. And you, you, my love come to tell me that *you* fear another child . . . even though the doctor confirms the dangers. Shadi, our beloved Shadi, is not yet two. My mother has a bad heart and cannot look after two children at the same time. What is the answer? Do you have a solution? I have a job. I am not prepared to give it up as long as my work is needed and as long as you are so extravagant. Listen . . . can you hear it? I can hear a buzzing in my head. Can't you hear the buzzing? For a whole week it has been buzzing. Now I am thinking about an abortion. Is that all right with you? Thank you, my love.

I am full of embarrassment. What can I say? What can I call it? Would it be correct to call it a problem? The same process is repeating itself: the dizziness, the nausea, the retching, the same symptoms as before. Oh my love, I did not realize that I am like a cat. One after another.

This time the doctor has refused to give me an abortion. He says it's too dangerous. Two abortions in only a few months would have a damaging effect on my womb. The upshot? My future life would be ruined. Do you understand? That's what the doctor says and then, then, then I still have anaemia because of all the blood I lost in the last abortion. As for my mother, oh my poor mother, her heart is worse and she is no longer capable of helping with children. And Shadi, Shadi, our pampered son has turned into an irritable, hyperactive child who likes to break things, to eat dirt and rummage in the rubbish with the neighbourhood cats.

What should I do? Shall I tear up my degree and resign from my job? I would do it. I would make the sacrifice. I would renounce my right to work even though I don't want to, if only you didn't chew *qat*, didn't smoke so much, didn't drink so much.

Two babies, boy and girl, Shadi and Shadia . . . look at her, she'd be a living picture of Cupid if she weren't so small. Her eyes are her most beautiful feature. No, her lips. No, her cheeks, her neck, no, her hair. Everything about her is beautiful and sweet. Sometimes I feel I could devour her, she is so delicious, especially when she laughs or when she cries.

Where shall I take her? My mother went to the hospital yesterday and it looks as if she may not come back. My maternity leave is almost over and it's six more months before Shadi will be old enough to go to nursery school. Oh, what a silly mistake. In our country we don't have any nursery schools. I'm mixing up nursery schools and kindergartens. Sorry, these days I sometimes find myself talking about things that don't actually exist . . . The important thing is that Shadi really doesn't pose a problem. Six more months and he'll be in kindergarten. I might manage six months leave without pay by using the little savings I have.

But oh, my love, what can we arrange for Shadia when those six months are up? What will happen if that old, sick woman, my poor mother, should die . . . What will happen if the doctor refuses to give me an abortion this time too? What nest can I find to hatch my new egg? Don't you see that I am too fertile? I wonder how many working women are like me?

I don't believe that you want this to happen, my love.

The alarm clock rings for the first time . . . It is six o'clock. But it should have rung at a quarter to five . . . do you hear me? You, who are the man, the master, who spread and fold your wings as you please . . . But it is the second ring. How is it that you have wings but don't seem to be able to fly, my love?

I'm sorry, but I can't move this morning . . . I'm unable to come over to your bed and give you the usual pinch. Oh, if only the bed had not been split in two my love. I'm sorry your clothes are scattered around and I was too sick to polish your shoes . . . last night . . . I apologize because the kitchen is still dark. And the baby . . . what about the baby, my love?

I can almost see Shadia drowning in her morning excrement. What is sad, my love, is that you seem to be overwhelmed with disgust whenever you see her in that state.

Forgive me, you virile man. Yes, I'm weak. I'm exhausted, my strength is gone but the alarm keeps on ringing . . . won't you wake up, my love?

I'm bleeding, oh how I'm bleeding. It seems as though half my blood poured out during yesterday's operation . . . what remains seems to be slowly seeping away. Soon, I may join my mother . . . and you, my love, will live on, a real stallion, your job to inseminate. Yes.

The alarm . . . the alarm is ringing for the last time. This time the ringing is weak, feeble, the spring must have wound down, let go, stretched to its limit, my . . . love.

Translated by May Jayyusi and Elizabeth Fernea

Waleed al-Rujaib   **KUWAIT**

Drip Drip

One of the men said: 'Your friend was arrested a week ago and will certainly be deported. His residence permit expired some time ago. You know what usually happens when it's a question of illegal residence.'

Mustafa (feeling rather lost): 'What about me?'

Another said: 'There is somebody who can get a residence permit for you, but you need a substantial sum of money.'

Mustafa (with triumphant joy): 'I've got money, I've got it.'

They're sitting around him in the bachelor flat. On the walls are girlie photos cut from magazines and clothes hanging on nails.

One of them offers Mustafa a cigarette: 'But I warn you', he says, 'you'll have to give him the money without any guarantees.'

Mustafa does not seem to understand.

Another of them explains: 'You might never get your money back, or get your residence permit either. What I, personally, have is a forged residence permit.'

Mustafa: 'Do you mean he might rob me? Didn't you say he was a senior employee?'

'It has happened many times. You've got to risk it.'

Mustafa exhales the smoke of his cigarette and says, as if talking to himself: 'If that happens what do I do?'

One of them: 'Having no residence permit means that you have to work at the hardest jobs, a porter, a construction worker, a ditch-digger and get minimum wages. Of course, you're under constant threat of arrest, of being deported.'

'What, then, are my chances of ever getting rich?' Mustafa asked, feeling defeated.

'I've been working here for four years and I've earned only enough to barely survive, to rent a room to live in, and eat and smoke,' one of the men answered.

'But I've already made promises to my son and daughter,' Mustafa answered, dejectedly.

A drop of water clings to the mouth of the tap. It is stuck there . . . it falls.

The water is stuck . . . it falls.

Drip, drip.

He cannot see the drops of water, but he can hear them.

Drip . . .

He keeps his mind busy, he pretends to be busy, he tightens his lips on the cigarette but the damn drop of water keeps him alert, and his alertness makes him wait in expectation, and waiting turns time into something like these drops of water, slow and provocative.

A drop of water gathers . . . it falls.

Drip, drip.

A drop gathers, seems to be stuck in the tap.

– It's three weeks since I handed the man the money . . .

Drip, drip, drip.

– He told me then that I was to have the residence permit in three days . . .

That drop is stuck again in the tap.

– Three weeks have passed while I sit in this prison waiting. I live by sharing the little food my friends bring in, and I share their cigarettes, too. They've hinted several times, however, that the cigarettes are very expensive here.

Drip, drip.

He turned on his back and the makeshift bed creaked under him. – I'm living in this room without paying my share. By God that's embarrassing.

A drop of water is stuck . . .

– To work without a residence permit means a hard job and poor pay.

Drip, drip, drip.

– And what about my children?

A drop is stuck in the tap.

He straightened his back.

– I've got to do something, anything. I don't want to go home in defeat, after having lost everything, including the money I've saved all my life. I could steal . . .

Drip.

He put his legs on the floor and removed two cigarettes from under the sweat-stained pillow.

He left the room.

424

A drop of water gathered at the mouth of the tap and seemed suspended there.

The street is empty. He walks between the dim street lights and the fences of elegant villas. He keeps an eye on everything: the parked cars, the windows of unlit rooms. His shadow, broken in half at the meeting point of the wall and the ground, sometimes seems to go ahead of him, sometimes moves as he moves, sometimes lags behind him, depending on the position of the lamp-posts. The headlights of a car flash over him for a moment. He shudders, his heart beats fast, the car speeds by. He lights a cigarette.

– I wonder if somebody noticed my confused footsteps?

He holds the cigarette within his palm, to hide the glow of the cigarette when he inhales.

– Or are my footsteps normal?

He draws on his cigarette again and looks apprehensively at his shadow, then turns into a street even darker than the one where he has been walking. Some of the street lights are out and the darkness and silence increase his nervousness. His cigarette falling on the asphalt makes an unexpected noise. He has a sense that he is being watched and that forces him to keep looking behind him. He tries to walk more lightly on the pavement. But his footsteps can still be heard.

He tries to step even more carefully. Then his foot makes a loud noise as it hits something in front of one of the luxurious villas. He freezes, looks carefully around him once more. The street is silent except for the distant barking of a dog. Something soft, liquid and cold covers his foot and he looks to see what it is. His foot is jammed in a rubbish bag. Slowly he pulls his foot out; it feels heavy because of what is stuck on his shoe.

– Damn them! Do they have to cook more than they need to eat? . . .

He moves away from the fences, walking somehow differently because of his soiled shoe.

The objects about him, the lamp-post, the iron doors of the villas, the cars with their bright lights and their inner darkness, seem to him extremely quiet, as if they are waiting for the right moment to attack him.

– I'm in a tight spot, but I must venture.

He hears panting, a rustling which seems to be coming closer. Startled, he looks back and his eyes widen. A dark shadow is following him. Then he realizes, in spite of the darkness, that it is a dog. Immediately his heartbeat speeds up. He stops, frightened. The dog stops too.

'Shsh . . .'

The dog stands still.

He points with his hand and whispers, 'Go away.'

The dog wags his tail.

– What if . . .

He spots a little stone.

– But if I hit him, he might attack.

He bends his knees, keeping his eyes on the dog.

– I must try, I have no choice . . .

His fingers feel along the ground, his eyes still fixed on the dog. He grasps the stone and straightens up.

'Shsh . . .'

He does not throw the stone.

'Come on, move off!'

The dog retreats a little and stands there. Mustafa keeps the stone in his hand, just in case.

– For an emergency, he tells himself.

He feels the sweat break out under his arms. He quickens his footsteps.

– Exile, bankruptcy, danger!!

His shadow goes ahead of him, it seems to grow larger and longer. He hears the noise of an engine behind him, the engine of a small car. The noise grows louder and higher as it approaches him.

– Don't panic . . .

The whining noise of the car engine indicates that it is speeding. It comes closer and closer, and Mustafa's shadow stretches longer and longer ahead of him.

– Don't look around.

The car passes so close to the curb that it stirs dust and leaves in the road. A hand reaches out of the car window and throws something that breaks when it hits the pavement. As he comes closer, he sees that it is an empty whisky bottle. The car's whine recedes into the distance. He stops in the middle of the pavement to light a cigarette.

'Oh, my son, my daughter!' he whispers to himself.

The street led him around a corner, straight ahead and around another corner. He found himself in front of the bachelor flats.

As soon as he walked in, one of his friends snapped at him, 'Where have you been?'

Mustafa did not answer. Exhausted, he threw himself on the makeshift bed and said, in despair, 'Tomorrow I will go to the building of the sewage contractor . . .'

Drip, drip, drip . . .

Translated by Salwa Jabsheh and Elizabeth Fernea

Amin Salih   **BAHRAIN**

The Butterflies

Beware of lowering your head lest the nightwatchman should say:
'There goes a woman who's ashamed of the road
   her husband paved for her.'

– Mubashshiri, a Persian poet

A woman looks out from her balcony and gazes at the sailors crowded inside and outside the tavern. (You sail between the two gates of presence and absence. Always present in my eyes. When, my husband, will you light up my forehead with your hands?) The sailors are redolent of the smell of shells, in their pockets there are particles of sand from strange shores, and in their hands they hold the braids of beloved girls who wait for them in far-off harbours. Memory is a familiar road, thronged with birds. (Longing has a colour like that of light on spring evenings, like the colour of the eyes of your little girl who asks about you all the time . . . Do you remember the colour of your little girl's eyes? She has turned into a real little devil.) The sailors' noise erupts here and there. They sing and there are tears in their voices. They lean on one another's shoulders.

They imagine that they are a flock of birds wet with the fragrance of dew and fog, who feel the pulse of the damp night. She listens to the silence that is uppermost for a moment, that is then suddenly broken by the noise of empty glasses and bottles. She turns her head to the other side of the public square. The mad young woman is still there, running the length and breadth of the square without stopping for a single moment. It seems she never gets tired. Or so it looks to the wife. (I told you about her in the previous letter. I do not believe that she is mad. The waiter who works in the tavern insists that she is mad, but he does not know who she is, or where she came from, or how she originally looked. I can imagine her as a sun sometimes. Yes, I know that my imagination can go astray, but . . . why shouldn't she be a rebellious sun? It surprises me to see her only at this hour . . . I don't know where she goes during the day. I have never seen her clearly. I would like to see her face, her feet, her arms.)

The mad woman's hair scatters rebelliously at the edge of the night. She moves like a troubled sea, as if there were frightening shadows following her. Her movements are violent and never calm down. She looks startled and nervous like the claws of a wounded beast caught in a trap. She invents a fiery alphabet. Is she an illusion or a manifestation of something real that is revealed from the silence under the cloak of the night? (I can see obscure voices pour out of her flaming heart. They touch the stones and windows, but no one listens. And I, too, do not listen. I imagine many things, particularly when I write to you. On one occasion, I could not prevent myself from going down and trying to find out the girl's secret. But she disappeared suddenly. And when I returned to the balcony, I saw her again. Isn't that strange? Tomorrow I shall cook an appetizing meal for you, and I hope you will not eat your fingers with the food.)[1] Sorrow engulfs her for a few minutes. She sends winged images through the labyrinths of time. Her lips part, smiling, as she imagines her husband coming towards her in his rose-coloured shirt, his chest bare, while the sea breezes pass through the locks of his hair and the folds of his shirt . . . She runs in front of him, laughing sweetly, sometimes hurrying, sometimes slowing down, while he continues to follow her, to catch her. When he reaches her, he takes hold of her wrist, she loses her balance and falls on the soft sand, he falls over her while they laugh. He kisses her and she kisses him. Then they roll on the sands that are white as the down of birds. A playful wave approaches her, touches her fingers gently. They feel embarrassed. He suggests that they build houses with the sand and foam, and she agrees. Her body is kindled with joy when the seagulls alight on these houses without caution or fear.

(You used to sit on that chair and read until late at night. Do you still read? I tried to send you the books you had asked for, but they refused. They said, 'These books are prohibited.' It's alright. Reading books like *The Empty Pillow* won't hurt you, especially when you are forced to do so. You have no choice. This is, of course, painful. You used to write sometimes in the dark, while lying in bed, lest the lamp light should wake me up. But I used to feel the movement of the bed . . . You were unable to

1. This is a translation of an idiomatic sentence in Arabic meaning that, when the food is really delicious, a person can even eat his own fingers with the food.

suppress your feelings while you wrote. This is why I used to wake up always and put the light on for you. You used to apologize. Do you still write? Last month I received your poem, and cried.)

Her eyes fall on a loafer searching through a rubbish bin. He finds an empty tin of sardines but he stretches out his finger to extract the last few bits. He finds an unsquashed cigarette butt and smokes it with pleasure while he sweeps the place with his eyes. Then he sits leaning on the wall and sings in a hoarse voice about Eden-like cities, whose gates are of marble, and where no keeners or mourners are allowed to enter because it is empty of widows, of orphans, of persons demented with platonic love, of mystics and poor people. In these cities a peasant would squat watching the revolution with pride as it ripens and blooms, then he would gather the fruits in a brightly coloured basket and carry it to his wife who waits for him at the threshold of their house. They will distribute them now. And in these cities one would see a mechanic who repairs the damage and greets his comrades and smiles, and there would be working men and children who carve their names on the tree trunks of the forest. And there would be snow and rituals for joy, and suns for weddings.

(Do you remember the songs of our friends on our first picnic? They were standing round a pool, making up warm, childlike songs, watching the flow of melody as it went beyond the usual boundaries of ordinary songs. I remember you told me then that such songs will one day flow out of the cells of grasses and enter the gardens of the body. And now, I sit on our balcony and yearn for another such picnic . . . O God! I should talk to you about happier things! You have your own worries. Alright. Our little girl is proud these days because she has learned how to read and write a complete sentence. Dawn is about to break, and I am a little tired. I love you.)

Translated by May Jayyusi and Dick Davies

Abdallah al-Salmi   SAUDI ARABIA

The Bridge

I had nothing to do that morning and, as usual, I'd left the house and made my way to the bridge. The weather was grey and cloudy and, as I watched the clouds constantly floating by, I felt a lump in my throat; for no rain fell any longer, even though the clouds passed overhead nearly every day. I thought back to the times when the rain did fall, each drop like a big lemon, and we'd plunge half-naked into the cold water.

It was then, I remember, that the bridge was built. Those were the days when people had begun to smile a good deal and exchange words that were kind and full of hope; for they'd been told how the bridge would change the face of the land, how the water would run beneath it marvellously, in a wider canal, and how vast fields would suddenly sprout with ears of purple grain.

I'd shared in the happy atmosphere of those days. We constantly put off our work and went down to the bridge – in fact, it hadn't been built yet, but we called the rectangular hole there a bridge – and we'd watch open-mouthed as the huge machines and vast army of workmen created a new, larger canal. As the canal grew, the smiles on people's faces grew broader too, and some of the men started to abandon their work completely and spend the whole day watching the bridge. Even the women started going there, on the pretext that they were looking for their children, and they'd stay there for hours on end, watching it and talking together.

Rumours abounded even before the bridge started to take shape. One evening a venerable old man said that the bridge was a holy thing, a thing of mystery, which would bring great blessings; and another wise man said that it was a finely honed machine which would take hold of the clouds, pour rain into the huge canal and spread it over the land. Some of the men had seen the bridge take strange shapes in their dreams and, when they woke in the morning, they found lasting pleasure in the wondering looks of their good-natured wives.

And so the bridge became a thing of mystery and wonder, taking on, as it grew, the aspect of a myth. I thought about it a good deal myself, and the longing to see the other side of things gave me no rest. I was on the point, once or twice, of asking one of the workmen about the bridge, but they spoke a strange language which I couldn't understand at all; and, quite apart from that, their foreman was a fierce man who cracked the whip all day and wouldn't let anyone near the place. Finally, when I'd worn myself out with pointless speculation, I just watched it grow, marvelling like all the others; it took a long time to build, I remember, and during this time people spent all the money they'd saved over many long years. Since the men weren't working for the most part, being content just to watch the bridge, they didn't get to sleep early – which meant that there were almost as many children as there were flies.

Then the splendid day came and, ignoring the sun which beat down on us, we gathered to look at the bridge. It seemed like a vast, grey mass clutching the two banks of the canal; it certainly was a most amazing sight, and people said nothing for a considerable time. Then there was a celebration in red and green and silver, and the men danced and ululations rang out from the women. We stayed there a long time that night dancing on the bridge, and some of the boys didn't leave until morning. Then came a long period of waiting, but what happened was hard to believe – the rain stopped falling and the clouds would flit away from the vast canal. All we'd catch sight of, from time to time, would be small cars speeding across the bridge, and people lost hope completely. They stopped visiting the bridge and, little by little, they forgot the whole affair and took to dreaming other dreams instead.

I didn't forget about it, though, and went on visiting the bridge; and I'd gaze into the empty depths beneath it and see how they were gradually filling up with dirt and refuse. I saw huge numbers of insects crawling about, eating up the dirt and multiplying at an appalling rate. Then the time came when the insects couldn't find anything to eat any more, and they started gnawing at the supports of the bridge. I'd often see their steely teeth gnawing at the iron and cement, and I realized that the bridge had become a mere trap, luring people to their destruction; I wanted to say this, but the people in the speeding cars never stopped to listen. Then, one morning, I found that the insects had eaten the supports right through.

I sensed disaster coming; then I caught sight of a big, brightly coloured car, and I heard the sound of clapping and laughter. I ran, waving my hands and crying out to warn them of the danger, but they didn't hear me – perhaps they thought I just wanted a ride. Then, in the twinkling of an eye, I saw the bridge collapse like a heap of earth.

Then the laughter became mixed with tears.

Translated by Lena Jayyusi and Christopher Tingley

Summer and Ashes

My hair was a wet sponge and little, sticky, acid drops were running down my temples and settling in my dirty collar. I took my handkerchief out, for something to do, and dried my face with it. My shoes rang out on the pavement – a mournful, nervous sound, like my own small thoughts. Grey thoughts had begun to spread through my head a few minutes before, and my feet were moving mechanically, their monotonous rhythm fading away without meaning in my ears. I watched my shadow moving over the pavement. It was following me silently, sticking to me like glue, and it struck me that my whole life was nothing more than a shabby, illusory shadow I couldn't get rid of. I smiled bitterly; one more bend and the old café would come into sight. The café and the brassy noise, then the return to limp silence – the flaccid, rubber wheels round which my empty days revolved. I smiled once more, as the sticky little drops continued their strange, twisting descent. My collar was full of the night and the smell of damp salt.

I undid another button on my shirt and walked on. The night brought no taste of pleasure to my lips, and yet I didn't want to go back – my room, I knew, would be steeped in its own sweat now, and I wouldn't get to sleep before two in the morning. I had nothing to do. Oh no, I'd forgotten those damned exercise books! They'd take two hours at least, two hours brimful of heat, intolerable heat, heat that makes your blood boil like a cauldron. Those damned exercise books! I'd started to hate them from the depths of my heart. Fifteen years face to face with exercise books and heat – always one or the other. What a life this was, almost enough to make you throw up! I felt a taste of rust in my mouth and I spat, but the taste in my mouth didn't change; still the rust lay stretched over my tongue, like a layer of lime, as if it had sprung from inside me. I hurriedly searched in my pocket. It was empty; I must have forgotten my cigarettes. I must have a cigarette, I thought, to get rid of this damned rust. I must have one!

I made my way towards the man. He was hurrying to close up his shop, as he had every reason to do with someone waiting for him – the gleaming house, the children, the wife and all the other things soaked in warmth. He won't be pleased to see me, I thought; he'll think I'm a nuisance, I know that. But what can I do? I need a cigarette. I went up to him and, trying to make my voice sound apologetic, said politely:

'A packet of Abu Bass, please.'

The man turned and threw me a hard look, then he moved, slowly and deliberately, trying to make me feel that I was a late-night customer he could do without. Then he came back, with the same hard look boring into me. I knew exactly what that look meant and I felt something or other opening up inside me like a cyst that was malignant and full of pus. You're not young any more, the look said, and yet you're still roaming the streets, into the night. I wanted to tell him that I was a single man on my own, abandoned and without a proper home, that I didn't have anything or anyone waiting for me. But things are never as easy as that. I swallowed my resentment with some difficulty and let my eyes fall on the brightly coloured packet.

'Okay,' I said. 'Thank you.'

I walked off without saying anything further. Why didn't I tell him the way things are? The swine think's he's better than I am because he doesn't roam the streets at this hour. Why didn't I tell him my only home was four walls as gloomy as his dirty face? I plunged back into my resentment. They all look down on you like that; they leave you to fight against unfair odds and face the bitterness of defeat. The match blew out, for the second time at least – it didn't look as if this damned cigarette was ever going to be lit. My fingers moved in a more and more agitated way, while the cigarette still drooped indifferently from between my lips. The thought struck me that my whole life was nothing more than a useless cigarette which had never been lit – a worthless childhood, and then long hours among creased yellow pages. What now? Nothing. Just a teacher at forty, a middle-aged man of forty with no memories or ties, half-forgotten, living alone in a rented room. One day, perhaps, I'll fall asleep for good and rot before they even find me.

I felt a sharp tightening in my chest and the tip of my cigarette glowed in a depressed kind of way. I breathed the smoke right down and walked on. The city was asleep early, the street sticky with heat and silent as the grave. The shops, emptied by the heat and the night, were all locked up and the street lamps looked tired, like eyes worn out with sleeplessness, as they threw their yellow light into the grey air. The sky was a faded cloud gazing despondently down. It was summer.

A fragrant perfume met me, from some gay, urbane laughter nearby. My clothes felt damper and stickier than ever, and I realized that these people must certainly have an air conditioner because their clothes were dry and as clean as soap. A reckless fury seized hold of me because I knew I'd never own an air conditioner and my clothes were always going to be damp and wet. I blew hard on my cigarette as I thought how unfair it all was. My shoes grated irritably on the pavement and the eyes of an old cat gleamed as it crossed the tarmac road, yawning lazily.

Then the young man came round the corner, bright and elegant, like an ornamental box. I noted his features in a vague, incoherent way, then they began to coalesce mysteriously, making up a small ruddy face. I may have clipped his ear once, or made him stand facing a wall, but the face approaching me now presented a completely different picture. It wasn't a small, ruddy face any more, but full, with a thin black line running across the centre. I looked straight ahead. If he speaks to me, I thought, my head's going to start spinning. My steps became nervous, as if I was wading in a shallow pool of mud. He was almost passing me now. He turned calmly towards me and smiled, revealing a row of marble teeth, and the black line stretched out in a quicksilver movement. I really was in a miserable spot.

'Good evening, sir,' he said.

'Good evening,' I said.

He was still smiling and the wall of shining marble teeth was now more clearly visible. I licked my own teeth – yellow, rotten teeth, covered with tobacco stains and failure. I stared at my shoes as his gaze bored into my face, as cold as a bucket of ice.

'Don't you know me, sir?'

The black line waved gaily up and down. They all started with thin, ruddy faces, then they changed in this amazing way. I hated those faces – they made me think of insects crawling ambitiously upwards – and I used to take a perverse pleasure in wiping the innocent gaiety out of those small eyes with a resentful slap. 'You there! Why are you talking?' 'Me?' The pale, frightened features would tremble with fear and my resentment would flash out in a single blow, a wretched blow that was crueller than it needed to be. It was the resentment of a man who'd been abandoned, whose gaze, day after day, strikes up against loneliness and cunning faces and the miserable blackboard, and nothing else. Day after day! Oh, God! I'd follow the little tremblings of their faces with concealed delight; I wanted to destroy those insects who seemed to be sucking away at my life like leeches. But they weren't destroyed because the same faces would meet me afterwards, solid and firm – making me feel fragile and old. The thought strikes me that these faces were still growing, still developing, whereas mine would never grow any more. He spoke up again, and I felt my head spinning.

'Hope you haven't forgotten me, sir?'

'No. But you've changed a lot.'

'Everybody changes, sir!'

He laughed lazily. It's true; everyone changes except me. I'd remain that middle-aged teacher, solitary, half-forgotten, abandoned beyond hope. The cigarette started wilting and drooping and I suddenly felt cold, yellow depression sweeping into me. I glanced down the length of the street; there was nothing but silence and the light of the spiritless street lamps, dripping with dampness. And across the utterly silent tarmac, just at the point where my glance fell, there it was stretched out in the middle of the night – the old, greying image of a life which, fifteen years ago, I'd expected to give birth to marvellous things: warmth and tenderness and the smile which had kept me waking through nights brimming with hopes and great dreams, the dreams of a young man in his twenties. But the child was born deformed. The smile, the smile fragrant with the scent of lemon blossom, vanished, and a harsh wrinkle had appeared on the delicate lips. What's the use of a third-rate teacher?

In a second the image had collapsed and shattered like a pane of brittle glass. As the fever raged, the wonderous pulse of life in the pock-marked face ceased to beat and the fire devoured image and shadow together; I had to seek out some modest corner to bury my roseate dreams. I'd been sunk in bitterness and decay and failure for fifteen years, fifteen years spent rotting among piles of exercise books, criticized daily by the headmaster when I arrived late as usual.

I nervously threw away the butt of my cigarette and turned my head aside in dejection, filled with the gloom of the image which lay shattered deep inside me.

The handsome face said:

'Are you all right?'

'Yes,' I answered. 'I'm all right, thank you.'

'Okay. Goodbye then, sir.'

I forced out a reply:

'Goodbye.'

I let my feet lead me on as usual and, in a little while, the café appeared at last. I speeded up my walk. Here was my drug at last: an oasis of pleasure and night-fleeting joys. But I didn't feel my usual cheerfulness stirring in me; for some strange reason the café didn't, this time, fill me with the surging joy of the confirmed addict given a rare dose of his drug.

Depression still swept through me, like a whirlwind. I went in. Not an eye turned to look at me; I'd become a relic in a deserted museum. I sank into my usual seat. The place had a distinctive smell, mingling with the thick cigarette smoke in the air and the muttering sound of the water-pipes, and it excited me as if I was experiencing it for the first time. I fixed my gaze on the top of the table in front of me. The same old faces bent over their cards and dominoes, the same stares at the clouds of white smoke up under the ceiling.

I was able to see all these things without lifting my eyes. They're all abandoned, I thought to myself, just like you; it's the same old story. I imagined myself, for ten more long years perhaps, sinking into this same seat, smelling this cursed smell, accompanying these same glances on their barren journey that led nowhere. Or going back to my cold, gloomy solitude, to be assailed by the old, old image of my spiritless life. The same thing, night and day. God, what a life! It's almost enough to make you throw up.

I picked up the glass of tea, then moved it away from my lips and put it back down on the table. The body of a small, blue fly was floating on the surface, a stupid fly that had been lured to the dark, sticky fluid. It had hovered round it eagerly then, before long, it had sunk quickly down, a bloated corpse, without even tasting a drop. I felt, for some reason, that I was like this miserable fly; and in fact we had more than one thing in common – the worthless beginning, the barren pursuit and the final bloated end. There was just one, fine difference between us: the fly had ceased to exist, whereas I was still waiting passively for the approaching end.

But why was I waiting? The question welled up from me all of a sudden, wounding me like a sharp knife, and the cold pallor of my depression gave way to a surge of overwhelming anger. I thrust the glass away with a single movement and it fell to the ground, smashing noisily. For the first time since I'd come in, people glanced at me, vacantly but with annoyance. Life had crept back into the disregarded old relic and the cold museum had filled with visitors. As I looked at the pieces of smashed glass, I felt a mysterious pleasure, as though I was seeing my former life transformed into scattered fragments and a new life unlocking its doors and flinging them open in front of me. A swift but complex thought sprang up in my mind – I'll start looking for a new job tomorrow – it'll be a different sort of life, of course – that doesn't matter, I'll start from scratch. A small, radiant glow began to fill my heart. I walked firmly, taking no notice of all the irritated glances, a many-sided joy coming to life in my soul.

The street outside looked, to me, as if it had been shaken by an earthquake; it wasn't still now, and my steps were no longer hollow when I struck it. The clear summer sky seemed wonderful to me and I breathed in deeply, wondering how I'd managed to wait so long. I thrust the question aside: it had no meaning now, now that I was making a new start. At the corner I threw a last glance back at the café which had been my opium. Then my feet began once more to move lightly over the pavement and this time their rhythm held a deep meaning which sent its warmth into the depths of my soul.

I was very late. My watch wasn't working but I knew it must be past nine o'clock because of the sun's rays in the room, gleaming, golden rays filling the room with the smell of a new day – something I'd never experienced before. I didn't get up because I wanted to savour this unique moment. I lay back in my splendid bed. This, I thought, is the last time I'll see that headmaster, with his lousy face and lifeless eyes and his words all mixed up with spittle. 'Why are you late, sir? You're here to work.' That's what he always said, and other things too, and the daily apologies I concocted would fall to the ground; the swine beat me every time. But today! I laughed to myself. Today was my day! I conjured up the picture, how his furious face would drop; I'd let him go through his routine right to the end, then, suddenly, I'd hit him with my decision. I jumped out of bed, burning to win once, just once, in a life which had always been soaked in defeat. A few moments later my footsteps were striking the pavement firmly. I got on the bus and let my body sink into the packed crowd; it was a small bus and our faces would almost come together at the slightest lurch. I gazed, with simple curiosity, round the silent faces, wondering to myself whether they'd known the taste of failure and deprivation. I looked into their eyes, eyes that gazed into emptiness. Had these people ever known joy, I wondered, or did they just surrender without a struggle? The thought hurt me – what if they had submitted? I looked quickly away, with a strange fear tugging at my heart.

The bus stopped and I got off, my nerves taut. The building appeared in front of me with its forbidding walls and its windows smashed by mischievous children. I came nearer; it was silent, like a broken machine. They must have reached the second lesson at least. I shrugged my shoulders: what did it matter if they'd reached the second lesson, or even the third? I walked past the lazy, lifeless gaze of the porter and was met by the atmosphere of decay – the smell of dust mixed with the smell of damp, gloomy places where the sun never penetrated. My nerves grew still more taut; the hour of eager decision had arrived. I went in.

438

'Good morning.'

'Hello.'

He didn't look up as he said it. Then he raised his eyes with his usual deliberateness.

'Where have you been?'

And he added:

'Late, of course. As usual.'

I didn't answer.

'Why are you late, without good reason? Eh?' His face hardened. 'To be frank, I think I've been more than patient with you.'

I waited quietly. Let him go through his routine right to the end.

'Now look, either you start doing your job properly or there's going to be trouble!'

I raised my eyes defiantly and began to feel a glorious prickling sensation on the edge of my tongue. I tried to smile calmly. Words began to surge up inside me. Then, all at once, like a sudden shot in the middle of the night, I caught sight of a hazy image reflected in the small, shabby mirror that was hanging straight in front of me on the wall – the image of a pale, dissipated, washed-out face, with blackened lips and sunken eyes surrounded by dark blue rings. Something inside me shrank back and my lips tightened painfully. In that wordless moment I felt, I don't know why, that I was an old man, a mass of burnt-out ashes in the heart of a deep furnace which had grown cold. Time had consumed the last spark of warmth and I'd never make a fresh start now; I'd missed my train and I'd have to spend the night alone, in the open, on the empty platform of the station. The old familar terror crept into my veins and a thousand thorns pricked in my throat. I said, as usual:

'I'm very sorry, sir.'

I turned round without another word, the small, false glow extinguished. My footsteps, as always, rang out monotonously, without meaning.

Translated by Lena Jayyusi and Christopher Tingley

Khayriyya al-Saqqaf   **SAUDI ARABIA**

Coal and Cash

'Here's forty *riyals*. That's all I'm paying.'

'It's not enough.'

'How much do you want then?'

'More than that.'

'Here's fifty. That's all I've got.'

'That'll do then. Thanks very much.'

The man checked the money, then went over to a corner of the shop, picked up something heavy and came back. He handed the other man a second-hand blanket smelling of coal, cooking and strange scents. The buyer only needed it because of the situation he was in at the moment; in a few hours he'd be back in his own home where he'd find warmth again, security and clean sheets.

He wrapped the blanket round him but still felt chilled to the bone. Other people had no covering at all. How would it be, he wondered, if he asked for some coal?!

'Hey, you!' he shouted.

The fat man in the soiled clothes was busy with other customers and trying to keep warm himself, but he came over again.

'Yes, what do you want?'

'Some coal to light a fire so we can all keep warm.'

'I haven't got much. It costs a hundred *riyals* a bag now.'

'Bring a quarter of a bag.'

The other man looked annoyed, but took the fifty-*riyal* note.

'Here you are,' he said. 'Here's your change. Twenty-five *riyals*.'

The man hurried away and came back with a quarter of a bag of coal. They lit a fire and huddled round it, trying to warm their limbs which felt as though they'd come apart with all the shivering.

They were between Makkah and Jeddah and it was one of those winter nights when ice storms arrive suddenly, without warning. Our friend had decided to go to Makkah to perform the minor pilgrimmage rituals. He'd done the circumambulation of the Kaaba, the running ritual, and the drinking of Zamzam well-water. Then he'd set out for Jeddah immediately; he was in a hurry, trying to keep one step ahead of the night.

If only I hadn't been in such a rush, he thought to himself. I could see the weather looked threatening. But there was something more urgent than that spurring me on. My teenage son has got ambitions and he's going abroad; we hope he'll come back after a few years as a doctor and know how to cure the disease I'm suffering from. He'll be able to get rid of this exhaustion I feel all the time. That's why I went on the pilgrimage . . .

The road was congested and the weather stormy. Then it started pouring with rain; there was a lot of thunder, and lightning struck the earth in a series of tremendous flashes. Nature was raising her voice and the hand of the storm was lashing out at everything in sight, the whole thing expressing a fierce, unparalleled fury. Nature's anger far outstrips the anger of man. When a man shouts, his voice only reaches as far as the walls of his house or his neighbour's house. When he hits out, his hand goes only as far as his body can reach. When he loses his temper, it can touch only the strictly limited range of people and things he controls. But with thunder and lightning and storms and winds, the range is far wider, encompassing man and his possessions. They can reach his most cherished, beloved objects, even his own clothes. All they leave him is a body shivering with cold and a little money; and with that money he's supposed to bargain with another man, a fellow human being with whom he happens, by force of circumstances, to be thrown together.

The long road had become a thing of fear and hope, of beauty and terror. The rain came down still harder, and the ground turned to mud. You can have too much of a good thing. Whole areas had been drenched and washed away, and everything was flooded. He was sitting in a car with a number of other people; this particular moment had brought them all together and so they were talking to one another and sharing their wretched experience. Then, suddenly, the car broke down.

'How are we going to get out?' one of them asked.

'The ground's flooded and I'm no swimmer,' replied another.

'The water's flowing pretty fast. Do you think we'd have the chance to swim even if we knew how?'

'What are we going to do then?'

'Look over there,' he said. 'There's another car there right next to us. Suppose we asked the driver to stop and take us with him? He might do it.'

441

'We haven't got much choice,' replied one of the passengers with a shiver. 'We're all like prisoners of war. Nothing we own belongs to us any more.'

'Okay then,' said another man, whose hands were firmly gripped under his armpits. 'Try it and see what happens.'

'Who me? If only you knew how bad my rheumatism is! I'm nearly sixty. Why don't you make the effort? You're all healthy youngsters. Okay, okay, I'll do it.'

He slid slowly out of the car and put his feet into the strongly flowing water; then, striving desperately to control his racing emotions, fighting to conquer fear and every cautious instinct, he paddled across for a few paces, losing his shoes in the process. Every now and then the force of the water would try to stop him.

He reached the other car and knocked on the window. After a while the driver opened the window just a crack.

'Could you take four of us in your car? Ours has broken down.'

'I've got enough problems of my own,' the driver replied irritably. 'I'm worried my car's going to break down too.'

'Couldn't we just go some of the way with you?'

The other driver didn't answer. He turned away, wound up the window and started to move off.

The whole situation was unbearable. He gestured to his fellow passengers then opened the back door of the other car. He didn't wait for permission from the driver but threw his soaking-wet body onto the back seat.

'What are you doing?' the driver asked. 'I didn't say you could get in!'

'I don't care. It's a matter of life and death.'

A few moments later his fellow passengers arrived, opened the door and crammed into the car alongside him. They were all shivering with cold; all the rain had left them was enough clothing to cover up some of their bodies, with the rest left exposed.

'Maybe we could find somewhere to stop soon,' one of the men suggested – his teeth were chattering and making a clicking sound – 'we could shelter there till the rain stops.'

The driver of the car didn't say a word; he seemed to be submitting to fate without a fight. He drove the car towards a place nearby which was lit up from time to time by flashes of lightning and had a red light outside. After a good deal of difficulty, the car finally drew up in front of the building and everyone rushed to get out, feeling exhausted and cold. They avoided the main path, heaped up with every kind of object – household utensils, barrels, clothing and rubbish – which, if not tied down, was being washed away in the tremendous flood. They threw themselves to the ground and found that they were under a warm ceiling.

'Have you got any coal?' he asked; he felt depressed and exhausted. He gestured to the man who'd come towards him; a fat man with a Mediterranean Arab accent, wrapped up in several layers of clothing with a cap on his head and thick shoes on his feet. They all looked at him, each of them wishing he could have an article of his clothing, which wasn't soaking wet and didn't feel like a lump of ice.

'It's a hundred *riyals* a bag.'

'We'll take half a bag.'

'Have you got a blanket?' another of them asked.

'No. I haven't got anything . . .'

The man kept saying no to every question he was asked. Meanwhile, a young man, who looked exactly like the owner and wore the same kind of clothes, came up to our friend.

'I see you're shivering, sir,' he whispered. 'I've got a blanket, but I can't lend it to you without asking my father first . . .'

'Is that man your father?'

'Yes.'

'I'll pay you for it.'

'How much?'

'Forty *riyals*.'

The father came over. 'That's not enough.'

'Fifty then. That's all I've got.'

The owner turned to his son. 'Okay, take it then,' he shouted.

The young man hurried off and fetched the blanket. Before he handed it over, he held out his hand for the fifty *riyals*.

So here I am, thought our friend, wrapping myself up in you, even though you smell disgusting. Here I am squatting by the lighted coals which cost me another fifty. My God, how cruel things are when you're really up against it.

He sat close to the fire and fixed his gaze on a piece of coal which had changed into a burning ember. He looked into it, deep in contemplation.

As they warmed themselves, he exchanged words and mumblings with his fellow-travellers.

How wonderful the warmth felt! How much they all needed it!

He chuckled loudly and everyone looked up and stared at him in amazement. He didn't notice anything; he was too busy laughing hysterically.

'These days,' he shouted through his laughter, 'everything in the world has its price. People are all apart from one another now; the only thing which brings them together is money and that's just made of paper . . .'

He stood up, still laughing; he was shaking with laughter as much as with the cold. He went over and stood by the window.

Outside the rain was still pouring down in torrents. Cars were being washed away by the flood, there were people being drowned, hands were waving frantically at the drivers of lorries passing by. But the drivers all went on without stopping for anyone; in circumstances like these, after all, no one has any money . . .

He felt a hand being placed on his shoulder and turned round to find himself looking at the silent man who'd been driving the other car. For the first time he heard his voice clearly, without any interruption.

'Pay me for the ride you and your friends had.'

He took just one look at the outstretched palm and started laughing all over again.

He didn't have anything in his pocket to give the man. He kept on laughing.

'Now listen,' the other man said, shaking him by the shoulders. 'Stop that, will you! If you haven't got any money, then you'll have to do some work for me by pushing the car to the nearest service station! That can pay for the ride you and your friends had!'

He didn't reply. He stared down at his bare feet and stroked his white beard. He could feel the rheumatism aching in his joints. He laughed and laughed and laughed . . .

Translated by Roger Allen and Christopher Tingley

Zayn al-Saqqaf   YEMEN

The End of Old Amm Misfir

Fierce winds were buffeting the mountains. They seemed to penetrate even the rocks with the cold breath of a bitter mountain winter. Old Amm Misfir stood up, chewing what remained from his supper, licking his lips and peering with regret into the empty bowl on the floor of the room.

'Thank you, Lord, for your bounty,' he murmured, rubbing his hands.

'What bounty are you talking about, unlucky wretch?' responded his wife.

'It is our duty to give praise to God in all circumstances.'

He pushed his fingers between his scalp and the tattered, dirty *kufiyya* that covered his small grey head, and pulled its torn, scattered threads away from his forehead. He peered through the window, then sat down, easing the burden of his sixty years onto an ancient mattress that was stuck to the floor in an age-old embrace. He fingered the pocket of his rough waistcoat, brought out his snuff box, removed the stopper; he placed some of the dark powder between his lower lip and his jaw, pushed it gradually over to the left side of his mouth while spitting again and again. The silence in the room was broken only by the clearing of his throat and the small sounds of his fidgeting on the mattress.

Enjoying the taste of snuff, he stretched out a hand and picked up the hose of the water-pipe. He inhaled and cocked his ears to the sound of the water bubbling in it. He stood up, fixed the hose more firmly into the neck of the water-pipe and began to breathe in and out. When he was happy with the result, he sat back on the old mattress, the tip of the hose between his lips. He turned his scrawny neck and called out to his wife.

'Aatika . . . hey Aatika! Come on, where's the charcoal burner?'

'I'm coming,' she answered in a voice so hoarse its feminine tones had almost disappeared. 'Why are you in such a hurry? Has your soul reached your gullet already, unlucky wretch!?'

The old man calmed down and curbed his impatience. His attention was drawn to the flies competing at the rim of the empty *aseeda* dish. He remembered the rich meals of the past and was possessed by an uncontrollable urge to laugh. The laughter became confused with coughing which increased in intensity until his chest almost burst. Aatika, coming toward him with the burner in her hand and arranging the coals on it, said in a tone indifferent from long familiarity, 'Why are you laughing, old man?' Then she added: 'Perhaps hunger's made you see the water-pipe as a beautiful dancing girl?'

The old man, overcoming his coughing fit, turned round, his face bilious with irritation. He regained his breath and tried to rearrange his exhausted body on the mattress. He turned his eyes away from the buzz of flies circling within the empty bowl, and looked into Aatika's face.

'Hmm, what did you say, you unlucky old woman?'

'What's so funny that you almost died laughing?'

He took hold of the hose of the water-pipe which had fallen from his hand during the coughing and laughing fit.

'Take this damned bowl away,' he growled in a mixture of annoyance and indifference. 'It reminds me of my empty stomach.'

Aatika leaned over to pick it up. 'Always issuing orders,' she grumbled. 'Is that soldier still lurking inside you?'

'Shut up,' he said, drawing on the water-pipe again and blowing smoke rings into the air of the room. 'Let me ease the pangs of hunger in the pleasure of smoking!'

Aatika sat down opposite him and adjusted her tattered head scarf. 'Come on,' she said. 'Tell me . . . old cock . . . what in God's name made you laugh like that?'

He stretched out his legs and relaxed, leaning his head on the wall behind him. The clouds of smoke from the water-pipe seemed to blend with his thoughts. He lifted his hand and scratched his head. Like one who has firmly grasped fleeting memories he smiled, revealing yellow, decayed teeth; he passed his tongue over dry lips.

'Woman, my thoughts have taken me far away, back to the days of fat chickens, rich spicy soup and that fine wheat *fatta* drenched in pure butter we used to have; to the tender legs of young goats . . . the smell of good food.'

He talked on, describing different dishes he'd eaten or heard of, his mouth watering, the veins in his forehead protruding, his eyes fixed on the ceiling of the room, his limbs trembling in the grip of emotion, while

Aatika, open-mouthed, listened in amazement and confusion. Different expressions passed over her face. She became so absorbed in the pleasure of the talk, she did not notice that her husband had come to a stop. Before her thoughts could take her too far, however, she came to and raised her eyes to look at her husband. The hose of the water-pipe rested on his cheek, and the relaxed wrinkles on his face told her he had fallen asleep.

Old Amm Misfir had been a soldier in the Imam's[1] tax-collection unit, a unit devised by the government. The work had taken him to all parts of the country. Age and ill health had overwhelmed him finally and he'd returned to his village, living in his stone hut in the distant mountains, regretting the banquets of chickens – but, at the same time, alleviating, against his will, the loneliness of his wife Aatika. Aatika had been alone since the departure of their only son, Salih, who had gone abroad many years before and had not been heard of since.[2]

He and his wife lived on a few measures of grain wrested from the dry, sparse land and on a miserable pension that was all that remained from forty years of army service. Not enough to fill a chicken's gullet, as he was wont to say, whenever he felt like complaining to his wife and other relatives in the half-deserted mountain village. This year, after several seasons of near drought, things were even worse. The harvest dwindled, animals died from lack of pasture, epidemics and famine spread. The Imam had left the people and the crops to the worms of the cemeteries. In their old age, old Amm Misfir and Aatika had no one to turn to unless Misfir could think of a solution to their miserable plight.

Aatika woke up and rose heavily, dragging her feet. She opened the door. A slow, sleepy morning in the desolate village. Another day ahead to be added to the ancient times of hunger. There was nothing left to eat in the hut except a handful of discoloured flour.

She collected her breath as she gathered sticks of wood, brought them back and placed them in the fireplace; she busied herself with preparing breakfast. Old Amm Misfir was awake but still lay in bed, rubbing his

1. The Imams of Yemen were regarded as kings. It is not clear when this particular story is supposed to have taken place, whether during the rule of Imam Yahya (d. 1948) or his son, Ahmad, who died in 1962, the year of the revolution against the Imam and his royalist forces.
2. The economic and political situation in pre-1962 Yemen induced many Yemenis to emigrate not only to neighbouring, oil-producing Arab states, but also to other countries.

eyes with his fingers to wipe away the traces of sleep. He pulled himself up and adjusted his head on the straw pillow, crossed his legs, laid one hand lethargically on his head, and picked his nose with the other. His wife recognized this posture; he only positioned his limbs in such a harmonious fashion when an important idea took hold of him.

Their situation was, beyond doubt, desperate. After all traces of sleep had fled his eyelids, he began to think. While he was still deep in thought, his eyes fixed on the ceiling, his wife's cracked voice broke into the silence of his contemplation.

'Hey man, get out of bed and come and have breakfast. The day is half gone.'

He ignored her call and went back to his thoughts. When she brought the food and bent down to place it on the ground, she scrutinized him carefully.

'Why don't you answer, you unlucky wretch?' she asked. 'Don't you want breakfast? Get up, man, I have important things to talk to you about.'

Muttering in exasperation, he collected his worn-out body, and stood up.

'What a curse!' he grumbled. 'Hunger and an evil-tongued old woman all at the same time.'

'Stop complaining and come to, old cock,' answered his wife. 'It's time for breakfast! I'm about to die from hunger.'

Glancing at the dish of food on the floor, he sighed in frustrated anger. '*Mateet* and dry bread – the same tragedy every day!' He went on muttering as he grabbed a tin ladle full of water and stood at the doorstep. He poured water out to wash his face and hands.

'*Mateet* and *aseed*, *aseed* and *mateet* – every day! Till when?'

Sighing once more, he added: 'What a miserable existence! What's the use of still having teeth in my head when there's nothing more to eat than *mateet* and *aseed*!'

Aatika, losing all her patience, sat down to eat. 'Why are you so slow today, old man?' she called. 'Hurry up or I'll eat all the food myself . . . There, I've already started.'

He sat opposite here and began to share the *mateet*.

'You said you had something to talk about. What is it?'

She said, with her mouth full, 'Only that our provisions are almost gone. We have to do something.'

'Yes, I know,' he answered. 'We'll kick the bucket, no way out, but what else can we do? You don't leave me time to think.'

'What's this "time to think" that you need?'

'All last night I was thinking . . . and this morning . . .'

'Thinking?' she inquired sarcastically, interrupting him. 'Like last night? That's thinking? You think, while you're asleep, about feasts of chicken, warm bread, soft wheat *fatta* drenched in butter and . . .'

'Stop your nonsense. I tell you, we're going to die of starvation.'

A dog howled in the distance.

'Our corpses will be torn to pieces by dogs while you are sitting here chewing empty words,' said Aatika, wiping the bottom of the plate with her fingers and then licking them clean.

He said nothing.

'Well?' she asked. 'After all this thinking, what's the word?'

He sighed, then lifted his head, signs of determination on his face. 'I have decided on something.'

She was still for a moment and, before she could interrupt, he hurried on. 'I've resolved to return to my job.'

'What job do you mean? Soldiering?' she said, in irritation. 'What are you talking about? At your age and in your condition?'

'Yes,' said old Amm Misfir. 'I'm going to Hadi, Ghuthaim and Nasir and ask them to join me. There's no other way to keep us from perishing.'

People in the villages shivered with hunger and cold. The drought had become a bottomless chasm swallowing its victims, like a cat devouring its offspring. The calamity had become so bad that it had even dried the tears in people's eyes. Life had become like a terrible grindstone, grinding out fear, sorrow and death. Even those who had once concealed grain in their secret storage places, slammed the doors in the face of the hungry and kept to themselves – even they had by now become besieged by the same fear. Death was knocking even at the mighty citadels of the rich. The Imam, his ministers and others in authority had let worms eat much of the country's buried grain; now they would occasionally exchange some for its weight in gold or silver. Those who were able bought a little, but most were unable to buy anything but starvation.

People fought over edible shrubs and grasses and what remained of the leaves on the trees; bodies wasted away, teeth closed over nothing and their eyes reflected only fear, fear of starvation and of the Imam and his soldiers.

Amm Misfir and Aatika spread out on an old tattered sheet all the old pieces of clothes and other necessities which he owned. They hurriedly tied them up.

With one hand old Amm Misfir held the knotted bundle and, with the other, he reached out for his old rifle. He lifted it, his body trembling, and slung it over his shoulder, panting with the effort. He looked right and left before peering at Aatika, her face wrapped tight in sorrow. Old Amm Misfir recovered his breath and dragged himself shakily toward the door. He turned toward his wife. Two old heads facing each other, the old veined hands clasped, the two worn-out faces looking at each other. Their eyes met for a moment, a moment like a lifetime, which seemed to hold their eyes together for an instant and then was swept away by the bitter winter winds. Amm Misfir, hunched under his load, went his way, trying in vain to straighten his body. Aatika turned back to curl up all alone in the hut.

Old Amm Misfir and his companions formed a procession, passing along the lonely mountain paths on the way to the government centre at Amil. Their thin legs stomped over the rocks. The desolate atmosphere seemed to offer nothing but thirst. Over the men's shoulders were slung waterskins and small bags of fried corn and dried bread, provisions for the trip, from which, every now and then, hands would draw out a piece to gnaw on, or some corn to crunch. Conversation went on all the time, a continuous nourishment to the band on the move.

Old Amm Misfir was already worn out with the journey and he would pause to rest at every possible opportunity. He stretched out his hands very often to his waterskin, and poured a little water down his burning throat. Occasionally, he would collapse under the weight of his rifle and the fatigue of his sixty-odd years, stopping the group's procession to catch his breath. His companions were sympathetic and indulged him. After all, Amm Misfir was the oldest and held the highest rank among them; besides, it was he who had had the bright idea to go to Amil in the first place.

The way is long and hard for the men on foot. Old Amm Misfir drags his feet under the weight of his burden. The sky is pale and the wind whistles and the spectre of death seems to loom over the villages scattered along the way.

The tune of an old folk song rises from the men's throats. Old Amm Misfir tries to join in, but his throat dries up. He resorts once more to his waterskin, wringing from it the nectar of life, his hands trembling, his heart pounding. Exhaustion overwhelms him and he collapses on the ground like a bundle of hay. He gasps, cursing, his hand on his rifle, his thin legs splayed out on the ground. His companions surround him anxiously, feeling his forehead and stretching out his legs so he is more comfortable. Questions pour out of their hungry, thirsty mouths:

'What's the matter with you, Sergeant Misfir?'

'Do you feel better?'

'Be strong, man! There's only a little way left to go.'

'Amm Misfir!'

The old man, twitching, moans and sighs, almost unable to answer. Words seem to grow heavy on his tongue and his eyes sink back in their sockets with fatigue. He looks round at his companions but his eyes are clouded by a veil of exhaustion. He moves his right hand and lifts his index finger in supplication.[3] His heart beats faster. His companions' anxiety increases. A few tears roll down his dry cheeks, into the furrows and wrinkles. Hands feel his forehead again; the man is aflame with fever. He gestures toward the waterskin. They give him a drink and moisten his face. He calms a bit, his hands relax. Ghuthaim bends over the old man, listening to his heart and feeling his chest.

'His heart is still beating,' he reports.

The road is empty and the sun about to set. On the horizon a village beckons, a mountain village where the dome of a shrine gleams.

Heads come together and the companions lift old Amm Misfir up on their shoulders and resume their procession. The faint moans of the old man echo above them.

Into one of the huts at the edge of the village the friends carry old Amm Misfir and set him down on a couch. An old woman with a rusty lantern in one trembling hand places a frayed mat on the floor. Her movements and her appearance seem to indicate impending disaster. The voices of the group rise, asking for food and water. But the old woman turns over her hands and shakes her head. She murmurs, with the fear of a helpless person.

'There's nothing except a little water.' As she went out to fetch it, the companions looked around at the hut and were convinced that her answer was honest.

The old man awakens. Gathering his energy into a terrible moan, he calls for water . . . water . . . They give him a drink and feel him all over. The fever still seems to be consuming his body in its fury. The old woman squats near the door, her hand on her cheek, her eyes full of curiosity and fear.

3. The lifting of the index finger in prayer (whether voiced or silent as when a man is dying) signifies that 'there is no God but God and Muhammad is His Prophet'.

'Can we find some sesame oil and some mustard?' asks one of the companions.

She nods her head and goes out. After a short while she comes back with a container of oil and a handful of mustard, then leaves them. The companions arrange the old man on the worn-out mat and bare his chest. His breathing sounds painful and exhausted. Ghuthaim and Hadi rub his chest, neck and back with the oil and with the mustard powder. His body seems like that of an immobile dummy. When the massage is finished they stretch him in place. He is completely still except for the feeble breathing. Then they turn to their own provisions of food and munch some leftover bread – a dinner that does not appease their hunger. They drink what is left of the water, each stretches out in his place and a deep sleep overwhelms them.

The night is pitch black, a deathly quiet envelops the village, arousing loneliness and gloom. The sounds of insects echo among the stones. Inside the hut, silence reigns like a king, except for the sound of faint moans forced from the lips of the old man as if from a deep pit. The weary bodies of the companions are heavy with sleep but the old man has no more control over his body; the fever is consuming him, his eyes are closed but sleepless; sleep and wakefulness mingle in his mind. He would like to scream with the full force of his voice but his heavy wooden tongue defeats him. He feels thirsty unto death and, while water is nearer to him than his own jugular vein, he cannot reach it. His strength is failing, he is powerless, fixed to the ground of the hut. But in his mind he hears the cocks crowing, he thinks that a jug of cool water is nearby, he believes he can hear the crackle of a wood fire in the stove. A smile returns to his lips and his saliva begins to flow. He can hear men bringing out a young goat, honing their knife to slaughter it. The voice of an old woman rises in his ears as if she cries out to her children to catch the red cock on the roof.

'Dinner for the sergeant, kids!' she shouts, and the barefoot children clamour and race about. The whole village is competing to prepare a feast for Sergeant Misfir. Everybody gathers round, to look at old Amm Misfir, seated at the head of the *diwan*, one hand holding a coffee cup, the other holding the stem of the water-pipe. The smoke curling up from the oven arouses a childlike pleasure in him. A delicious expectation for dinner tickles his insides, and he is filled with a feeling of contentment. He stretches out a leg and contemplates the smoke of the water-pipe. The merriment in the village increases and cries of the boys rise higher, mingling with the cries of the red cock on the rooftop.

Curiosity gets the better of old Amm Misfir. In his dream, he goes up to the window to find out what's causing the commotion. At that moment the cock flies up and perches on the edge of the windowsill. Old Amm Misfir looks out at the boys watching the cock and calmly rolls up his shirt-sleeves, revealing his arms. The hunted cock, panting with exertion, is hanging onto the window edge as a nearby hand, that of Amm Misfir, advances calmly toward it; the boys' eyes, many eyes, stare eagerly and a cunning smile plays over the lips of the old man. His hand stretches out towards the cock's neck, the boys' cries rise higher, but the bird suddenly pecks at the outstretched hand, strong and sharp like a well-aimed bullet.

The old man screams at the top of his voice, shattering the silence of the hut. His cry explodes in the ears of the sleeping men who wake, terrified, and quickly converge on old Amm Misfir. Their frightened hands feel him over. But he is already cold . . . a faint glow on his frozen face, the eyes transfixed as on a great fear. The hands of the three terrified men compete to close those eyes and then from their breasts arise deep sighs of sorrow.

In the early morning old Amm Misfir's companions hurried out in search of the old woman. They met her coming towards them and told her what had happened. She sighed, a neutral sigh, not revealing any emotion because a burden had been lifted from her own life, but busying herself with adjusting her black headscarf. She indicated that they should carry the corpse to the village mosque next to the saint's shrine at the top of the mountain. There the custodian would ritually prepare the old man's body for burial.[4]

The three companions returned to the hut, reciting invocations to God. They wrapped Amm Misfir's body in an old cloak and then carried it off to the mountain top, their heads bowed, repeating their invocations and prayers. Near the mosque an old Shaikh sat fingering his rosary beads and murmuring prayers. They explained their sorrowful errand and he motioned them toward the door of the shrine.

The Shaikh followed them across a small open square paved with fine stones and into the washing room where they set old Amm Misfir's body down on a bed-frame of bare wooden boards. Then the companions returned to the square, leaving the Shaikh alone with the body.

The washing room was a small enclosure with the sky for a roof, its

4. Unless a person has died a martyr for either God or country, his corpse must be ritually washed before burial.

453

floor simply an extension of the square. Next to the wooden bed-frame where lay the body of old Amm Misfir a low basin had been built for the ritual washing. From the basin, the water ran out through an opening in the wall, its edges eaten away by time and use, to flow over the mountainous cliff on which stood the shrine and the mosque into the deep chasm below.

The custodian took off his patched robe and his turban, and rolled up his shirt-sleeves. Yes, the ladle was in its place at the edge of the basin. From a small crack in the wall he brought out a bundle of dirty cloth and a piece of black soap. He stripped the corpse and began to wash it, murmuring invocations as he did so.

Old Amm Misfir's body was small, thin, slippery from the oil and mustard with which his companions had earlier rubbed him, in a vain attempt to ease his fever. The custodian of the shrine soaped the body, turning it over and over, washing it continuously, the soapy lather mixing with the oil and mustard on the pale cold skin. As he reached with one hand to the water basin, while steadying the corpse with the other, his foot slipped, the soap fell, the corpse slipped from his hand, slid towards the opening in the wall and, in a few incredible seconds, was gone. The custodian stood still, contemplating the disaster, all solutions and strategems deserting him. His heart pounded, terrified at the horror of the calamity and at the prospect of what awaited him outside. What could he say? How could he get out of this fix?

Just as the event had taken place in an instant, an idea flashed suddenly through his mind. He cleared his throat and raised his voice in sounds of rejoicing, his face lifted to the sky, his hands raised high and all his body trembling. The companions, waiting in the square, were taken aback by the sound of the continuous resounding prayers. They came close to the entrance of the washing room where the custodian's voice was loudly proclaiming the Lord's omnipotence, his cries rising up to the vault of the sky. Curiosity overwhelmed them, they pushed open the door and went in. The Shaikh paid no attention to them but went on praying, wholly engaged in loudly calling upon God. The astonished group cried out to him. They looked from him to the washing boards. Old Amm Misfir's clothes were all piled up but there was no trace of his corpse. In terror and amazement, they caught hold of the custodian and shouted at him: 'What's happened, Shaikh?'

The Shaikh stepped back . . . his face pale, his body trembling . . . his eyes staring, with his hands gesturing towards the sky.

'The body', he mumbled, 'was snatched from my hands . . . amazing, unbelievable, but it happened . . . the man ascended to the sky! God be praised! The Lord sent angels to take him from my hands. There was a noise like thunder deafening my ears, lightning blinding my eyes. In the twinkling of an eye the body flew up to the sky. Oh, there is no power and strength except in God!!!'

The Shaikh once more broke out in prayer and invocation, oblivious to all, his face turned to the sky, one hand on his ear, the other raised high, his body shaking like a storm-swept tree.

The three companions whispered together, their eyes fixed on the sky, their thoughts and feelings in a turmoil as they tried to understand the incredible event. Then they withdrew to the court and, from them also, came a cry to heaven!

'Oh God, grant us an end like the end of old Amm Misfir.'

Translated by May Jayyusi and Elizabeth Fernea

Waiting

The sun was setting and the trees had begun to gather in their families of birds. The village streets swarmed with people. Every house had its door wide open; there were cries of joy, hugs and kisses; hearts danced, rejoicing. It was festival-time: time for perfume, incense and prayers for the Prophet . . .

Maryam gazed at the horizon. As the sun sank towards it, so did her heart.

Where was he?

Everyone else who had left – people, birds, the last of those who were coming from far away across the sea – had returned home. In every household, stoves were burning, the thick smoke of cooking rising into the sky, pots were being washed and smiling faces looked down from the rooftops. Food was being prepared, tea was boiling, and the people on the roofs were laughing as they thought about the long, joyful evening ahead:

'How are things?'

'Fine!'

'Are you going to stay up?'

'Of course! Till dawn!'

Everywhere in the village people were preparing rooms and lighting festival lanterns. Maryam stood alone on the roof of her small house as though frozen to the spot. For her, the fire was in her heart and her lantern looked gloomy. Her son would be the only one not to laugh and look forward to the night ahead. All around her was cold rain, falling in darkness. Her heart and eyes stared through the void towards the sunset.

Where had the boy gone to?

One of the returning men had told her he had seen the brown-skinned boy walking, with a book in his hand and a pen in his pocket, along a pavement in the city:

'He shook hands with me briefly and told me he had work to do.'

'How was he?' she had asked.

'He looked fine, just fine . . . He asked me to say hello to you.'

'I saw him one evening!' another man told her excitedly.

'Where?'

'In a small café,' came the reply. 'In one of the old quarters.'

'How was he?'

'He shook hands with me briefly and told me he had work to do.'

'How was he?'

'Fine, just fine. He asked me to say hello to you.'

A third man told her. 'I saw him one evening.'

'Where?'

'In a small café, in one of the old quarters.'

'How was he?'

'He was frowning and seemed preoccupied about something.'

'I heard he was well!' whispered another, guardedly . . .

'The boy's gone, Maryam,' she said to herself. 'He's flown the coop and gone, and your mind's gone with him . . .'

Maryam gave a sob. She felt very sad, longing for her son. Where had he gone? Hadn't he said, on that morning, that nothing would stop him from coming home for the festival? That he would not be late? Wasn't that what he'd said? And something else, too . . . What had it been? . . .

No. He had not said anything else. He had kept staring at the ground in gloomy silence. And, as he hurried down the road, she had chased after him, his travelling bag on her head; her heart had raced ahead of her, trying to catch up with him . . .

Who was it that had said something else that morning?

His eyes. They had spoken. At the very last moment, after he kissed her goodbye. 'Nothing will stop me from coming home for the festival,' they had said.

If he did not get back tonight, then, he would tomorrow morning: it would be a moment of sunrise and joy.

Translated by Roger Allen and Thomas G. Ezzy

Ali Sayyar   **BAHRAIN**

The Staircase

This wasn't the first time I'd been up these stairs; I'd climbed them nine times before, not counting this time. Now I had to go up for the tenth time . . . I reached the first floor, my legs moving from one step to the next. There was a staircase of memories in my mind, which I leaped up, one stair after the other.

I was a man without a job now . . . unemployed. My brawny muscles hadn't persuaded the managers of building sites to employ me, and the shop owners shunned me because I'd got muscles like that. Once I'd been standing humbly in front of a shop owner, waiting for him to tell me if he'd employ me, and he'd said:

'You look more like a wrestler than a shop assistant.'

Householders, too, looked at my huge body sarcastically as they listened to my entreaties to be employed as a houseboy. And they were right too; who wants a houseboy with a moustache and muscles like mine? And here was the end of my long search, on the staircase of the Ministry more than two months ago, carrying an application form for any job, even if it was just an office boy – and I've got a high school diploma! What if I did work as an office boy? People would probably say that I was too educated, that I was degrading myself. Let them say what they liked, I wouldn't mind; after all, their talk wouldn't fill my hungry stomach and it wouldn't pay the rent for the miserable room I shared with five other people in a tenth-rate hotel.

I reached the second floor . . . Oh my God! Why wasn't I using the lift? I was even stupid about a thing like climbing stairs! The lift went up and down carrying all sorts of people. Some of them seemed to be people of wealth and status, while others were carrying papers and parcels. But when I succeeded in getting a job in this Ministry I wouldn't hesitate to use the lift; I'd be as good as any other respectable civil servant in this

458

grand Ministry. But God, when would that happen? When? I'd already walked up the same stairs ten times, and I'd met the same faces passing me as I made my way to the fourth floor . . .

I'd come ten times to check the progress of my application with the head of the Personnel Department. That had eaten up two months of my life, but every time he saw me he turned away as if he was looking at some deformed freak.

'Come back and check again in ten days,' he'd say.

Every time I heard him repeat that phrase I felt as if a knife had been plunged deep in my breast, and I'd get a vivid picture of the vicious hotel owner who daily threatened to throw my belongings out. My belongings, did I say? What I meant was that he threatened to throw me out. After all, I didn't own anything except this threadbare suit that covered my body and hid it from people's eyes.

I'd reached the third floor now.

I passed a dignified-looking man with a serious expression on his face; he was carrying some files and papers. He must be one of the important Ministry officials, I thought. I greeted him after some hesitation, then waited for his answer with naïve cunning because to have a man as respectable as that answer my greeting would certainly be a plus in this sealed-up place. I haven't used the wrong word there; it was a closed place for someone like me who'd been hanging about the streets looking for anyone who'd believe I belonged to the human race and that I had to assuage the dreadful screaming sensation people call hunger. But no, the man passed by without even opening his mouth. Was my voice lower than it should have been, so that he couldn't hear me? That was really very unlikely, as the office boy, sitting on the other side, answered me, thinking the greeting was meant for him.

I climbed some more stairs, on my way to the fourth floor.

I passed many faces as I climbed those marble stairs, the faces of people who seemed to be from a higher world. It's usually the important people, after all, who come to the fourth floor. As I dragged my feet from one step to the next, I felt I was getting tired, that my strength was being drained and that something heavy, like lead, was pulling my feet downwards. I must be exhausting myself, I thought, with all this tiring climbing. The problem was that I'd need more food today because of the energy I'd used up climbing like this. But it didn't matter; all this hard effort I was putting in was for a good cause.

When I'd reached the top of the stairs I didn't have the energy to move another step; there was nothing for it but to stop and rest. People passed by me with light, graceful steps. I was the only one who was standing still, but no one seemed to notice me; they were all busy with their own affairs or with their papers, or else they were busy with each other. I moved towards the office of the head of the Personnel Department and reached it after a few tired steps. How tired I was!

When I touched my knees I felt they weren't part of me, that they were only half alive. But I'd resolved, even so, to make the journey from the first to the fourth floor and meet this Head of Personnel who could decide my fate with a word. One word of his could relieve me of all the misery and suffering I was going through. One word could spare me all the cruel, painful words that were like a slap in the face every time I went to one of the heads of personnel in this company or that. I was a human being; nobody could deny that or say I was something else. Yet I had been ready to deny this humanity, to deny it to such an extent that I just couldn't express things any more. At that time I looked exactly like a tame animal. What was the point of being a human being in a society that had no respect for the humanity of man? A society that did nothing to assuage the aching hunger screaming in my stomach? What was this whole universe worth anyway? I wasn't going to be mad enough to say the universe was created just to honour me, but I wanted to live, I just wanted to survive. I wasn't asking for a marble palace that dazzled the eyes with its candles and bright colours, or for a fast car so that I could flash past people and stir up feelings of humiliation in them. I didn't even want a beautiful wife to hang on my arm and dazzle people's eyes and turn their heads. I wasn't asking for any of this. I just wanted to live. I wanted to make my destined journey in life like other people. Sometimes I felt that even animals were luckier than I was. They could at least find something to eat, or at least so I imagined. But where could I, a human being, find food?

Should I stand on the streets and beg? It was a tempting idea for someone like me, whose stomach was howling out for a crust of bread. But even begging seemed to be excluded for me because I was cursed with a body strong enough to carry bulls. What charitable person was going to reach out his hand and give me money?

I'd reached the fourth floor; in fact, I was now outside the office of the Head of the Personnel Department. The door was closed and, in front of it, was a person who seemed to be a kind of master himself. It was the office boy who was carrying a glass of tea in his hand. My God, at this moment, even a glass of tea looked like the elixir of life to me! I was willing to cling on to life even with a glass of tea carried by one of the office boys.

I stood there in front of him. Should I laugh at my situation? In my

460

pocket I had a beautiful, decorated diploma that I'd been given at one time; it was, I'd been told, my passport to getting on in life, a thing which would open closed doors to me. Well, here was a closed door that I was only a step away from, and even then I could only get inside with the permission of the office boy who seemed to me, at that moment, like a giant able to play his part in humiliating me if he wanted to, or able to grant me his blessing and open the closed door. And when I reached the place where this man who granted benediction was sitting, drinking his tea with obvious pleasure, I had no alternative but to greet him humbly and submissively.

'Good morning.'

He pushed his glass of tea to one side.

'Good morning,' he answered.

I spoke again.

'Could I possibly see the Head of the Personnel Department, please?'

'Yes, of course. Just a moment.'

He disappeared for a second, then came out of the office and held the door wide open.

'Come on in.'

I went in, my feet moving forward and my hands held tightly together, a storm of thoughts and hopes and expectation and desperation and sadness and disappointment swirling around inside my head. Every step I took was deciding my destiny in this world; and, while I was taking those little hesitant steps, the memory of the interview two weeks before sprang into my mind. Two weeks ago I'd stood in front of him after taking those same steps and he hadn't looked at me. I'd cleared my throat, but even then he hadn't stopped reading the newspaper in his hand. After more than two minutes he'd moved the newspaper away from his face, and he knew at a glance who I was and what I wanted. He hadn't wasted any time in useless discussion as he'd done the first time asking who I was, or what my qualifications were, or through what channels I'd submitted my application. He hadn't said any of those things, just: 'We haven't finished going through your papers yet. Come and check again in two weeks.'

I counted the days of those two weeks, day by day; then I counted the hours, hour by hour. I even counted the minutes. It wasn't easy for my stomach to wait for two whole weeks – a total of three hundred and thirty-six hours in all. I'd been so hungry over those two weeks, I simply hadn't known what having a full stomach meant. In fact, I'd almost forgotten what hunger was. It became a matter of strange routine to me. Every day I sold something – my jacket, my watch, even my school books. There was nothing left to sell except the diploma and, if I'd had the chance to sell that, I wouldn't have hesitated for long. Yet, for all that, I never had a full stomach for a single day. Didn't I tell you I didn't know what it was any more to be full?

Now, at last, I was standing face to face with the little god sitting in his chair, the man who – may God forgive me for saying so – had the power to grant me life or death. Here I was standing in front of his desk, exactly as I'd done two weeks before. Nothing in the room had changed. The last time he'd been reading a newspaper; now, this time, he was talking on the telephone. My heart had turned into a band playing jungle songs. Everything in my body was beating fiercely and my head had turned into a huge drum as well. The man was talking on the phone. Talking, did I say? He was raving! It couldn't be talk because what he was saying had no meaning. He was talking about fish, and his new car, and the new furniture he'd bought for his villa the day before because he'd decided to replace the old furniture. He was talking about such trivial things that he could only be wanting to waste time – killing time, while I stood there like a statue looking at him with glassy eyes. Just imagine, I couldn't look away for fear of not meeting his eye the moment he'd finished his conversation, before he became entangled with some other responsibility. My suffering was over at last, as the telephone call ended with an invitation to a substantial lunch. I forced a wan smile as I watched him put the receiver down and look at me. This was the tenth time I'd stood like that and the tenth time he'd looked at me in the same way but, even so, I had the feeling every time I stood there, that I was a guilty man standing in front of a judge and waiting to hear my sentence. The feeling increased as the decisive moment approached. He stretched back in his elegant swivel chair, as far as he could, just as he'd done the other nine times. I thought he'd never speak. That fleeting moment was transformed to eternity in my mind, a long eternity with no beginning or end. The objects in front of me seemed meaningless and worthless. The fan hanging from the wall turned into a frightening bird ready to pounce on me. The telephone dial became a black coal, like the heart of this cruel society which refused to find a place for a human being who carried, in his head and in his pocket, something called a diploma. This little god who'd just finished speaking into the telephone and become a terrifying giant, was crushing me to fragments under his feet, like a helpless ant too insignificant even to have a shadow on the earth.

Through the beating of the drums, and the storms of desperation, across the flood of destruction and ruin, his voice reached me:

'You can start work tomorrow.'

The drums started beating in my head again. My outcast journey was over at last. I was a human being again.

Translated by Salwa Jabsheh and Christopher Tingley

Ruqayya al-Shabeeb   SAUDI ARABIA

The Dream

At the crack of dawn each day, he arrives with his anxious footsteps, pacing the streets up and down, up and down. A kind of bewilderment dwells in the furrows of his face, and a pain seems planted in his soul. 'I lean on you, my companion, and feel protected from sorrow. Your steps accompany my lazy feet in wiping clean these streets.'

He leans on a wall and props his companion next to him, gazing at it tenderly. 'In the moments we are alone, we possess the world. The whole universe is ours. We are surrounded with silence, as if these moments are exempt from time.' He touches his companion gently, drawing near. Leaning his bony forehead on his rough hand, he speaks. 'You alone can give me comfort, my mute one. I speak to you always, but you do not answer. How I love your silence.'

He continues talking as he rests. 'You and I are both strangers. We have been estranged from others for so long! The earth swallows you little by little, but don't be sad, the day will come when it swallows me too. Ah, only with you do I feel secure and forget my isolation a little. Only with you do I dream . . . how plentiful are my dreams!

'When I was young I dreamed of sweets and candies. I used to imagine streets littered with candies, the skies raining candies, my bed turning into a bed of sweets. Yet when I stretched my hand to take the candy from the neighbour's little boy, I was slapped and kicked, my mother pinched my ear harshly in a way that stunned me. I did not understand then that other people had rights and there were limits beyond which one should not go. When I became an adolescent, I planted my nights with dreams . . . I often dreamed of a long sword that glittered in the sun, and a wonderful horse like the one they described in old heroic tales.'

He gazes around him. His emaciated hand looks dark and he thinks of

Antara,[1] the black hero of that ancient folk tale. He remembers how often he wished to be like Antara, looking for Abla[1] in the eyes of the neighbourhood girls, hoping to find one that would mean what she meant to him. But all he received was sarcastic laughter from the girls. It's true, he was ugly. Now his hand feels the furrows left by smallpox in his face, and he thinks, 'What a rotten landscape that blasted illness left me with!' Looking at his companion, he exclaims, 'Only you accept me, you are my sole companion on this long road, the road that has been mine all these years! While I grow older and weaker, this road keeps getting more beautiful. When I was prevented from cleaning it for several months, I returned to find it as black as Antara's face. Then I came to it every sunrise with you, my dear companion, and together we made it beautiful again.'

He looks now at his companion, recalling the times he ran away from his teachers' and stepmother's sticks. His companion became his link to life. And whenever he shuddered in the scorn of people's glances, he found in his companion's silence a way to forget the sorrow, to see it being scattered from his soul on to the street. A tear falls down his cheek and settles in a valley on his face. He takes hold of his companion, as footsteps approach. He trembles. His friend asks him what the matter is and he answers, 'Nothing!'

'I was the one who put a hand on your shoulder,' his friend says. 'So why do you look so gloomy?'

He remains silent. 'You've taught me to remain silent,' he says in his mind, looking at his companion, and he hears his friend's voice. 'What's happened? I see you are lazy today. I've finished the whole pavement opposite here and now we need to go together to the other street to sweep it before passers-by increase. Come on, help me drag the cart.'

But he hears nothing. The sunlight dazzles him. The squealing cars stop him short in the road. He turns around and lifts his dear companion, his broom, quickly sweeping away the dust from the street, his other companion, and heavily dragging his tired footsteps to another one of life's roads.

Translated by Salwa Jabsheh and Naomi Shihab Nye

1. See footnote on p. 374.

Sharifa al-Shamlan   SAUDI ARABIA

A Secret and a Death

She sat on a stone beside a tranquil pool squeezing clothes against a rock,
dipping them back into the pool, pulling them out and wringing them
again. She repeated the process over and over. After the last rinse, she
threw them into the deep basin next to her. Winding a ragged cloth into a
circle, she wrapped it around her weary head, crammed with a thousand
fantasies. She wiped away the beads of sweat that had accumulated on her
chapped brow. Placing the basin on her head, she began to heave herself
up, but a palm thorn had pierced the big toe of her right foot. Putting her
load down again, she bent over, pulled out the painful thorn and tossed it
aside indifferently – her feet, which had never known shoes, were quite
accustomed to such things. She replaced the basin and wound a faded
wrap around her skinny, stick-like form. The only distinguishing marks
of her sex were the two bulges on her chest.

She walked heavily, droning a sad folk tune, until a gang of boys cut
her off in jest, 'Look, there's the madwoman! Here comes the madwoman!'

They pelted her with stones. Some landed in the basin, clattering
noisily. She screamed, 'You sons of . . . am I mad or are your mothers
who leave you roaming the streets?'

The meanest boy tried to reply, 'You . . . you . . .'

'A madwoman doesn't wash clothes,' she shouted, the veins bulging in
her neck. 'I wash your clothes, I clean your filth . . .'

The same boy retorted derisively, 'Because you're a madwoman!'

Fuming with rage, she yanked down the hem of her dress. Her wrap
had fallen off and the basin of clothes had tumbled to the ground.
Gripping a large stone, she ran after the boy, who hid behind one of the
houses. Suddenly, a young man dressed in working clothes appeared
from an alley. Her hand loosened its hold on the stone and she dropped it.

466

'What's the matter, Zahra?' he asked her affectionately.

'They are insulting me by saying I'm a madwoman! I'm not mad, the madwoman is your sister who gave me this nickname, your wicked sister who was able to make people believe her. No, I'm not mad, I just say what I feel.'

The young man's sister was married to Zahra's father. Fearing her brother would marry Zahra, she had spread the rumour of her madness and people believed it. Observing Zahra, they thought her actions were substantiating evidence.

The young man patted her shoulder, speaking tenderly, 'No Zahra, you are not mad. You are good at a time when goodness is considered to be madness.'

She felt as if the heavens had opened up, as if the world were staging a wedding celebration especially for her. Drums were beating, the rounds of singing growing louder . . . She was running to the wedding house while he rode the bus that would carry him to work . . . The drum beat and singing transported her with joy. She danced and danced and the boys gathered round, clapping for her. Their mothers came out of the houses. The owner of the clothes exclaimed, 'What a pity! My children's clothes . . .'

An old, one-eyed woman kept repeating, 'Don't you realize she's mad?'

'Her madness only materializes when it concerns me,' replied the owner of the clothes. 'I have bad luck.'

Exhausted from dancing, Zahra collapsed on the ground. A girl with dust-covered hair went to her brother's house to inform them. Her brother and his wife arrived holding out their hands to her – his hands were warm and compassionate, his wife's were cold, with fingers like piercing nails. As they entered their house, the wife remarked in disgust, 'It's my lot to have to live with crazy people.' A sharp look from her husband silenced her, but poor Zahra retreated within her shell. Her eyes stared unwaveringly without absorbing anything. Her brother and his wife left the room and even after half an hour she was still weeping fitfully.

From that day forward, Zahra entered a new era of life, going out every day to the calm pool, washing the clothes and returning to meet the beloved. Then she would dance and collapse. Finally, the women refused to give her any clothes to wash. So she went to the pool empty-handed. After school started, she was freed from the youngsters' stones and their amused shouts.

The dusty quarter was buried in silence one day when the beloved whispered to her about an isolated place where they could meet on the following day, Thursday. Her thin breasts expanded with delight! She noticed that the repetitive beat of the drums had transformed into soft music. She didn't dance; she didn't fall to the ground. She went cheerfully to her brother's house with the coyness of a fourteen-year-old girl. She washed her best dress, stole perfume, rouge and *kohl* from her brother's wife and hid them in her narrow bed.

While everyone in the house slept, she sprinkled perfume on her chest, put *kohl* on her eyes and rouge on her cheeks, slipped out of the building and went to the appointed corner. Her face was like a picture drawn by a playful child whose hand had slipped with the colours. She met her beloved and her breasts tingled excitedly. Thursday became a holy day in her life.

She calmed down, grew self-possessed and no longer roamed the streets. She no longer danced. And she no longer slept on two nights of the week – Thursdays and Fridays.

As time passed, two things about Zahra's body changed: her belly and her leg swelled up. As for the belly, everyone noticed it. The moustaches and beards of the elders and young men of the village wagged rapidly.[1] But no one paid any attention to the leg.

Whispers grew to announcements: 'The madwoman is pregnant!' Every wall and palm frond in the village trembled with the echoes. Her brother tried to extract the truth from her, entreating, saying he would know what to do, he would take care of her. But she told him nothing.

In her bed she would cry silently, until her silence rose to a howl like that of a suffering wolf. The authorities, learning of the affair, tried to investigate the matter with her, but did not succeed. She would not speak. They questioned her brother but he was more ignorant than they were.

On a damp, downcast morning, a car stood at the head of the alley. A wooden door creaked mournfully to let Zahra pass through. Village boys and women were gathering around the car as she climbed into it. Amongst them was a lady holding her child up high so he could witness the spectacle.

The workmen's bus, filled with men, was parked nearby. One of them sat with a bowed and silent head as the car set off on its sad procession. Looking up to his father in the bus, a child called, 'Father, they are taking away the madwoman!'

1. An Arab woman's dishonour is a stigma on her male relations: father, brother, son (not the husband). In a small village such as the one described, all men seem to feel an affront to their manhood, to their capacity as guardians of women to protect them from dishonour.

His father looked at him with brimming eyes. He wanted to shout to the world, 'No, she isn't mad! She is the sanest of the sane!' She had upheld his name and reputation. She had protected him, the sane man, while he abandoned her to an unknown destiny.

Time moved forward. The memory of the madwoman grew dim: the men's moustaches stopped wagging. Women's gossip was overtaken by more ordinary topics. Only two people did not forget her – the young man and her brother. Her silence had left a hole in the young man's heart. The brother searched the eyes of every man for the criminal who had dallied with his unstable sister.

The Feast of Sacrifice[2] arrived; the wealthy of the village slaughtered animals in honour of their dead. People rejoiced at having meat to eat. One evening the *Umda* knocked on the same door through which Zahra had exited two months earlier. Her brother invited him in, his heart beating so wildly it seemed it would burst his ears. The *Umda* held out an envelope to him – it was open, despite its being addressed to him. Removing the letter, the brother read with eyes that would not focus, not comprehending its contents until he had read it three times.

Sighing deeply, he threw it aside. His last hope for his sister was broken – she had died from blood poisoning in her leg. The little one had died in her belly. A secret that would never be disclosed was laid to rest with her.

Translated by Olive Kenny and Naomi Shihab Nye

---

2. This is called the Adha Feast in Arabic. Another name is 'the Feast of Immolation'. It takes place on the 10th of Dhu al-Hijja, immediately after the completion of the annual pilgrimage to Makkah.

Sulaiman al-Shatti   **KUWAIT**

The Voices of Night

He shot up . . . jerked off the bedcover in a sudden panic. He had been in the first torpor of sleep when the sound of the doorbell, shattering the silence of the night, pierced his ear. That, then, was the irritation he had tried to avoid when he had chosen a doorbell with a gentle, tinkling sound. But here, nonetheless, was his violent reaction, arousing every nerve and muscle . . .

His wife, who had beaten him to the intercom, tossed the earphone over. Her face, lined with sleep, had drained of blood. In a voice crackling with fright she said:

'Someone's dying!'

A current of fear tingled in his knees; he took hold of the earphone:

'Who is it, who are you, what do you want?'

The voice of a wounded man in the throes of agony pervaded his whole being.

'Open the door . . . I shall die . . . Aah, someone . . . aah.'

He'd been in a dazed state between daydream and the first embrace of sleep. His mind had wandered, recalling the images of the day, adding to them, dressing them up with an imagination that spread and expanded until it dissipated in sleep. One image engrossed him: a large sitting-room where voices cut across, each speaking with rigorous logic. Endless talk about ways and means for social services. His mind had selected a few points that he intended to raise whenever the argument around him grew intense, or the scope of the discussion widened. Then he would put forward a precise word or considered opinion . . . which would attract eyes like a magnet. His person would swell, become prominent, and his voice rise:

'We have to rebuild the bridges that this age has broken. The individual has become isolated in the crowd. Our alienation in the midst of our own city, and our sense of isolation, wears us out. Look at the desert: there man's warm heart had been able to fill its furthest bounds and create a marvellous range of values . . .'

He stopped to see the effect his words were having. What he saw pleased him and he plunged on:

'Vast emptiness containing nothing but man's voice! Yet it spread eternal values: chivalry, solidarity, hospitality. Even collective social responsibility found its unquestioned place, all this resting on the noble ethos of the age. A human being's warmth of heart surpasses imagination. Take your fellow-man to your bosom and life will be changed.'

Enthusiasm kindled in him, and found an echo in his voice.

'But we now live in alienation: all these cars and human masses have not demolished man's isolation. We suffer the ache of solitude and isolation. It is strange how one can be alone among multitudes. We must revert to the continuity of tradition, to nature.'

He wanted to take a breath and follow up the gleam of an idea that had come to him, but someone cut into the conversation;

'Yes . . . yes, sound reasoning. And we can add to what our friend has said, when we go on to examine this great human heritage that has begun to slip from our hands.'

Smiling pleasantly, he retrieved the thread of his argument before attention could wander or the talk be steered away from the direction he wished it to take. In a most impressive manner he affirmed:

'I am with you! I am with you in what you say! What you say is good, but we must try not to live in the stagnation of the past. I did not mean to glorify the past; rather I would modernize its values. We have to live in our own time and must understand its logic, and resurrect the humanity of man. In this way those who are educated will know how to cooperate to build their society.'

He could still see the smiles of approbation emanating from shining eyes, from people of standing . . . His imagination began to expand, to prepare to organize and welcome other similar gatherings. He would say many things . . . his mind began to arrange a little project . . .

The doorbell screamed!

The shrieking voice of the man ripped through the membrane of his ear from two sources – no longer the earphone alone, for the man's pain had transcended the instrument and was now tearing the silence apart.

He felt weak, surprise and fright loosening every taut muscle.

'Tell me . . . What's the matter with you? Tell me!'

'Open the door . . . help me . . . I'm going to die . . . aah . . . someone.'

He did not dare press the buzzer: weakness invaded his knees, his tongue rattled woodenly between his jaws.

'You didn't tell me . . . What's wrong with you? Tell me.'

'I shall die . . . help me. God protect you.'

'Has someone beaten you up?'

'Aah. Aah. I'm going to die . . . to die . . . open the door . . .'

His hand did not have the strength to press the buzzer. He banged the earphone into position, looked at his wife.

'Someone's screaming!'

He tried to stretch a hesitant hand out to the intercom.

'Shall I open the door?'

His wife said hesitantly:

'Wait, I'm afraid, wait a minute . . .'

The situation froze, staccato bursts from the voice disturbing the stillness from moment to moment. His wife moved.

'We'll call Emergency. It's better. The number?'

'In the directory.'

With staring eyes his wife quickly flipped through the pages. He stood looking at her, overtaken by impotence, the distant voice still ringing in his ear.

'Here's the number . . . !'

Time in slow motion, no one answering, the phone ringing on and on. He pushed the curtain aside and peered into the darkness, in the direction of the door. The anguished voice became sharper. He had to do something.

'Shall I go out to him?'

'Wait. I'm trying to make contact. I'm afraid it might be a trap. We are in an isolated spot.'

And again she busied herself dialling. Two sounds. The intercom and the intermittent cries of panic. Two eyes peering into the dark.

His mind filled with insistent misgivings. It certainly is a plot. Really, why not? It's an attempt to kidnap him. He remembered his persistent efforts, the attitudes, often extreme, which he was sometimes forced to take up when harried by the hot temper of a crowd. He was assailed by the memory of a previous position he had maintained when he'd been worked up. He had said dangerous things despite misgivings about the people present. Theirs were eyes that told tales: nevertheless, he had thrown caution to the winds. A burning enthusiasm had propelled him and he had ventured much further than most of those who adopted a rationalistic position. The tide was with him. That day he had pleaded for the universalization of the awareness of humanity and the abolition of all discrimination which could only be achieved by means of a clear-cut

472

policy which attempted to provide solutions for social problems. That day he had said that it was the duty of people to transcend fear, because we live with others and for them; that we must nourish co-existence and help it to develop, instead of allowing it to disintegrate and die. Therefore, self-sacrifice and submergence into the commonality was essential and this could only happen by putting self-interest aside and clearly establishing one's position, dotting the i's and crossing the t's. Courage in confronting critical situations asserts our existence and the fact that we are a living body.

Without a doubt this was the position: it was a trap. His active imagination was kindled. News whispered from mouth to mouth. A mysterious kidnapping. Stealthy hands reach out in the darkness of night and one is suddenly one of the missing. And not a word more is heard. That was certain. Perhaps the plot was hatched that day when his spoken opinions overstepped the limit . . . They are cold-blooded, their patience is infinite. So he must be careful.

He imagined the pain and bewilderment that would strike his family. When the news spread he would be the talk of the town. They would look for his photograph. 'Here he is. He was a sound man.' Perhaps they would look for the hidden motive behind the kidnapping. As for himself, where will they take him? A shudder went through him. Those who had been abducted before had never been heard of again.

His wife heaved a sigh of irritation:

'Where are they? Sons of . . . ! Nobody answers. What Emergency is this?'

Having ebbed a little, the agonized voice renewed. He must screw up his courage – this can't be a plot. Those ideas he had projected weren't all that dangerous; and, if they had wanted to do something, it wouldn't have been in this open way. That would have been ridiculous. Was it an attempt to embarrass him? No. The suffering voice was authentic, it couldn't be a trap.

'Shall I go out to him then?'

His wife said:

'Wait. I'll come with you. I'll put on my dressing-gown.'

He picked up the intercom once again.

'You still haven't told me who you are.'

'A watchman – your neighbour . . . the guard at the next building.'

'What's the matter with you . . . has someone beaten you up . . . have you been stabbed?'

'Aah . . . help me!'

It was evident that someone had got him on his own and stabbed him, for he was alone in that huge building. Someone, then, had really meant to rob him. He visualized the scene: stopping, no, crawling on the ground, the victim reaches up his hand for the dangling doorbell: the stoop increases his pain. In the middle of the back, the blade of a sharp knife sticks out, some of it gleaming in the night, blood gushing forth and flowing over the edges. The victim falls prostrate on his face, filled with agonizing pain . . . only his great strength has enabled him to crawl as far as the threshold.

No – the murderer was not a robber. There is nothing there worth stealing; the building was new and empty. Therefore! . . . It was a vendetta, yes, a vendetta. Vendettas are two a penny in the watchman's hometown. He remembered the story of a former watchman. A long time ago he had been guarding a nearby house. They had all heard the story. He'd hit a rival of his on the head with an axe. His large family had been unable to protect him. The man's uncle had said:

'You killed him treacherously. We aren't going to protect you. Don't oblige us to hand you over to them. Run away, for they'll never leave you alone. You're a wanted man and have no protection.'

He'd seen the man a month ago, every inch of his body gone flabby, no longer able to see. He'd pitied the man's miserable condition – prosperity had overflowed the watchman's hometown, but he had not had any share of it. Even after wave after wave of his townsfolk had emigrated to share the sudden riches, he alone remained, haunted by his ancient crime. Some of his fear had left him, but he could not return. Thirty years had not erased the stain of blood.

Why shouldn't this watchman be like the other? His vigorous youth, forceful masculinity, wary eye and scarred face mark him for what he is. His glances are indicative of slyness and cunning. Perhaps he had committed a similar crime. But his pursuers were too quick for him. Modern means had enabled them to achieve their vengeance swiftly. They had stabbed him. Perhaps they had not been completely successful? Then they would pursue him and once again plant a dagger in him, this time right in the heart.

That is how it was, then. The situation must be as he envisaged it. What if the man's pursuers were on his track at this very moment?

What will happen to me? I could be hurt!

The couple stirred irresolutely. His wife made the first move, saying with obvious concern:

'Let's go to this poor man!'

She moved and he followed her. To show his courage he tried to precede her to the courtyard of the house. Louder rose the rattling voice, as strong as before, ripping apart the silence.

'Aah . . . Aah! . . . Folks . . . aah!'

'Wake up the servant.'

'Good idea. Two men are better than one.'

She went . . . caution was needed; one had to be alert. The situation was a frightening one and needed precise handling. He thought: our response must be to initiate events rather than react to them, otherwise we'll be lost. They haven't come back yet – that servant of ours never gets enough sleep – all servants are like that. He was now alone with the agonized voice – he felt he could not go on hesitating. The voice was coming from the main gate. He would go to the other door and open it slowly and look – if there was anything suspect about the affair he would see it and have plenty of time to lock the door again. Slowly and cautiously he walked to the far corner. He decided to raise his head and peer between the bars of the fence. He turned his head and looked. The man was bent over, leaning against the outside lamp-post, his hand on his bosom. Everything seemed distorted. His moans made a din while all the houses stood mute, wrapped up in the silence of the small hours. He could not see any dagger – was it a plot? Yet the man was in pain. He moved closer, hugging the wall, and let out a hesitant word:

'What – what's the matter with you?'

The voice answered, hope grown strong again:

'Help me . . . I'm going to die!'

The door opened – it was his wife rushing out with the servant behind her. She reached her hand out to support the watchman. In the distance was the figure of a man, with a woman running behind him. His energy renewed itself and he lifted the watchman up.

'My chest is being torn apart.'

His wife asked:

'Does your left hand feel numb?'

'I can't breathe . . .'

'Perhaps it's a heart attack.'

'I'm going to die . . . My children are lost.'

The other man said:

'Remember God . . . remember God . . .'

Many hands came to help, and a speeding car approached.

Two hours later he returned with the watchman beside him, now in the best of health. As he got down he turned and said to him:

'Take care of yourself! There's nothing wrong with you!'

With the first light of dawn he was standing firm and upright, confidently telling his wife:

'Nothing. An allergy. He'd eaten some fish that didn't agree with him. Human frailty!'

And he began to think about the incident.

Translated by Lena Jayyusi and David Wright

Ahmad al-Siba'i

Auntie Kadarjan

Her name wasn't Kadarjan,[1] that was a nickname. You'll pity her when you understand how it superceded her real name until nobody ever called her anything else.

Although she was over fifty according to some of her women neighbours, others were convinced that she was older than Amm Idrus, the itinerant saffron hawker. Idrus himself was sure of this. He would say, 'She was wearing a head covering[2] when I was a child attending the Mughraby Quran School near her mother's house.' His opinion was that she was only two or three years short of sixty.

Auntie Kadarjan, however, wasn't concerned about all that. She thought that reckoning the years was an unnecessary fuss. She would easily say that she remembered the year of the great flood,[3] that she had seen the elephant in Makkah and had attended the wedding of the Sharif[4] when she was young. When she was told that there were years and years between these events she replied with smiling face, 'Get off my back! I like peace and quiet, this fuss makes my head ache.'

She considered herself not much over thirty bar a few years, she'd forgotten how many. She would say this with absolute certainty, assuring you about it as she walked proudly in her neat dress and hairdo between the vestibule of the large central hall she lived in and the door of the small

1. Kadarjan is a nickname meaning 'a person of great sorrow', *kadar* meaning 'sorrow' or 'spleen'.
2. A girl begins to wear a head covering just before or around puberty.
3. A flood which took place in Makkah in the nineteenth century.
4. This is probably a reference to a nineteenth-century ruler of Makkah, the Sharif Abdallah ibn Muhammad ibn Awn, who ruled for around twenty years, ending with his death in 1877. He is reputed to have had a great wedding and to have brought an elephant to Makkah.

room or niche that she had made into a kitchen, her wooden clogs slapping against her feet as she strutted with the coquetry of a twenty-year-old girl.

We boys used to play hide-and-seek those days in the nooks and corners of our alley. Being her pampered favourite, I would refuse – when the game reached fever pitch – to hide anywhere but in her house. When she saw me rushing to her out of breath she would think I was frightened of someone chasing me to beat me up. She would then point to the couch in the front of the hall so that I could hide under it behind the fringe. Having recovered my courage I'd creep out on hands and knees. But when she caught sight of me, she'd stand in front of me to stop me leaving.

'How many times have I told you, boy, not to let the children gang up on you? They are naughty and you are little.'

In her simplicity she could not comprehend that it was all a game, and that whoever was the seeker had to discover the hiding-place of one of the others to make him take his turn as seeker.

I used to notice that Auntie Kadarjan took great care of her *kohl* jar. Next to the *kohl* jar she kept a small box that I would often see her reaching for. From it she'd take something that she'd rub between her hands, then cover her face with. What she was doing didn't mean anything to me.

Many times I saw her sitting down at the low tea table. When she was finished she would remove the tray and cups, and prop up a mirror in their place. Then, picking up the scissors, she would go over her hair, plucking out a snow-white hair here and there. As she attached no great importance to me as a child, she would ask me to help her by examining her hair. Whenever I came upon a white hair she would thrust in the scissors to remove it. I used to tell my mother about this of an evening in the company of her women neighbours. They would laugh, wink at each other, and one of them might give a deep sigh: 'Poor soul!' she'd say. Sucking in their lips, they'd agree she was indeed a poor soul.

I could not get the point of this 'poor soul' business or of their lamenting comments on Auntie Kadarjan. It seemed to me that she was kinder and more affectionate than any of her neighbours, including my mother. I perceived in her concern for herself and for people in general, a quality which I did not find in the neighbours whose houses I visited. Her dwelling, despite its smallness, was so clean that it attracted attention. The back rests of the couch upon which she received her guests were bedecked with shiny gold and silver spangles, while the cushions in the middle of the couch were embroidered with trees gleaming with lapis lazuli and yellow lights. Along the border was a line of Arabic script that appealed to me although I could only manage to read the word 'Ah' amongst the syllables on it.

She did her housework decked in her best, wearing a long robe of delicate diaphanous material, her hair fastened by a comb sparkling with gems. As for the slippers she swayed about in so proudly, they looked as new as if she had put them on that very day.

When she was doing her housework I noticed her actions were more graceful than I was used to seeing in our house or those of our neighbours. She picked things up daintily with her fingertips. When I reported this to my mother and her neighbours, I was startled by their expressing pity for Auntie Kadarjan. Sucking in their lips they repeated, 'Poor soul, my boy – Good heavens, you don't say!'

I don't remember if, at that artless age, anything about Auntie Kadarjan preoccupied me more than the attempt to reconcile her elegant way of life, which made her shine in my childish eyes, with the pity that I observed in the eyes of my mother and her neighbours every time she was mentioned.

Many weary years passed, in the course of which my mother died, followed by most of her neighbours, leaving me no longer a child. As I kept myself away from Auntie Kadarjan's hall, the scene of my childhood games, I heard no more of her. Then news reached me one day that she had lost her mind and had been moved to the home of one of her relatives, where she died not long after.

The final word about her came from an old woman, the last remaining of my mother's neighbours. I entreated the old lady to tell me the story of Auntie Kadarjan over whom they used to grieve and lament in spite of her elegant way of life. Thus I came to understand much that had been inexplicable to me.

Auntie Kadarjan grew up in her father's care, a slim, extremely beautiful young girl. Because she had lost her mother when she was a baby at the breast, she lived with him in his big house alone. After losing her sister when she was an adolescent, there was no one left in the family but her and her father, all of whose needs she looked after. He in turn spoiled her, granting her every wish.

The father, a wealthy landowner, was advanced in years. When she reached the age of puberty, her face radiant with the captivating bloom of youth, he was living with her in a mansion, one of his properties.

Despite the father refusing to let her marry on the plea that she was his only child, all he had to look after him in his old age, requests for her hand increased. But those who understood the underlying reasons for his attitude knew that he dreaded having a stranger get hold of his property.

The young girl lived in her father's house looking after his needs. In time death overtook him while she was still in the bloom of youth. The days of mourning were scarcely ended when her cousin on her father's side asked for her hand. Following her father's death he had assumed the position of her guardian. She refused his offer because he had children of her own age. When he insisted, she stuck stubbornly to her refusal. He repaid her with the same obstinacy, refusing, in his role of guardian, anyone who sought to become engaged to her. To each of her suitors he would invent some defect in her upon which to base his refusal, until in the end he condemned her to living the rest of her life as a spinster.

Her livelihood was guaranteed by the share that fell to her from her father's property. Nevertheless, hers was an empty life, spent waiting, as all young girls do, for something to fill her heart, and dreaming of a knight on a white charger, even in her waking hours.

Her time of waiting having stretched out fruitlessly, the mansion she lived in became too large for her cruel solitude. Having moved some of her furniture to the hall on the ground floor, she put the rest of the house up for lease. There she lived, choking on the bitter dregs of her solitary existence.

Time passed. One morning she was awakened by a knock on the door. It turned out to be guests from Indonesia who were making their *Hajj* that year – a man and two women carrying a message from some relatives of her father. Wearing a thin veil as was the custom of Makkan women when receiving pilgrims, she welcomed them, trusting in their sincerity as pilgrims. After they had drunk a hospitable cup of coffee, she became aware of the young man furtively stealing longing glances at her. She did not set too much store by that, although it gratified her to surprise him by letting her glance rest on his lidded eyes for a second or two.

Only a few hours after the guests had taken their leave there was a knock on the door. This time it was *Shaikhat al-Hujjaj* that she welcomed. She had come to convey her guests' desire to ask for her hand in marriage to their son, the young man who had accompanied them on their visit some hours before.

This met with the girl's fancy. They went into details but they led, inevitably, to the question of her cousin, her guardian, who tried every means he could think of to prevent her marrying.

But the Shaikha was a sharp old lady. As she was saying goodbye, she exclaimed encouragingly, 'Look, my daughter, after the *Hajj* the boy will return home with his mother and sister and obtain permission from his father, and get whatever he can from him for a dowry and other expenses.

His father wants him to study here, get married and settle down. Don't ask your cousin's permission. You aren't a youngster. Run off secretly, the two of you, to the judge; he'll tie the knot, since you are willing and aren't under age, eh? We're agreed.'

'Whatever you say!'

'It's settled, then?'

'As you say! You are just like a mother to me.'

The season of the *Hajj* was over. The last boat to Indonesia set sail, taking them back to their country. She spent the new year counting the months, for she got no rest from her taut nerves. 'It's the chance of a lifetime! I'm not going to let it slip through my fingers. The bridal dowry doesn't matter to me, be it large or small. What a wonderful woman the Shaikha is! How marvellous her ideas! The day he knocks on my door I'll tell him of my resolve, and go with him to the judge. What a joy to find someone to kill the emptiness in my house after all these years. May God have mercy on you, father! While you lived you chained me to your wishes. Afterwards you abandoned me to this bitter solitude and allowed that despicable nephew of yours to use me for his own advantage and put new locks on the chain. I'll break that chain no matter how strong it may be. So come, come, my soul's companion. Would to God you could hear me!'

But he did not hear her, it seems. In the new year the first ship carrying Indonesians landed at Jeddah. After that the boats arrived in succession without her hearing anything from him. The pilgrim season ended, followed by another and another, leaving our girl still waiting and hoping.

She tried to find out what the Shaikha thought was keeping him away. But where was the Shaikha? Her visit had been like some strange dream. She never returned. On the day of her visit, in her great astonishment she had neglected to learn the Shaikha's name and address. She still kept on hoping, however.

Year after year she lived on in these expectations. Meanwhile, middle age crept over her comely face, leaving its tracks on her wrinkled cheeks. Despite that she refused to acknowledge her advancing years. She went on living in a daydream, expecting her lover when any commotion echoed through the long alley, and listening to every knock, even if it were on her neighbours' doors, lest he should have lost his way to her door. For this reason she was always decked in her best while doing her housework, picking everything up with her fingertips, with the graceful-ness of a bride on her wedding night.

Her neighbours were amused by the trouble she took in making herself so neat and trim at inappropriate times, in dresses so unsuitable to one of

481

her age. Those who know how tribulation can affect the personality lamented her state, laying blame on her father who had made her a target for this kind of delusion. In the eyes of the old women, however, her odd conduct made her a laughing-stock. Therefore they called her 'Auntie Kadarjan'.

Translated by Olive E. Kenny and David Wright

Layla al-Uthman   **KUWAIT**

Pulling up Roots

He gently patted her shoulder as she squatted among the contents of the metal trunk.

'Have you finished yet, Umm Hijran?' he asked.

She shrugged her shoulders helplessly.

'By God, Abu Hijran, I am still confused about what I should take and what I should leave.'

He squatted down beside her, feeling a sudden pang when he noticed the hunting rifle. He lifted it out. 'Umm Hijran, why do we need this? It would be better and safer to leave it hanging in its place on the wall.'

She sighed and heaved her thighs into a cross-legged position.

'Abu Hijran', she replied with troubled eyes, 'this was a gift from your father. We have kept it near us all these years, so I'm going to take it with me.'

'We won't need it, so it's better for it to stay here.'

She sighed. 'Who knows?'

He laughed, shaking his head, glancing toward the other side of the room. 'And this other metal trunk – I wonder what's in it?'

Despite her weariness, she leapt to her feet, hurried over to the other trunk and sat down on it. She lifted her arms and swore.

'By God, Abu Hijran, even if you cut off my head from my body, I won't let you leave behind what's in this box!'

He laughed again hoarsely, realizing her seriousness.

'Just tell me what's in the box.'

'Things that are precious to me.'

'Like what? They may be precious to me too.'

'It's not important for you to know. They are precious and that's enough.'

Gently approaching her, he lifted a lock of hair which had slipped down over her forehead and seated himself next to her on the trunk. 'Don't I have a right to know the contents of this box which will travel with us?'

'Certainly,' she said reluctantly. 'But I'm afraid you'll get angry and empty out what's in it.'

'I promise you we'll discuss it together. Let me see.'

He moved her gently aside and opened the trunk. Raising his eyebrows in astonishment, he stared at her, his eyes meeting her own which were glinting with determination and warning, as if to remind him of what he'd said.

'What's this, Umm Hijran?'

She pointed deliberately from item to item.

'These are cooking pots dear to me – they were part of my mother's trousseau, made of pure copper. You will not find any similar ones in this world of swindlers and robbers. This is an old jerry can my mother used to boil my father's clothes in, I still use it for boiling yours. These are silver spoons and knives which I inherited from my mother, and this is . . . Hijran's doll . . .'

She was sobbing. 'Or do you want me to bury it just as we buried Hijran?'

'Don't bring up the tragedy – but darling, there is no need to transport all this. We'll find each of these things in the other country.'

'No, we'll never find any like these,' she insisted.

She held the box of silverware in front of him like a challenge.

'You may find better forks and knives', she said, 'yes, more expensive than these, but you will never find any *like* these. These are antiques.'

His roving eyes noticed something else.

'And what is all this in here?'

'Books.'

'Whose books?'

'Your old books which you always like to read.'

He took a deep breath. 'What on earth do we need these for? The world is full of books, and we'll find plenty of them wherever we go.'

'Not like these, my good man,' she cried.

His patience was running out. He sat down with his head between his hands, his eyes gazing at the bare floor.

'Where is the carpet?' he asked.

'There.'

'Where?'

She pointed to the corner of the room where the carpet was rolled up and roped.

'I hope you're not going to say you're taking that too?'

'Of course I'm taking it, and inside it is our woollen quilt.'

He rose, raising his voice. 'Umm Hijran, you act as if we were leaving the house forever!'

'Who knows?' she replied sorrowfully. 'You may be happy in a foreign country and choose to stay there, so shall I abandon my precious things behind me?'

'My dear, it will only be for a year, one year. We'll try out our luck as others have done. We may be able to save enough money to buy back the piece of land we were forced to sell a while ago.'

Her tears flowed silently down her cheeks.

'A year! Who knows? It may be one year and it may be a hundred.'

He shook his head emphatically. 'I wish you would believe me and trust what I say!'

'I trust you, but I don't trust circumstances.'

She left him bewildered and stalked out of the room.

In bed she was fidgeting and turning. He was tormented by her tension, seized by a strange premonition she might die that night – maybe she wanted to die. Or she might get up in the morning having decided not to leave.

She heaved a deep sigh, kicked and threw the quilt off her body.

'What's the matter, Umm Hijran?'

'I feel a sudden hot flash.'

'But the weather is cold.'

'I know that, but I feel it anyway.'

He turned toward her, leaning on his elbow. 'Something you'd like to talk about?' he whispered close to her ear.

'Yes.'

'What is it?'

'I say to myself, what about you travelling alone and I'll stay here to wait for you? It's only a year, as you say, and I shall endure it.'

'No, absolutely not, I cannot leave you alone.'

'I'll be amongst my own family, in my own city. I won't lack anything.'

Without thinking, he replied, 'Who knows? Our absence may be an extended one.'

She shuddered. These candid words made her shiver and her heart pound. Nameless fear churned deep inside. She sat up in bed, frantic.

'See – you're doubtful how long we'll be gone! I knew it. You may like it too much in a foreign country. Years may go by without your being able to save the money you are dreaming about. Do you blame me, Abu

Hijran, do you blame me?'

'My dear, will anyone who loves his own land enjoy living in a foreign country? Believe me, it will only be for a year. Let's risk it.'

'And our house?'

'It will be here when we get back.'

'Do you guarantee it will remain safe from all the robbers who have multiplied in the city?'

'Oh, you have just reminded me of something I need to speak to you about.'

She sat up straight. 'What is it? Tell me!'

He scratched his head, then rubbed it. 'As a matter of fact, Umm Hijran, I prefer that the house be occupied at all times. I am afraid the rosebush might wither up without anyone caring for it, likewise the henna tree and the jasmine. I have therefore asked Musa to stay in the house and care for it, and . . .'

'Musa?' she groaned.

'Yes,' he said, knowing he would be faced with an outburst. 'Is there anything wrong with that?'

'Of course – Musa, this vagabond young fellow from the desert!'

His voice was persuasive. 'Musa is a good young man. It is true he came here mysteriously, without anyone knowing his origins, but he is industrious and clever. He has been able to work and win people's confidence. Haven't you seen how the city merchants put him in charge of certain operations? Some even entrust their finances to him.'

'I know and see, but that is one thing and his living in our house is something else. It shouldn't be allowed at all, at all. Our belongings, and . . .'

'And what?' he interrupted. 'Everything will remain as it is. He will bring his own bedding and personal items, and live in the room on the east side. He'll have no connection with the rest of the house other than guarding and looking after it.'

'East side or west side – all are part of my house and I won't allow it.'

'Umm Hijran, Musa will care for the garden – it will flourish, which is better than its withering away. I want our place to remain green.'

'Oh Abu Hijran, how can this vagabond occupy our house? I don't like him or the look of his face.'

'In any event you won't be seeing his face.'

She was silent, then said emphatically, 'I *will* take the gun with us – I won't leave it hanging on the wall, he might use it.'

Abu Hijran laughed, gently patting her cheeks, 'Don't be ridiculous! He has a big gun and a pistol as well.'

'Even so – I shall take our gun.'

He was cheerful despite their disagreement. Smiling, he kissed her cheek before falling asleep.

She could not relax. She kept imagining she was touring their beloved home, inspecting each corner, remembering and sorrowing tearfully each time the ghost of their infant daughter, Hijran, passed through like a dream.

'It won't be easy for me to leave this place', she whispered to herself, her eyes haunting the room, 'but it is his desire which I must accept.'

Their neighbours' eyes were filled with tears.

'We'll miss you, good people!'

'We'll miss you too.'

Umm Kifah from next door was weeping openly. 'Write to us,' she begged.

Abu Hijran nodded, a lump in his throat preventing any words.

'Let us know constantly how you are getting along,' called out Abu Sharara warmly. He was the owner of their local grocery store.

Abu Hijran nodded again, summoning up the courage to say, 'We'll do that. And we'll appreciate your watchfulness here.'

'I'll keep an eye on your house, and on Musa, even if . . .'

Abu Hijran tried to quiet him, but he continued:

'Even though you have entrusted your affairs to a stranger. I was more entitled to this honour.'

'It's a small matter, Abu Sharara. I didn't want to add to the responsibilities of any of our neighbours, and Musa will not neglect his duty.'

The neighbours were carrying their bundles to the car, while the women wiped away tears. One offered a Koran as a present, another brought a scenic picture, while a third presented them with a beautifully tinted bunch of artificial grapes.

'Remember us, Umm Hijran – don't forget your friends!'

She cried harder when Abu Hijran called to her to get into the car. All the belongings had been loaded. No sooner had she lifted her foot to place it in the car, than she drew back.

'I have forgotten something important!'

'What?' asked Abu Hijran, astonished. Surely she had everything by now.

'I forgot the key to the house.'

Abu Hijran sighed, 'What key? Why do you want a key?'

'Don't you think I'd like to take the key to my own home with me?'

'Why do we need it when Musa will be here?'

'I certainly will take it. Suppose we return suddenly after a year and this Musa isn't at home – would we have to sleep in the street?'

Their neighbour Abu Kifah interjected gallantly, 'If that happened, Umm Hijran, you would never sleep in the street! All our houses are yours. We would be the guests!'

She shook her head sadly, then hurried to where Musa stood with his hard gaze. 'Give me a key and keep the other one,' she demanded.

A strange smile traced itself on his lips. Only Umm Hijran could see it. He unfastened his bunch of keys and handed her the one she wanted. She hid it in her bosom, pressed the spot and sighed contentedly.

The car's engine started. Abu Hijran called out to her, but she turned back toward the house. Sorrow was flooding her bosom which also embraced the key and a handful of earth which she had bound up in a piece of paper and hidden beside it.

She moved toward the car, her eyes fixed on the house, memorizing the shoots of jasmine she had planted a few months earlier. She stared at the thriving henna tree, the green window of her room, all the love planted within it. The tender fragrances painfully penetrated her lungs.

Still the neighbours' voices were pursuing them, insistent, entreating, 'Write to us – reassure us – don't forget us.'

But she couldn't hear them. She stretched out her hand to beckon Musa, calling, 'Come here.'

He approached with the same hard eyes.

'Listen, don't you dare neglect the garden . . . don't forget to clean the rooms . . . don't use our private possessions – I mean, our pitchers and dishes . . .'

The car shifted into gear, so she raised her voice louder. 'Don't leave the house without a light – leave the entrance light on. As for the grapevine trellis, don't forget to give grapes to the neighbours as we always do, and . . .'

The wheels began turning before she was finished. Musa stood motionless as the orders rolled toward him. She waved at the neighbours, goodbye, goodbye, her eyes still embracing the house as her voice echoed for the last time, 'Musa, don't forget the henna tree, and the mimosa, and the jas . . .'

Musa changed the locks that same night, and the arrangement of the rooms.

Translated by Lorne M. Kenny and Naomi Shihab Nye

Siba'i Ahmad Uthman   **SAUDI ARABIA**

Silence and the Walls

He threw his bedding down in a corner and sat staring at the room. 'The ventilation here is terrible. Nothing but silence. And the walls, and restlessness.' One dark light-bulb strung from the ceiling. 'Somebody's sleeping in the opposite corner – that's wonderful.'

He felt slightly better, but looked up irritably at the ceiling. The scent of blood still clogged his nostrils. 'But where am I now? What's happening here? Everything is silent as these walls. Why?' His withheld shout echoed loudly within him. Despair engulfed him so heavily he felt dead.

He glanced across at his sleeping companion. 'Only the silence speaks here. And when silence speaks, all other speech is ended. Why? A dead man tumbled – blood gushed from his nose like oil from a well. Poor man! He fell like an unarmed warrior in an unequal battle. But what else could I have done? Weightiness, heaviness – and I don't remember what happened next. Then I stood stupidly in front of the over-tired night officer. My eyes were immobilized. I spoke with great difficulty:

– Officer, there's been a murder in the street. The officer sat up very straight.

– What? Did you say a murder?

– Yes sir. And I am the murderer and, if you like, the victim too.'

He had said this last sentence in a blur. He paced the hallway. It was a terrible mission. Afterwards, his steps were as heavy as if they already belonged to the earth. He was silent, impassive, his mind completely empty. His eyes blinked in an enormous vacuum. On the way there he could not concentrate on anything at all. Perhaps he didn't try. In front of the large building he stopped for a moment, taking a last look around. The policeman accompanying him urged him forward. He turned to him apologetically, then continued to walk, with regret. He lingered at the door of an isolated room. The policeman gestured, 'Please, go in.'

With difficulty, he swallowed. 'Thank you –'

It was a truly bitter moment. He could define nothing. At that moment, the whole world seemed futile and worthless.

'Please.' What a polite word! He felt, for the first time, how much significance it carried. Suddenly it was of immense value, it meant so much more to him than ever before. Another time, another place, and the word would surely have had a different taste and smell. Was it truly different? Or did it only seem different in the misery of the moment?

And so he set off on that journey into night, silence and the walls. As he examined the contents of the room he thought, 'But he kept on breathing. Insistently. Yet he lay there unresisting. Why did death drag his feet as if bargaining?'

He was dazed. His head ached. He clenched his jaw. Some old filth lay congealed on the bottom of the ashtray. His companion snored loudly, in a tone as lax as this dull night. A cockroach chirped in a corner of the room. He rose to trace the sound. Damn it, I must destroy it! He examined each crack in the wall, listening hard, but couldn't find the source. Ha! He got away, the wretch! (Only a roach would assert its presence in such desolation!) The policeman at the door removed his bulky socks and stuffed them into his pocket. He threw his huge boots to one side.

'What are you looking for?' he asked, massaging his own, tired feet.

'Can't you hear this racket?'

'Don't exhaust yourself. You won't find it.'

'Do you know anything about cockroaches?'

'I told you, you won't find it. That's all I know.'

'Have you tried?'

'And failed. I've taught myself to think of it as something dissolved in the silence.'

He went back to his seat. 'Nothing is clear now.' He tightened his jaw again. Sleep would not come. He lifted the ashtray, now full of cigarette butts, and tossed its contents out of the barred window. He banged it twice against the sill and returned it to its place. He liked that. He had destroyed some of the silence pervading the room. He stared at the bars on the window: 'Does anyone escape? How exciting. But where to?' He smiled vacantly. A man surrendering to – nothing. Somewhere an engine was running. Damn. His companion stirred and turned to face the wall. He looked at him and wondered what sort of person he was. He was snoring like a ox. 'Nothing matters.' He felt a strong desire to scream. Let all hell break loose – nothing but silence. The need to scream had been with him since the night began. A sharp pain jabbed him as he tried, again, to relax. He pushed the thought away from him. Smoke darkened the room like fog in a coastal city. He moved his pillows aside and stared at the cover of the one book which had been under them. He opened it. His eyes were sluggish. The black letters danced in front of them. Everything felt empty. The moon rose into the window. 'What a lie the moon is. My girl slapped me when I said she had a face like the moon. Science has exposed everything. What can I compare her face to after this? They are ruining all things of beauty.' He roamed round the page. 'Damn and curse them all. What will they do on the moon? It's a restlessness that is tearing the world apart.' He threw the book aside. 'How can I read in this dreadful silence?' He felt suspended between motion and silence. Concepts swam into one another. No shorelines. No definite tides. He remembered the man sleeping near him. 'Still snoring like an ox? He doesn't even know that someone is sharing his room.' He felt a surge of confidence. 'It's time to break the wall of silence.' He roused the man gently. 'Good. Right now I must appear very polite.' The man opened his eyes, stared around him and asked, 'Who are you?'

'A new colleague.'

'Welcome.'

'Thank you.'

The man lay back on his bed and yawned. He asked, 'What time is it?'

'Time has no meaning here.'

'I guess we're still at the beginning of night?'

'What's the difference? What do you plan on doing at the end of the night? Or even tomorrow? Night and day, day and night: words that have no meaning here. They swim into each other. You should know that by now.'

He felt lost, gazing at his comrade who all at once had drowned the room in a flood of despair. He wondered, 'Why does he speak with such bitterness? Now he lies on his back as though he will never speak again.'

He had to ask, 'Why so silent, as if you were dead?'

'Pardon me? Did you say something?'

'How dirty the room is.'

'The whole world is dirty.' He spat mechanically into the ashtray.

'You speak in a disgusting manner.'

He laughed coldly. 'Doesn't it suit our situation?'

'How?'

'Sometimes a man must adapt to circumstances, make concessions . . .'

He was quiet for a moment, then added, 'Anyway, be glad I didn't hit you.'

'Hit who, you madman?!'

'Never mind. It was just an idea. I apologize.'

'Is this a concession?'

'Maybe. But don't expect too many of them.'

He hated his coldness. But he needed words to shed this silence. He waited a while, then asked, 'Tell me. What's your problem?'

'So you realize there's a problem. If you'd asked, "Why are you here?" I'd have answered, "Because of a problem." So, since you already know the answer, why ask?'

'I don't know anything. I'm only guessing.'

The man suddenly rose and came over to his bed. 'Listen, mister. What's a man doing lying on his bed in a guarded room unable to go out, eh? You know the answer, of course?'

He returned to his own bed and threw himself down.

'Freedom is always wonderful, mister. It's the only thing that can't be bought or sold.'

He laughed bitterly. To his astonished companion, the word appeared inflated, as if he were hearing it for the first time. He thought, 'Freedom is always wonderful.' He asked, 'When do you expect to get out?'

'I haven't thought of that yet. Have you?'

'No.'

'It's better.'

('Better? What does he mean, this madman?')

But he cried only, 'What do you mean?'

'Can you see it any other way?'

'What exactly do you mean?'

'Oh, nothing. But sometimes I don't think a man can form an opinion.'

'I might not see it that way yet, but I can understand you.'

'Ah! We agree at last. Now you can lie on your bed and forget everything.'

He turned to the policeman. 'What time is it?'

'Three a.m.'

'Time here is longer than it is outside. Do you know anything about that?'

'About what?'

'About time, and . . .'

'And what?' he interrupted eagerly.

'And restlessness. Do you know about it?' He stared at the ceiling.

'I thought I was the only one who did.'

The emptiness expanded around them.

'Restlessness. How I've fought it. And finally I killed it with indifference. It's the best sponge to mop up aggressive feelings.'

He stated this simply and turned his face to the wall.

His imagination reached out: the corpse in the hospital morgue like a mummy; the blood on the pavement; the astounded police officer; his own quick words; obscuring fog in the street; and death, like a giant, dominating the scene. He shivered slightly. 'It's hot.' He could tell the time now. It wasn't difficult. There were so many connected things to think about his mind had no more room for them. Sometimes differences between things dissolved. Comparisons became difficult. But area and volume are always the same. The fourth dimension had become reality and a mummy was now freezing in the hospital morgue like a Danish chicken. Everything gets lost in indifference. He knew that well.

The moon receded from the window. The halo of light was growing – and growing. 'What a lie the moon has been!' His headache came back. 'My head feels like it is bursting. Why?' He lit a cigarette. He offered one to the policeman, who accepted it hesitantly.

'Thank you.'

The policeman lit up and went back to his seat. He turned to the policeman and asked, 'May I go to the rest-room?'

'Of course! Please –'

'Thank you.'

He sat motionless. The policeman asked him, 'So why don't you go?'

'Because I don't really want to.'

'Then why did you ask me?'

'Just to find out whether you had the authority to give me permission. And whether I had the freedom to ask.'

The policeman smiled. 'You are strange.'

He took a long drag, 'But it is freedom that is always wonderful.'

He stubbed out his cigarette and lay back. 'When I write my memoirs I'll omit this depressing chapter.' His lids grew heavy and he closed his eyes. He thought, 'A man should have more glorious memories.' He yawned lengthily, and the silence took him in.

Translated by Ahdaf Soueif and Naomi Shihab Nye

The Mud (a Play)

SCENE I

The curtain rises on an elegant reception room, decorated with beautiful paintings which have thematic motifs. Upstage it extends to a spacious balcony, with blue silk curtains screening the garden. Downstage right, three steps lead to an upper floor. Downstage left a door leads to the garden. Luxurious furniture, antiques – everything in the room gives an impression of opulence.

Early evening. Mariam is lying on a sofa quietly reading a book. Tariq is at the table, eating, making a lot of noise. Suddenly Mariam stops reading and turns to look at Tariq, quietly. He smiles, but does not stop chewing.

Tariq: What do you think of the book?

Mariam is silent at first; then, without glancing at the book, mutters to herself incoherently. Tariq goes on chewing.

Now Mariam places the book over her face. Tariq walks over and lifts it away again.

Tariq: Didn't I tell you this book was much too difficult for you? It's such a shame to waste that radiant look of yours on such complicated books.

Mariam is silent. She moves away from him towards the balcony; on her way she switches on the lights.

494

Tariq: I can see it has upset you – I advised you not to read it.

She toys with the curtains; is silent.

Tariq (pointing at her): Haven't you noticed? Even the way you move
        your hands isn't relaxed.

She parts the curtains.

Tariq: Are you trying to throw off the depression you brought on
        yourself by reading that?
Mariam: I am trying to throw off the depression *you* inflict on me.
Tariq: How?
Mariam (quoting):   'The moon is fast asleep and the night is hateful.'
Tariq: I feel just the opposite.
Mariam: It's such a gloomy evening – it reminds me of the night my
        grandmother died. It reminds me of her staring eyes in
        death.
Tariq: Quite the contrary – look, there are stars up there, shining so
        brightly – as if they were dancing.
Mariam: That is what you see. All I can see up there is gravestones.
Tariq: I can't see any graves up there.
Mariam: That is because you can't see me.
Tariq: But I thought we were close to each other, Mariam?
Mariam: There are vast distances between us.
Tariq: Mariam! This book has made things complicated for you.
Mariam: You, myself, and the book.
Tariq: I can't understand what you are trying to say.
Mariam: I thought you did understand. A moment ago you were
        interpreting every movement I made as if you were the
        wisest of men.
Tariq: Mariam, don't complicate things for me.
Mariam: Don't *you* complicate them for me.
Tariq: Mariam. I've never heard you talking this way before.

She is silent.

Tariq: Mariam.

Still silent.

Tariq:	What's going on?
Mariam:	That's very strange. *(She comes downstage.)*
Tariq (following):	You frighten me when you speak like this.
Mariam:	I am not a ghost, to frighten you – I am your wife.
Tariq:	Do you mean to torture me?
Mariam:	Forgive me, please.
Tariq:	Talk sense, you are still torturing me.
Mariam:	But I am quite calm, I haven't as much as touched you. Look – I am nowhere near you.
Tariq:	Mariam, is there something you are hiding from me?
Mariam:	The million moments lost in a lifetime!
Tariq:	What are you talking about?
Mariam:	Nothing out of the ordinary.
Tariq:	Mariam! You're definitely not normal tonight. Why don't we go and see a doctor?
Mariam:	Whatever for?
Tariq:	For – for –
Mariam:	For the million moments lost? That's it, isn't it!
Tariq:	OK – yes, the million moments lost.
Mariam:	Hard luck, the doctor won't be able to help us there.
Tariq:	He might try; he might find them again for you.
Mariam:	He might as well search for the million moments lost to him!
Tariq (cannot keep calm):	Oh! for heaven's sake, speak properly – don't be so vague, you're killing me.
Mariam:	You have killed me over and over again a million times. Can't you even take it once?
Tariq:	I have never hurt you.
Mariam:	You have, Tariq, every second I live with you I am murdered and brought back to life again.
Tariq:	Is this really what's been happening?
Mariam:	Do you think I am beautiful, or not?
Tariq:	Why do you suddenly ask me that?
Mariam:	It's only a question. I want you to answer it with absolute frankness.
Tariq:	I love you dearly.
Mariam:	That is not the issue.

Tariq is silent.

Mariam:	Why are you suddenly quiet?
Tariq:	I do love you.

Mariam:	Answer me for one moment in that million. Release me from one moment of murder.
Tariq:	Release me from one moment of embarrassment.
Mariam:	You mean I am ugly. I know the truth. People are kind to me, but the mirror always tells the truth.

Tariq is silent.

Mariam:	You don't have to say anything – I know the truth. What's the point in deceiving myself? I am ugly. Other girls all envy me because you're my husband. You must know they would all like you for themselves.
Tariq:	No one on earth is more precious to me than you.
Mariam:	Why don't you behave arrogantly with me?
Tariq:	But whatever for?
Mariam:	Because of all the beautiful girls who would like you for themselves.
Tariq:	But I told you – there is nobody more precious to me than you.
Mariam:	In any case, you know my weak points, and I know yours. We complement each other. None of the other girls can take you away from me.
Tariq:	What are you talking about?
Mariam:	It's a fact, and running away from it is impossible. You've got to pay in order to receive.
Tariq:	All day you've talked in mysteries.
Mariam:	And your silence is a mystery to me. You make me go on talking and you answer me with complete and utter silence.
Tariq:	What are you trying to say, Mariam?
Mariam:	Nothing – how beautiful were the moments we spent together at the beach!
Tariq:	Indeed, but what brings back these memories now, at a moment of such misery?
Mariam:	Our home at 'Al-Fintas' – the night – eating that supper of flounder with my family. Those are all beautiful memories. Those very hot summers, and the sea; the seaweed and the light summer clothes.
Tariq:	Have you forgotten the ship, Mariam? How we both toppled over the side? How funny your dress looked when you struggled out onto the beach?
Mariam:	Did you think it looked funny? Is that how you feel about

	me? Laughing about everything that concerns me – even your own feelings about me?
Tariq:	Mariam – you've got to have more faith in me.
Mariam:	I believe you're selling me nothing but falsehoods.
Tariq:	Mariam – no! It isn't true!
Mariam:	I accept it – I *do* accept it, Tariq, believe me – you don't love me, Tariq, and I've known it for a long time.
Tariq:	Whoever gave you that idea?
Mariam:	Whisper to me Tariq – something poisonous that will bring back life to me again. Feed me some lovely fantasies about your emotions. I need all your filth – all your falsehood brings me back to life. Let me lie down on you and be told things like how you need me, or how you can't leave my side. Feed me your sweetened poison. I need you.
Tariq:	You are mixing up the issues.
Mariam:	On the contrary, I am trying to clarify the issues.
Tariq:	Do you call it clarifying when you accuse me of not loving you?
Mariam:	Yes, you *don't* love me.
Tariq:	Mariam – please do try to understand me.
Mariam:	I do understand you.
Tariq:	Mariam, don't let me blaspheme! How would you like me to prove my love to you?
Mariam:	It's impossible – you *don't* love me.
Tariq:	In the name of God I *do* love you. I love you. I love you. Is that enough?
Mariam:	You drain me out and I drain you out. All the silence and all the obstinacy involved in revealing all this is killing me. I know you so well – yet I can't bring myself to tell you that.
Tariq:	What is it that you know about me?
Mariam:	There is no point in talking about it.
Tariq:	Mariam, please tell me.
Mariam:	I know some things that would embarrass you.
Tariq:	What things?

Mariam is silent.

Tariq:	Please do tell me.

She sighs.

Tariq:	If you don't want to tell me, suit yourself. *(She is silent.)* The important thing though is that I love you – even though you don't believe me. I swear to you that I love you. *(A short silence.)* Mariam – what are you saying to yourself, what are you blabbering?
Mariam:	I am only feeling sorry for myself.
Tariq:	Feeling sorry? For what?
Mariam:	For the deal.
Tariq:	What deal?
Mariam:	The deal between us two.
Tariq:	I didn't know there was a deal between us.
Mariam:	You can deny it because there are no documents to prove it.
Tariq:	Deny it?
Mariam:	Both of us are losers.
Tariq:	What's wrong with you tonight?
Mariam:	And both of us are winners – as long as there is an element of winning, loss is endurable.
Tariq (pats her on the shoulder):	Why don't we go and see a doctor?
Mariam (holds him tight):	I love you – I love you, Tariq – I can't rid myself of my love for you, for all your baseness. I go on loving you, because there is a lot of your filth in me – I love you – I love your handsomeness and I wish I had it – I am so ugly – I needed something new – you sold it to me for a price – I am thrilled that I bought myself something new and beautiful, although in a way what I had was once very precious to me – All the girls envy me because you're my husband – They think there must be a secret quality in me that makes me attractive. They had looked down on me for thirty years, but now, it is my turn to look down on them, because I am confident that my new outer shell, which I bought for such a lot of money, is beautiful.
Tariq:	You love the way I look – my outer shell – but I love you for your spirit and idealism, and for your deep humanity.
Mariam:	Which one of us is deceiving the other now?
Tariq:	You are the reason for my pride.
Mariam:	Perhaps.
Tariq:	Believe me – you're all I've got in this world.
Mariam:	Not me, Tariq.
Tariq:	Yes, you – Mariam – you are all I've got.
Mariam:	It's the filthy money that this world has given me that makes you say that. It's the price I've paid to have you. Filthy

money *moves* people, Tariq – filth, give me your filth – touch me – may my body tremble – inflame all the cells of my body – *(passionately)* destroy me with your filth!

Tariq moves towards the exit door.

Mariam: Tariq, please come back.
Tariq: I am going out to spend the evening with my friends.
Mariam: To gamble?
Tariq: No. To see Muhammad. I haven't seen him for a long time, he's just back from a trip. I want to go and say hello to him.
Mariam: But after that you will be gambling.
Tariq: I don't think so.
Mariam: I know you well enough. But why are you leaving now? Can't we go on talking? Whenever I need you, you get up and go.

Tariq leans in the doorway, looking weak and tired.

Mariam: Tariq – come and sit down, let's talk a bit, and then you can go later. Why are you standing there like that? Come on – do I bore you?
Tariq (weakly):   I've got to go.
Mariam: It's still early. *(Silence.)* What are you thinking about? What's possessing you, Tariq?
Tariq: Mm?
Mariam: Why shouldn't we gamble together?
Tariq: You don't know how to.
Mariam: What do you mean? Of course I know. Come, I'll show you – I can even teach you.
Tariq: We don't have any playing cards.
Mariam: We don't need them.
Tariq: How can we play without playing cards?
Mariam: For a long time we have been gambling without cards – now you're saying we can't. Come on, play with me. If you go to your friends, the chances are you'll lose; with me you're bound to win – always.
Tariq: I should really be going now.
Mariam: I need you. Please stay. How can you leave me now?
Tariq: But you are questioning my loyalty to you.
Mariam: No, I am not, don't reject me. Kill me, but don't leave me,

500

tear me apart if you wish, but stay.

Tariq (stands straight, preparing to leave):   I am too late already, I'm keeping them waiting.

Mariam: But I am always kept waiting. Tariq, please don't leave me, the girls will look down on me. You hide all my ugliness and, without you, I can't survive. Don't be so proud with me. *(She jumps at him and pulls him.)* Either I keep you to myself or I'll die. Come here – don't ever leave me.

Tariq: But my friends – I've got to go to my friends, Mariam.

Mariam: I am frightened that if you go you'll never come back. I won't let you go – without you there is nothing left for me in life. *(Pulls him towards the stairs.)* Come – let's go up to our bedroom.

Tariq: Mariam, for heaven's sake, let me be.

Mariam: I won't leave you – I'll chase you – I'll keep following you. *(She rests her head on his chest.)* I need you. *(Silence.)* Why are you standing there? I want you to make love to me.

Tariq: I am too tired.

Mariam: Only because we are downstairs. Come on, let's go upstairs. This place is not right any more because we've spoken the truth in it, about ourselves. This place is scary – whisper to me while we're going up. Come on –

He holds on to her and goes up with her.

Mariam (repeats, in a dreamy voice):   Upstairs – upstairs –

Fahd (entering through the garden door, carrying some files):   Wafa' – Wafa' – *Wafa'*!

Mariam (from upstairs):   She went to her folks, Father.

Fahd: Who with? Who took her there?

Mariam: The driver.

Fahd: The driver? And you allowed it? Why didn't you go with her? Suppose something developed between them on the way? Why don't you answer me? *(Silence.)* Typical! Each of us keeps quiet. No one cares for anyone else, everyone minds his own business. *(Silence.)* Your silence forces me to go on talking for as long as three hours when I really don't feel like opening my mouth. *(He looks through the files.)* My wife goes out alone. How can that happen?

Marzouq enters, carrying some bottles of medicine.

Fahd (still looking through the files: Where is the original? It must be lost. So that's another problem on my hands. When the original's lost the documents are useless – it's easier to cut through rock than it is to carry the burden of useless papers.

Marzouq puts the medicine bottles down on the files.

Fahd: What's happening? The world is turning upside down. Don't put the bottles there – have some care!

Marzouq picks them up again.

Fahd: Is there any news of the war? Human life is getting cheaper every day. *(Goes to the radio, switches it on, then off again.)* Oh! It's out of order, even the radio that usually has some life in it has gone silent. The house is as quiet as a cemetery. There's only me around – I talk like Azrael. *(Looks at Marzouq.)* Have you asked the driver to bring what I told you to?

Marzouq nods, eagerly.

Fahd: Come on, give me that medicine.

Marzouq hands him a bottle.

Fahd (opens the bottle):   Nowadays, illness doesn't show on a person's face – it just eats him up from inside. Even sickness is becoming cunning – you can never tell the difference nowadays between the sick and the healthy. It is all so scary. *(He gulps the medicine and looks disgusted, then wipes his mouth on his sleeve.)* Ugh! – It's bitter, more bitter than wormwood. *(Places the cap on the bottle and puts it down.)*

Marzouq hands him the other bottle.

Fahd: *That's enough* – put them down there. What do you think my stomach is? A storeroom, or a factory?

Marzouq puts the bottle back on the table.

Fahd: These medicines have aggravated my illness. I don't have just one illness – I have a family of illnesses: rheumatism, nerves, the colon. One's dead without dying. What am I waiting for, how long do I have to wait? I suppose I know – I am waiting for Azrael. But I wonder why Azrael's so long in coming.

Marzouq makes to leave.

Fahd: Please don't leave me alone, Marzouq. I am so depressed. This house is enormous, yet there isn't one human sound in it.

Marzouq lingers.

Fahd: Marzouq, I am probably going to die soon. Life does not want me any more. The doctor says I am unable to have any more children. I am no good. I am going to die without having any sons.

Marzouq is silent.

Fahd: I have bored you with my problems. It doesn't matter. *(Silence.)* It's been a long time since my father wanted me to name a son after him, and here I live to be seventy and I have never accomplished it. What good am I?

Marzouq is silent.

Fahd: Let's sit on the floor the way we used to and have a talk. *(Sits down and puts his hand on Marzouq.)* Why aren't you wearing enough clothes? You will catch a chill and fall sick.

Marzouq: I haven't any money to buy clothes.

Fahd: Money? You knew me before I knew money. You knew how strong I was – you would tire while I would be climbing the mast.[1] But now, everything's changed. The blue sea's

---

1. This is a reference to the pre-oil days when pearl diving was the major means of livelihood.

turned stormy and grey; the clouds in the sky have turned red; the black beard's turned white, and the good days are over. When did we last sit like this?

Marzouq: Twenty years ago.

Tariq's laughter is heard from upstairs.

Fahd (agitated): We can't even sit like this in peace any more. Listen! Listen, and you'll realize that life's not what it used to be, it has all changed.

Tariq's laughter gets louder and louder.

Fahd: Can you hear that mule? *(He addresses Tariq, loudly).* Who are you laughing at? I can't stand listening to your laugh any more. Shut up, will you! *(Tariq's laughter dies away.)* What does the doctor mean when he says that there's something wrong with my nerves? Why am I always frightened? I dream of frightening faces and I talk in my sleep. Sharks never used to scare me when I went pearl diving. I was never scared of being short of breath when diving to the sea bed, so why am I always scared now when I know I'm on dry land and there are people all around me?

Marzouq: It's been so ever since we had cement houses instead of our old mud huts.[2] We've been hearing this laughter every night since then. It's no use, the world's changed.

Fahd: Why should Wafa' go out alone with the driver? That is frustrating! Me – the highly-respected man – becoming everyone's joke. She does what she pleases and I can't stop her. And my daughter marries a degenerate against my wishes! What is there left for me? I try to avoid trouble but I fall right into it. I swear I know what'll happen long before it does happen. But she married him, she married him, she did. Oh Marzouq, I have so many problems! When I leave this house nothing seems to be done properly. Have you seen Wafa'? Wafa' is always out – who's bringing her back? Heh!

Marzouq takes a deep breath.

2. With the oil boom, architecture also changed and, instead of the old mud houses, people built houses of cement and mortar.

Fahd:	I don't know what goes on in this house! I work in the Souk fourteen hours a day. If this place burnt down I wouldn't know. Don't you see, Marzouq, that Mariam doesn't love me any more? No one really wants me. I am so lonely.

Marzouq is silent.

Fahd:	Answer me! I am so scared. Are you deaf? Are you still angry with me? Every one of you is angry with me, without any reason. My first wife despises me and my daughters are scattered around at their uncles' houses. You can see for yourself that this house is nothing like it used to be – if only I could get it back to what it used to be. But I can't. Of course I can't. Marzouq, answer me, say something or I'll die talking. I just can't stop *talking*.
Marzouq:	Ever since cement took the place of mud, we've been hearing this laughter every night. The world has changed. It's no use my saying anything.
Fahd:	Life has not changed drastically. You, for example, you haven't changed. The way you dress is the same and you're still being smitten by the cold.
Marzouq:	That's because I say nothing.
Fahd:	Why don't you speak up!
Marzouq:	I am afraid I might change.
Fahd:	Why don't you want to change?
Marzouq:	Because all of you prefer me to remain silent.
Fahd:	Speak up, Marzouq. A lot of people owe me money and don't pay it back when I ask for it. They want to eat me alive.
Marzouq:	That's not important, you'll end up poor, like me.
Fahd:	You are still angry with me even now. But I'm like a brother to you. We've lived together for the past seventy years, we don't need any bitterness now. Remember, my father freed your father. You're free. What's wrong, Marzouq?

Mariam appears at the top of the stairs and Marzouq makes to leave.

Fahd:	Marzouq!

Marzouq is standing up very straight.

Fahd:	Where are you going?

Marzouq:	Home.
Fahd:	Stay with me, don't leave me alone. This is your home as well.
Marzouq:	You only know me when you're in trouble. (*Prepares to leave.*)
Fahd:	Please don't go.
Marzouq:	Your father freed my father. (*Attempts to leave.*)
Fahd:	But this is your home, Marzouq.

Marzouq stops, in silence.

Mariam (*coming to Marzouq*):	What's for dinner tonight?
Marzouq:	Meat.
Mariam:	Is it ready?
Marzouq:	Not yet.
Mariam:	When it's ready bring it upstairs – Tariq and I are not coming down. (*She goes back upstairs while Marzouq and Fahd watch her silently and, as soon as she reaches the top –*)
Fahd (*shouts*):	Mariam!

Mariam stops, but does not turn round.

Fahd:	Mariam, I am your father. Wafa' is not home yet. Why don't you look at me?
Mariam (*without moving*):	Yes?

Marzouq tries to leave through the door leading into the garden.

Fahd:	Wait, Marzouq.

He stops at the door.

Mariam:	I am late. Tariq's waiting for me.
Fahd:	Where's your prayer outfit, I haven't seen it for a long time?
Mariam:	What are you talking about? (*Attempts to move again.*)
Fahd:	Wait.
Mariam:	I am late enough as it is.
Fahd:	If you don't stop, I'll burn this house down and you with it. Don't you try to rule me!
Mariam (*looking at him*):	What is it you want, Father? I know all that you're hinting at.

Fahd:	If you know it, why just say nothing? You are killing me with your own two hands. You know very well that, to me, Tariq's presence in this house is exactly like Azrael's. I've told you a thousand times that I can't stand him.
Mariam (shouts):	You can't even stand yourself! What do you expect *me* to do?
Fahd:	I don't want to see your child. I don't want you to have Tariq's child.
Mariam (coming downstairs):	But why?
Fahd:	Why are you asking me a second time? I told you to get rid of it.
Mariam:	Should I murder my own child? How many times you have asked me to do this!
Fahd:	What happens if you do kill it?
Mariam:	It would be murder, cold-blooded murder, filthy murder that I could never live with.
Fahd:	That's a lie, you won't die. Every day I am slaughtered ten times over, and those who kill me survive. And who'd call it a crime, anyway, when there are no witnesses and no proofs?
Mariam:	There *are* witnesses and proofs.
Fahd:	You are a liar. There are none.
Mariam:	But I keep count of them in my heart, *Yubah*. In my heart.
Fahd:	Your heart is no better than waste ground. It's a graveyard – it contains only the dead. *(He holds her firmly).* Abort this child – or I'll kill it myself.
Mariam:	You long to have a son, Father – you married Wafa' hoping she'd bear you a son.
Fahd (looking at Marzouq):	Wafa's not back yet. I am sure something is going on between her and the driver on the way. She's one of those who are slaughtering me ten times a day and she seems to get away with it.

Marzouq puts his hand on the garden door, planning to leave.

Fahd:	Stop! *(to Mariam)* You get rid of it – or I will!
Marzouq:	I have to go and bring the food in for Mariam and Tariq. I have work to do.
Fahd:	What about all this we've been discussing? Doesn't it concern you?

Marzouq exits without attempting to answer.

Fahd:	Stop, Marzouq, stop!
Mariam:	You want to stop everything, Father – even the life thriving inside me. You want things stopped at your command. Stop! Stop! But nothing ever stops.
Fahd:	It does – there's a limit beyond which things *do* stop.
Mariam:	But things in this house are limitless. What you've longed for all your life I might be able to give you now. I might have a son.
Fahd:	I'll kill it.
Mariam:	How can you kill what you've always wanted?
Fahd:	What I longed for died a long time ago – and my soul has died with it. Don't you realize, you fool, that my wife sleeps by herself? I went to the doctor and he said *(pause)* I – I can't have any more children.
Mariam:	But my son will be yours, Father.
Fahd:	I don't want your son, he'll probably be the spitting image of his father.
Mariam:	His father! His father! You always speak badly of his father. You haven't any good reason for such hatred.
Fahd:	I hate him – that's good enough.
Mariam:	Why do you hate him? Is it because he hit Walid or because he went to prison? Well! Neither are good enough reasons as far as I'm concerned.
Fahd:	How do you know what I feel? There are a thousand reasons for me to hate him. Do you understand? The minute I see his face I feel uneasy.
Mariam:	You seem to hate everything I love.
Fahd:	I hate him. Divorce the father – then you can keep the child.
Mariam:	You repeat those words every single day. *(She walks towards the stairs.)* The father, the child – I don't know what you're after.
Fahd:	You do. You do.

Mariam stands by the stairs.

Fahd (going after her): You know that he's a swindler and a drifter, don't you? See, he has left his filthy traces all over the house.

She stops at the top of the stairs.

508

| Fahd: | You know, of course, that his family has disowned him, and you've heard of all his past exploits? Why do you keep him around? He's dirtied the house. Don't you know what he did to his brother and sister? And this drifter makes fun of me in my old age! Aren't you aware of that? |

Mariam nods.

Fahd:	Talk to me with your tongue! Don't just nod your head; you realize that he doesn't love you, don't you?
Mariam (*coming down the stairs one at a time*):	I know . . . I know. Is there anything else you want to tell me?
Fahd:	What are you waiting for? Divorce him.
Mariam:	Why did you approve our marriage?
Fahd:	You caused a scandal. You were going out with him like a mad woman. You were crazy about him – the people were talking. They warned me: 'Your daughter! Your daughter!' I was scared that you would become lovers without marrying, so I covered up the scandal with another scandal. I had to approve your marriage.
Mariam:	You always used to force me to do whatever you wanted. Why didn't you prevent me that time?
Fahd:	Nowadays I can't stop anything happening in this house!
Mariam:	Why is that?
Fahd:	Can't you see that things in this house have changed? Everything seems to be upside down.
Mariam:	Why don't you like the change you have been responsible for?
Fahd:	Because it has worked against me. You have all turned against me.
Mariam:	Why don't you divorce Wafa' and bring my mother and sisters back to the house?
Fahd:	I can't.
Mariam:	And I can't divorce Tariq either.
Fahd:	But my circumstances are different – you should understand that.
Mariam:	So are *my* circumstances. I've had enough years of deprivation and misery.
Fahd:	You just want to defy me.
Mariam:	Either your circumstances overrule mine – or you make out I am defying you.

Fahd (holds his head in his hands and walks towards the garden door):

> Oh! My head is going to burst, it is full of filth, like a sewer.
> *(Looks at Mariam.)* Since you know that he doesn't love
> you, why do you cling to him? Leave him, Mariam.

Mariam (coming closer to him): Wafa' isn't home yet, Father. Why
don't you leave her?

Fahd: I am unable to – my head is spinning – but he doesn't love
you.

Mariam: He doesn't hate me either.

Fahd (sits down): Enough! Don't talk any more. My liver is hurting me.
(He presses hard on his side.) My hands are numb and
tingling – they hurt me – my nerves are on edge. Massage
me!

Mariam massages him.

Fahd: I'm scared that if I divorce Wafa' everybody will understand
that I am impotent. My nerves are shattered! Stop! – you are
making it worse. I'd like to hit someone – I'd like to hit
someone! Oh! Only if – don't shake me like that. Tariq is up
to something. He might cut my throat. Either he leaves this
house or I will.

Mariam: We – create problems out of nothing.

Fahd: No, the problems come of their own accord. Since he neither
loves nor hates you what do you want with him?

Mariam: I'm in love with him, Father. I'm in love with him. I'd like to
rid myself of him but I can't. That is my weakness. I know
what he wants of me, but I don't know how to respond. I
want to leave him but can't. When he pays me a compliment
I know he is making fun of me, he's so dishonest –

Fahd: Since you realize he is just filth, leave him, get rid of him.

Mariam: His filth doesn't harm me because I *am* aware of it.

Fahd: How can it not harm you when you know that he only
married you because of your money – in order to rob you?

Mariam: I'm also married to him because of *his* wealth.

Fahd: Wealth – what wealth?

Mariam: His handsomeness – that's his wealth.

Fahd: Have you sunk so low? I'll have to kill myself or kill both of
you.

Mariam: Kill me but don't kill my handsome half – without him I

	can't live. I live in a society where appearance is the only thing that matters.
Fahd:	Is that why you fell in love with Tariq?
Mariam:	Tariq fell in love with me.
Fahd:	Don't you dare say those words in front of me!
Mariam:	What would you want me to say, then?
Fahd:	Say nothing.
Mariam:	Truth is like fire. It burns – no one can take it.
Fahd:	You want to squander my money on that drifter? He's just waiting for me to die.
Mariam:	Loving a handsome figure is like having beautiful, blind eyes. None of us can see the truth with them.
Fahd:	My money, my wealth. It will all get squandered just because you love a handsome man.
Mariam:	But what about you, Father? What have you ever loved except an appearance? You have spent your life of seventy years worshipping money, caring about nothing else but money. Where are my sisters? Where's my mother? I tried to convince myself that it's the essence of things that's important. Wrinkles crept into my face because of my faith in the importance of the spirit. I found out that I was mistaken, that the world cares only for appearances. Trinkets alone attract us; the outer shell speaks aloud; whereas faith in the human spirit is hidden and people don't look for it because they are too lazy. Appearances, appearances, they have destroyed you and me, Father. Give me faith, give me the spark of the spirit! What worthwhile thing have you ever given the world in your whole lifetime?
Fahd:	Stop it! Don't say any more.
Mariam:	I will say it! Thirty years have gone by. The girls were giggling all the time. I could hear them with my own ears: 'Mariam is a laughing-stock. Her nose is crooked. Look at the way she walks – look at her legs!' The girls made fun of me. My legs! What's wrong with my legs? Aren't they God's creation? I am like this. I was born like this. Is that my own fault? *(Pause.)*
Tariq (coming downstairs):	Hey, Mariam! – isn't dinner ready yet? *(A silence.)*

Mariam looks from one to the other.

Tariq (uneasily):   You were late coming up again. If dinner isn't ready I'll go out and get some takeaway food. *(Pause.)* What's wrong with you? *(Silence. Tariq puts his hand on her.)* What's wrong Mariam? Won't you tell me? What's wrong with you?

Mariam looks at her father; Fahd dashes over to the stairs and goes up.

Mariam (following him):   Father! Father! Stop, Father, stop!

Silence. Then, eventually, the sound of the father's painful crying is heard at intervals from upstairs, accompanied by intermittent bursts of talk.

Fahd: He's waiting for me to die. He'd like to do away with me. Every time he looks at me, it is as if he is saying, 'Go on. Die!' *(More crying is heard.)*
Mariam (from upstairs):   Calm down, Father – calm down.

The crying goes on. Tariq walks towards the balcony, goes out and draws its curtain behind him. Marzouq suddenly enters, carrying the dinner tray.

Fahd (we can hear him upstairs):   Why, Mariam? Why has the house become like this? Why can't I change it back to what it used to be? *(Goes on crying.)*
Marzouq (pointing upstairs):   Ever since cement replaced mud we hear that crying, every night. It's no use, life has changed. *(Music is heard.)*

SCENE II

A month later. The room as before. Early morning. Tariq is sunk in one of the armchairs drawing heavily on a cigarette. Footsteps are heard coming down the stairs. Wafa' enters, walking with exaggerated feminine indifference and charm. Tariq ignores her.

Wafa':   Where's your wife?

He glances up at her absentmindedly.

Wafa':	What's wrong with you?
Tariq:	What?
Wafa':	I'm asking you where your wife is.
Tariq:	What are you saying?
Wafa':	Can't you hear me?
Tariq:	No.
Wafa':	Tariq, don't be foolish! Where's Mariam?
Tariq:	Eh?
Wafa':	Don't be tedious! I am not joking with you. Oh my God!
Tariq:	How nice that word 'God' sounds coming from your lips. Say it again.
Wafa':	Where's Miriam?
Tariq:	She has burnt down. Mariam has burnt down.
Wafa':	No, really, where is she?
Tariq:	Wafa', why are you so high and mighty with me nowadays?
Wafa':	At this moment I am only asking you about Mariam.
Tariq:	She is in the bath. Why are you asking about her?
Wafa':	Her father wants her.
Tariq:	Where were you yesterday?
Wafa':	I went out for a walk.
Tariq:	Who with?
Wafa':	What's that to you?
Tariq:	Wafa'!
Wafa':	I mean it! What's that to you?
Tariq:	I don't think I've heard you speaking in this dry way before.
Wafa':	You'd better get used to it.
Tariq:	So we're enemies now?
Wafa':	Perhaps.
Tariq:	Please yourself.
Wafa':	Of course I'll please myself.
Tariq:	Aren't you going to tell me who you went out with?
Wafa':	What good will that do you?
Tariq:	It'll make me feel better.
Wafa':	But it'll make me feel tired.
Tariq:	Wafa', why do you like to torment me? Do tell me who you went out with.
Wafa':	It's none of your business.
Tariq:	It *is* my business.
Wafa':	What are you to me? My husband? My brother? My cousin?

Tariq:	No. But I love you.
Wafa':	I don't like men who ask too many questions.
Tariq:	I don't like women who won't answer. What were you doing yesterday? Who did you go out with?
Wafa':	Don't worry yourself.
Tariq:	I love you.
Wafa':	Thank you!
Tariq:	Don't be unkind, Wafa'. You haven't been yourself for the past two days. What's happening?
Wafa':	Nothing.
Tariq:	Maybe you've heard some gossip – or maybe I've done you some wrong without realizing it.
Wafa':	You pretend you have no idea of what you've done!
Tariq:	No. You tell me.
Wafa':	Why did you tell Badriya about our relationship, yesterday?
Tariq:	She'd been asking. She'd asked me on the phone a hundred times or more.
Wafa':	But why did you tell her? Don't you realize that she'll gossip it around and create a scandal?
Tariq:	She can't.
Wafa' (sarcastically):	Oh no, of course she can't – out of consideration for your good looks.
Tariq:	Believe me, she can't possibly do it.
Wafa':	Why should I believe you?
Tariq:	Because she's told me all her secrets. If she created a scandal for us, we'd create one for her.
Wafa':	Why did you get in touch with her?
Tariq:	She was the one who phoned me.
Wafa':	Why didn't you hang up on her when you heard her voice?
Tariq:	Because she is your friend.
Wafa':	She's not! How could I be friends with a hyena like that?
Tariq:	So this is what's been eating you up all this time!
Wafa':	How do you expect it not to? Tell me what am I to do if the news reaches my father? Badriya will spread it around tomorrow as if she was Reuters sending out news reports.
Tariq:	Don't you worry.
Wafa':	Maybe my reputation doesn't matter to you, but it matters to me!
Tariq:	But what have we done?
Wafa':	Tariq, don't make me angry!
Tariq:	Is it our fault that we love each other?

Wafa':	It's a thousand times our fault! Whatever there was between you and me – it's over now.
Tariq:	You are just being neurotic. Why are you fretting yourself about something of no importance?
Wafa':	I am not being neurotic –
Tariq:	How can you say you're not neurotic when you're trying to destroy the most precious thing we possess?
Wafa':	That dirty little affair? The most precious thing we've got?
Tariq:	Naturally.
Wafa':	No!
Tariq:	Then you do love me – don't you?
Wafa':	Yes. I love you – but don't ask for anything else.
Tariq:	Say that beautiful word I like to hear you speak.
Wafa':	I don't feel like it.
Tariq:	Say it. Say, 'Oh my God!'
Wafa':	Not now.
Tariq:	Yes. Say it now.
Wafa':	I told you I don't feel like it.
Tariq:	Say it. Say it. Wafa', please.
Wafa':	Oh my God, you're hurting me.
Tariq:	That's beautiful! *(He imitates her.)* 'My God, you've hurt me.' Say it again.
Wafa' (smiling):	No. Not again.
Tariq:	Say it again and you'll hypnotize me.
Wafa' (moves her lips):	Oh my God!
Tariq:	Say it louder.
Wafa' (raising her voice a little):	My God!
Tariq:	My God!
Wafa' (clearly):	My God!
Tariq (tenderly):	What am I going to do with you? *(He fondles her lovingly.)* How beautiful she is. So delicious! So lovely!
Wafa':	What are you getting at? Stop this! *(She walks over to the garden door, intending to go out.)*
Tariq:	Where are you going?
Wafa':	To call Mariam.
Tariq:	You want to call that nag!
Wafa':	Have you forgotten? She's your wife.
Tariq:	Wafa'!
Wafa':	Yes, my dearest?
Tariq:	Don't mock me.
Wafa':	May God forgive you.

Tariq (lovingly): 'May God blast you!'
Wafa': Let Him, then.
Tariq (lovingly): 'May God blast you!'

She is silent.

Tariq: I hope I didn't offend you.
Wafa': Not really.
Tariq: Are you angry with me? Angry with your Tariq?
Wafa': A little – just a little.
Tariq: You shouldn't get angry with me.
Wafa': Then make it up with me.
Tariq: I am scared you might get angrier if I try to make it up with you.
Wafa': No, I won't.

He tries to kiss her.

Wafa' (trying to prevent him): Tariq – I'll be cross with you. Marzouq or Mariam might come in at any moment and see us.
Fahd (from upstairs): Wafa' – Wafa'.

Tariq stops. A silence.

Fahd (he sounds very ill): What are you doing? Haven't you called Mariam yet? I want Mariam – I'm calling her. I've sacked the driver. Who else is down there? Is Tariq there? He's waiting for me to die. *(Pause.)* Wafa'! Wafa'!
Wafa': Why don't you just die and leave me alone! Do you own me? *(To Tariq)* He's been dying for a long time – he's like a cat with nine lives.
Tariq: That's not a nice thing to say, Wafa'.
Wafa' (sarcastically): Honestly?
Tariq: You ought to treat him gently. With a little humanity.
Wafa': Had there been any humanity in the world that man wouldn't have become my husband.
Tariq: That's your destiny, Wafa'.
Wafa': Is it my destiny that my father, a man like my father, married me? That my father sleeps with me instead of sleeping with my mother? Why do I have this feeling every time I sleep with Fahd? Isn't it a crime? I don't feel he's my husband – I

516

	feel he's my father. How can I get rid of the feeling?
Tariq:	All the same, try to treat him well, just as I treat Mariam.
Wafa':	Should I treat sickness well? It is a sickness, the whole room has become damp with his dirt. His filth kills me – I am haunted. The air I breathe is polluted. The food I eat is polluted. My life is a waste ground.
Tariq:	These are the signs of pregnancy – maybe you're expecting?
Wafa':	Are you making fun of me? *(Laughs sarcastically.)* That's wonderful, it really is!
Tariq:	You think it is so far fetched to be pregnant?

She does not reply.

Tariq:	What's wrong with you? If Fahd is not capable of giving you children, you could still be pregnant with someone else's child.
Wafa':	You are without shame.
Tariq:	Why? You and I should have been married.
Fahd (from upstairs):	Mariam, where are you? Wafa'– call her! Wafa' –
Wafa':	'You who take life away, have mercy on my youth!' I wish you would die and leave me alone!
Tariq:	True, if he died he'd be at rest, and leaving others at rest.
Wafa':	When will you free me of him, God? When?
Tariq:	From a humanitarian point of view he's better off dead than alive.
Wafa':	But he's resisting, he just refuses to die. He wants to squander my life away.
Tariq:	He won't squander your life away or squander anything. He can't resist much longer. When we want him to die, he'll die.
Wafa':	Is it our choice?
Tariq:	Well – is it to be *his* choice?
Wafa':	What are you trying to say?
Tariq:	We would be doing him a great favour.
Wafa':	I don't understand.
Tariq:	Letting him find his peace, so that everyone else around him can find theirs.
Wafa':	You want us to kill him?
Tariq:	No. Care for him. Give him some medicine.
Wafa':	How can we care for him and kill him at the same time?
Tariq:	We can kill him with care – with the medicine prescribed by his doctor. When it is time for him to take his medicine,

increase the dosage a little and poison him.

Wafa':	I can't believe that you would go as far as that.
Tariq:	Only a suggestion.
Wafa':	But it's a crime.

Marzouq appears on the right-hand side of the balcony and pauses to listen.

Tariq:	From a humanitarian point of view it can't be considered a crime. It will be just a treatment – because it is the only solution that will bring relief both to you and to him.
Wafa':	But that's no reason. I could never think of it like that.
Tariq:	You say it is your one wish to be rid of him?
Wafa':	It is.
Tariq:	Then it's settled.
Wafa':	But not in the way you are thinking of; it's impossible.
Tariq:	Why?
Wafa':	Do you think I'm made of stone and have no conscience?
Tariq:	You're kidding yourself! What conscience? If people had consciences, he would never have become your husband.
Wafa':	But you were just telling me to treat him with compassion and kindness.
Tariq:	But if his illness has no cure, what can you do? Leave him to suffer? It's only natural you should relieve him by helping him to die.
Wafa':	And that is compassion and kindness?
Tariq:	Of course it is! Don't you want to be freed?
Wafa':	So, in order to free myself of a burden I have to kill a human being?
Tariq:	Sometimes we can only achieve peace of mind by killing others.
Wafa':	Your thoughts frighten me.
Tariq:	The important thing is that I'm thinking of your own good.
Wafa':	You're lying. You're not thinking of my good. You want to get rid of him because you want his money to pass on to Mariam, and then you can play around as you like.
Tariq:	I am sorry to think I have any respect for someone like you.
Wafa':	I don't need your respect.
Tariq:	Do you suspect me of greed? It's my fault if I worry about you.
Wafa':	Why shouldn't I suspect you when his presence annoys you

518

	more than me? You want him out of the way so you can have a free hand! You want me to be the means of committing your crime.
Tariq:	But why should that ever cross your mind?
Wafa':	I just – thought it.
Tariq:	Wafa' – I'll expose you!
Wafa':	My humanity is above your thoughts and your threats! You're thinking, 'She's married to an old man and so I can exploit this weak point in her.' You can stop thinking that!
Tariq:	Don't try slandering me, you'll regret it! Do as I say.
Wafa':	I am not a means to your end. (Walks towards the door.)
Tariq (holding on to her):	And what about the driver? What about the driver! You're a means, despite what you say – a means to everything.
Wafa':	Leave me alone, Tariq.
Tariq:	First I told you to do it for your own good, but now I tell you to get rid of him, for both your own good and mine.
Wafa':	Someone'll hear you. You'll start everyone talking.
Tariq:	I'll start them talking about you. What do you think I am waiting for in this house? Do you think I like looking at Mariam's face day after useless day? My presence here is meaningless unless you do as I say.
Wafa' (trying to release herself from his grip):	It's impossible! Leave me alone!
Tariq (trying to stop her attempts to free herself):	Listen to me – wait!
Fahd (his voice is heard from above):	Where's Mariam? Wafa'!
Tariq:	Don't you shout up there! I won't let her come up! If you want her, come down and get her. Wafa' is with me, Wafa' is unfaithful to you and wants to kill you! Come down, invalid!
Wafa':	Leave me alone.
Tariq:	I won't leave you, you can only go if you agree to my suggestion.
Wafa' (shouts):	Tariq!
Tariq:	Shouting won't help you.
Wafa':	Let me go!
Tariq:	You'll do as I say.
Wafa':	No!
Tariq:	I'll break your bones – I'll throw acid in your face. I'll tell your father about all your exploits in the past.
Wafa' (shouts):	Mariam – come here!

Tariq tries to shut her up by putting his hand over her mouth.

Wafa':   Mariam – come and look at your husband! Save me from your husband!

Marzouq now enters and puts a hand on Tariq's shoulder. Tariq looks at him and releases Wafa'. She goes upstairs, but is still watching both of them.

Tariq: What's wrong Marzouq? What did you take hold of me for?

Marzouq is silent.

Tariq: It's been your habit not to interfere. How long have you been standing there? What have you heard? Eh? How dare you intrude!

Marzouq: Because I hate the sound of your laughter at night, and I hate the cement that has taken the place of the mud.

Tariq: Why does my laughter bother you? I've never heard you express yourself like this before.

Marzouq: Because of the mud in my throat. I took the mud for some people to change into cement and they stuck it in my throat and blocked it.

Tariq: What mud are you talking about?

Marzouq: The mud inside my throat.

Tariq: Who did you take it to?

Marzouq: To some people who turn mud into cement. I took it to them and they stuck it in my throat.

Tariq: Your silence is strange, but your words are even stranger. You are the only one I completely fail to understand.

Marzouq: It's not only me you don't understand. You're at a loss in this house because you're a stranger in it. This house was built by people who are dead now. See – their veins are in the walls!

Tariq: You're senile!

Marzouq: Look – there! My father's veins are in these walls and, when I die, my own veins will grow around his. This house was built by my father's sweat and mine.

Tariq: You and your father built this house?

Marzouq: Yes, but not us alone. There were others with us – but the owner of the house, before he gave them cement, put mud in

	their throats so they would not eat the cement. We built it with the cement he gave us and its owner built it with the mud he put in our throats. We are from those who turn mud into cement.
Tariq:	Why didn't you change your own mud into cement?
Marzouq:	I made it, but I can't eat it. They have put mud in my throat.
Tariq:	Who are they?
Marzouq:	Those who want their cement to increase. It does them more harm than good. Every time it increases and grows in size, like a mountain, the wind blows it over us. It gets into our lungs and hurts us. Their cement destroys us.
Tariq:	What has made you talk today?
Marzouq:	The laughter!
Tariq:	What laughter?
Marzouq:	The laughter you laugh every night – I hate it.
Tariq:	What is it to you?
Marzouq:	You laugh for Mariam so that she gives you cement.
Tariq:	You mean money?
Marzouq:	I've cried a lot and sweated a lot but never got any, and you get it just by your laughter. Why?
Tariq:	Because my skin happens to be smoother than yours. Mariam adores it.
Marzouq:	I hate your skin and I hate whoever loves it. They ate up my father's toil and threw him into the sea to be eaten by fish, and I am eaten alive and burned with petrol.
Tariq:	Marzouq – did you hear what I was saying to Wafa'?
Marzouq:	All of it.
Tariq:	Although you are always silent, you know very well what's going on. No one in this house scares me except you. You're the opposite of my mother. My mother annoys me with her chatter and you scare me with your silence. I don't think you'll tell Mariam what you've heard. Don't you dare tell anyone!
Marzouq:	Are you threatening me?
Tariq:	I am not threatening you.
Marzouq:	I'm not going to tell anyone, but don't dare hurt Fahd. If you don't abandon that plan of yours, I will hurt you.
Tariq:	Why, Marzouq?
Marzouq:	You plan to kill him and take his money away from Mariam. You tried to lure Wafa' today, but that didn't work. I have worked hard for the money he has, how can I allow you to

take it? I will stuff your mouth with dirt before you take it.

Mariam (appearing through the balcony door, drying her head with a
towel):   Father Marzouq, you haven't brought the food up
yet.

Marzouq: I had some business with Tariq.

Mariam: What kind of business do you have with him?

Marzouq: Why don't you ask him? *(Leaves.)*

Tariq: Marzouq is a good man. He's been chatting about the sea
and the days of pearl diving. *(He pulls her by her arm.)*
Come on, let's sit down, I feel like chatting with you.

Mariam: My hair's wet, I have to go and comb it.

Tariq: It doesn't matter – you can do that later. If we can chat
together, I'll relax. Let's sit down.

Mariam: I can't.

Tariq: Don't you realize how I miss you?

Mariam is silent.

Tariq: What's wrong? Are you still upset with me? I didn't mean to
hurt your feelings. I lost my temper yesterday – I didn't
intend to.

Mariam: You didn't only lose your temper, you beat me up.

Tariq: It was out of my control. When I get into a state of
depression I lose my self-control. It's a chronic habit with
me, and it is not something new to you. You've always
known it, Mariam.

Mariam: What I know for sure is that you're tired of me, Tariq.

Tariq: Quite the contrary – you're the one who's been neglecting
me. You treat me so coldly.

Mariam: I treat you coldly because I am consumed by jealousy. I
suffer inside myself and say nothing because I long for you
to ask what's wrong with me.

Tariq: I have asked you more than once, but you didn't answer me.

Mariam: Until I made you angry – isn't that so?

Tariq: The way you treat me nowadays always makes me angry.

Mariam: And because it upset you yesterday, you beat me up!

Tariq: I told you it was beyond my control. It's a fit that seizes me
sometimes.

Mariam: But *I* caused it this time, I was the reason you were so
anxious!

Tariq: Can't you see that you're so cold to me that you've stopped

522

	caring? If you don't want me, I'll go.
Mariam:	No – I love you. I lost interest in you for one reason alone.
Tariq:	I can't think of any reason.
Mariam (loudly):	Because of Wafa', my stepmother.
Tariq (after a moment's silence):	What about her?
Mariam:	Wafa' is my stepmother, and I'm your wife, Tariq.
Tariq:	Of course.
Mariam:	Of course, but you carry on with her. You have a relationship with her.
Tariq:	Have a relationship with who?
Mariam:	My stepmother. How can you desire your father-in-law's wife?
Tariq:	Me? Whoever told you that?
Mariam:	My soul burns when I see you two together. I have been patient about everything you have ever done. I knelt at your feet and you trampled on me. But to think that she deceives my father with you! I can't accept that!
Tariq:	There's nothing between us, woman. Our relationship is innocent.
Mariam:	You can't deny it. I see it with my own eyes. Late at night you wait for her near the bathroom and she leaves my poor father in his bed and comes to you.
Tariq:	There was a small problem on her mind . . . She wanted some help with it.
Mariam:	One night, two nights, not a whole month. What kind of problem is it that can only be solved late at night and near the bathroom? For a whole month I have suffered this misery because of your ugly behaviour. Every night you leave our bed and go to her. Every night the house screams with your shameful, filthy deceit. What wrong has my father done? What has he done to you to hurt him like this?
Tariq:	She's been running after me. I didn't run after her.
Mariam:	But she's my father's wife, don't you understand? That means she's like my mother. The heavens tremble with anger at what you do when you deceive me with her. Deceive me – but don't deceive me and my father at the same time. Don't deceive me with my mother.
Tariq:	You have a mother younger than yourself? What sort of mix-up is that?
Mariam:	You treat the question as if it's of no importance.
Tariq:	How can I treat it as important when she's the cause of all

523

	this trouble and you blame me for it?
Mariam:	Is she really the cause of it all?
Tariq:	Of course she is.
Mariam:	Then why don't you get away from her?
Tariq:	Don't you know her? How many drivers have you had to sack because of her?
Mariam:	The bitch! She never gives up. I try to make her see sense but it's no use.
Tariq:	It's no use trying to make that kind see sense. If you want, I'll prove to you that there's absolutely nothing between us. I tell you, kick her out, save me from her so she won't create trouble for me. Wherever I go I see her waiting for me. She does things to tempt me, she's like the devil.

Wafa' enters, coming downstairs.

Mariam (simultaneously):   It doesn't matter, I know how to cure her. I'll put her in her place this time.

Wafa' stands at the foot of the stairs. She is silent. After a moment or two Mariam approaches her.

Wafa' (when Mariam is close to her):   Mariam, he's dead.
Mariam (after a pause):   My father? Dead?

Wafa' nods. Mariam pushes her out of the way and goes upstairs.

Tariq:	Wafa'.

She turns to him.

Tariq:	I had a feeling you would do it. You acted stubbornly but you couldn't resist my suggestion for long. You carried it out right away. Well done.
Wafa':	He took his own life.
Tariq:	That's true. You've helped him to his rest, but we must say that he committed suicide.
Wafa':	He killed himself with his own two hands.
Tariq:	Whether he killed himself with his own two hands or you killed him with yours is no concern of mine. The only person who worries me is Marzouq. That bastard, he's

always so silent. That blackguard! He wants to ruin everything for me.

Wafa' walks towards the garden door.

Tariq:	Where are you going?
Wafa' (stops):	Do you want anything from me?
Tariq:	No, I'm just asking you –
Wafa':	Fahd is dead, what else is left for me here? Why should I stay?
Tariq:	If you're going home, I'll give you a lift.
Wafa':	Thank you, I have a lift.

Mariam's crying is heard from upstairs. Tariq and Wafa' stand in silence, listening. Now Marzouq enters and stops at the door as soon as he hears Mariam's crying. The crying stops. Wafa' makes to leave.

Marzouq (standing in her way):	So you've carried out Tariq's orders? You've killed him, Wafa'?
Wafa':	No, by God, Father Marzouq! I didn't kill him! He died by God's will.
Marzouq:	We all die by God's will, but I'm afraid that the devil might have turned your head and tempted you to kill him.
Wafa':	No, by God, no, Father Marzouq, I left the room and, when I came back, I found that he had drunk all the medicine. The bed was empty and he had fallen onto the floor.
Marzouq:	So you didn't obey Tariq's orders?
Wafa':	No! How could I tempt fate by listening to Tariq?
Marzouq:	Tell me the truth.
Wafa':	Do you doubt my honesty, Father Marzouq? I swear to you he died by his own hand.
Marzouq:	I'll soon know the truth. Where are you going now?
Wafa':	I'm going home. God be with you, Father Marzouq.
Marzouq (without answering her, looks at Tariq):	Whether he died naturally or Wafa' killed him, you're still not going to profit from it. So long as I'm around, don't try and, if you try to argue, I'll stick sand in your throat.

Tariq walks over to the garden door and, after opening it, hesitates for a second and looks briefly at Marzouq. Then he rushes out, slamming the door behind him. Low, sad music is heard. Now Mariam comes down, looking utterly exhausted. She walks to the balcony and stands gazing absently into nowhere. Marzouq concentrates all his attention on her. Then he walks silently over to the balcony and stops. Mariam half-turns towards him.

Marzouq: You have my sympathies.

Mariam turns to face him slowly, then turns back to her previous position.

Marzouq (again):   You have my sympathies.

She turns to face him again, then moves over from the balcony towards the door.

Marzouq: You have my sympathies for the loss of Tariq, not your father. *(Walks over and looks upstairs.)* My sympathies to you, as well. I've just given my condolences to your daughter but she didn't answer. She's silent. She's become like you. She is dead while still moving around. You can't hear me because you're asleep, but why can't she hear me? Is it because of the laughter? Your daughter's sad because she misses Tariq's laughter, that laughter which turns mud into cement. I can't laugh that way, that's my problem. My mud can't turn into cement. Hey! Why is this house so quiet? Where are you people upstairs? Where's your laughter, Tariq? None of you wants to laugh any more. It's so silent. I'll do your laughing for you, Tariq. *(He laughs, and it is clear from his laughter that he is in agony.)* My laughter is no use because there's no one to hear it. I don't have anyone like Mariam. My crying doesn't do any good either. Why don't you cry, you upstairs? *(The light dims slowly.)* You! – are you really dead, or are you deceiving me? But you're dead, you can't possibly lie to me. See . . . see my father's veins are growing in the wall . . . Where are your veins? Why didn't they grow like this in the wall? Where are your veins? . . . My father's veins are here, they have no blood in them. *(It is now completely dark.)* Don't swallow me in darkness as you swallowed my father's blood . . . Don't use my own dark colour to kill me, or I'll throw my colour on you and let it kill you . . . I'll take revenge on you with my colour . . . In the past I could speak more eloquently while I was silent, better than I am able to speak now when I speak . . . Hey *(to Tariq, sarcastically, who is offstage)* . . . owner of the cement, why do you want to alter the world to suit your own wishes? Because you are upstairs and you control the electric switch? I'm coming up to you.

Translated by Salwa Jabsheh and Alan Brownjohn

Glossary of Foreign Terms

Amm: Uncle, also a vocative for any older man.

aseeda: A popular dish made up of flour and some broth, usually a poor man's dish.

azad: A type of high quality date.

Azrael: The angel of death.

bajilla: or *baqilla*, broad beans sold either boiled or fried, usually by street vendors.

dashdasha: A long wide robe worn either by men or women in the Gulf area and Iraq, very similar to the *jallabiyya* or *gallabiyya* in Egypt.

dinar: The highest monetary unit in Iraq, Kuwait, Jordan, Tunisia and some other Arab countries. It was also the highest monetary unit in Classical times in the Arab world.

diwan: The men's drawing room.

djinn: or *jinn*, spiritual beings of the middle kind, i.e., between angels and devils, among whom are good and evil spirits. Unlike the other two, they figure greatly in folk stories and legends in both their negative, destructive capacities, and in their positive, constructive powers.

faqih: A learned man, usually in religious matters; also a teacher.

fatta: A rich man's dish in Yemen made up of specially kneaded pastry mixed with butter, honey and eggs.

fils: The smallest monetary unit in certain Arab countries.

ghutra: The large square headgear usually worn by men in the Gulf countries. It is called *kufiyya* in such countries as Jordan, Syria and Lebanon, a term also used in the Gulf countries.

Haj: The man who has performed the pilgrimage to Makkah, one of the five holy duties of every Muslim. A woman is called *Hajja*.

Hajj: The annual pilgrimage to Makkah.

Hazeen: This word was kept in its original form because of its complex meaning in Arabic which signifies sad, unfortunate and miserable, at one and the same time.

houdaj: A seat, usually canopied, on the back of a camel, in which women ride.

igal: The head band which keeps the *kufiyya* or *ghutra* in place.

janbiyya: A dagger worn by Yemeni men. It is attached to a belt, sometimes elaborately and expensively made, which is worn around the waist with the *janbiyya* placed above the middle of the abdomen. *Janbiyyas* can be very expensive.

jubba: A wide cloak worn by learned men over their clothes.

kohl: Black eyeliner used to line the eyelids from time immemorial. In English it is known as 'pulverized antimony'.

kufiyya: See *ghutra*.

kuttab: The lowest elementary Koranic school.

mateet: Flour, mixed with yoghurt and spices, including cumin and hot pepper; a poor man's dish.

meyzar: A wrap around the waist worn on such occasions as attending a *qat* social gathering in Yemen or, and this is also done in other Arab countries, in a public bath.

Mu'azzin: The caller to prayer from a minaret or other high place.

mawwal: A song written in colloquial language, sung often to the accompaniment of a reed pipe.

qat: A plant with green leaves chewed as a narcotic in Yemen.

riyal: The highest Saudi and Yemeni monetary unit.

rubbiyya: or *rupee*, the Indian monetary unit which was also used in Yemen and some Gulf countries prior to the present period.

rupee: see *rubbiyya*.

Salaam: The usual Muslim greeting, meaning 'Peace'.

Saqifat al-Safa: The covered market of al-Safa. Al-Safa, together with al-Marwa are the two spots near al-Kaaba between which the Muslim pilgrim is commanded to run or walk seven times during the pilgrimage. Before the modernization of the pilgrimage area by the present Saudi government, there was a covered *souk* or market near al-Safa.

Shaikh: An old man, or a title of dignity given to men of high breeding or great learning; it also means a teacher or a man who performs clerical duties.

Shaikha: A title of rank to women, but could also mean a *kuttab* teacher.

Shaikhat al-Hujjaj: The woman who used to help women pilgrims to Makkah during the *Hajj* season.

sharshaf: The outer black garment worn by traditional Yemeni women over their clothes.

souk: Market, market place, centre of business.

umda: A village mayor.

Um or Umm: Mother. Women in many Arab countries are called by the name of their first-born child, the male having ascendancy over the female even if younger. Thus the mother of Ahmad is called Um Ahmad.

ustadh: A teacher, a university professor, a learned man. It may also mean 'Sir' when used in the vocative.

Yubah: Papa, Daddy, in Gulf colloquial speech.

Biographies of Authors

Muhammad Abd al-Malik (b. 1944)
Bahraini short story writer. An experimental and sensitive author, Abd al-Malik is deeply concerned with the plight of down-trodden individuals and pervasively describes the various reactions of these people to all kinds of exploitation, including class exploitation, and the way they interact with their own deprivation and insecurity. He writes in a vivid and effective style, usually free of mawkishness and redundancies, but sustaining a sufficient emotive appeal. He published his first collection, *The Death of the Cart Owner* in 1972 and his second, *We Love the Sun* in 1975. Two other collections, *The Fence* and *The River Flows* appeared later.

Mayfaᶜ Abd al-Rahman (b. 1951)
Yemeni short story writer from the south. He first studied agriculture then went to the Gorki Institute in Moscow where he obtained an M.A. in 1982. One of the committed Yemeni writers of the south, he writes on both social and political issues. Despite the sombre reality he discusses in his work, a real mitigating effect is achieved through his sense of suppressed humour and realistic knowledge of human frailty and vulnerability. Two collections have appeared by him to date, the first in 1975 and the second, which represents his more mature work, in 1983 titled *Bathing in the Rose Water of Joy*. He now works at the Ministry of Information in Aden.

Muhammad Abd al-Wali (1940–1973)
Yemeni novelist and short story writer. Born in Abysinnia, he studied in Cairo and did his higher studies at the Gorki Institute in Moscow. After the success of the 1962 revolution in Yemen, he returned to his country and held several important positions such as the Chargé d'Affaires of Yemen in Moscow and Berlin. The last position he held was Director General of Aviation in Yemen. Abd al-Wali is one of the most distinguished writers of fiction in the Arabian Peninsula. His work reflects a preoccupation with the human condition in its more tragic or at least more pathetic situations, treating, cogently and with sensitivity, problems of alienation, loneliness, artistic dedication, oppression and the opposing aspects of human behaviour, speaking of vulnerability and of strength, of failure and of noble endeavour. His premature death in an aviation accident while still in his prime put an end to a most promising career. He published three collections of

531

short stories, *The Land, Salma* (1966); *Something Called Longing* (1972) and *Uncle Salih*. His two novels are, *They Die Strangers*, and *Sanaa, an Open City*.

Abd al-Hameed Ahmad (b. 1957)

Short story writer from the United Arab Emirates. He studied up to secondary level and has acquired much of his literary education through his readings. One of the foremost writers of fiction in the Gulf area, his work reflects a deep insight into the problems of change and transformation that have resulted from the sudden oil riches in the area. He has a keen sensibility for the tragic aspects of this new life, which he delineates with poignancy and compassion, but sometimes also with a comic apprehension of experience. His first collection, which appeared in the early eighties, was entitled, *Swimming in the Eye of a Savage Gulf*. A second collection, *The Farmer*, appeared in 1987. Abd al-Hameed Ahmad is now deputy-head of the Union of Writers in the United Arab Emirates.

Muhammad Alwan (b. 1948)

Saudi short story writer. Born in Abha in Saudi Arabia, he obtained a B.A. in Arabic literature from King Saud University in Riyadh where he now holds a responsible position in the government. He has participated in many literary activities in Saudi Arabia and in the Arab world and has travelled widely. Regarded as one of Saudi Arabia's foremost writers, he has shown great concern in his experimental writings for human suffering and the paradoxical results of newly achieved wealth in the area. He has published two collections to date, *Bread and Silence* (1977) and *Thus Begins the Story* (1983).

Khadija al-Amri (b. 1959)

Saudi poet. Born in Karak, Jordan, she lived there until the age of nine then came with her family to Saudi Arabia in 1968. She studied in Tabuk and has worked as an elementary school teacher in Riyadh where she lives now with her poet husband, Muhammad Jabr al-Harbi. She has published her verse in various periodicals but has no collection to date. Her poetry, written in the modern poetic tradition, abounds in complex imagery and language. It carries a deep feeling of disappointment in the general conditions in the Arab world, and harbours a dream of a beautiful yet out-of-reach world.

Abd al-Qadir Aqeel (b. 1954)

Bahraini short story writer. Born in Manama, he studied commerce in Bahrain and works at the office of the UNICEF in Manama. Aside from membership in the Union of Bahraini writers, he is also member of the editorial board of *Kalimat*, the quarterly which the Union publishes. Aqeel is greatly interested in children's literature and has published several works for children. His first collection of short stories, *Cries in the Savage World* was published in Bahrain in 1979, and his second collection, *Evening of Crystals* is in press.

Fahd al-Askar (1914?–1951)

Kuwaiti poet. He is accredited with having changed the direction of Kuwaiti poetry in the thirties and forties, bringing in romantic streaks and moving away from the rigid inherited traditionalism which had characterized Kuwaiti poetry before him. He died before publishing his poetry in a single volume. This was accomplished after the poet's death by Abdallah Zakariyya al-Ansari who collected al-Askar's verse and wrote about his life and work in a book entitled, *Fahd al-Askar, his Life and Poetry*, which has already run into many editions.

Abd al-Kareem al-Auda (b. 1952)
Saudi poet. Born in the district of Qasim in Saudi Arabia, he studied first in the religious schools before going to the University of Imam Muhammad ibn Saud where he obtained a B.A. in Arabic language and literature. He travelled in the Arab world and Europe and lived three years in the United States as editor of *Al-Mubtaath*, the review published by the Saudi educational mission. At present he lives and works in Riyadh. His poetry has been published in papers and reviews and a collection is now due for publication.

Saeed Aulaqi (b. 1940)
Yemeni writer and dramatist from South Yemen. One of the finest authors of Yemen, he writes on a wide range of subjects including the two revolutions of North and South Yemen. Whether on political or social themes, his writings are based on reality but a reality made thrilling and imposing through fiction. His short story collection, *Emigrating Twice* was published in 1980. He also published a play entitled, *The Inheritance* and a literary history of drama in Yemen titled, *Seventy Years of Theatre in Yemen* (1980).

Muhammad Hasan Awwad (1902–1980)
Saudi poet. Born in Jeddah, his talent as poet appeared early in life when he wrote his first poems at the age of ten. Despite the fact that this poet writes mostly in the two-hemistich monorhymed form, his poetry reflects much originality and a deep sensitivity for human suffering and the human condition in general. He has published several collections of poetry which he republished in three large volumes entitled, *Diwan al-Awwad* (1953).

Salih Saeed Ba-Amer (b. 1925)
A Yemeni short story writer from Hadramaut. He works at the Ministry of Information and Culture in South Yemen.

Abd al-Ilah al-Babtain (b. 1951)
Saudi poet. One of the group of young Saudi poets who write in the modern tradition of contemporary Arabic poetry, he is a graduate of the University of Imam Muhammad ibn Saud where he read Arabic Literature. He has published no collections of poetry, but it is clear to the critic from the poems published in various periodicals that al-Babtain is capable of playing an innovative role in the technique and outlook of contemporary Saudi and Gulf poetry.

Fawziyya al-Bakr (b. 1957)
Saudi short story writer. She studied in Riyadh obtaining a B.A. in psychology and history and an M.A. in education from the Girls' University College of King Saud University. She now teaches at the same institution. Three books are now under publication, a collection of short stories, a collection of journalistic

articles entitled, *Engraving on the Face of the City*, and a study in her field of specialization entitled, *The Historical Development of Women's Education in Saudi Arabia*. Al-Bakr is an experimental writer with a purpose and an ability to describe her characters' innermost feelings and frustrations, dwelling more on the negative aspects of contemporary life in her country.

Abdallah al-Baraduni (1929)

Yemeni writer, literary historian and one of the most famous poets of the Peninsula. He was born in Baraddun in north Yemen, and had a restricted childhood because of his blindness after contracting smallpox at the age of six. Despite this handicap, Baraduni was able to excel in his studies, obtaining a degree in Arabic Language and Sharia in 1952. He has taught for some time, but currently works in the cultural section of the Broadcasting Service in Sanaa. He has published at least eight collections of poetry to date and several books on literary history. Among his poetry collections are *From the Land of Belkis* (1961); *City of Tomorrow* (1970); *Journey to the Green Days* (1974); *Faces of Smoke in the Mirrors of the Night* (1977); *A Time without Quality* (1979) and *Sand Translation for Dust Weddings* (1983). In his poetry, al-Baraduni is a dedicated social and political critic whose criticism transcends the boundaries of his own country to speak of the ills and tragedies that have taken place in the contemporary Arab world. On the artistic level, he excels in paradox and irony, qualities well represented in the selections chosen for this Anthology.

Hamza Bogary (1932–1984)

Saudi novelist and short story writer. Born in Makkah, he did his early education in his home town then went for his higher studies to Cairo, reading Arabic Literature, Pharsi and Hebrew. His M.A. thesis on *The Short Story in Egypt and Mahmoud Taymour* was later published in 1979. Before establishing his own prosperous trading agency, he worked for many years in broadcasting, becoming director general of broadcasting in 1965. In 1962, he was appointed Deputy Minister of Information, a post which he held until 1967. Deeply involved in culture, he co-founded in 1967 the University of King Abd al-Aziz in Jeddah (which was initially founded and funded by private individuals then turned over to the government in 1971). Bogary published many short stories, articles and radio talks in various periodicals. His original, partly autobiographical novel, *Saqifat al-Safa*, on Makkah life before oil, was published in 1983. It abounds with a rare sense of humour and describes a bygone way of life which has now irreversibly changed. These qualities give the novel a special importance, and PROTA is preparing it in English translation. Bogary's premature death put an end to a promising career in Arabic letters. He has left another novel in manuscript form.

Zayd Mutee^c Dammaj (b. 1943)

Yemeni novelist and short story writer. Born in Abb in Yemen, he did his secondary and his university studies in Cairo. On his return to his country, he was appointed member of the Shura Council in Yemen and occupied various prominent positions in the government. He comes from a revolutionary family who lost many members in the war against the Imam and his writings are full of descriptions, artistically presented, of the corruption and injustice of the rule of the Imams and their high officials, and of the struggle against them. His lovely novel, *The Hostage* (1984) is a fine exposition of the cruel practices that were carried on in pre-revolutionary days. He has two collections of short stories, *Tahish al-Hauban* and *The Scorpion* (1982). Another collection, *The Bridge*, is under publication.

Ali al-Dumaini (b. 1953)
Saudi poet. Born in al-Baha, he lives and works now in Dhahran. He studied mechanical engineering, but his literary interests eventually took the upper hand and he opted for literary journalism only four years after his graduation, editing various literary reviews. His poetry has been collected in a volume entitled *Winds of Places*, forthcoming.

Muhammad al-Dumaini (b. 1958)
Saudi poet. After obtaining a degree in library studies from the University of Imam Muhammad ibn Saud in Riyadh, he went to work in Dhahran where he still lives. He has participated in many literary activities in Saudi Arabia and is deeply involved in pan-Arab issues in his poetry. Aside from poetry, he also writes essays and articles for various journals. Two collections of his verse are now ready for publication.

Abd al-Rahman Fakhri (b. 1936)
Yemeni poet from the south. Born in Aden, he did his higher studies at the American University of Beirut reading political science after which he held several government positions in his country including the position of counsellor for culture and information at the Ministry of Culture and Information in Aden. Since 1978 he has been Information Officer at the United Nations Secretariat. He writes in the modernist tradition of contemporary Arabic poetry and has published one collection of verse, *Etchings on the Stone of the Age* (1978) and is preparing his second. He has also published a book of criticism, *Words and Other Words* (1983).

Muhammad Hasan Faqi (b. 1912)
Saudi poet. Born in Makkah, he studied in both Makkah and Jeddah, and taught at the Falah School in Makkah then worked as editor-in-chief of the *Saut al-Hijaz* paper. Later on he occupied various other prominent positions in the Saudi government, becoming his country's ambassador to Indonesia. His love of literature prompted him to seek early retirement after which he dedicated his time to reading and writing. He published several collections of poetry and many other books on various literary, religious and legal issues, as well as a collection of short stories in two volumes. His best poetry is characterized by a deep and a genuine involvement in the human condition, especially achieved in his large collection, *Rubaiyyat* (1980) which contains 474 quatrains.

Muhammad al-Fayiz (b. 1938)
Kuwaiti poet. Born in Kuwait, he studied up to the intermediate level and works in the literary section of Radio and Television in the Ministry of Information in

Kuwait. He began writing in the early sixties and published his first collection, *A Sailor's Memoirs* in 1964. He has since published several other collections. His poetry, particularly in his first volume, is deeply involved in the problems of change that have been a major issue in the oil rich countries, accentuating the differences between pre-oil and post-oil times. A nostalgia for the pre-oil past permeates his verse as it permeates the verse and fictional writings of many other authors in the area.

Abdallah al-Faysal (b. 1922)

Saudi poet. Born in Riyadh a son to Prince Faysal who later became King Faysal of Saudi Arabia, and grandson to King Abd al-Aziz to whom the young prince was a favourite. Prince Abdallah studied in Hijaz and occupied the positions of Minister of Health and Minister of the Interior. However, he eventually left the government to concentrate on business. He soon became known as the poet-prince, writing a poetry mostly dedicated to the love experience. His first collection was entitled *The Inspiration of Denial*. A later collection is entitled *The Autumn of Life*.

Sulaiman al-Fulayyih (b. 1953)

Kuwaiti poet. Born in the desert of Kuwait to a bedouin family, he studied up to the secondary level and works now in the Kuwaiti army. His bedouin affinities have not influenced his poetry toward a continuation of a conventional desert tradition, whether folk or formal, for he writes a poetry well versed in the modern tradition and is as original as it is powerful. Two collections of his works have appeared so far, *Singing in the Desert of Pain* (1979) and *Sorrow of Migrating Bedouins* (1981). Two other collections are now ready for publication.

Khalil al-Fuzay[c] (b. 1944)

Saudi short story writer. He works in journalism in the Eastern province and, like so many other writers from the area, writes much about the past but also about universal human experience, sometimes mixing realism with nostalgic notions, and at others offering a comic description of human behaviour. He has published several collections among which are *The Clock and the Palm Tree* (1977) and *Women and Love* (1978).

Ghazi al-Gosaibi (b. 1940)

Saudi Arabian poet and anthologist. He comes from an influential family in eastern Saudi Arabia where he was born. While a small child, his family took him to Bahrain. He did his higher studies in various countries, obtaining a B.A. in law from the University of Cairo in 1961, an M.A. in international relations from the University of Southern California in 1964 and Ph.D. in political science from the University of London in 1970. Returning to his own country, he occupied several important positions, first as Minister of Industry and Electricity (1976–1983), then as Minister of Health (1983–1985), after which he became his country's ambassador to Bahrain where he remains. A prolific poet who is widely read in classical and modern Arabic literature, he has been very active as poet and anthologist. To date, he has at least twelve books in print including *Verses of Love* (1975), *Fever* (1980), a volume of selected poems which appeared in 1980 and *Return to Old Places* (1985). In his poetry, there is a deep yearning for simple, uncomplicated human relations and for spontaneity and truth. He is at present preparing a selected volume of modern Arabic poetry in English translation.

Qasim Haddad (b. 1948)

Bahraini poet and one of the foremost modernist poets of the Peninsula. Born in Bahrain, he is largely self-educated and has been able to transcend his lack of formal higher education through his own erudition and fine literary sensibility. He is at present Director of Culture and Art at the Ministry of Information in Bahrain. A prolific poet, his poetry developed with the years to arrive at an authentic modernist outlook and style, achieving at times a rare beauty and sophistication. His first collection was *The Good Omen* (1970), followed by several others among which are *The Heart of Love* (1980); *Doomsday* (1980); *Belonging* (1982) and *Shrapnel* (1983).

Ibrahim al-Hadrani (b. 1915)

Yemeni poet. Born in Dhamar, he studied up to the secondary level, but augmented his well-rounded education through his own readings. He is prominent in the field of politics and was one of the founders of the Liberation movement founded in 1944. After the failure of the first Yemeni revolution of 1948, he was imprisoned for several years in the notorious Hajja prison. After the success of the 1962 revolution in Yemen, he was appointed Minister of Information, then as ambassador, after which he retired. A large volume of his abundant poetry is still awaiting publication.

Muhammad Hasan al-Harbi (b. 1951)

Novelist and short story writer from the United Arab Emirates. He studied aviation engineering and electronics but has opted for a literary career and works as a journalist in the *Khalij* paper in Sharja. He has travelled widely and has participated actively in the literary movement in the Emirates. His writings reflect a deep and contemplative creativity which has tended lately towards a more modernist method and style of writing, away from the classical, chronological method followed by most writers in the area. His first collection of short stories, *Rebelling Against the Tattoo of the Tribe*, appeared in 1981 and was followed in 1985 by his second, *The Tales of a Tribe, Now Dead*. A novel entitled, *Events in a City On the Shore* was published in 1985.

Muhammad Jabr al-Harbi (b. 1956)

Saudi poet. Born in al-Ta'if, he did his secondary studies in Saudi Arabia and was sent to England in 1975 to study medicine. However, he discovered after three years that his preference was to follow up a literary career, and he returned to his country to work in journalism, particularly in literary journalism. He is now responsible for the cultural section of *Al-Yamama* literary review which comes out in Riyadh, where he lives with his wife, the poet Khadija al-Amri. Al-Harbi leads an active literary life, and participates in many cultural events on a pan-Arabic scale. His first collection of poems, *Silence and Madness*, appeared in 1983.

Muhammad Ubaid al-Harbi (b. 1955)

Saudi poet. Born in the holy city of Madinah, he studied civil engineering, graduating in 1979, then spent a year studying English in Wellesley, Mass. On returning to Saudi Arabia he worked in journalism and is now editor-in-chief of the cultural section in *Al-Sharq* Review in Dammam. He is one of the young group of modernist poets who are now contributing to the changing poetic scene in the Arab world, and writes his poetry in the medium of prose. His first collection of poems is now in press. Al-Harbi has been working on a translation into Arabic of a large selection of Walt Whitman's *Leaves of Grass*.

Kamal Haydar (1933–1980)

Yemeni short story writer from South Yemen. His short stories are concerned mainly with social issues. He published one collection of short stories entitled, *Signpost* (1978).

Muhammad Salih Haydara (b. 1952)

Yemeni short story writer from South Yemen. He did his early education in Aden then went to Cairo University where he studied communication. He has worked in journalism and is regarded as one of the foremost committed writers of the country. His first collection, *A Wanderer from Yemen* appeared in 1974, followed by two others, *Very Much an Adolescent* (1978) and *Migrating Clouds* (1980).

Mansour al-Hazimi (b. 1935)

Saudi short story writer, poet and scholar. Born in the holy city of Makkah, he did his elementary and secondary studies in his birthplace then took his B.A. in Arabic literature from Cairo University in 1958 and his Ph.D. also in Arabic literature from the School of Oriental and African Studies of the University of London in 1966. Since then he has worked at the King Saud University lecturing in Arabic literature and occupying the position of Dean of the College of Arts from 1973 to 1976, then chairman of the Arabic Department, then Dean of University College for Girls (1981–1984), and is now again Chairman of the Arabic Department at King Saud University. He has also been editor-in-chief of the *Review of the College of Arts* which he himself founded in 1970, and is very active in Saudi Arabia's cultural life, occupying many sensitive positions in various cultural institutions. He published his first collection of poetry, *Tales and Desires* in 1981 and a collection of short stories and essays, *Essays and Images* in 1984. He has also published several books in literary history and criticism. Al-Hazimi has a fluent, clear style and exhibits a mastery in the ironical mode of writing which he accomplishes with great sensitivity and skill.

Saad al-Humaidin (b. 1943)

Saudi poet. Born in Ta'if, he studied up to secondary level and has worked in teaching and in journalism, first as editor-in-chief of *Al-Yamama* literary review in Riyadh and now as editor in one of Saudi Arabia's most prestigious papers, *Al-Riyadh*. His first collection of poems, *Drawings on the Wall* appeared in 1975 and another, *You are the Tent, I am the Threads* is in press now.

Husain Ali Husain (b. 1950)

Saudi Arabian short story writer. He studied land surveying but works in journalism. One of the foremost short story writers in Saudi Arabia, he has published widely in the various periodicals of his country and his first collection appeared in 1983, titled, *Song of the Hunted Man*. Like so many writers of his generation, he is deeply involved in social problems in general but shows great sympathy with human frailty, and with the problems of poverty and failure.

Abd al-Rahman Ibrahim (b. 1954)

Yemeni poet. Born in Aden, in the south of Yemen, he took his university degree from the University of Algiers in 1979. He belongs to the modernist group of poets in Yemen and is involved in his poetry in major Yemeni and Arab political and social issues. He published his first collection under the title of, *Tropical Symphony to the Face of my Beloved*.

Ismail Fahd Ismail (b. 1940)

Kuwaiti novelist and short story writer and one of the best known authors outside the Peninsula. Aside from his various specializations in commerce, psychology and public administration, he obtained a B.A. in literature and drama criticism and is deeply involved in the dramatic and cinematographic activity in his country. He is a prolific writer with many collections of short stories and a good number of novels to his name, as well as a number of books of criticism and literary history. Among Ismail's collections of short stories are, *The Dark Spot* (1965) and *Cages and the Common Language* (1975); and other than his lovely novella, *Lightspots of Stagnation* (1971), his novel in two volumes, *The Nile Flows Northward* (1981, 1982) has earned him an added reputation. He is now head of a company of cinematographic products in Kuwait.

Muhammad Fahd al-Issa (b. 1924)

Saudi poet. He was born in Unaiza and studied in Madinah after which he worked in various government positions, moving eventually to Riyadh. He has two published collections, *On the Outskirts of the Road* (1963) and *Lydia* (1963).

Abdallah Muhammad Jabr (b. 1932)

Saudi poet. Born in Makkah, he is a self-educated man and leads a quiet life in Makkah, concentrating on reading and writing. His poetry reflect a great involvement in the particular human condition brought about by the sudden change in the pace and quality of life after oil, and betrays a wistful tone as the poet watches the social developments around him. Two collections have been published, *The Price of Civilization* (1983) and *I Want a Wonderful Life* (1983).

Muhammad Saeed Jarada (b. 1923)

Yemeni poet from South Yemen. He had a traditional education and has worked in teaching then in research at the Centre for Yemeni Studies in Aden. He is regarded as one of the foremost poets of the old school which adheres to the two-hemistich form and the rhetorical expression of inherited poetry. Aside from his verse, which he only collected into book form in 1976 under the title of *To Yemen My Love*, he has written much on the cultural history of Yemen.

Junaid Muhammad Junaid (b. 1955)

Yemeni poet. One of the generation of modernist poets in Yemen, he works as a teacher in Aden. He has published one book of poetry, *A Garland for a Qaitbani Woman*.

Fawziyya Abu Khalid (b. 1955)

Saudi poet. Born in Riyadh, she did her higher studies in the United States reading sociology, and now teaches at the Girls' University College of King Saud University. She is a sensitive poet with vision and deep faith in human possibilities and in the capacity of other women to achieve knowledge and strength. Her first collection, *Until When Will They Abduct You on Your Wedding Night* came out in 1973 when the poet was very young. Her second collection. *Secret Reading in the History of Arab Silence*, which has a preponderance of political themes, came out in 1985.

Abdallah Ali Khalifa (b. 1948)

Bahraini novelist and short story writer, and one of the most committed authors of the Gulf area. He deals pervasively with class conflict and various kinds of oppression, revealing a genuine zeal for progress and for a better life for all, particularly the long-suffering and deprived members of society. From his early experiments as a writer of fiction such as in his collection, *Winter Melody* (1975), his style has developed to a fine artistic level as in his novels, *Pearls* and *The Pirate and The City*, both in 1982.

Ahmad Muhammad Al Khalifa (b. 1930)

Bahraini poet. Born to the ruling family of Bahrain, he studied Arabic literature and lives in the Western section of his country. His poetry, written in the traditional two-hemistich form, reflects a diversified thematic interest moving from nationalism, to love, to nature, to personal reflections. He has published four collections of poetry, *Songs of Bahrain* (1955); *Noonsun and Mirage* (1962); *Remnants of Fountains* (1966) and *Moon and Palm Trees* (1980) which he collected in one volume in 1980 titled *The Book of Four Clusters* (1980). A fifth volume, *Clouds in Summer* is under publication.

Ali Abdallah Khalifa (b. 1944)

Bahraini poet. He has been active in the literary life of his country and has helped found the Union of Bahraini Writers, which he headed for three years. He also founded a publishing house and in 1976, the literary review, *Kitabat (Writings)*. During the last few years, he has helped found the Center of Folk Culture for the Arab Gulf States in Qatar, where he still works. His poetry stems from the very heart of his Bahraini experience, employing images from the surrounding landscape. He has to date published three collections, among which are *The Moaning of the Masts* (1969) and *Illuminating the Memory of the Motherland* (1977).

Dhabya Khamees (b. 1958)

Poet from the United Arab Emirates. Born in Abu Dhabi, she obtained her B.A. in political studies and philosophy from the University of Indiana and did her higher studies in politics and anthropology at the same university, and is now doing a Ph.D. at the University of London. She has worked in the government and in literary journalism coediting *Awraq*, a literary review which was published for a few years in London. Her poetry is written in the medium of prose and reflects a deep love of freedom and great confidence in the poet's own role as a woman conscious of the needs and pressures of life. Her first collection, *A Step Over the Earth* was published in 1981 and her second, *I Am the Woman, the Earth, All the Ribs*, in 1983. She has several other collections in press as well as a collection of short stories.

Hamda Khamees (b. 1946)
Bahraini poet. Born in Bahrain, Hamda Khamees studied political science at the University of Baghdad, graduating in 1968. She worked in teaching before moving on to journalism working first as journalist at *Al-Azmina Al-Arabiyya* review in the United Arab Emirates then at *Al-Fajr* paper also in the Emirates where she still is. She publishes widely in Gulf and Arab periodicals and has won acclaim for her strong stand on the side of justice and progress. Her poetry reflects depth and sensitivity and is at the forefront of women's writings in the area. Her collection, *An Apology for Childhood*, appeared in 1978.

Hasan al-Lawzi (b. 1952)
Yemeni poet and short story writer. Born in Sanaa, he studied at the University of al-Azhar in Cairo and occupied several important government posts the most recent of which is the post of Minister of Culture in Sanaa. Al-Lawzi has published several collections of poetry and short stories, and is a powerful writer with diversified themes and interests. Among his major themes is his deep and committed involvement in the issues of the Yemeni revolution and his aspiration for its success on both the political and the social levels. He has published several collections of short stories and poetry among which are his verse collection, *Poems for the Difficult Woman* (1979) and his collections of short stories, *The Woman who Ran in the Glow of the Sun* (1976) and *Hymns in the Temple of Love and Revolution* (1978).

Abd al-Aziz al-Maqalih (b. 1939)
Yemeni poet, writer and scholar. He read Arabic literature at the University of Cairo and, on his return to Yemen, became very active in Yemen's literary life, promoting Yemeni literature and culture in his capacity as poet and critic, and also in his capacity as the president of Sanaa University and of the Centre for Yemeni Studies. His poetry has won fame and recognition all over the Arab world, and is concerned in the political and social issues of both Yemen and the vast Arab world. Writing in the modernist trend, he has been able to incorporate into his verse a great number of historical legends and to connect present day Arab (and particularly Yemeni) life with ever recurring patterns in Arab history, achieving a mythic sense of time of real sophistication. Among his many collections of poetry are *Ma'rib Speaks*; *A Letter to Sayf Ibn Dhi Yazin*; and *The Return of Waddah al-Yaman*. A collection of all his works to date has been published in 1977 under the title of *Diwan Abd al-Aziz al-Maqalih*. In October, 1986, al-Maqalih was awarded the Lotus prize for literature.

Muhammad al-Murr (b. 1954)

Short story writer from the United Arab Emirates. Born in Dubai, he studied at Syracuse University in the United States and now works in journalism in his own country, a profession which has given him great scope in expressing his ideas on culture and on general social issues. One of the generation of modern writers in the Gulf, he reflects in his short stories great involvement in the issues of poverty and human suffering. He has published five collections of short stories to date among which are *Friendship* (1984); *A Little Tenderness* (1985) and *The Surprise* (1985).

Muhammad al-Muthanna (b. 1945)

Yemeni novelist and short story writer. Born in al-Hudaida of a poor family, he studied in Cairo and has worked in the government as well as in journalism. Two collections of short stories have appeared so far, *In The Heart of the Night* (1976) and *The Mountain also Smiles.* (1979).

Ibrahim al-Nasir (b. 1933)

Saudi novelist and short story writer. Born in Riyadh, he studied up to intermediate level, and now lives and works in the capital. His fiction favours a realistic approach and he is one of the many writers in the area who have addressed the contradictions that have mushroomed with the advent of oil wealth and the topographic and social change which it imposed. He treats his subject often with a nostalgic tone for the bygone days and way of life. Aside from his short stories which he continues to publish in the various periodicals, he has written many serialised features for radio and television. He has published several books including, *Our Mothers and the Struggle* (1960), *Land without Rain* (1965) and *The Girls' Fountain* (1976), all collections of short stories. Among the novels he has published are *A Hole in the Night's Garment* (1961) and *Ship of the Dead* (1969).

Abd al-Majeed al-Qadi (b. 1934)

Yemeni short story writer and dramatist. Born in the district of Taaz, he works now at the ministry of culture in Aden. In his writings, he reflects an involvement in social issues, particularly the issues of progress and change, expressing a yearning for a better life in his country. He has published two plays, *Al-Daudahi's Daughter* and *Young Man Mansour*. His short stories have been published in various periodicals in Yemen.

Ahmad Qandeel (1911–1979)

Saudi poet. Born in Jeddah, he studied at its Falah School then taught there before he was appointed editor-in-chief of one of the country's prestigious papers. After that he occupied several government positions, then left in order to concentrate on business. His first collection was entitled *Aghadeer* and he has also attempted writing verse in the colloquial. Other collections are *The Towers* and *Fire*.

Maysun Saqr al-Qasimi (b. 1958)

A poet from the United Arab Emirates. She studied political science at Cairo

University and she is still living in Cairo. In her original and experimental poetry, she is deeply involved in the problems of Arab life on both the social and the political levels, and imparts a message of freedom and emancipation from the ills that she sees impairing her life. She has published one volume of her poetry, *Thus I Call Things* (1983).

Hasan Abdallah al-Qurashi (b. 1926)
Saudi poet. Born in Makkah he studied first in his birthplace then obtained a B.A. in history from the University of Riyadh (now King Saud University). He occupied several prominent positions in the government the last of which was the rank of ambassador. He is a famous book collector and his interest in literature and culture supercedes all other interests. He has participated in many pan-Arab literary meetings and has published widely in Saudi and Arab reviews. Several collections of his poetry have appeared to date among which are *When Lamps Burn Out* (1974) and *Etchings on the Remains of the Age of Jesting* (1979). A two volume collection of his poetry has appeared entitled, *Diwan al-Qurashi*.

Abd al-Rahman Rafee^c (b. 1938)
Bahraini poet. Aside from formal poetry which he writes in both the traditional two-hemistich form as well as free verse, he also writes folk poetry which he has published in a separate volume. He has published several volumes of formal poetry including *Songs of Four Seas* (1970, 1982).

Sayf al-Rahabi (b. 1956)
Omani poet. Born in Masqat, Oman, Rahabi studied in Cairo, specializing in journalism, and now works as a journalist in Paris and the Gulf. He is a promising young poet whose poetry, all written in prose form, clearly reflects the unity of contemporary Arabic culture and the shared aspirations of Arab poets everywhere for internal order and external liberation. He has published three books of poetry, *Sea Gull of Madness* (1981), *The Green Mountain* (1982), and *Bells of Estrangement* (1983).

Muhammad Hashim Rasheed (b. 1930)
Saudi poet. Born in Madinah of Syrian origin, he was exposed early in life, thanks to his father who was himself interested in literature, to the company of many men of letters in Madinah. He studied at the Shari^ca School of Religious Studies but acquired much of his literary knowledge from his father's distinguished friends. He later studied journalism and, aside from his work as a government official, he has worked in journalism all his life. His first collection, *Behind the Mirage* appeared in 1953, and he has since published several others.

Abd al-Kareem al-Razihi (b. 1947)
Yemeni poet. He is one of the young Yemeni poets who write in the modern tradition of Arabic poetry and are leading the trend toward a more original poetry. He has worked in literary journalism and has published a collection of poetry entitled, *The Need for a Second Heaven and an Additional Hell*. At present, al-Razihi is working at the Ministry of Culture and Information in Sanaa, and edits *Al-Yaman Al-Jadid* magazine.

Waleed al-Rujaib (b. 1954)

Kuwaiti novelist, dramatist and short story writer. He has a B.A. in social studies and an M.A. in education and works at present at Kuwait University in the sociology department. He is also editor of the cultural section of *Al-Amil* review, which is the review of the general union of workers in Kuwait, and his fictional work reflects his understanding of and sympathy with the situation of workers and their problems. His first short story collection appeared in 1983 titled, *Drip Drip*. A novel, *Badriyya*, has been appearing in serialised form in *Al-Amil* review. A new short story collection entitled, *God's Will Concerning a Man of Limited Means* and a play titled, *Attachés to a Boxed City* are in press.

Saqr al-Rushud (1944?–1978)

Kuwaiti playwright. Born in Kuwait, he obtained a degree in commerce and economics from Kuwait University. His talent for drama absorbed much of his energy and he wrote and directed several successful plays. During his short span of life, he was able to benefit and greatly raise the standards of a fledgling Kuwaiti theatre, helped in this by another Kuwaiti playwright, Abd al-Aziz al-Surayyi[c], and deeply influenced by his readings in Western theatre. He found in the many problems of modern life in Kuwait rich material for his themes, and he wrote much on the changes that have taken place in his country describing how the new awakening clashed with deep-rooted traditional hang-ups, especially in people's attitudes toward women. Among his well-known plays are, *I and Fate* (1964), *The Big Fang* (1965), and *The Barricade* (1966). *The Mud*, which he wrote in 1965 is regarded as one of his best.

Suad al-Mubarak al-Sabah (b. 1942)

Kuwaiti poet from the family of al-Sabah, the rulers of Kuwait. However, she has distinguished herself in her own right not only through her poetry but also through her deep interest in freedom and human rights (she is a member of the Executive Board of 'The Arab Human Rights Organization' in Cairo and is on the Board of Trustees of the 'Arab Thought Forum' in Amman, Jordan, as well as a supporting member of the prestigious Center for Arab Unity Studies in Beirut), and her support of literary activity among which is her recent sponsorship of the republication of the forty volumes of the important review, *Al-Risala*, which was at the heart of Arab literary activity in the thirties and forties. Suad al-Sabah did her higher studies in Cairo and England, obtaining her Ph.D. in Planning and Development from the University of Surrey in 1982. She has published two collections of poetry, *A Wish* (1972) and *To You, My Son* (1982) and is preparing her third which contains her recent, much revolutionized verse. From its conservative beginnings, her poetry has developed in both form and content towards greater modernity, deeply expressing both the joy in love, life and human freedom as well as anger and frustration at the many tragedies and relapses in present-day Arab life. In the field of her own specialization, she has published several books among which is *Kuwait, Anatomy of a Crisis Economy* (1983) in English, and *Opec, Past Experience and Future Trends* (1986) in Arabic.

Ali al-Sabti (b. 1934)

Kuwait poet. Born in Kuwait, he studied up to intermediate level, then worked

544

in journalism after trying his hand at commerce. He is now an editor on *Al-Siyasa* in Kuwait. His poems are published in various periodicals and in two collections to date *A House of Summer Stars* (1969) and *In the Open Air* (1980).

Abdallah al-Saikhan (b. 1955)
Saudi poet. He was born in Ha'il and studied up to secondary level in Tabuk after which he moved to Riyadh, working as a literary journalist, where he is cultural editor at *Al-Yamama* literary review. He is one of the modernist poets of the Gulf area and writes an experimental poetry that reflects a progressive vision not free, however, of frustration and a wistful attitude. His first collection, *Anxiety in the Motherland's Climate* is in press now.

Ahmad Salih al-Salih (b. 1946)
Saudi poet. He was born in Runya where he did his early studies then moved in 1960 to al-Ta'if where he finished his secondary schooling and left with his family to Riyadh. In the capital, he worked and continued his studies reading sociology at the University of Imam Muhammad ibn Saud. He works as a government official in Riyadh. His first collection of poetry is entitled, *Bewildered Dreams*.

Amin Salih (b. 1950)
Bahraini novelist and short story writer. Born in Manama, he studied up to secondary level but has augmented his knowledge of literary forms and techniques by his wide readings. One of the most modernist of the Arabian Peninsula writers of fiction, his experimental work imparts a message of real human significance as well as a great aesthetic pleasure. He has published four short story collections to date among which are, *Royal Game* (1982) and *The Fugitives* (1983). A fifth collection, *The Elements*, is in press. His first novel, *First Song of A.S.* was published in 1982.

Abdallah al-Salmi (b. 1950)
Saudi Arabian short story writer. Born in Riyadh, he did his early studies in Makkah and after studying at the Police Academy in his country went to the United States where he studied civil engineering for six years, returning home in 1986. He now works with the Boarders Security Police in Riyadh. His first collection of short stories, *Cubes of Dampness* was published in 1981. He resorts at times to a symbolic representation in his fictional work, and often reflects great concern for human failure and for the suffering of those who fall victim to their own or their society's shortcomings.

Khayriyya al-Saqqaf (b. 1951)
Saudi short story writer. Born in the holy city of Makkah, she obtained a B.A. in Arabic literature from the Girls' University College of King Saud University in 1973, and obtained an M.A. from the University of Missouri in 1976. She is now studying for her Ph.D. and lectures at the Girls' University College in Riyadh. She is also editor of the women's section of the prestigious *Riyadh* paper, and is active in literary journalism. She participates in Saudi Arabia's literary life through her articles, radio talks and public lectures which she gives at various

women's institutions in her country. Her collection of short stories, *Sailing toward the Distances* appeared in 1982.

Zayn al-Saqqaf (b. 1940)
Yemeni poet and short story writer. Born in the village of Hadarim in the district of Taaz, he obtained a B.A. from Cairo University in economics and political science. He has travelled widely in the Arab world and has visited Ethiopia and France, and holds now an important position at the Ministry of Culture in Sanaa. He writes in the modern tradition of poetry and has a fine grip of the fictional mode in his short stories, mixing pathos with a comic representation of reality. He publishes in various periodicals in Yemen.

Muhammad Saeed Sayf
Yemeni short story writer from the north. He lives and works in Sanaa, and publishes his short stories in various Yemeni periodicals, addressing problems and experiences in Yemen before and after the Yemeni revolution.

Habeeb al-Sayigh (b. 1955)
Poet from the United Arab Emirates. Born in Abu Dhabi, he obtained his B.A. in philosophy from the University of Alexandria and worked in the Ministry of Information, then in journalism first editing the *Al-Fajr* daily then *Awraq* literary review which was founded in London in 1983. He is one of the more sophisticated poets of Arabia and has published several collections the first of which is *Here is the Bar of Banu Abs, the Invitation is General* (1980), and *Poems to Beirut* (1982). Other collections are in press now.

Ali Sayyar (b. 1928)
Bahraini poet and short story writer. Born in Manama, he has a diploma in industry from Cairo and works as editor-in-chief of *Sada Al-Usbu^c* magazine. His short stories reflect an involvement in social problems which has characterized much short story writing in the Arab world. He has a fine power of description and a capacity to follow up, cogently, the psychological and emotional development of his characters. His first collection, *The Master*, appeared in 1976. A second, *An Ink Drop*, is now in press.

Ruqayya al-Shabeeb (b. 1952)
Saudi Arabian short story writer. Born in the northern part of Saudi Arabia, she came with her family to Riyadh where she studied history and works now in the field of education. In her work, she expresses genuine interest in women's issues, but discusses also other crucial points of general interest. Her first collection, *The Dream*, appeared in 1984.

Shawqi Shafeeq (b. 1950)
Yemeni poet from the south where he has studied up to the secondary level and where he still lives in its capital, Aden. He is a modernist and an innovative poet with depth and passion employing complex imagery and a fresh and original language.

546

Ahmad al-Shami (b. 1924)

Yemeni poet. Born in Ab, Yemen, with an early education in Sanaa he then depended on a self-planned program of education through reading. He worked in politics early in life and was one of the founders of the liberation movement in the forties which caused him to be imprisoned by Imam Yahya from 1948–1953. After his release, he worked in several government posts the last of which was ambassador to Britain in 1961. He opposed the 1962 revolution and worked instead with the ousted shadow government of Imam Muhammad al-Badr, and remained in opposition to the actual revolutionary government until 1969 after which he was appointed by this government a member in the highest Republican Council in Yemen. However, in 1973 he left all official duties and came to live in London. He has published several collections among which are *The First Breath*; *An Iliad from Sanaa*, and *Shadows* which appeared in London in 1981. He has also published several books on Yemeni history and on the history of literature.

Sharifa al-Shamlan (b. 1947)

Saudi short story writer. She read journalism at the Girls' University College in Riyadh graduating in 1968, and works now in the eastern section of the country as head of social services. She reads widely and has benefited from her readings both in her short stories as well as in her many articles on society. Her short stories have been published in various periodicals, but a collection of these is being prepared for publication.

Ali al-Sharqawi (b. 1948)

Bahraini poet. Born in Manama, Bahrain, he did his secondary studies there, then studied human science at the University of Baghdad, graduating in 1979. After that, he did a course on veterinary science in Britain in 1981 and works now at the veterinary laboratory in Manama. He is one of the experimental poets of the Gulf area who has combined modern sophistication with an ardent commitment to the cause of human justice and freedom. His best poetry stems from the heart of the modernist tradition in contemporary Arabic poetry, in which he uses complex imagery and a rather difficult technique. He has published at least seven collections of poetry among which are *Thunder in the Season of Draught* (1975); *Palm Tree of the Heart* (1981); and *Psalm 23 for the Singers' Nectar* (1985). At present, Sharqawi is the head of the Bahraini Union of Writers.

Sulaiman al-Shatti (b. 1943)

Kuwaiti short story writer, critic and scholar. Born in Kuwait, he studied for his B.A. and M.A. at Kuwait University, then obtained a Ph.D. in Arabic literature from Cairo University. He is now an assistant professor at the University of Kuwait and is also head of the Kuwaiti Union of Writers whose literary review, *Al-Bayan*, he edits. He is also a member of the prestigious National Council of Culture, Arts and Literature in Kuwait and a very active member of the Kuwaiti literary scene, representing Kuwait in many pan-Arab conferences. Aside from his critical studies, he has published two collections of short stories, *Low Voices* (1970) and *Men from the Upper Echelon* (1983). In his fictional works, al-Shatti is preoccupied with the tremendous change that has taken place in Kuwait after oil, and speaks, with a nostalgic tone, about the past.

Hamza Shihata (1910–1971)

Saudi poet. He was born in Makkah but grew up in Jeddah where he also studied. He worked in trading and lived many years in India before returning to Jeddah as secretary of the Council of Commerce there.

Muhammad al-Shurafi (b. 1940)

Yemeni poet and dramatist. Born in the district of Hajja, he graduated from the School of Science at Cairo University in 1961 and has worked as a Yemeni diplomat. A prolific author, he has published to date more than twenty volumes of poetry and plays some of which, such as *In the Land of Two Edens* and *Seasons of Migration and Madness* are verse plays. Among his many poetry collections are *Women's Tears*; *To Her I Sing*; *Songs on the Long Road* and *Love is Tears and Revolution*. He has won considerable fame because of his effective involvement in the question of feminine freedom and progress, a major theme in his poetry.

Ahmad al-Sibaᶜi (1905–1983)

Saudi writer. One of the most highly regarded essayists, short story writers and social critics, al-Sibaᶜi, a Makkan by birth and early education, also studied in Alexandria then returned to his country to work first in teaching, then in journalism and other responsible government positions. His autobiographical book, *My Days* (1955) is a fascinating record of life in Makkah before oil and, with Hamza Bogary's autobiographical novel, *Saqifat Al-Safa* (1983), which is another magnificent account of this life, fills a gap in our knowledge of the traditions, customs and outlook of the people of Makkah before oil changed most aspects of life. Among al-Sibaᶜi's short story collections are, *Auntie Kadarjan* and *An Idea*, and among his collections of essays are *Let us Walk On* and *Diary of a Madman*. Just before he died, al-Sibaᶜi won the High State Award for literature.

Husain Sirhan (b. 1913)

Saudi poet. Born in Makkah he studied at its schools but left studying early, and he is mainly self-taught. He worked in various government posts and rose to fame as a poet with revolutionary ideas. His collection of poetry is entitled, *Featherless Wings*.

Muhammad al-Thubaiti (b. 1952)

Saudi poet. Born in al-Ta'if, he obtained a B.A. in sociology and works now in teaching. He also participates in literary activities both within Saudi Arabia and on a pan-Arab scale. One of the more interesting poets of the new generation in the Arabian Peninsula, he writes a robust and original poetry, with deep roots in both the social and literary traditions of his country, yet preserving a modern outlook on life. Two collections have appeared to date: *The Lover of Rosy Times* and *I Spell a Dream, I Spell an Illusion*.

Ahmad al-Mushari al-Udwani (b. 1923)

Kuwaiti poet. Born in Kuwait, he studied at the Islamic University of al-Azhar in Cairo and held many responsible positions in his own country. At present, he is the director of Kuwait's famous National Council for Culture, Arts and Literature which has made, through its monthly book series, a great contribution towards the dissemination of ideas and knowledge through the Arab world. His poetry reflects an unorthodox critical stance towards the ills he detects in Kuwaiti and Arab contemporary life, revealing a skeptical mind and embodying an ironical tone and an individual method of approach. He has published one collection of poetry, *Wings of the Storm* (1980).

Ibrahim al-Urayyid (b. 1908)
Bahraini poet. Born in India the son of a Bahraini father from the well-known tribe of al-Urayyid and an Iraqi mother, he lost his mother while still an infant and was brought up with the help of Indian women in Bombay where his father was a pearl merchant. The boy grew up in an Indian environment hardly exposed to his native language until he returned to live in Bahrain at the age of twenty. There he got married and studied Arabic language and grammar with a reputable Bahraini teacher. His first attempts at poetry were in Urdu and English, but he quickly excelled in Arabic, reading avidly in classical and modern Arabic literature and distinguishing himself by his writings on both. He has several collections of poetry, but it was his third, *The Brides* (1946) which drew the attention of readers in the Arab world. It was followed by several others and by such books on literary criticism as *Poetic Methods* (1950) an excellent discussion on the element of tone in poetry; and *Issues in Poetry* (1955) and *A Trip in Contemporary Arabic Poetry* (1962), two books which made an early link between Gulf writers and mainstream Arabic literature, reflecting the author's deep interest in poetic innovation and progress. In 1979, a volume of the poet's collected verse was published.

Abdu Uthman (b. 1936)
Yemeni poet. Born in al-Zubaira, he studied in Aden and Cairo returning to hold several responsible positions in his country's government including ambassador to Ethiopia, China, Baghdad and Moscow where he is at present. His poetry is involved in his country's as well as in general Arab political situations, and he has published a volume of poetry, his second, titled *Palestine in the Heart* (1971). This appeared at the same time as his highly nationalistic volume, *Ma'rib Speaks* (1971). A third volume, *The Wall and the Noose* was published in 1977.

Layla al-Uthman (b. 1945)
Kuwaiti short story writer and novelist. Born in Kuwait, she studied up to secondary level, but has augmented her education through her wide readings in Arabic as well as Western literature in translation. She is one of the Peninsula's foremost women writers of fiction whose short stories reflect skill, economy and a diversified outlook, ranging from local issues to general Arab, particularly Palestinian experience. Her first collection of short stories, *A Woman in a Vessel* appeared in 1977 followed by several others among which are, *Departure* (1979); and *Love has Many Images* (1984). Her first novel, *The Woman and the Cat* was published in 1985 and a second novel, *Wasmiyya Comes out of the Sea* is in press. Several of her short stories have been translated into East European languages

and a full collection of these was translated into Yugoslavian. Al-Uthman is completely dedicated to her writing, despite her many family responsibilities.

Sibaᶜi Uthman (b. 1938)
Saudi short story writer. Born in the Sudan, he studied for two years at the College of Arts in Khartoum then left to work in journalism in his own country. Two collections of short stories have appeared so far, *Silence and the Walls* and *Circles in the Book of Time*. His work reflects the author's interest in psychological states which he describes with poignancy and in detail.

Ismail al-Warith (b. 1950)
Yemeni poet. Born in Dhamar, he studied Arabic literature at the University of Sanaa. He has occupied several administrative positions at the Ministry of Culture in Yemen and is now a research scholar at the Center for Yemeni Studies in Sanaa. He is one of Yemen's foremost young poets and writes in the modern tradition with a preponderance of political themes. His first collection, *Presence in the Alphabet of Blood* (1984), won him general acclaim and he has another collection in press now.

Khalifa al-Wugayyan (b. 1941)
Kuwaiti poet. He had his early education in Kuwait and his higher education in Cairo, where he obtained a Ph.D. from Ain Shams University in 1980, specializing in Arabic literature. He is now a high ranking official at the National Council for Culture, Arts and Literature in Kuwait and has helped greatly in the Council's programme of disseminating Arabic and world culture among a wide Arab audience. His poetry reflects a deep sensitivity to life's vulnerabilities in general and to the many political problems that confront the whole Arab world. He has published two collections of poetry, *Those Sailing with the Winds*, (1974) and *Metamorphosis of Time* (1983) and is preparing his third collection for publication.

Tahir Zamakhshari (b. 1913–1987)
Saudi poet. He was born in Makkah where he also studied. He has worked for the government in various capacities including the directorship of the Broadcasting Station, and in the diplomatic corps. He has published several collections of poetry among which are, *From the Tents* (1968); *A Window on the Moon* (1978) and *A Stranger's Melodies* (1982). His poetry is collected in a large volume entitled *The Green Collection*. He has also written short stories and essays on social ethics.

Khalid Saud al-Zayd (b. 1938)
Kuwaiti poet. Born in Kuwait, he studied to the secondary level in his own country, then left school to work. His greatest interest, however, has always been in books and he is largely self-taught, having taken great advantage of his father's large private library. Aside from being a poet, he is a researcher and his first book was a collection of Kuwaiti folk proverbs. He has also written a history of Kuwaiti literature in three volumes titled *Kuwaiti Authors in Two Centuries* (1867, 1981, 1982). His poetry collection, *Prayers in an Abandoned Temple* was

published in 1970 and republished in 1983. Al-Zayd has travelled widely and has represented his country in various literary conferences in the Arab world.

Muhammad Mahmoud al-Zubairi (1909–1964)

Yemeni poet and one of Yemen's most celebrated authors. Born in Sanaa, he studied at its religious schools then spent time at the University of Cairo. His main preoccupation was his country's political plight under the rule of the Imam and he was one of the founders of the Movement of Liberals in the forties, and the leader of opposition against the Imam's rule. This led to his persecution and he suffered destitution and exile outside his country, settling finally in Pakistan where he worked at its Broadcasting Station and had the opportunity to translate into Arabic the poetry of Pakistan's major poet, Muhammad Iqbal. Finally, in 1962, when the revolution against the Imam erupted in North Yemen, he went back to his country and became the Minister of Education there and a member of the Executive Council, the highest authority in the country at the time. However, he fell victim to the royalist forces in 1964 and has been regarded since as one of Yemen's most acclaimed martyrs. Al-Zubairi published several collections of poetry among which was his *Prayer in Hell* and *The Revolution of Poetry*. In 1978 a volume of his collected poems was published entitled *Diwan al-Zubairi*. Although al-Zubairi wrote along conservative lines, resorting to the terse sentence construction, sonorous tone and balanced structure of classical Arabic poetry, his work reflects a real originality of themes, ideas and method of treatment.

Biographies of Translators

First Translators

Roger Allen

Roger Allen is professor of Arabic at the University of Pennsylvania and chairman of the department of comparative literature there. He studied Arabic at Oxford University and has been active as editor, translator, anthologist and scholar of Arabic, specializing in particular in Arabic fiction. His book, *The Arabic Novel, an Historical and Critical Introduction*, was published in 1982, and he has written widely on contemporary Arabic drama, and the short story. Among his translations is *The Ship*, a novel by the Palestinian novelist, Jabra Ibrahim Jabra (1986), and *Search for Walid Masu'ud* by the same writer, as well as Abd al-Rahman Muneef's novel, *Endings*, both forthcoming. His latest published work is a large anthology of modern critical writings in Arabic, titled *Modern Arabic Literature*, in *A Library of Literary Criticism*, the reference series by Ungar, (1987). A member of the Administrative Board of PROTA, Roger Allen is co-editing with Salma Khadra Jayyusi PROTA's large anthology of contemporary Arabic theatre.

Issa J. Boullata

Born in Jerusalem, Palestine, he graduated with a Ph.D. in Arabic Literature from the University of London in 1969. He taught at Hartford Seminary in Connecticut, then joined McGill University, where he is now Professor of Arabic Literature and Language. His publications include *Outlines of Romanticism in Modern Arabic Poetry*; *Badr Shakir al-Sayyab: His Life and Poetry*, both in Arabic, and *Modern Arab Poets 1950–1975*, an anthology of poetry in English translation; and, as editor, *Critical Perspectives on Modern Arabic Literature*. He is a member of the Editorial Board of PROTA.

Sargon Boulus

Iraqi poet and short story writer. Born in Habbaniyia, Iraq, he left for Beirut in 1967 where he worked as journalist and translator and published both poetry and fiction in major literary reviews. An accomplished poet and translator who writes in the modern tradition, he has translated into Arabic selections from the poetry of W. S. Merwin, Snyder, Ginsberg, McClure and others. He has lived in San Francisco since 1968 where he studied Comparative Literature at UC

552

Berkeley, and Sculpture at Skyline College, San Mateo. A selection of his poems were published in Washington in 1982 under the title *Arrival in Where City*. In 1972, he published and edited *Tigris*, a magazine of poetry and graphics.

Sharif Elmusa

Born in Palestine, Sharif Elmusa came to the United States in 1971, and has obtained a Ph.D. in Urban Studies and Planning from the M.I.T., in Cambridge, Ma, in 1986. His poems in English have been published in several periodicals and will soon appear in an *Anthology of Arab-American Poetry*. He is one of PROTA's readers and reviewers, and has reviewed, among others, the final version of Emile Habiby's famous novel, *The Secret Life of Saeed, the Pessoptimist* (1982, 1985) and Sahar Khalifeh's novel, *Wild Thorns* (1985).

Salwa Jabsheh

Salwa Jabsheh studied biology at Beirut University College. She is well acquainted with the culture and dialects of the Gulf countries where she lived with her husband for nine years. She is co-director of MINWAR, an Arabic Language publishing firm specializing in educational literature. She is a Palestinian who is now living with her husband and two children in London.

Lena Jayyusi

Born in Amman, Jordan, to Palestinian parents, Lena Jayyusi was educated first in England where she obtained a Ph.D. in sociology from the University of Manchester, then at Boston University, where she obtained an M.S. in Film Studies. Her first book, *Categorization and the Moral Order* was published by Routledge and Kegan Paul in 1984. She writes on cine-semiotics, poster-semiotics, and language and communicative action. She was assistant to the producer on three documentary films about women in the Middle East in 1981. She worked as assistant professor of sociology at Wellesley College and is now a research assistant professor at the Language Behaviour Program at Boston University. Lena Jayyusi is one of PROTA's readers and reviewers and has translated, with Naomi Shihab Nye, selections from the poetry of the Tunisian poet, Abu al-Qasim al-Shabbi (forthcoming), and is now preparing an English language version of the well-known epic folktale, *Sayf ibn Dhi Yazin*, part translation, part re-telling, with an introduction. She lives with her husband and daughter in greater Boston.

May Jayyusi

Born in Amman, Jordan, May Jayyusi did most of her studies in London, and read philosophy at University College of London University. She later did graduate film studies at Boston University. Widely read in European thought and literature, especially the novel, she is one of PROTA's readers. She has worked as production assistant on *Wedding in Galilee*, a film made by Michel Khleifi, and has been working on a translation of selections from Ghassan Kanafani's works entitled, *What Has Remained For You and Other Stories* for PROTA. She lives with her husband and two children in Jerusalem.

Lorne M. Kenny

Professor Emeritus at the University of Toronto, he has taught for many years at the Department of Middle Eastern and Islamic Studies of this University, and was its chairman from 1975–1979. One of the most informed specialists on modern Arab and Egyptian history and on modern Islamic thought with a special emphasis on al-Afghani, Muhammad Abdo and Rashid Rida, he has written and lectured extensively on subjects pertaining to the areas of his specialization, including many presentations on Palestinian issues addressed to various groups, organizations and societies. In 1982, he was chosen to be the first chairman of Toronto Universities Middle East Group (TUMEG), which is a group of academics concerned with contemporary Middle Eastern issues on behalf of justice for the Arabs. Professor Kenny has also done many translations and has participated with his wife, Olive Kenny, on the translation of three novels for PROTA: M. Y. al-Qaid's *War in the Land of Egypt* (1986), Hanna Mina's *Fragments of Memory*, and Hamza Bogary's *Saqifat Al-Safa*, both forthcoming.

Olive E. Kenny

Olive Kenny spent many years in Egypt where she taught English and studied Arabic at the School of Oriental Studies of the American University of Cairo. Her work among pupils and contacts afforded her a great opportunity to absorb Arabic culture and thought and understand the Egyptian scene. Mrs. Kenny is the translator of two of Najib Mahfouz's famous trilogy, *Bayn al-Qasrayn*, and *Qasr al-Shauq* which latter she translated with her husband, Lorne M. Kenny. She also revised the translation of the third book, *Al-Sukkariya*. Another Najib Mahfouz novel which she translated was *Wedding Song (Afrah al-Qubba)* published in 1984. She is now an active translator and works extensively with PROTA for which she has translated three novels in participation with Lorne Kenny: M. Y. al-Qaid's *War in the Land of Egypt* (1986); Hanna Mina's *Fragments of Memory*, and Hamza Bogary's *Saqifat al-Safa*, both forthcoming.

Christopher Nouryeh

Christopher Nouryeh has a Ph.D. in comparative literature from the City University of New York and has taught English language and literature. At present he is director of the Advisement Office at Touro College, where he also teaches courses in Medieval and Renaissance literature. He has written papers on various subjects, including one on 'Troubadour and Arab Love Lyric', and another on St. Augustine for Villanova University's *Collectania Augustiniana*, forthcoming. Recently, he has translated ten pre-Islamic odes and has written an introduction to them.

Al-Sayyid Ishaq al-Khalifa Sharif

One of Sudan's most erudite intellectuals and lovers of literature, he has been active as poet, thinker and translator. He is proficient in several languages, and is highly versed in classical Arabic poetry and thought and in Islamic traditions. For several years, he worked as English language coordinator at the Secretarial General of the Muslim World League in Makkah before he went back to Khartoum to participate in the new activity generated by the recent changes in the Sudanese political and social scene.

Ahdaf Soueif
Ahdaf Soueif was born in Cairo to Egyptian parents active in the cultural scene in Egypt. She was first educated at Cairo University then at Lancaster University where she obtained a Ph.D. in linguistics. She taught English at Cairo University and is also an editor at the publishers Collier Macmillan in London. Her first novel, *Aisha*, published by Jonathan Cape in 1983 was a best seller. She is married to the British poet and critic Ian Hamilton and lives with her husband and son in London.

Second Translators

Alan Brownjohn
Alan Brownjohn studied for his degree at Merton College in Oxford. He taught at various schools and lectured at a College of Education and a Polytechnic, and is now a full-time writer. He has published several volumes of poetry, and his *Collected Poems* appeared in 1983. In 1979 he received the Cholmondeley Award for Poetry. His translation, with his wife Sandy Brownjohn, of Goethe's play *Torquato*, was broadcast by Radio 3 in 1982.

Dick Davies
Dick Davies read English at Cambridge University and lived for eight years in Iran. He has published three books of his own poems, *In the Distance*, *Seeing the World*, and *The Covenant*, and with his Iranian wife, Afkham Darbandi he has translated Farid al-Din al-Attar's *Conference of the Birds* from Persian, published by Penguin Classics in 1984. He is at present Literary Fellow at the Universities of Durham and Newcastle.

Diana Der Hovanessian
Diana Der Hovanessian, an award-winning American poet, is the translator and co-editor (with Marzbed Margossian) of *Anthology of Armenian Poetry*; *Sacred Wrath, Selected Poems of Vahan Tekeyan*; *The Arc, Poems of Shen-Mah*; and *Land of Fire, Poems of Charents*. She has also translated the works of the medieval poet Nahabet Koutchag, *Come Sit Beside Me and Listen to Koutchag*; and Gevorg Emin, *For You on New Year's Day*; as well as the poems of Vahan Derian, *Coming to Terms*, forthcoming. Her own work, which has appeared in various literary periodicals, is collected in *How to Choose Your Past*, and has been translated into Armenian and published in the Soviet Union. She has worked as visiting lecturer and writer-in-residence at many universities, and has been president of the New England Poetry Club since 1979. She has recently become a member of the National Board of Columbia University Translation Center.

Thomas G. Ezzy
A dual (U.S.-Canada) national, he was born to a Lebanese-American father and a French-Canadian mother, and received an M.A. in English from the University of Toronto. Poet and writer of fiction, he has so far published two volumes of

poetry *Parings*, and *Arctic Char in Grecian Waters*, but is now exclusively working in fiction. Currently he resides in Montreal, where he teaches English at Dawson College. He has co-translated with Michael Young as first translator, Bechir Ben Slama's novel, *Aisha*, for PROTA, (forthcoming).

Elizabeth Warnock Fernea

Elizabeth Fernea lectures in the Department of English and the Center for Middle Eastern Studies of the University of Texas at Austin. She specializes in cross cultures such as Middle Eastern and Western cultures, or men-women cultures. With her husband, the anthropologist, Robert Fernea, she has lived two years in Iraq, six years in Egypt and fifteen months in Morocco, sojourns which have afforded her rich first-hand material for her books: *Guests of the Sheikh* (1968); *A View of the Nile* (1970) and *A Street in Marrakech* (1975). Her continued interest in Middle Eastern society, particularly in the life of women, has informed much of her later activity in both writing and film making. It resulted in two large anthologies, *Middle Eastern Muslim Women Speak* which she edited with Basima Q. Bezirgan (1977) and *New Voices: Women in the Muslim Middle East* (1984). Her latest work on Middle Eastern Women was a series of three and a half hour films on social change in the Arab world: 'A Veiled Revolution' (religious change), 'The Price of Change' (economic change) and 'Women Under Seige' (political change as seen in the Rashidiyya Palestinian refugee camp in the south of Lebanon). Elizabeth Fernea has co-translated poems and selections from fiction including Sahar Khalifeh's novel, *Wild Thorns* which she has co-translated with Trevor LeGassick for PROTA (1985).

John Heath-Stubbs

English poet, critic and translator, he gained a first class degree in English from Queen's College, Oxford, in 1942 and lectured at the universities of Alexandria, Michigan and the College of St. Mark and St. John in London. He now lectures at the University of Oxford. Among his many writings is his long poem, *Artorius*, for which he won the Queen's Gold Medal for poetry in 1972. In 1978, he won the Oscar William-Gean Durwood Award. He has published a number of volumes of criticism, plays and poetry collections the most recent of which was *Naming the Beasts*, 1983. He has also translated *Selected Poems and Prose of Giacomo Leopardi* with Iris Origo, from Italian; and with Peter Avery has translated *Hafiz of Shiraz* and *The Rubaiyat of Omar Khayyam* from Persian.

Christopher Middleton

English poet and translator. His most recent book of poems is *111 Poems* (Manchester and New York, 1983). Essays: *The Pursuit of the Kingfisher* (Manchester and New York, 1983). Translations: Goethe, *Selected Poems* (Suhrkamp-Insel Verlag, Boston, 1983), Gert Hofmann, *The Spectacle at the Tower*, New York, Fromm International, 1984. Forthcoming from Oasis Press, London: *Serpentine* (short prose). He teaches German Literature and Comparative Literature at the University of Texas, Austin.

Naomi Shihab Nye

Poet and musician. Born in St. Louis to a Palestinian father and an American mother, she graduated from Trinity University, San Antonio. Between 1966–1967 she lived in Jerusalem. She worked as a poet-in-the-school for ten years in Texas, as Holloway lecturer at the University of California, Berkeley, and Lecturer in Poetry at the University of Texas at San Antonio. Her publications include *Hugging the Jukebox* and *Different Ways to Pray* as well as poems published in numerous journals and anthologies. Her next book, *Yellow Glove*, is due to appear in the spring of 1987. She has co-translated, with Lena Jayyusi, selections from the poetry of the Tunisian poet, *Abu al-Qasim al-Shabbi*. She lives with her husband and son in San Antonio, Texas.

Jeremy Reed
Jeremy Reed was born in Jersey, Channel Islands, but now lives in London. Among his publications are two books of poetry, *By the Fisheries*, 1984, and *Nero*, 1985. He has received an Eric Gregory Award, and Somerset Maugham Award for *By the Fisheries*, and Cape are to publish his novel, *Blue Rock* in 1987. Penguin will also publish his selected poems. He has co-translated, with May Jayyusi as first translator, Ghassan Kanafani's *What has Remained for You and Other Stories* and, with Olive and Lorne Kenny as first translators, Hamza Bogary's novel, *The Covered Bazars of Al-Safa*, both for PROTA.

Christopher Tingley
Born in Brighton, England, he received his education at the universities of London and Leeds. Following initial teaching experience in Germany and Britain, he lectured in the fields of English Language and Linguistics at the University of Constantine, Algeria, the University of Ghana and the National University of Rwanda. In the field of translation, he collaborated with the author on the translation of the extracts of Arabic poetry in S.K. Jayyusi's two volume work, *Trends and Movements in Modern Arabic Poetry*. He has translated, with Elizabeth Hodgkin, Mohamed Mzali's book in French, *La Parole de l'Action* and with Olive and Lorne Kenny as first translators has co-translated Muhammad Yusuf al-Qaid's novel, *War in the Land of Egypt* (1986), for PROTA.

David Wright
David Wright was born in Johannesburg and educated at Oriel College, Oxford. He is Fellow of the Royal Society of Literature and was Gregory Fellow in Poetry at the University of Leeds, 1965–1967. His publications include *To the Gods the Shades* and *Metrical Observations*, both published by Carcanet, and he translated *Beowulf* (Penguin) and *The Canterbury Tales* (Random House). He has also published *The Penguin Book of English Romantic Verse*.

Transliterated List of Arab Authors

Muḥammad ʿAbd al-Malik

Mayfaʿ ʿAbd al-Raḥmān

Muḥammad ʿAbd al-Wali

ʿAbd al-Ḥamīd Aḥmad

Muḥammad ʿAlwān

Khadīja al-ʿAmri

ʿAbd al-Qādir ʿAqīl

Fahd al-ʿAskar

ʿAbd al-Karīm al-ʿAuda

Saʿīd ʿAulaqi

Muḥammad Ḥasan ʿAwwād

Ṣāliḥ Saʿīd Bā-ʿAmer

ʿAbd al-Ilāh al-Bābṭain

Fawziyya al-Bakr

ʿAbdallah al-Baradūni

Ḥamza Boqari

Zayd Muṭīʿ Dammāj

ʿAli al-Dumaini

Muḥammad al-Dumaini

ʿAbd al-Raḥmān Fakhri

Muḥammad Ḥasan Faqi

Muḥammad al-Fāyiz

ʿAbdallah al-Fayṣal

Sulaimān al-Fulayyiḥ

Khalīl al-Fuzayʿ

Gosaibi (see al-Quṣaibi)

Qāsim Ḥaddād

Ibrāhīm al-Ḥaḍrāni

Muḥammad Ḥasan al-Ḥarbi

Muḥammad Jabr al-Ḥarbi

Muḥammad ʿUbaid al-Ḥarbi

Kamāl Ḥaydar

Muḥammad Ṣāliḥ Ḥaydara

Manṣūr al-Ḥāzimi

Saʿd al-Ḥumaidīn

Ḥusain ʿAli Ḥusain

ᶜAbd al-Raḥmān Ibrāhīm

Ismaᶜīl Fahd Ismaᶜīl

Muḥammad Fahd al-ᶜĪsa

ᶜAbdallah Muḥammad Jabr

Muḥammad Saᶜīd Jarāda

Junaid ᶜAbdallah Junaid

Fawziyya Abū Khālid

ᶜAbdallah ᶜAli Khalīfa

ᶜAli ᶜAbdallah Khalīfa

Aḥmad Muḥammad Āl Khalīfa

Dhabya Khamīs

Ḥamda Khamīs

Ḥasan al-Lawzi

ᶜAbd al-ᶜAzīz al-Maqāliḥ

Muḥammad al-Murr

Muḥammad al-Muthanna

Ibrāhīm al-Nāṣir

ᶜAbd al-Majīd al-Qāḍi

Aḥmad Qandīl

Maysūn Ṣaqr al-Qāsimi

Ḥasan ᶜAbdallah al-Qurashi

Ghāzi al-Quṣaibi

ᶜAbd al-Raḥmān Rafīᶜ

Sayf al-Raḥabi

Muḥammad Hāshim Rashīd

ᶜAbd al-Karīm al-Rāziḥi

Saqr al-Rushūd

Walīd al-Rujaib

Suᶜād al-Mubārak al-Ṣabāḥ

ᶜAli al-Sabti

ᶜAbdallah al-Ṣaikhān

Aḥmad Ṣāliḥ al-Ṣāliḥ

Amīn Ṣāliḥ

ᶜAbdallah al-Sālmi

Khayriyya al-Saqqāf

Zayn al-Saqqāf

Ḥusain Sarḥān

Muḥammad Saᶜīd Sayf

Ḥabīb Ṣāyigh

ᶜAli Sayyār

Ruqayya al-Shabīb

Shauqi Shafīq

Aḥmad al-Shāmi

Sharīfa al-Shamlān

ᶜAli al-Sharqāwi

Sulaimān al-Shaṭṭi

Ḥamza Shiḥāta

Muḥammad al-Shurafi

Aḥmad al-Subāʿi

Muḥammad al-Thubaiti

Aḥmad Mushāri al-ʿUdwāni

Ibrāhīm al-ʿUrayyiḍ

ʿAbdu ʿUthmān

Layla al-ʿUthmān

Subāʿi ʿUthmān

Ismāʿīl al-Warīth

Khalīfa al-Wuqayyān

Ṭāhir al-Zamakhshari

Khālid Saʿūd al-Zayd

Muḥammad Maḥmūd al-Zubairi